Dráma

CE

Kavála

Komotiní

THRACE

Alexandroúpoli

níki

*Aegean
Sea*

Northern Greece
Pages 236–261

AROUND
ATHENS

ENS

ATTICA

Lávrio

Athens
Pages 66–139

Around Athens
Pages 144–161

EYEWITNESS TRAVEL

GREECE
ATHENS &
THE MAINLAND

RAVEL

GREECE
ATHENS & THE MAINLAND

Main Contributor **Marc Dubin**

DK

LONDON, NEW YORK,
MELBOURNE, MUNICH AND DELHI
www.dk.com

Project Editor Jane Simmonds
Art Editor Stephen Bere
Editors Isabel Carlisle, Michael Ellis, Simon Farbrother,
Claire Folkard, Marianne Petrou, Andrew Szudek
Designers Jo Doran, Paul Jackson, Elly King, Marisa Renzullo
Map Co-Ordinators Emily Green, David Pugh
Visualizer Joy Fitzsimmons
Language Consultant Georgia Gotsi

Contributors and Consultants
Rosemary Barron, Marc Dubin, Mike Gerrard, Andy Harris,
Lynette Mitchell, Colin Nicholson, Robin Osborne, Barnaby
Rogerson, Paul Sterry, Tanya Tsikas

Maps Gary Bowes, Fiona Casey, Christine Purcell (ERA-Maptec Ltd)

Photographers Joe Cornish, John Heseltine, Rob Reichenfeld,
Peter Wilson, Francesca Yorke

Illustrators
Stephen Conlin, Paul Guest, Steve Gyapay, Maltings Partnership,
Chris Orr & Associates, Paul Weston, John Woodcock

Printed in China

First American Edition, 1997

14 15 16 17 10 9 8 7 6 5 4 3 2 1

Published in the United States by
DK Publishing, 345 Hudson Street,
New York 10014

**Reprinted with revisions 1998, 1999, 2000, 2001,
2002, 2003, 2004, 2006, 2007, 2009, 2011, 2013, 2015**

Copyright © 1997, 2015 Dorling Kindersley Limited, London
A Penguin Random House Company

ISSN: 1542-1554

ISBN: 978-1-46542-796-0

Throughout this book, floors are referred to in accordance with European usage; ie the
"first floor" is the floor above ground level.

MIX
Paper from
responsible sources
FSC
www.fsc.org   FSC™ C018179

**The information in this
DK Eyewitness Travel Guide is checked regularly.**
Every effort has been made to ensure that this book is as up-to-date as possible
at the time of going to press. Some details, however, such as telephone numbers,
opening hours, prices, gallery hanging arrangements and travel information are
liable to change. The publishers cannot accept responsibility for any consequences
arising from the use of this book, nor for any material on third party websites, and
cannot guarantee that any website address in this book will be a suitable source of
travel information. We value the views and suggestions of our readers very highly.
Please write to: Publisher, DK Eyewitness Travel Guides, Dorling Kindersley,
80 Strand, London, WC2R ORL, UK, or email: travelguides@dk.com.

Front cover main image: Porch of the Caryatids, Acropolis, Athens

◀ Picturesque village of Oia Santorini

Contents

How to Use
This Guide 6

Black-figure bowl depicting
the god Dionysos

Introducing
Athens and
Mainland Greece

Ancient
Greece

Three gateways at the entrance to Acrocorinth

Fresco at Varlaám monastery at Metéora, Central Greece

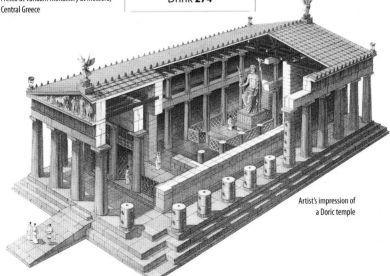
Artist's impression of a Doric temple

HOW TO USE THIS GUIDE

This guide helps you to get the most from your visit to Mainland Greece. It provides expert recommendations and practical information. *Introducing Athens and Mainland Greece* maps the country and sets it in its historical and cultural context. *Ancient Greece* gives a background to the many remains and artifacts to be seen. The four regional chapters, plus *Athens*, describe important sights, with maps and illustrations. Restaurant and hotel recommendations can be found in *Travellers' Needs*. The *Survival Guide* has tips on everything from using a Greek telephone to transport.

Athens

Athens has been divided into two sightseeing areas. Each has its own chapter, opening with a list of the sights described. All sights are numbered on an area map, and are described in detail on the following pages.

Sights at a Glance gives a categorized list of the chapter's sights: Museums and Galleries; Squares, Parks and Gardens; Churches and Historic Buildings.

All pages relating to Athens have red thumb tabs.

A locator map shows you where you are in relation to the rest of Athens.

1 Area Map
The sights are numbered and located on a map. Sights in the city centre are also shown on the Athens Street Finder on *pages 126–39*.

2 Street-by-Street Map
This gives an overhead view of the key areas in central Athens. The numbering on the map ties in with the area map and the fuller descriptions that follow.

A suggested route for a walk is shown in red.

Story Boxes highlight special aspects of a particular sight.

Stars indicate the sights that no visitor should miss.

3 Detailed Information The sights within Athens are described individually. Addresses, telephone numbers, opening hours and information concerning admission charges and wheelchair access are given for each entry. Map references to the Athens Street Finder are also provided for orientation.

1 Introduction
An introduction covers the history, character and geography of each region, showing how the area has developed over the centuries and what it has to offer the visitor today.

Mainland Greece Area by Area

Mainland Greece has been divided into four regions, each of which has a separate chapter. A map of these areas can be found inside the front cover of the book.

Each region can be identified by its colour coding, shown on the inside front cover.

A locator map shows you where you are in relation to the other regions in the book.

2 Regional Map
This shows the region covered in the chapter. The main sights are numbered on the map. The major roads are marked and there are useful tips about the best ways of getting around the area.

3 Detailed Information
All the important towns and areas to visit are described individually. They are listed in order, following the numbering on the *Regional Map*. Within each entry, there is detailed information on all the major sights.

A Visitors' Checklist provides the practical information you will need to plan your visit.

4 Greece's Top Sights
These are given one or more full pages. Historic buildings are dissected to reveal their interiors. Many of the ancient sites are reconstructed to supplement information about the site as it is seen today.

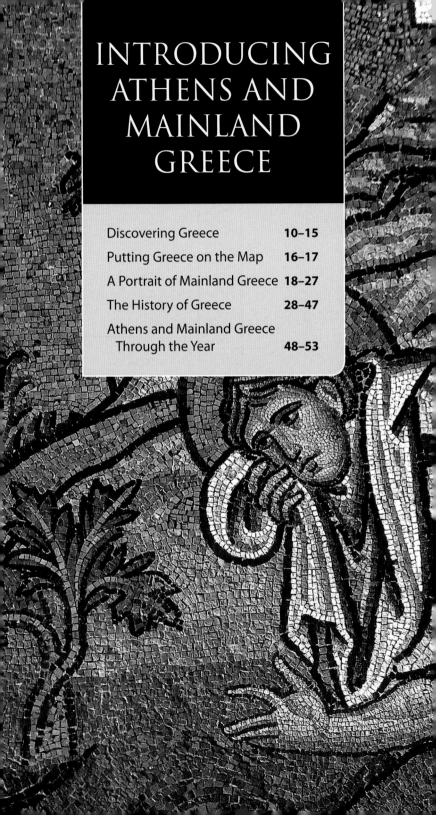

INTRODUCING ATHENS AND MAINLAND GREECE

DISCOVERING GREECE

The following tours have been designed to take in as many of the country's highlights as possible, while keeping long-distance travel to a minimum. The first itinerary outlined here is a two-day tour of Athens, followed by five days spent in the Attica region and the Peloponnese. These itineraries can be followed individually or combined

to form a week-long tour. Next, come two week-long tours, covering Central, Western and Northern Greece, including Thrace and Macedonia. Additional suggestions are included for those who want to extend their stay. Pick, combine and follow your favourite tours, or simply dip in and out and be inspired.

One Week in Central and Western Greece

- Explore the beautiful, rugged **Pílio** peninsula and visit its unspoilt villages.
- Admire the powerful mosaic, *Washing of the Apostles' Feet*, at the **Monastery of Osios Loúkas**.
- Imagine what life was like at **Ancient Delphi**, once considered the centre of the earth.
- Marvel at **Metéora's** huge sandstone towers topped by monasteries and dwellings.
- Enjoy a leisurely stroll along the theatre-shaped waterfront of **Párga** and see its Venetian-style fortress.
- See the spectacular scenery of the **Víkos Gorge**, carved over millions of years by the Voïdomátis river.

Key

━━━ One Week in Central and Western Greece
━━━ Five Days in Attica and the Peloponnese
━━━ One Week in Northern Greece

Préspa Lakes · Edessa · Ancient Pélla · Lefkádia · Thessaloníki · Kastoriá · Véroia · Vergína · Siátista · Mount Olympos · Kónitsa · Víkos Gorge · Zagória · Vale of Tempe · Métsovo · Metéora · Dodóni · Ioánnina · Trikala · Vólos · Párga · Kassópi · Arta · Préveza · Lamía · Thermopylae · Ancient Delphi · Aráchova · Náfpaktos · Mesolóngi · Galaxídi · Monastery of Osios Loúka · Ancient Corinth · Ancient Neméa · Ancient Olympía · Mycenae · Anci Tiry · Argos · Loúsios Gorge · Náfplio · Ancient Tegéa · Mystrás · Outer Máni · Monemvasi · Inner Máni

Ancient Delphi
Once home to the famous oracle, these ruins mark what was believed to be the centre of the earth in ancient times.

◄ The beautiful *Tranfiguration* mosaic depicting the apostles, Peter and John at the Monastery of Dafní

Thássos
Around 12 km (7 miles) from the mainland, this beautifully situated resort island is known for its sandy beaches and mountain villages.

One Week in Northern Greece

- Admire the distinctive Neo-Classical, Byzantine and Ottoman architecture of **Xánthi**.

- Visit the fascinating **Thessaloníki Archaeological Museum** to see its priceless gold treasures.

- Ascend **Mount Athos** for dramatic views of the coast and explore the Orthodox monasteries around.

- Relax in the unspoilt wilderness of the **Olympos National Park** or the pretty **Préspa Lakes**.

- Explore **Alexandroúpoli's** labyrinth of narrow streets lined with traditional craft workshops.

- Take a boat trip to the island of **Thássos**.

Xánthi
Famous for its annual spring carnival, the lively market town of Xánthi also has an interesting folk museum.

Five Days in Attica and the Peloponnese

- See the spectacle of dozens of ferries leaving Kentikó Limáni in **Piraeus** for the islands every morning.

- Be captivated by the magnificent mosaics and cloisters at the **Monastery of Dafní**.

- Discover the Peloponnese's ancient sites, including **Mycenae**, **Epidaurus** and **Olympia**.

- Dine on sumptuous fresh fish in the picturesque town of **Náfplio**.

- Visit the **Attica Zoological Park**, home to one of the world's largest collections of birds.

- Admire the visually stunning ancient towns of **Monemvasía** and **Mystrás** and wonder about the lives of the people who lived here.

Two Days in Athens

- **Arriving** Flights from around the world arrive everyday at the modern Elefthérios Venizélos – Athens International Airport, which lies around 27 km (17 miles) from the city centre. A metro service connects the airport with Plateía Sýntagma and Monastiráki. Buses and taxis operate from outside the terminal. Athens can also be reached by road and rail, or sea via the port of Piraeus.

- **Transport** The main sights of Athens are all within easy walking distance. The city also has an efficient bus network.

- **Booking ahead** Some museums, including the Acropolis Museum, are closed on Mondays.

Day 1
Morning Start the day early with a trip to the **Acropolis** (pp98–105). Follow the pathway up from the entrance and be sure to stop at the **Theatre of Herodes Atticus** (p101), which dates from AD 161. Ascend the steps to the **Propylaia** (p100). Take a minute to admire the **Temple of Athena Nike** (p100), before moving on to see the mighty **Parthenon** (pp102–103) dominating the scene ahead. Enjoy spectacular views of Athens and the coast from here. Later, make your way back down to the pedestrianized Dionysiou Areopagitou, turn left and follow the path for a selection of lunchtime eateries.

Afternoon Head for the ultra-modern **Acropolis Museum** (p104), which is as stunning as the ancient treasures that are on display. Spend an hour here, and visit the **Parthenon Gallery** (pp102–103), which has a glass roof on the top floor. Admire the outstanding exhibits. Next, explore vibrant **Pláka** (pp106–107), but before losing yourself in its labyrinth of tiny, picturesque lanes, take a quick detour to

Hadrian's Arch and the **Temple of Olympian Zeus** (p115). In the evening, try the authentic *Kléftiko* (goat meat cooked in parchment paper) in one of Pláka's traditional tavernas.

Day 2
Morning Spend the morning exploring the superb **Benáki Museum** (pp82–3) or the nearby **Museum of Cycladic Art** (pp78–9), both are full of interesting Greek treasures. Keep an eye on your watch so that you're in time outside the parliament building in **Plateía Sýntagma** (p116) to witness the pageantry of the changing of the guard. It begins at 11am and continues for about half an hour (longer on Sundays). From here, take a short walk to the **National Gardens** (p116), one of the most peaceful spots in the city, before enjoying an early lunch in one of the area's fine restaurants.

Afternoon Make your way along Ermou Street, lined with shops such as Gucci and Dolce & Gabbana, to **Monastiráki** (pp88–9). Just off to your left, along Fokionos, is Plateía Mitropóleos, a bustling square dominated by the little 12th-century church, **Panagía Gorgoepíkoos** (p109). **Monastiráki** is famous for its **Flea Market** (p91, open daily until 2pm) and the ruins of the marketplace or **Ancient Agora** (pp94–5), where Athenians would once engage in bartering goods. The marketplace dates from 600 BC. Among

the ruins is the interesting octagonal **Tower of the Winds** (p90). End the day with a romantic meal in Thiseio where almost every restaurant has a pretty view of the famous flood-lit **Acropolis**.

> **To extend your trip...**
> The **National Archaeological Museum** (pp72–3) in the district of Exárcheia houses fabulous treasures, including sculptures from Kerameikós, the ancient cemetery in Thiseio.

Five Days in Attica and the Peloponnese

- **Arriving** Piraeus is just 10 km (6 miles) SW of Athens and is therefore served by the Elefthérios Venizélos – Athens International Airport.

- **Transport** The best way to explore Piraeus and the Peloponnese is by car.

Day 1: Piraeus to Soúnio
Begin the day by enjoying the fascinating spectacle of dozens of ferries departing for the islands from the main ferry port, Kentikó Limáni, in **Piraeus** (pp158–9). This popular event takes place every morning so be sure to get there early, just after breakfast. Explore **Piraeus** with its elegant Neo-Classical architecture, parks and museums, including the theatre-inspired Pános Aravantinoú Museum of Stage Décor. Follow the signs

The imposing Roman Theatre of Herodes Atticus

Temple ruins in Ancient Corinth

to the **Mikrolímano** harbour and stop for a quiet lunch at any of the fish restaurants here before heading out of town and along the Attic Coast strewn with marinas and resorts to **Soúnio** (pp152–3). A charming coastal town, **Soúnio** serves as an ideal overnight stop.

Day 2: Soúnio to Athens
Begin early from **Soúnio** and make your way to **Ancient Brauron** (pp150–51) via **Làvrio** (p152) and the picturesque fishing harbour of **Pórto Ráfti** (p151). Watch out for the ruins of ancient temples and tombs here. Continue along the coast to **Rafína** (p149) and sample fresh fish for lunch. In the afternoon, take the road to Athens. Along the way, visit the **Attica Zoological Park** (p154), home to one of the world's largest collections of birds, and enjoy the peaceful countryside that inspired monks to build the Moní Kaisarianís Monastery in the 11th century.

Day 3: Athens to Corinth
Just 10 km (6 miles) outside Athens is the **Monastery of Dafní** (pp156–7). Look out for its wonderful mosaics and cloisters. A few miles further on is **Ancient Eleusis** (pp160–61), which was once an important religious sanctuary. There's an interesting museum that tells its story. The Peloponnese 'island' comes into full view as you make your way along the coastal road to the

Corinth Canal (p171). Spend the afternoon visiting the site of **Ancient Corinth** (pp166–7), once a prosperous Roman city. End the day in Corinth, which offers a good choice of hotels.

Day 4: Corinth to Náfplio
Get acquainted with the Peloponnese's history by stopping first at **Ancient Neméa** (p171), then the mighty fortified palace of **Mycenae** (pp182–4), built around 3,500 years ago. Next, head to the historic market towns of **Argos**, **Ancient Tiryns**, and **Epidaurus** (pp188–9), with its spectacular theatre, and the remains of **Ancient Troezen** (p185). Round the day off with dinner in **Náfplio** (pp186–7).

Day 5: Ancient Olympia
Set out to explore **Ancient Olympia** (pp174–7), one of the most religious, political and athletic centres in the ancient

Bust of Roman Emperor Marcus Aurelius at Ancient Eleusis

world. From **Náfplio**, follow signs for Trípoli and **Ancient Tegéa** (p181). Opt for the picturesque, but windy mountainous road through **Loúsios Gorge** (pp178–80), or the highway and coastal road.

> **To extend your trip...**
> The ancient towns of **Monemvasía** (pp190–92) and **Mystrás** (pp196–7), and the rocky plains of **Outer Máni** (pp198–9) and **Inner Máni** (pp202–203) lie towards the south of the Peloponnese.

One Week in Central and Western Greece

- **Arriving** The Nea Anchialos National Airport serves the east coast of Central Greece. Taxis and the Magnesia Intercity Bus Company connect the airport with the city of Vólos.

- **Transport** The best way to explore Central and Western Greece is by car.

Day 1: Vólos to Argalastí
Before exploring the beautiful, rugged **Pílio** (pp222–3) peninsula, do visit to the **Vólos Archaeological Museum** (p224), which offers plenty of insight into the history of the region. Next, head southeast from Vólos and stop for the night at Argalastí. The route via Afétes will reveal unspoilt villages, such as cobbled Vyzítsa, and stunning scenery.

Day 2: Argalastí to Aráchova
Get an early start, take the coastal road back to Vólos and the motorway to **Lamía** and **Thermopylae** (p228), where be sure to visit the Catalan Kástro and the Battle of Lataiai site. After a break, continue on to **Thebes** (p225) and visit the museum, which stands alongside a 13th-century Frankish tower and the remains of a castle. Nearby, is the site of the legendary Fountain of Oedipus. Enjoy the 40-km- (25-mile)-long drive to Aráchova, which lies on the southern slopes of **Mount Parnassus** (p225). Soak up views of the Pleistos valley from here.

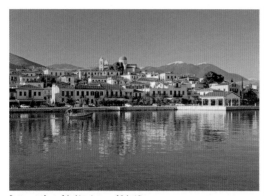

Pretty waterfront of the historic town of Galaxidi

Day 3: Aráchova to Galaxidi

Aráchova is famous for its wine and cheese, so be sure to buy some before following the signs to the enchanting **Monastery of Osios Loúkas** (pp226–7). Look out for the wonderful mosaic, *Washing of the Apostles' Feet*. Later, set out for **Ancient Delphi** (pp232–5). Regarded as the mighty god Apollo's home, this ancient site was once considered to be the centre of the earth. Opt to spend the night either in historic Galaxidi or Náfpaktos, where most hotels offer panoramic views of the **Gulf of Corinth** (pp228–9).

Day 4: Galaxidi to Párga

Take the coastal road to **Párga** (p216) and stop enroute at several attractions such as the picturesque fishing harbour of **Mesolóngi** (p229), the charming

town of **Préveza** (pp216–17), where visitors will come across several waterfront fish restaurants, and the traditional town of **Arta** (p217). On the hillside between **Arta** and **Párga** are the ruins of the 4th-century BC city of **Kassópi** (p216).

Day 5: Párga to Kónitsa

Start the day with a leisurely stroll along the theatre-shaped waterfront of **Párga**. A Venetian fortress stands proudly to the west side of the harbour. Next, take the highway to **Dodóni** (p215) with its theatre, one of the largest in Greece, and **Ioánnina** (p214), which is the capital of the region. Take time out to explore **Ioánnina** before taking the road through the **Víkos Gorge** (p212) to Kónitsa. Spend the night in the busy, rural town of Kónitsa.

Day 6: Kónitsa to Ioánnina

The **Víkos Gorge**, which has been carved by the Voïdomátis river over millions of years, together with the **Zagória** (p211), offer spectacular scenery, hikes and around 45 traditional villages to explore. End your day in one of **Ioánnina's** elegant hotels, where you must sample the famous feta cheese and baklava dessert.

Day 7: Ioánnina to Tríkala

Métsovo (p213) was once home to the region's Vlach shepherds, along with merchants who availed themselves of the town's unusual tax privileges. Today, mansions and museums testify to **Métsovo's** historical importance. Continue along the highway and notice how the landscape changes to reveal huge sandstone towers topped by monasteries and dwellings. This is the peaceful and enchanting **Metéora** (pp220–21). If you have time, conclude your tour with a trip to **Tríkala** (p217), around 25 km (15 miles) away, to see its fine fortress and exquisite Byzantine churches.

> **To extend your trip...**
> The **Vale of Tempe** (p217) lies close to Central Greece's border with Macedonia, and is believed to have been where Apollo purified himself after slaying the serpent, Python.

The awe-inspiring monasteries at Metéora

For practical information on travelling around Greece, see pp314–23

One Week in Northern Greece

- **Arriving** The Alexandroúpolis International Airport is one of several airports serving Northern Greece. Buses and taxis make it easy to access Alexandroúpoli.
- **Transport** The best way to explore Northern Greece is by car.

Day 1: Alexandroúpoli to Komotiní

Start the day by taking a stroll along **Alexandroúpoli's** *(p261)* attractive waterfront before heading inland to explore its labyrinth of narrow streets lined with traditional grocers, craft workshops and antique shops. The **Ecclesiastical Art Museum** *(p261)*, in the grounds of the Agios Nikólaos cathedral, is worth a visit. Nearby, are excellent fish restaurants. Stop for an early lunch at any one of them before heading out of town, through the village of Féres, to the scenic **Dadia Forest** *(p261)*. Among the sweet-smelling pine trees here, explore rare flora and fauna. Retrace your route to the highway and follow signs for **Komotiní** *(p260)*, which is perfect for an overnight stop. Along the way, take a short detour to see the ruins of the ancient town of **Maróneia** *(pp260–61)*.

Day 2: Komotiní to Kavála

The architectural combination of Neo-Classical mansions, Byzantine churches and Ottoman-built mosques gives **Xánthi** *(p259)* a distinctive look. Nearby, towards the coast, is the site of the ancient city of **Avdira** *(p260)*, while to the north is the **Néstos Valley** *(p259)*. A mix of rivers, mountainside dotted with hamlets, forest and views of the coastline dominated by the island of Thássos make it a heavenly place to while away a couple of hours. Next stop is **Kavála** *(p259)*, where St Paul is believed to have first set foot on European soil. Explore the museums, take a boat trip to Thássos and stop for the night in one of the town's harbourside hotels.

Day 3: Kavála to Thessaloníki

Follow the coastal road to reach Amfipoli and then head inland to explore central Macedonia. The peaceful area around Lake Kerkini makes an ideal midday picnic spot. Later, drive to **Thessaloníki** *(pp248–52)*, Greece's second largest city after Athens, for a two-night stay.

Day 4: Thessaloníki

The **Thessaloníki** city centre is a bustling place full of elegant buildings, fabulous Byzantine churches, including the largest church in Greece, **Agios Dimítrios** *(p252)*, plush hotels and shopping areas. The **Thessaloníki Archaeological Museum** *(pp250–51)* houses priceless treasures. Don't miss its collection of gold jewellery; some pieces are more than 2,000 years old.

Day 5: Thessaloníki to Chalkidikí

Set out to explore the Chalkidikí region. Take time out to visit the Petrálona Caves, the picturesque Kassándra peninsula with its sandy beaches and bays full of boats, and the peaceful **Sithonía** *(p253)*. Chalkidikí's highest point is **Mount Athos** *(pp256–8)*, which offers dramatic views of the coast and the monasteries. The region offers a good selection of hotels, including the chance to stay on the idyllic Ammouliani Islet.

Day 6: Chalkidikí to Lefkádia

Spend the morning exploring the ancient sites that lie to the west of **Thessaloníki**. Ancient

Pélla *(p247)* has some of the best-preserved pebble mosaics in Greece and is believed to have been where Alexander the Great was born in 356 BC. Nearby, **Lefkádia** *(p246–7)* is notable for its Macedonian tombs with well-preserved frescoes and **Vergína** *(p246)* for its Royal Tombs. Take time out for a detour to **Edessa** *(p247)*. Relax in the peacefulness of the countryside, famed for its waterfalls and be sure to visit **Véroia** *(p246)* to see its collection of more than 50 barnlike churches. Spend the night in one of the area's fine hotels.

Day 7: Lefkádia to the Préspa Lakes

Round off your trip with a visit to the beautiful and unspoilt **Préspa Lakes** *(pp240–41)*. Take the highway to the elegant towns of **Siátista** *(p244)* and **Kastoriá** *(p244)* until you reach the lakes' national park. It is one of the most important wildlife habitats in Greece and home to several rare and vulnerable species.

To extend your trip...
Mount Olympos *(p245)* and the unspoilt, verdant Olympos National Park lie around 80 km (50 miles) southwest of **Thessaloníki**. More than 1,700 plant species thrive here, along with roe deers and boars. Walking maps and overnight accommodation are available in the park.

View of Mount Athos, known as the "monk's republic"

Putting Greece on the Map

Occupying the southernmost tip of the Balkan peninsula, Greece divides into over 2,000 islands stretching from the Ionian Sea in the west to the Aegean Sea in the east. The mainland has borders with Albania, Bulgaria, Turkey and the former Yugoslav Republic of Macedonia and is home to most of Greece's 10.9 million people, with a third of these in Athens.

Key

─── Motorway

─── Major Road

----- Railway line

----- Ferry route

▬▬▬ National boundary

For keys to symbols *see back flap*

A PORTRAIT OF
MAINLAND GREECE

Greece is one of the most visited European countries, yet one of the least known. The modern Greek state dates only from 1830 and bears little relation to the popular image of ancient Greece. At a geographical crossroads, Greece combines elements of the Balkans, Middle East and Mediterranean.

For a relatively small country, less than 132,000 sq km (51,000 sq miles) in area, Greece possesses marked regional differences in topography. Nearly three-quarters of the land is mountainous, uninhabited or uncultivated. Fertile agricultural land supports tobacco farming in the northeast, with orchard fruits and vegetables grown further south. A third of the population lives in the capital, Athens, the cultural, financial and political centre, in which ancient and modern stand side by side.

Rural and urban life in contemporary Greece have been transformed despite years of occupation and conflict, including a bitter civil war *(see p46)* that would surely have finished off a less resilient people. The society that emerged was supported with US aid, yet Greece remained relatively underdeveloped until the 1960s. Rural areas lacked paved roads and even basic utilities, prompting extensive, unplanned urban growth and emigration. It has been said, with some justice, that there are no architects in Greece, only civil engineers.

For centuries, a large number of Greeks have lived abroad; currently there are over half as many Greeks outside the country as in. This diaspora occurred in several stages, prompted by changes in the Ottoman Empire late in the 17th century. Most post war emigration was to Africa, the Americas and Australia.

Backgammon players at the flea market around Plateía Monastirakíou in Athens

◀ Leading a mule on the streets of Monemvasía

The Píndos mountain range, from above the village of Vrysochóri

Religion, Language and Culture

During the centuries of domination by Venetians and Ottomans *(see pp42–3),* the Greek Orthodox Church preserved the Greek language, and with it Greek identity, through its liturgy and schools. Today, the Orthodox Church is still a powerful force despite the secularizing reforms of the PASOK government in the 1980s. The query *Eísai Orthódoxos* (Are you Orthodox?) is virtually synonymous with *Éllinas eísai* (Are you Greek?). While no self-respecting couple would dispense with a church wedding and baptisms for their children, civil marriages are now equally valid in law as the traditional religious service. Sunday Mass is very popular with women, who often use the services as meeting places for socializing much in the same way as men do the *kafeneía* (cafés).

Votive offerings in the Pantánassas convent

Parish priests, often recognizable by their tall stovepipe hats and long beards, are not expected to embody the divine, but to transmit it at liturgy. Many marry and have a second trade (a custom that helps keep up the numbers of entrants to the church). There has also been a renaissance in monastic life, perhaps in reaction to the growth of materialism since World War II.

The subtle and beautiful Greek language, another great hallmark of national identity, was for a long time a field of conflict between

Greek priests leading a religious procession in Athens

katharévousa, an artificial, written form hastily devised around the time of Independence, and the slowly evolved *dimotikí*, or everyday speech, with its streamlined grammar and words borrowed from several other languages. The dispute acquired political overtones, with the Right tending to champion *katharévousa*, the Left, *dimotikí*, with blood even being shed at times.

Tavernas in the town of Náfplio

Today, the supple and accessible *dimotikí* is the language of the nation. The art of storytelling is still as prized in Greece as in Homer's time, with conversation pursued for its own sake in *kafeneía* and at dinner parties. The bardic tradition has remained alive with the poet-lyricists such as Mános Eleftheríou, Apóstolos Káldaras and Níkos Gátsos. The continuous efforts made to produce popular and accessible art have played a key role in helping to keep *dimotikí* alive from the 19th century until the present day.

Selling fish at Vólos harbour, the Pílio

Both writers and singers, the natural advocates of *dimotikí*, have historically been important to the Greek public. During recent periods of censorship under the dictatorship or in times of foreign occupation, they carried out an essential role as one of the chief sources of coded information and morale-boosting.

Development and Diplomacy

Compared to most of its Balkan neighbours, Greece is a relatively wealthy country. However, by Western economic indicators, Greece is poor and languished at the bottom of the EU league table until the addition of ten new East European countries in 2004. The persistent negative trade deficit is aggravated by imports of luxury goods, an expression of *xenomanía* or belief in the inherent superiority of all things foreign. Cars are most conspicuous among these, since Greece is one of the very few European countries not to manufacture its own.

An archaeologist helping to restore the Parthenon

Greece still bears the hallmarks of a developing economy, with agriculture and the service sector accounting for two-thirds of the GNP. Blurred lines between work and living space are the norm, with professional brass plates alternating with personal bell-buzzer tags in any apartment block. There is a tenacious adherence, despite repeated campaigns against it, to the long afternoon siesta. As a result, some workers have to endure commuting twice a day.

Barrels in the Achaïa Klauss winery at Pátra

a severe crisis. Industry has shrunk and unemployment has risen sharply. Tourism ranks as the largest hard-currency earner, offsetting the depression in world shipping and the fact that Mediterranean agricultural products are duplicated within the EU. Greece's historically lenient entry requirements for refugees, and its pre-eminent status in the Balkans, have made it a magnet for Arabs, Africans, Kurds, Poles and Albanians for a number of years. Now protectionist procedures, such as stringent frontier clamp-downs and the deportation of all undocumented individuals, have been introduced.

With EU membership since 1981 and a nominally capitalist orientation, Greece overcame its resemblance to pre-1989 Eastern Europe. The state no longer invests heavily in antiquated industries, nor is the civil service of today overstaffed as part of a full-employment policy. After the turn of the millennium, Greece saw an initial growth in its economy above the EU average, but due to uncontrolled government spending and the world financial crisis that started in the late 2000s, the Greek economy faces

Statue of Athena standing beside the Athens Academy

The fact that the Greek state is less than 200 years old, and that it has had much political instability, means that there is little faith in government institutions. Life operates on networks of personal friendships and official contacts. The classic designations of Right and Left have only acquired their conventional meanings since the 1930s. The dominant political figure of the first half of the 20th century was Elefthérios Venizélos, an anti-royalist Liberal. The years following World War II have

Rooftops of Náfplio and Boúrtzi islet from the Palamídi fortress

House in the village of Psarádes, beside the Préspa lakes

been largely shaped by the influence of three men: the late Andréas Papandréou, three times premier as head of the Panhellenic Socialist Movement (PASOK), the late conservative premier Konstantínos Karamanlís, and the late premier Geórgios Papandréou (PASOK). Since 2012, Antonis Samaras has been the premier of Greece and the leader of the New Democracy.

Since the end of the Cold War, Greece has been asserting its underlying Balkan identity. Relations with Albania have improved since the collapse of the Communist regime in 1990. Greece is the biggest investor in Bulgaria, and after a rapprochement with Skopje, it seems poised to be a regional power, with Thessaloníki's port (second largest in the Mediterranean) seen as the future gateway to the southern Balkans.

Home Life

The family is still the basic Greek social unit. Traditionally, one family could sow, plough and reap its own fields, without need of cooperative work parties. Today, family-run businesses are still the norm in urban settings. Family life and social life are usually one and the same, and tend to revolve around eating out, which is done more often than in most of Europe. Arranged

marriages and granting of dowries, though officially banned, persist; most single young people live with their parents or another relative until married, and outside the largest cities, few couples dare to cohabit. Despite the renowned Greek love of children, Greece has the lowest birth rate in Europe after Italy: less than half its pre-World War II levels. Owing in part to reforms in family and inheritance law, urban Greek women have been raised in status. Better represented in medicine and the law, many women run their own businesses. In the country, however, macho attitudes persist and women often forgo the chance of a career for the sake of the house and children. New imported notions and attitudes have begun to creep in, especially in the larger cities, but generally, tradition remains strong and no amount of innovation or outside influence is likely to jeopardize the Greek way of life.

Man with a shepherd's crook
in the village
of Métsovo

Wednesday market in Argos

Byzantine Architecture

Medieval churches are virtually all that have survived from a millennium of Byzantine civilization in Greece. Byzantine church architecture was concerned almost exclusively with a decorated interior. The intention was to sculpt out a holy space where the congregation would be confronted with the true nature of the cosmos, cleared of all worldly distractions. The mosaics and frescoes portraying the whole body of the Church, from Christ downwards, have a dual purpose: they give inspiration to the worshipper and are windows to the spiritual world. From a mountain chapel to an urban church, there is great conformity of design, with structure and decoration united to a single purpose.

The Best of Byzantine Architecture

① Thessaloníki p252
② Mount Athos pp256–8
③ Arta p217
④ Monastery of Osios Loúkas pp226–7
⑤ Pátra p173
⑥ Moní Kaisarianís pp154–5
⑦ Monastery of Dafní pp156–7
⑧ Athens p84, p109, p112
⑨ Mystrás pp196–7
⑩ Geráki p193

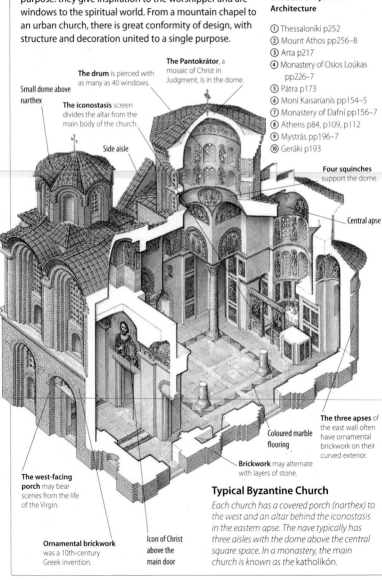

The drum is pierced with as many as 40 windows.

The Pantokrátor, a mosaic of Christ in Judgment, is in the dome.

Small dome above narthex

The iconostasis screen divides the altar from the main body of the church.

Side aisle

Four squinches support the dome.

Central apse

The three apses of the east wall often have ornamental brickwork on their curved exterior.

Coloured marble flooring

Brickwork may alternate with layers of stone.

The west-facing porch may bear scenes from the life of the Virgin.

Ornamental brickwork was a 10th-century Greek invention.

Icon of Christ above the main door

Typical Byzantine Church

Each church has a covered porch (narthex) to the west and an altar behind the iconostasis in the eastern apse. The nave typically has three aisles with the dome above the central square space. In a monastery, the main church is known as the katholikón.

Understanding Frescoes in a Byzantine Church

The frescoes and mosaics in churches' interiors were organized according to a standard scheme. Symbolically, images descended from heaven (Christ Pantokrátor in the dome) to earth (the saints on the lowest level). The Virgin was shown in the semi-dome of the apse, with the fathers of the church below her.

Choirs of angels

Windows in drum

Christ Pantokrátor

The dome is symbolically filled by the figure of Christ in Judgment, the Pantokrátor. Choirs of angels swirl around Him, and outside them stand the Old Testament prophets. This dome comes from Moní Perivléptou in Mystrás *(see p196).*

Prophets

The Virgin and Child are in the curve of the apse, symbolically between heaven (the dome) and earth (the nave).

Archangels Michael and Gabriel, dressed like courtiers of a Byzantine emperor, honour the Virgin.

The Fathers of Orthodoxy, here in their episcopal robes, defined Orthodoxy in the early centuries.

Upper register of saints

The apse is often hidden from public view by an elaborate iconostasis screen, through whose doors only the clergy are admitted. This apse is from Agios Stratigós in the Máni *(see p203).*

Lower register of saints

Sand-filled tray for votive candles

The side walls are decorated in registers. On the lowest level stand life-size portrayals of the saints, their heads illuminated with haloes. More complex scenes portraying incidents from the Gospels or the Day of Judgment fill the upper walls and vaults. This church is at Miliés in the Pílio *(see pp222–4).*

The Virgin Mary

Icons of the Virgin Mary abound in every Orthodox church, where she is referred to as Panagía, the All Holy. Her exceptional status was confirmed in 431 when she was awarded the title Theotókos "Mother of God", in preference to just "Mother of Christ".

Eleoúsa, meaning "Our Lady of Tenderness", shows the Virgin Mary brushing cheeks with the Christ Child.

The Virgin seated on a throne, flanked by two archangels, is a depiction usually found in the eastern apse.

Odigítria, meaning the "Conductress", shows the Virgin indicating the Christ Child with her right arm.

The Landscape of Mainland Greece

Greece is a land of rugged beauty. The narrow coastal belt is backed by cliffs in places, while inland, there are massive mountain ranges, gorges and cliffs, the haunt of eagles and vultures. The fantastic array of vegetation, including many species of spring wild flowers, is strongly influenced by the Mediterranean climate of long, hot and dry summers and mild, wet winters. Clearance of forests for agriculture and timber has produced a mosaic of flower-rich fields and areas of shrubs. This shrubland habitat is of two kinds: the dense aromatic bushes of *maquis* and the sparser *phrygana* with lower and more compact plants. Although the country's millions of goats destroy the vegetation with their constant grazing, one of the most romantic sights in Greece is that of flocks being herded through olive groves full of archaeological remains, as at Sparta in the Peloponnese.

Abandoned areas of cultivation soon revert to the wild. Larks and pipits feed and nest here and, in spring, wild flowers and butterflies are abundant.

Phrygana often covers bare slopes and rocky outcrops.

Hilly landscapes with stately cypress trees standing tall and dark against the steep slopes are closely associated with Greece's archaeological sites. These, including the Byzantine town of Mystrás above, are worth visiting for their wildlife alone, and in particular, the spring wild flowers that mix rare orchids with daisies, poppies and marigolds.

Olive trees harbour numerous birds and insects among their silvery-green foliage.

Spring flowers such as poppies and irises, have a brief but prolific season.

Maquis and Phrygana

Maquis *shrubland dominates the landscape in this view of Mycenae. It is a mixture of rockroses and aromatic herbs. The more barren* phrygana, *in the far distance, has clumps of spiny vetches.*

Olive groves are found all over Greece at low altitudes; this one is at Argalastí in the Pílio. In spring, flowers grow in profusion in the shade of trees and attract a wealth of butterflies and beetles. Lizards hunt for insects in the twisted trunks that also provide nesting places for birds such as masked shrikes.

Wetland areas, such as the margins of Lake Stymfalía in the Peloponnese, are often used for farming. Usually fairly dry underfoot, they are rich in birds, amphibians and plants.

Wild Flowers of Greece

Greece is blessed with an extraordinary wealth of flowering plants. At least 6,000 species grow in the country, quite a few of them found nowhere else in the world. The floral richness is due in part to the country's diversity of habitats, ranging from wetlands, coastal plains and lowland *maquis* to snow-capped mountain tops. The growing period for many plants is winter, the dampest, coolest season, and the flowering periods run from March to early June, and again in September. Coastal areas of the Peloponnese are perhaps the richest in wild flowers.

The wild gladiolus has several varieties that are among the most showy spring flowers.

The tassel hyacinth is aptly named for its appearance. It grows on open ground and flowers in May.

Cytinus hypocistus is a parasite plant found growing close to the base of colourful cistus bushes *(see below)*.

Sage-leaved cistus is widespread in *maquis* habitats. Its colourful flowers attract pollinating insects.

White asphodel is often seen growing on roadside verges in many parts of Greece. Tall spikes of white flowers appear from April to June.

Areas of *maquis* provide ideal habitats for nesting birds such as warblers, serins and hoopoes.

Between the shrubs in open areas of *maquis*, orchids, tulips and other native flowers appear in the spring.

Orchids

One of the botanical highlights of a visit to Greece is the range of wild orchid species that can be found in bloom between late February and May. All have strangely shaped, and sometimes colourful, flowers whose purpose is to attract pollinating insects.

The four-spotted orchid has spots on the flower lip. A plant of open hillsides, it flowers in April.

The naked man orchid has a dense head of pale pinkish flowers and favours open woodland.

The Greek spider orchid looks more like a bumblebee than a spider. It is found in *maquis* in early spring.

THE HISTORY OF GREECE

The history of Greece is that of a nation, not of a land: the Greek idea of nationality is governed by language, religion, descent and customs, not so much by geography. Early Greek history is the story of internal struggles, from the Mycenaean and Minoan cultures of the Bronze Age to the competing city-states that emerged in the 1st millennium BC.

After the defeat of the Greek army by Philip II of Macedon at Chaironeia in 338 BC, Greece was absorbed into Alexander the Great's Asian empire. With the defeat of the Macedonians by the Romans in 168 BC, Greece became a province of the Roman Empire. As part of the Eastern Empire, she was ruled from Constantinople and in the 11th century became a powerful element within the new, Orthodox Christian, Byzantine world.

After 1453, when Constantinople fell to the Ottomans, Greece as a political entity disappeared altogether. Eventually, the realization that it was the democracy of Classical Athens which had inspired so many revolutions abroad gave the Greeks themselves the courage to rebel and, in 1821, to fight the Greek War of Independence. In 1832, the Great Powers that dominated Europe established a protectorate over Greece which marked the end of Ottoman rule. Greece re-established itself as a sizeable state, but the "Great Idea" – the ambition to re-create Byzantium – ended after Greece's disastrous defeat in the Greco-Turkish War (1919–22).

The instability of the ensuing years was followed by the Metaxás dictatorship and then by the war years (1940–48), during which half a million people were killed. The present boundaries of the Greek state have only existed since 1948, when Italy returned the Dodecanese. Now, as an established democracy and member of the European Union, Greece's fortunes seem to have come full circle after 2,000 years of foreign rule.

A map of Greece from the 1595 Atlas of Abraham Ortelius called *Theatrum Orbis Terrarum*

◄ The beginning of the 1821 Greek Revolution as shown in 1825 by L Dupré

Prehistoric Greece

During the Bronze Age, three separate civilizations flourished in Greece: the Cycladic, during the 3rd millennium; the Minoan, based on Crete but with an influence that spread throughout the Aegean islands; and the Mycenaean, which was based on the mainland but spread to Crete in about 1450 BC when the Minoans went into decline. Both the Minoan and Mycenaean cultures found their peak in the Palace periods of the 2nd millennium when they were dominated by a centralized religion and bureaucracy.

Prehistoric Greece

Areas settled in the Bronze Age

Neolithic Head (3000 BC)
This figure was found on Alónnisos in the Sporades. It probably represents a fertility goddess who was worshipped by farmers to ensure a good harvest. These figures indicate a certain stability in early communities.

The town is unwalled, showing that inhabitants did not fear attack.

Multistorey houses

Cycladic Figurine
Marble statues such as this, produced in the Bronze Age from about 2800 to 2300 BC, have been found in a number of tombs in the Cyclades.

Minoan "Bathtub" Sarcophagus
This type of coffin, dating to 1400 BC, is found only in Minoan art. It was probably used for a high-status burial.

	7000 Neolithic farmers in northern Greece	**3200** Beginnings of Bronze Age cultures in Cyclades and Crete	**2000** Arrival of first Greek-speakers on mainland Greece
200,000 BC	**5000 BC**	**4000 BC**	**3000 BC** **2000**
200,000 Evidence of Palaeolithic civilization in northern Greece and Thessaly		"Frying Pan" vessel from Sýros (2500–2000 BC)	**2800–2300** Kéros-Sýros culture flourishes in Cyclades
			2000 Building of palaces begins in Crete, initiating First Palace period

Mycenaean Death Mask

Large amounts of worked gold were discovered at wealthy Mycenae, the city of Agamemnon. Masks like this were laid over the faces of the dead.

Forested hills

The inhabitants are on friendly terms with the visitors.

Where to See Prehistoric Greece

The Museum of Cycladic Art in Athens (see pp78–9) has Greece's leading collection of Cycladic figurines. The remains at Mycenae are extensive (pp182–4) and the museum at Náfplio (p186) displays finds from this and other Mycenaean sites, as does the National Archaeological Museum, Athens (pp72–5). Excavations at Nestor's Palace (p205) uncovered tablets written in Linear B script. These earliest examples of Greek language can be seen in the museum at nearby Chóra, together with frescoes and pottery from the palace.

Cyclopean Walls

Mycenaean citadels, such as this one at Tiryns, were encircled by walls of stone so large that later civilizations believed they had been built by giants. It is unclear whether the walls were used for defence or just to impress.

Oared sailing ships

Minoan Sea Scene

The wall paintings on the island of Santoríni were preserved by the volcanic eruption at the end of the 16th century BC. This section shows ships departing from a coastal town. In contrast to the warlike Mycenaeans, Minoan art reflects a more stable community which dominated the Aegean through trade, not conquest.

Mycenaean Octopus Jar
This 14th-century BC vase's decoration follows the shape of the pot. Restrained and symmetrical, it contrasts with relaxed Minoan prototypes.

| 1750–1700 Start of Second Palace period and golden age of Minoan culture in Crete | 1525 Volcanic eruption on Santoríni devastates the region | 1250–1200 Probable destruction of Troy, after abduction of Helen (see p58) | |
| | | 1450 Mycenaeans take over Knosós; use of Linear B script | Helen of Troy |

| **1800 BC** | **1600 BC** | **1400 BC** | **1200 BC** |

| 1730 Destruction of Minoan palaces; end of First Palace period | | | 1200 Collapse of Mycenaean culture |
| 1600 Beginning of high period of Mycenaean prosperity and dominance | *Minoan figurine of a snake goddess, 1500 BC* | 1370–50 Palace of Knosós on Crete destroyed for second time |

The Dark Ages and Archaic Period

After 1200 BC, Greece entered a period of darkness. There was widespread poverty, the population decreased and many skills were lost. A cultural revival in about 800 BC accompanied the emergence of the city-states across Greece and inspired new styles of warfare, art and politics. Greek colonies were established as far away as the Black Sea, present-day Syria, North Africa and the western Mediterranean. Greece was defined by where Greeks lived.

Koúros (530 BC)
Koúroi were early monumental male nude statues *(see p74)*. Idealized representations rather than portraits, they were inspired by Egyptian statues, from which they take their frontal, forward-stepping pose.

Bronze breastplate

Locator Map
Areas of Greek influence

The double flute player kept the men marching in time.

Bronze greaves protected the legs.

Solon (640–558 BC)
Solon was appointed to the highest magisterial position in Athens. His legal, economic and political reforms heralded democracy.

Hoplite Warriors

The "Chigi" vase from Corinth, dating to about 750 BC, is one of the earliest clear depictions of the new style of warfare that evolved at that period. This required rigorously trained and heavily armed infantrymen called hoplites to fight in a massed formation or phalanx. The rise of the city-state may be linked to the spirit of equality felt by citizen hoplites fighting for their own community.

Vase fragment showing bands of distinctive geometric line patterns

900
Appearance of first Geometric pottery

1100 BC	**1000 BC**	**900 BC**

1100 Migrations of different peoples throughout the Greek world

1000–850 Formation of the Homeric kingdoms

6th-Century Vase
This bowl *(krater)* for mixing wine and water at elegant feasts is an early example of the art of vase painting. It depicts mythological and heroic scenes.

Where to See Archaic Greece

Examples of *koúroi* can be found in the National Archaeological Museum *(pp72–75)* and in the Acropolis Museum *(p104)*, both in Athens. The National Archaeological Museum also houses the national collection of Greek Geometric, red-figure and black-figure vases. The first victory over the Persians in 490 BC was commemorated by the mound of Athenian dead which still dominates the plain at Marathon *(p149)*. The museum at Sparta *(p193)* contains a bust of Leonidas, the Spartan king, who with his 300 hoplite soldiers, was massacred by the Persians at Thermopylae in 480 BC.

Bronze helmets for protection

Spears were used for thrusting.

The phalanxes shoved and pushed, aiming to maintain an unbroken shield wall, a successful new technique.

Gorgon's head decoration

Characteristic round shields

Hunter Returning Home
(500 BC) Hunting for hare, deer, or wild boar was an aristocratic sport pursued by Greek nobles on foot with dogs, as depicted on this cup.

Darius I (ruled 521–486 BC)
This relief from Persepolis shows the Persian king who tried to conquer the Greek mainland, but was defeated at the battle of Marathon in 490.

---

776 Traditional date for the first Olympic Games

675 Lykourgos initiates austere reforms in Sparta

600 First Doric columns built at Temple of Hera, Olympia

Doric capital

490 Athenians defeat Persians at Marathon

800 BC	700 BC	600 BC	500 BC

770 Greeks start founding colonies in Italy, Egypt and elsewhere

750–700 Homer records epic tales of the *Iliad* and *Odyssey*

Spartan votive figurine

546 Persians gain control over Ionian Greeks; Athens flourishes under the tyrant Peisistratos and his sons

630 Poetess Sappho writing in Lésvos

480 Athens destroyed by Persians who defeat Spartans at Thermopylae; Greek victory at Salamis

479 Persians annihilated at Plataiaí by Athenians, Spartans and allies

Classical Greece

The Classical period has always been considered the high point of Greek civilization. Around 150 years of exceptional creativity in thinking, writing, theatre and the arts produced the great tragedians Aeschylus, Sophocles and Euripides, as well as the great philosophical thinkers Socrates, Plato and Aristotle. This was also a time of warfare and bloodshed, however. The Peloponnesian War, which pitted the city-state of Athens and her allies against the city-state of Sparta and her allies, dominated the 5th century BC. In the 4th century, Sparta, Athens and Thebes struggled for power, only to be ultimately defeated by Philip II of Macedon in 338 BC.

Classical Greece, 440 BC

Athens and her allies

Sparta and her allies

Fish Shop
This detail is from a 4th- century BC Greek painted vase from Cefalù in Sicily. Large parts of the island were inhabited by Greeks who were bound by a common culture, religion and language.

Theatre used in Pythian Games

Temple of Apollo

Siphnian Treasury

Perikles
This great democratic leader built up the Greek navy and masterminded the extensive building programme in Athens between the 440s and 420s, including the Acropolis temples.

The Sanctuary of Delphi
The sanctuary (see pp232–3), shown in this 1894 reconstruction, reached the peak of its political influence in the 5th and 4th centuries BC. Of central importance was the Oracle of Apollo, whose utterances influenced the decisions of city-states such as Athens and Sparta. Rich gifts dedicated to the god were placed by the states in treasuries that lined the Sacred Way.

Detail of the Parthenon frieze

462 Ephialtes's reforms pave the way for radical democracy in Athens

431–404 Peloponnesian War, ending with the fall of Athens and start of 33-year period of Spartan dominance

c.424 Death of Herodotus, historian of the Persian Wars

475 BC

450 BC

425 BC

478 With the formation of the Delian League, Athens takes over leadership of Greek cities

451–429 Perikles rises to prominence in Athens and launches a lavish building programme

447 Construction of the Parthenon begins

Bust of Herodotus, probably of Hellenistic origin

Gold Oak Wreath from Vergína
By the mid-4th century BC, Philip II of Macedon dominated the Greek world through diplomacy and warfare. This wreath comes from his tomb.

Where to See Classical Greece

Athens is dominated by the Acropolis and its religious buildings, including the Parthenon, erected as part of Perikles's mid 5th-century BC building programme (pp98–103). The Marmaria, just outside the sanctuary at Delphi, features the remains of the unique circular tholos (p234). In the Peloponnese, the town of Messene dates from 396 BC (p205); the best-preserved theatre is at Epidaurus (pp188–9). Philip II's tomb can be seen at Vergína in Macedonia (p246).

Votive of the Rhodians

Stoa of the Athenians

Sacred Way

Athenian Treasury

Athena Lemnia
This Roman copy of a statue by Pheidias (c.490–c.430 BC), the sculptor-in-charge at the Acropolis, depicts the goddess protector of Athens in an ideal rather than realistic way, typical of the Classical style in art.

Slave Boy (400 BC)
Slaves were fundamental to the Greek economy and used for all types of work. Many slaves were foreign; this boot boy came from as far as Africa.

387 Plato founds Academy in Athens

Sculpture of Plato

359 Philip II becomes King of Macedon

337 Foundation of the League of Corinth legitimizes Philip II's control over the Greek city-states

400 BC

375 BC

350 BC

399 Trial and execution of Socrates

371 Sparta defeated by Thebes at Battle of Leuktra, heralding a decade of Theban dominance in the area

338 Greeks defeated by Philip II of Macedon at Battle of Chaironeia

336 Philip II is assassinated at Aigai and is succeeded by h son, Alexander

Hellenistic Greece

Alexander the Great of Macedon fulfilled his father Philip's plans for the conquest of the Persians. He went on to create a vast empire that extended to India in the east and Egypt in the south. The Hellenistic period was extraordinary for the dispersal of Greek language, religion and culture throughout the territories conquered by Alexander. It lasted from after Alexander's death in 323 BC until the Romans began to dismantle his empire, early in the 2nd century BC. For Greece, Macedonian domination was replaced by that of Rome in AD 168.

Relief of Hero-Worship (c.200 BC) The worship of heroes after death was a feature of Greek religion. Alexander, however, was worshipped as a god in his lifetime.

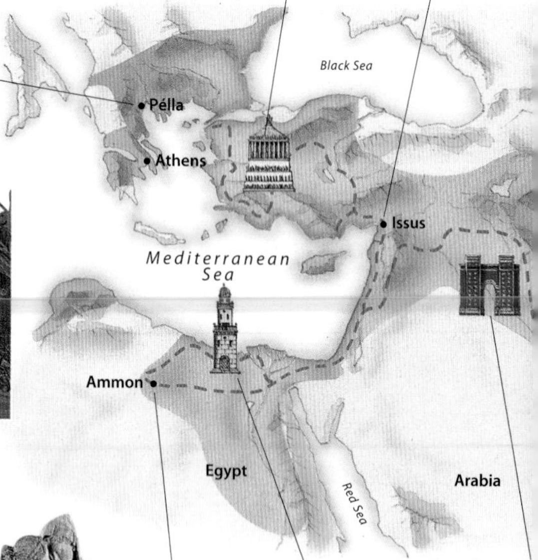

The Mausoleum of Halicarnassus was one of the Seven Wonders of the Ancient World.

Issus, in modern Turkey, was the site of Alexander's victory over the Persian army in 333 BC.

Pélla was the birthplace of Alexander and capital of Macedon.

Black Sea

• Pélla

• Athens

• Issus

Mediterranean Sea

Ammon •

Egypt

Red Sea

Arabia

Alexander Defeats Darius III
This Pompeiian mosaic shows the Persian leader overwhelmed at Issus in 333 BC. Macedonian troops are shown carrying their highly effective long pikes.

Alexander died in Babylon in 323 BC.

The Ammon oracle declared Alexander to be divine.

Alexandria, founded by Alexander, replaced Athens as the centre of Greek culture.

Terracotta Statue
This 2nd-century BC statue of two women gossiping is typical of a Hellenistic interest in private rather than public individuals.

Key

··· Alexander's route

▦ Alexander's empire

▦ Dependent regions

---

333 Alexander the Great defeats the Persian king, Darius III, and declares himself king of Asia

323 Death of Alexander, and of Diogenes

301 Battle of Ipsus, between Alexander's rival successors, leads to the break-up of his empire into three kingdoms

268–261 Chremonidean War, ending with the capitulation of Athens to Macedon

| **325 BC** | **300 BC** | **275 BC** | **250 BC** |

322 Death of Aristotle

287–275 "Pyrrhic victory" of King Pyrros of Epirus who defeated the Romans in Italy but suffered heavy losses

331 Alexander founds Alexandria after conquering Egypt

Diogenes, the Hellenistic philosopher

Fusing Eastern and Western Religion
This plaque from Afghanistan shows the Greek goddess Nike and the Asian goddess Cybele in a chariot pulled by lions.

Where to See Hellenistic Greece

The royal palace at Pélla (p247), capital of Macedon and birthplace of Alexander, and the palace of Palatítsia (p246) are exceptional. Pélla has outstanding mosaics, one of which depicts Alexander. Goldwork and other finds are in the museum at Pélla and the Archaeological Museum at Thessaloníki (pp250–51). In Athens, the Stoa of Attalos (p94) in the Greek Agora was given by Attalos of Pergamon (ruled 159 to 138 BC). The Tower of the Winds (pp90–91) in the Roman Agora, built by the Macedonian astronomer Andronikos Kyrrestes, incorporates a water clock.

Susa, capital of the Persian Empire, was captured in 331 BC. A mass wedding of Alexander's captains to Asian brides was held in 324 BC.

Alexander chose his wife, Roxane, from among Sogdian captives in 327 BC.

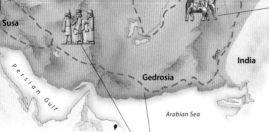

Caspian Sea

Sogdiani

Battle elephants were used against the Indian King Poros in 326 BC.

• Alexandropolis

• Taxil

Persia

Bactria

Alexander's army turned back at the River Beas.

• Susa

Beas

India

Gedrosia

The Persian religious centre of Persepolis, in modern Iran, fell to Alexander in 330 BC.

Arabian Sea

Alexander's army suffered heavy losses in the Gedrosia desert.

Alexander the Great's Empire

In forming his empire, Alexander covered huge distances. After defeating the Persians in Asia, he moved to Egypt, then returned to Asia to pursue Darius, and then his murderers, into Bactria. In 326 BC, his troops revolted in India and refused to go on. Alexander died in 323 BC in Babylon.

The Death of Archimedes
Archimedes was the leading Hellenistic scientist and mathematician. This mosaic from Renaissance Italy shows his murder in 212 BC by a Roman.

227 Colossus of Rhodes destroyed by earthquake

Colossus of Rhodes

197 Romans defeat Philip V of Macedon and declare Greece liberated

146 Romans sack Corinth and Greece becomes a province of Rome

225 BC	200 BC	175 BC	150 BC

222 Macedon crushes Sparta

217 Peace of Náfpaktos: a call for the Greeks to settle their differences before "the cloud in the west" (Rome) settles over them

168 Macedonians defeated by Romans at Pydna

Roman coin commemorating Roman victory over the Macedonians in 196 BC

Roman Greece

After the Romans gained final control of Greece, with the sack of Corinth in 146 BC, Greece became the cultural centre of the Roman Empire. The Roman nobility sent their sons to be educated in the schools of philosophy in Athens *(see p61)*. The end of the Roman civil wars between leading Roman statesmen was played out on Greek soil, finishing in the Battle of Actium in Thessaly in 31 BC. In AD 323, the Emperor Constantine founded the new eastern capital of Constantinople; the empire was later divided into the Greek-speaking East and the Latin-speaking West.

Roman Provinces, AD 211

Roman basilica

Bema, or raised platform, where St Paul spoke

Mithridates
In a bid to extend his territory, this ruler of Pontus, on the Black Sea, led the resistance to Roman rule in 88 BC. He was forced to make peace three years later.

Bouleuterion

Notitia Dignitatum (AD 395)
As part of the Roman Empire, Greece was split into several provinces. The proconsul of the province of Achaïa used this insignia.

Springs of Peirene, the source of water

Reconstruction of Roman Corinth

Corinth (see pp166–70) was refounded and largely rebuilt by Julius Caesar in 46 BC, becoming the capital of the Roman province of Achaïa. The Romans built the forum, covered theatre and basilicas. St Paul visited the city in AD 50–51, working as a tent maker.

Baths of Eurycles

A coin of Cleopatra, Queen of Egypt

49–31 BC Rome's civil wars end with the defeat of Mark Antony and Cleopatra at Actium, in Greece

AD 49–54 St Paul preaches Christianity in Greece

AD 124–131 Emperor Hadrian oversees huge building programme in Athens

| 100 BC | AD 1 | AD 1 |

86 BC Roman commander, Sulla, captures Athens

46 BC Corinth refounded as Roman colony

St Paul preaching

AD 66–7 Emperor Nero tours Greece

Mosaic (AD 180) This highly sophisticated Roman mosaic of Dionysos riding on a leopard comes from the House of Masks, on Delos.

Where to See Roman Greece

In Athens, the Roman Agora, Hadrian's library nearby (p88) and the Arch of Hadrian (p115), which leads from the Roman into the old Greek city (pp94–5), are examples of Roman architecture. The Temple of Olympian Zeus (p115) and the Theatre of Herodes Atticus (p101) are also in Athens. The triumphal arch of Galerius in Thessaloníki (p248) commemorates the Emperor Galerius's victories over the Persians in AD 297. The museum at Corinth (p170) contains fine Roman mosaics and other artifacts.

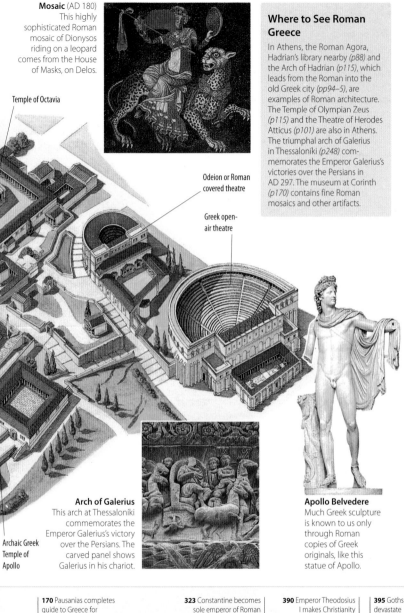

Temple of Octavia

Odeion or Roman covered theatre

Greek open-air theatre

Archaic Greek Temple of Apollo

Arch of Galerius This arch at Thessaloníki commemorates the Emperor Galerius's victory over the Persians. The carved panel shows Galerius in his chariot.

Apollo Belvedere Much Greek sculpture is known to us only through Roman copies of Greek originals, like this statue of Apollo.

170 Pausanias completes guide to Greece for Roman travellers

267 Goths pillage Athens

323 Constantine becomes sole emperor of Roman Empire and establishes his capital in Constantinople

390 Emperor Theodosius I makes Christianity state religion

395 Goths devastate Athens and Peloponnese

AD 200

AD 300

Coin of the Roman Emperor Galerius

293 Under Emperor Galerius, Thessaloníki becomes second city to Constantinople

393 Olympic Games banned

395 Death of Theodosius I; formal division of Roman Empire into Latin West and Byzantine East

Byzantine and Crusader Greece

Under the Byzantine Empire, which at the end of the 4th century succeeded the old Eastern Roman Empire, Greece became Orthodox in religion and was split into administrative *themes*. When the capital, Constantinople, fell to the Crusaders in 1204, Greece was again divided, mostly between the Venetians and the Franks. Constantinople and Mystrás were recovered by the Byzantine Greeks in 1261, but the Turks' capture of Constantinople in 1453 was a significant part of the demise of the Byzantine Empire. It left a legacy of hundreds of churches and a wealth of religious art.

Byzantine Greece in the 10th Century

Chapel

Watch-tower of Tsimiskís

Refectory

Two-Headed Eagle
The double-headed eagle was an omnipresent symbol of the power of the Byzantine Empire in this era.

Great Lavra
This monastery is the earliest (AD 963) and largest of the religious complexes on Mount Athos (see pp256–8). Many parts of it have been rebuilt, but its appearance remains essentially Byzantine. The monasteries became important centres of learning and religious art.

Defence of Thessaloníki
The fall of Thessaloníki to the Saracens in AD 904 was a blow to the Byzantine Empire. Many towns in Greece were heavily fortified against attack from this time.

578–86 Avars and Slavs invade Greece

Gold solidus of the Byzantine Empress Irene, who ruled AD 797–802

400	600	800

529 Aristotle's and Plato's schools of philosophy close as Christian culture supplants Classical thought

680 Bulgars cross Danube and establish empire in northern Greece

726 Iconoclasm introduced by Pope Leo III (abandoned in 843)

841 Parthenon becomes a cathedral

Constantine the Great
The first eastern emperor to recognize Christianity, Constantine founded the city of Constantinople in AD 324. Here, he is shown with his mother, Helen.

Where to See Byzantine and Crusader Greece

In Athens, both the Benáki (*pp82–3*) and the Byzantine (*p80*) museums contain sculpture, icons, metalwork and textiles. The medieval city of Mystrás (*pp196–7*) has a castle, palaces, houses and monasteries. The churches of Thessaloníki (*p252*) and the monasteries of Dafní (*pp156–7*) and Osios Loúkas (*pp226–7*) contain fine Byzantine mosaics and frescoes, as do the monasteries of Mount Athos (*pp256–8*). Chlemoútsi (*p173*), built in 1223, is one of Greece's oldest Frankish castles. There are important fortresses at Acrocorinth (*p170*) and Monemvasía (*pp190–92*).

Cypress tree of Agios Athanásios

Christ Pantokrátor
This 14th-century fresco of Christ as ruler of the world is in the Byzantine city and monastic centre of Mystrás.

Fortified walls

Chapel of Agios Athanásios, founder of Great Lávra

Combined library and treasury

The katholikón, the main church in Great Lávra, has the most magnificent post-Byzantine murals on Mount Athos.

1054 Patriarch of Constantinople and Pope Leo IX excommunicate each other

1081–1149 Normans invade Greek islands and mainland

Frankish Chlemoútsi Castle

1354 Ottoman Turks enter Europe via southern Italy and Greece

1390–1450 Turks gain power over much of mainland Greece

| **1000** | **1200** | | **1400** |

Basil the Bulgar Slayer, Byzantine emperor (lived 956–1025)

1204 Crusaders sack Constantinople. Break-up of Byzantine Empire as result of occupation by Franks and Venetians

1210 Venetians win control over Crete

1261 Start of intellectual and artistic flowering of Mystrás; Constantinople reoccupied by Byzantines

1389 Venetians in control of much of Greece and the islands

Venetian and Ottoman Greece

Following the Ottomans' momentous capture of Constantinople in 1453, and their conquest of almost all the remaining Greek territory by 1460, the Greek state effectively ceased to exist for the next 350 years. Although the city became the capital of the vast Ottoman Empire, it remained the principal centre of Greek population and the focus of Greek dreams of resurgence. The small Greek population of what today is modern Greece languished in an impoverished and underpopulated backwater, but even there, rebellious bands of brigands and private militias were formed. The Ionian Islands, Crete and a few coastal enclaves were seized for long periods by the Venetians – an experience more intrusive than the inefficient tolerance of the Ottomans, but one which left a rich cultural and architectural legacy.

Locator Map

Areas occupied by Venetians

Areas occupied by Ottomans

Battle of Lepanto (1571)
The Christian fleet, under Don John of Austria, decisively defeated the Ottomans off Náfpaktos, halting their advance westwards (see p229).

Cretan Painting
This 15th-century icon is typical of the style developed by Greek artists in the School of Crete, active until the Ottomans took Crete in 1669.

Arrival of Turkish Prince Cem on Rhodes

Prince Cem, Ottoman rebel and son of Mehmet II, fled to Rhodes in 1481 and was welcomed by the Christian Knights of St John. In 1522, however, Rhodes fell to the Ottomans after a siege.

1453 Mehmet II captures Constantinople, which is renamed Istanbul and made capital of the Ottoman Empire

1503 Ottoman Turks win control of the Peloponnese apart from Monemvasía

1571 Venetian and Spanish fleet defeats Ottoman Turks at the Battle of Lepanto

1500   **1550**   **1600**

1460 Turks capture Mystrás

1456 Ottoman Turks occupy Athens

1522 The Knights of St John forced to cede Rhodes to the Ottomans

Cretan chain mail armour from the 16th century

Shipping

Greek merchants traded throughout the Ottoman Empire. By 1800, there were merchant colonies in Constantinople and as far afield as London and Odessa. This 19th-century embroidery shows the Turkish influence on Greek decorative arts.

Where to See Venetian and Ottoman Architecture

Náfplio (pp186–7) contains many examples of the Venetian presence, especially the Naval Warehouse (now a museum) and the Palamídi fortress (p187). Following a pattern familiar throughout the Balkan states, enormous efforts were made after Independence to remove or disguise all Ottoman buildings. However, in Athens there are small but well-preserved Ottoman quarters in the Pláka district, and the Tzistarákis Mosque (now the Ceramic Museum, p90) is also Ottoman. The White Tower in Thessaloníki (p248) was built by the Turks in the 15th century. In Kavála (p259), there is an aqueduct built in the reign of Suleiman the Magnificent, and in Ioánnina (p214), the Aslan Pasha Mosque.

The Knights of St John defied the Turks until 1522.

The massive fortifications eventually succumbed to Turkish artillery.

The Knights supported Turkish rebel, Prince Cem.

Dinner at a Greek House in 1801
Nearly four centuries of Ottoman rule profoundly affected Greek culture, ethnic composition and patterns of everyday life. Greek cuisine incorporates Turkish dishes still found thoughout the old Ottoman Empire.

1687 Parthenon seriously damaged during Venetian artillery attack on Turkish magazine

1715 Turks reconquer the Peloponnese

Ali Pasha (1741–1822), a governor of the Ottoman Empire

1814 Britain gains possession of Ionian Islands

1650	1700	1750	1800

1684 Venetians reconquer the Peloponnese

Parthenon blown up

1778 Ali Pasha becomes Vizier of Ioánnina and establishes powerful state in Albania and northern Greece

1801 Frieze on Parthenon removed by Lord Elgin

1814 Foundation of *Filikí Etaireía*, Greek liberation movement

The Making of Modern Greece

The Greek War of Independence marked the overthrow of the Ottomans and the start of the "Great Idea", an ambitious project to bring all Greek people under one flag *(énosis)*. The plans for expansion were initially successful, and during the 19th century, the Greeks succeeded in doubling their national territory and reasserting Greek sovereignty over many of the islands. However, an attempt to take Asia Minor by force after World War I ended in disaster. In 1922, millions of Greeks were expelled from Smyrna in Turkish Anatolia, ending thousands of years of Greek presence in Asia Minor.

The Emerging Greek State

Greece in 1832

Areas gained 1832–1923

Massacre at Chíos
This detail of Delacroix's shocking painting *Scènes de Massacres de Scio* shows the events of 1822, when Turks took savage revenge for an earlier killing of Muslims.

Klephts (mountain brigands) were the basis of the Independence movement.

Weapons were family heirlooms or donated by philhellenes.

Declaration of the Constitution in Athens
Greece's Neo-Classical parliament building in Athens was the site of the Declaration of the Constitution in 1843. It was built as the Royal Palace for Greece's first monarch, King Otto, during the 1830s.

1824 The poet Lord Byron dies of a fever at Mesolóngi

1831 President Kapodístrias assassinated

1832 Great Powers establish protectorate over Greece and appoint Otto, Bavarian prince, as king

1834 Athens replaces Náfplio as capital

German archaeologist Heinrich Schliemann

| 1830 | 1840 | 1850 | 1860 | 1870 |

1827 Battle of Navaríno

1828 Ioánnis Kapodístrias becomes first president of Greece

King Otto (ruled 1832–62)

1862 Revolution drives King Otto from Greece

1874 Heinrich Schliemann begins excavation of Mycenae

1821 Greek flag of independence raised on 25 March; Greeks massacre Turks at Tripolitsá in Morea

1864 New constitution makes Greece a "crowned democracy"; Greek Orthodoxy made the state religion

Life in Athens

By 1836, urban Greeks still wore a mixture of Greek traditional and Western dress. The Ottoman legacy had not totally disappeared and is visible in the fez worn by men.

Where to See 19th-century Greece

Independence was proclaimed at the Moní Agías Lávras, near Kalávryta (*p172*). Lord Byron died at Mesolóngi (*p229*). Ioánnis Kapodístrias was assassinated at the church of Agios Spyrídon in Náfplio (*p186*). Pýlos is the site of the battle of Navaríno (*p204*).

Flag Raising of 1821 Revolution

In 1821, the Greek secret society Filikí Etaireía *was behind a revolt by Greek officers which led to anti-Turk uprisings throughout the Peloponnese. Tradition credits Archbishop Germanós of Pátra with raising the rebel flag near Kalávryta* (see p172) *on 25 March. The struggle for independence had begun.*

Corinth Canal

This spectacular link between the Aegean and Ionian seas opened in 1893 *(see p171)*.

Elefthérios Venizélos

This great Cretan politician and advocate of liberal democracy doubled Greek territory during the Balkan Wars (1912–13) and joined the Allies in World War I.

1893 Opening of Corinth Canal

1896 First Olympics of modern era, held in Athens

1919 Greece launches offensive in Asia Minor

1908 Crete united with Greece

1917 King Constantine resigns; Greece joins World War I

1922 Turkish burning of Smyrna signals end of the "Great Idea"

1880	1890	1900	1910	1920

Spyrídon Loúis, marathon winner at the first modern Olympics

1899 Arthur Evans begins excavations at Knosós

1912–13 Greece extends its borders during the Balkan Wars

1920 Treaty of Sèvres gives Greece huge gains in territory

1923 Population exchange agreed between Greece and Turkey at Treaty of Lausanne. Greece loses previous gains

Twentieth-Century Greece

The years after the 1922 defeat by Turkey were terrible ones for Greek people. The influx of refugees contributed to the political instability of the interwar years. The dictatorship of Metaxás was followed by invasion in 1940, then Italian, German and Bulgarian occupation and, finally, Civil War between 1946 and 1949, with its legacy of division. After experiencing the Cyprus problem of the 1950s and the military dictatorship of 1967 to 1974, Greece is now an established democracy and a member of the European Economic and Monetary Union.

Barber shop in Marousi, a painting by Tsaroúchis

1938 Death of sculptor Giannoúlis Chalepás, best known for his *Sleeping Girl* funerary statue

1946 Government institutes "White Terror" against Communists

1947 Internationally acclaimed Greek artist, Giánnis Tsaroúchis, holds his first exhibition of set designs, in the Romvos Gallery, Athens

1945 Níkos Kazantzákis publishes *Zorba the Greek*, later made into a film

1957 Mosaics found by chance at Philip II's 300 BC palace at Pélla

1967 Right-wing colonels form Junta, forcing King Constantine into exile

1933 Death of Greek poet Constantine (C P) Cavafy

1925	1935	1945	1955	1965

1925	1935	1945	1955	1965

1932 Aristotle Onassis purchases six freight ships, the start of his shipping empire

1939 Greece declares neutrality at start of World War II

1951 Greece enters NATO

1955 Greek Cypriots start campaign of violence in Cyprus against British rule

1948 Dodecanese becomes part of Greece

1963 Geórgios Papandréou's centre-left government voted into power

1925 Mános Chatzidákis, who wrote music for the film *Never on Sunday*, is born

1960 Cyprus declared independent

1940 Italy invades Greece. Greek soldiers defend northern Greece. Greece enters World War II

1946–9 Civil War between Greek government and the Communists who take to the mountains

1944 Churchill visits Athens to show his support for Greek government against Communist Resistance

1981 Melína Merkoúri appointed Minister of Culture. Start of campaign to restore Elgin Marbles to Greece

1993 Andréas Papandréou wins Greek general election for the third time

1973 University students in Athens rebel against dictatorship and are crushed by military forces. Start of decline in power of dictatorship

1974 Cyprus is partitioned after Turkish invasion

1988 Eight million visitors to Greece; tourism continues to expand

1994 Because of the choking smog (néfos), central Athens introduces traffic restrictions

1998 Karamanlís leaves office and Stefanopoulos succeeds him

2005 The Greek Parliament ratifies the EU constitution

2010 Economic crisis forces Greece to apply for financial support from the International Monetary Fund, European Central Bank and European Commission

1975	1985	1995	2005	2015

1975	1985	1995	2005	2015

1975 Death of Aristotle Onassis

1990 New Democracy voted into power; Konstantínos Karamanlís becomes President

2002 Euro becomes sole legal currency

2012 Greece's first coalition government in 60 years is formed by three parties, led by prime minister Antonis Samaras of the conservative New Democracy party

1974 Fall of Junta; Konstantínos Karamanlís elected Prime Minister

1981 Andréas Papandréou's left-wing PASOK party forms first Greek Socialist government

2003 Greek presidency of EU (Jan–Jun)

1997 Athens is awarded the 2004 Olympics

2009 Left-wing PASOK party voted into Power; George Papandréou becomes Prime Minister

2007 Wildfires in Peloponnese cause the death of more than 70 people

2004 Athens hosts the Olympic Games

1994 European leaders meet in Corfu under Greek presidency of the EU

1973 Greek bishops give their blessing to the short-lived presidency of Colonel Papadópoulos

1996 Andréas Papandréou dies; Kóstas Simítis succeeds him

ATHENS AND MAINLAND GREECE THROUGH THE YEAR

Predominantly rural, Greece is deeply attached to its locally produced food and wine, and chapels dotting the countryside serve as the focus for culinary, as well as religious, celebrations. Festivals of the Orthodox Church are deeply identified with Greekness, no more so than on 25 March, a date which commemorates both the Feast of the Annunciation and the start of the Independence uprising in 1821. Summer festivals are celebrated widely in rural villages, and expatriate Greeks return from across the globe. Organized arts events are a more recent phenomenon, paralleling the rise of tourism.

Spring

Spring is a glorious time in Greece. The lowland landscape, parched for much of the year, luxuriates in a carpet of green, and wild flowers abound. But the weather does not stabilize until late spring, with rainy or blustery days common in March and April. Artichokes ripen in March, and May sees the first strawberries. The fishing season lasts to the end of May, overlapping with the start of the tourist season. Spring festivities focus on Easter.

25 March, Independence Day

March

Apókries, Carnival Sunday *(first Sun before Lent)*. Carnivals take place for three weeks leading up to this climax of pre-Lenten festivities. There are parades and costume balls in many large cities, and the port of Pátra *(see p173)* hosts one of the most exuberant celebrations.

Katharí Deftéra, Clean Monday *(immediately after "Cheese Sunday" – seven Sundays before Easter)*. Kites are flown in the countryside.

Independence Day and **Evangelismós** *(25 Mar)*. A national holiday, with parades and dances nationwide celebrating the 1821 revolt against the Ottoman Empire. The religious festival, one of the most important for the Orthodox Church, marks the Angel Gabriel's announcement to the Virgin Mary that she was to become the Holy Mother.

Celebrating Easter in Greece

Greek Orthodox Easter can fall up to three weeks either side of Western Easter. It is the most important religious festival in Greece, and Holy Week is a time for Greek families to reunite. It is also a good time to visit Greece, to see the processions and church services and to sample the Easter food. The ceremony and symbolism is a direct link with Greece's Byzantine past, as well as with earlier and more primitive beliefs. The festivities reach a climax at midnight on Easter Saturday. As priests intone "Christ is risen", fireworks are lit, the explosions ushering in a Sunday devoted to feasting, music and dance. Smaller, more isolated towns, such as Andrítsaina and Koróni in the Peloponnese, and Polýgyros (the capital of Chalkidikí), are particularly worth visiting during Holy Week for the Friday and Saturday night services.

Christ's bier, decorated with flowers and containing His effigy, is carried in solemn procession through the streets at dusk on Good Friday.

Priests in their richly embroidered Easter robes

Candle lighting takes place at the end of the Easter Saturday mass. In pitch darkness, a single flame is used to light the candles held by worshippers.

Banners raised during a workers' May Day rally in Athens

April

Megáli Evdomáda, Holy Week *(Apr or May)*, including *Kyriakí ton Vaḯon* (Palm Sunday), *Megáli Pémpti* (Maundy Thursday), *Megáli Paraskeví* (Good Friday), *Megálo Sávvato* (Easter Saturday), and the most important date in the Orthodox calendar, *Páscha* (Easter Sunday).

Agios Geórgios, St George's Day *(23 Apr)*. One of the most important feast days in the Orthodox calendar, commemorating the patron saint of shepherds, and traditionally marking the start of the grazing season. Celebrations are nationwide, and are particularly festive at Aráchova, near Delphi *(see p225)*.

May

Protomagiá, May Day *(1 May)*. Also known as Labour Day, this is given over to a national holiday. Traditionally, families go to the countryside and pick wild flowers, which are made into wreaths with garlic. These

Firewalkers in a Macedonian village, 21 May

are then hung on doors, balconies, fishing boats and even car bonnets to ward off evil. In major towns and cities across the country, there are also parades and workers' rallies to mark Labour Day, usually led by the Communist Party.

Agios Konstantínos kai Agía Eléni *(21 May)*. A celebration throughout Greece for Constantine and his mother, Helen, the first Orthodox Byzantine rulers *(see p41)*. Firewalking ceremonies may be seen in some Macedonian villages.

Análipsi, Ascension *(40 days after Easter; usually late May)*. This is another important religious feast day.

Easter biscuits celebrate the end of Lent. Another Easter dish, *magirítsa* soup, is made of lamb's innards and is eaten in the early hours of Easter Sunday.

The procession of candles in the very early hours of Easter Day, here at Lykavittós Hill in Athens, celebrates Christ's resurrection.

Egg loaves, made of sweet plaited dough, contain eggs with shells dyed red to symbolize the blood of Christ. Red eggs are also given separately as presents.

Lamb roasting is traditionally done in the open air on giant spits over charcoal, for lunch on Easter Sunday. The first retsina wine from the previous year's harvest is opened. After lunch, young and old join hands to dance, Greek-style.

Summer

Warm days in early June signal the first sea-baths for Greeks (traditionally after Análipsi, Ascension Day). The peak tourist season begins, and continues until late August; after mid-July, it can be difficult to find hotel vacancies in the more popular resorts. June sees the arrival of cherries, plums and apricots, and the collection of honey from beehives can begin. The last green leaf vegetables are soon totally replaced by tomatoes, melons and cucumbers. By July, much of the Aegean is buffeted by the notorious *meltémi*, a high-pressure northerly wind, which – though more severe on the islands – can be felt along the mainland coast.

Various cultural festivals – programmed with an eye on the tourist audience, but no less impressive for that – are hosted in major cities and resorts. Outdoor cinemas are also well attended *(see p123)*. Urban Greeks retreat to mountain villages, often the venues for musical and religious fairs.

Beehives for summer honey production, near Mount Parnassus

June

Pentikostí, Pentecost or Whit Sunday *(seven weeks after Orthodox Easter)*. This important Orthodox feast day is celebrated throughout Greece.

Consecrated bread, baked for festivals

Agíou Pnévmatos, Feast of the Holy Spirit or Whit Monday *(the following day)*. A national holiday.

Athens Festival *(mid-Jun to mid-Sep)*. A cultural festival encompassing a mix of modern and ancient theatre, ballet, opera, classical music and jazz. It takes place at various venues, including the Herodes Atticus Theatre *(see p123)* and the Lykavittós Theatre *(see p76)*. The Herodes Atticus Theatre, on the slopes of the Acropolis, hosts performances of ancient tragedies, concerts by international orchestras and ballet. The Lykavittós Theatre, spectacularly situated on Lykavittós Hill, with extensive views across Athens, hosts performances of modern music – jazz and folk – as well as drama and dance.

Epidaurus Festival *(Jun-Aug)*. Affiliated to the Athens Festival, though sited 150 km (90 miles) from the capital at the Epidaurus Theatre *(see p188)* in the Peloponnese, this festival includes open-air performances of Classical drama.

Agios Ioánnis, St John's Day *(24 Jun)*. A day celebrated throughout Greece commemorating the birth of St John the Baptist. However, it is on the evening of the 23rd that bonfires are lit in most areas, and May wreaths consigned to the flames. Older children jump over the fires. This is an equivalent celebration to midsummer's eve.

Agioi Apóstoloi Pétros kai Pávlos, Saints Peter and Paul *(29 Jun)*. A widely celebrated name day for Pétros and Pávlos.

July

Agía Marína *(17 Jul)*. This day is widely celebrated in rural areas, with feasts to honour the saint, an important protector of crops.

Ioánnina's Cultural Summer *(through Jul and Aug)*. A wide range of music, arts and cultural events.

Profítis Ilías, the Prophet Elijah *(18–20 Jul)*. Widely celebrated at hill-top shrines, the best known being Mount Taÿgetos, near the town of Spárti. Name day for Ilías.

Agía Paraskeví *(26 Jul)*. There are many big village festivals on this day, but it is particularly celebrated in the Epirus region.

Musical performance at the illuminated Lykavittós Theatre

Agios Panteleímon *(27 Jul)*. As a doctor-saint, he is celebrated as the patron of many hospitals, and as a popular rural saint, he is celebrated in the countryside. Name day for Pantelís and Panteleímon.

Strings of tomatoes hanging out to dry in the autumn sunshine

August
Metamórfosi, Transfiguration of Christ *(6 Aug)*. For the Orthodox church, this is an important feast day. Name day for Sotíris and Sotiría.
Koímisis tis Theotókou, Assumption of the Virgin Mary *(15 Aug)*. A national holiday, and an important and widely celebrated feast day. This is traditionally a day when Greeks return to celebrate in their home villages. It is also a name day for Mary, María, Pános and Panagiótis.

Pátra Summer Festival *(Aug–Sep)*. This festival offers events such as Classical drama and art exhibitions, as well as music concerts in the Roman theatre.
Vlachopanagía *(19 Aug)*. This is a day of celebration in many Vlach villages located in the mountainous Epirus region.
Apotomí Kefalís Ioánnou Prodrómou, beheading of John the Baptist *(29 Aug)*. The occasion for festivals at the many country chapels that bear his name.

Autumn

By September, most village festivals have finished. The sea is at its warmest for swimming and, though the crowds have gone, most facilities are still available. There is a second, minor blooming of wild flowers, and the fine, still days of October are known as the "little summer of St Dimítrios", randomly punctuated by stormy weather. Grapes, and the fat peaches *germádes*, are virtually the only fruit to ripen since the figs of August, and strings of onions, garlic and tomatoes are hung up to

Girl in national dress for 15 August festivities

dry for the winter. The hills echo with the sound of the September quail shoot and dragnet fishing resumes.

Ceremonial dress on Ochi Day

September
Génnisis tis Theotókou, birth of the Virgin Mary *(8 Sep)*. An important religious feast day in the calendar of the Orthodox church.
Ypsosis tou Timíou Stavroú, Exaltation of the True Cross *(14 Sep)*. This is an important Orthodox feast day, and, although it is almost autumn, it is regarded as the last of Greece's major outdoor summer festivals.

October
Agios Dimítrios *(26 Oct)*. This marks the end of the grazing season, when sheep are brought down from the hills. Celebrations for Dimítrios are particularly lively in Thessaloníki, where he is the patron saint. Name day for Dimítris and Dímitra.
Ochi Day *(28 Oct)*. A national holiday, with patriotic parades in cities and plenty of dancing. It commemorates the Greek reply to the 1940 ultimatum from Mussolini calling for Greek surrender: an emphatic no *(óchi)*.

November
Ton Taxiarchón Archangélou Michaïl kai Gavriíl *(8 Nov)*. Ceremonies at the many rural monasteries and churches named after Archangels Gabriel and Michael. It is also name day for Michális and Gavriíl.
Eisódia tis Theotókou, Presentation of the Virgin in the Temple *(21 Nov)*. An important feast day in the Orthodox calendar, celebrated throughout Greece.
Agios Andréas, St Andrew's Day *(30 Nov)*, Pátra. A long liturgy is recited for Pátra's patron saint in the opulent cathedral named after him.

Celebrating the Assumption of the Virgin Mary, 15 August

View over a snow-covered Herodes Atticus Theatre, Athens

Public Holidays

Agios Vasíleios (1 Jan)

Independence Day (25 Mar)

Protomagiá (1 May)

Megáli Paraskeví (Good Friday)

Páscha (Easter Sunday)

Deftéra tou P9scha (Easter Monday)

Christoúgenna (25 Dec)

Sýnaxis tis Theotókou (26 Dec)

Winter

Many mountain villages assume a ghostly aspect in winter, with their seasonal inhabitants returned to the cities. Deep snow accumulates at higher altitudes and skiing can begin; elsewhere, rain falls several days of the week. Fishing is in full swing, and at the markets, kiwi fruits and exotic greens abound. Cheese shops display a full range of goat and sheep products, and olives are pressed for oil. The major festivals cluster to either side of the solstice. New Year and Epiphany are the most fervently celebrated festivals during winter.

Branch of olives

December

Agios Nikólaos, St Nicholas's Day *(6 Dec)*. The patron saint of seafarers, travellers, children and orphans is celebrated at seaside churches. Name day for Nikólaos and Nikolétta.

Christoúgenna, Christmas *(25 Dec)*. A national holiday and, though less significant than Easter, it still constitutes an important religious feast day.

Sýnaxis tis Theotókou, meeting of the Virgin's entourage *(26 Dec)*. A religious celebration and national holiday.

January

Agios Vasíleios, also known as *Protochroniá*, or New Year *(1 Jan)*. A national holiday. Gifts are exchanged on this day and the traditional new year greeting is *Kalí Chroniá*.

Theofánia, or Epiphany *(6 Jan)*. A national holiday and an important feast day. Blessing of the waters ceremonies take place by rivers and coastal locations throughout Greece. Youths dive to recover a cross that is thrown into the water by a priest.

Gynaikokratía *(8 Jan)*, Thrace. Matriarchy is celebrated by women and men swapping roles for the day in some villages of Thrace.

February

Ypapantí, Candlemas *(2 Feb)*. An Orthodox feast day all over Greece, at a quiet time, prior to pre-Lenten carnivals.

Diving for a cross at a blessing of the waters ceremony, 6 January

Women playing cards on Gynaikokratía day, Thrace

Name Days

Greeks celebrate their name day, or *giortí*, the day of the saint after whom they were named when baptized. Children are usually named after their grandparents, though in recent years, it has become fashionable to give children names deriving from Greece's history and mythology. When someone celebrates their name day, you may be told, *Giortázo símera* (I'm celebrating today), to which the traditional reply is *Chrónia pollá* (many years). Friends tend to drop in, bearing small gifts, and are given cakes and sweet liqueurs in return.

The Climate of Mainland Greece

The mainland climate varies most between the coastal lowlands and the mountainous inland regions. The mountains of western Greece and the Peloponnese get heavy snow in winter, rain during autumn and spring, and hot days in summer. The Ionian coast has milder temperatures, but is the wettest part of Greece. In Macedonia and Thrace, rainfall is spread more evenly across the year, with the North Aegean exerting a moderating influence on coastal temperatures. Around Athens, temperatures are hot in summer and rarely drop below freezing in winter, when rainfall is at its greatest.

NORTHERN GREECE

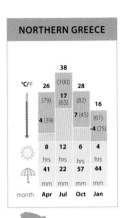

°C/°F		38 (100)		
	26 (79)	17 (63)	28 (82)	16 (61)
	4 (39)		7 (45)	-4 (25)
☀	8 hrs	12 hrs	6 hrs	4 hrs
☂	41 mm	22 mm	57 mm	44 mm
month	Apr	Jul	Oct	Jan

CENTRAL AND WESTERN GREECE

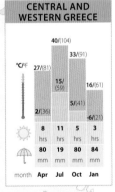

°C/°F		40/(104)	33/(91)	
	27/(81)	15/ (59)		16/(61)
	2/(36)		5/(41)	-6/(21)
☀	8 hrs	11 hrs	5 hrs	3 hrs
☂	80 mm	19 mm	80 mm	84 mm
month	Apr	Jul	Oct	Jan

THE PELOPONNESE

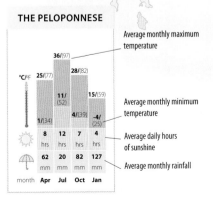

°C/°F		36/(97)	28/(82)	
	25/(77)	11/ (52)	15/(59)	
	1/(34)		4/(39)	-4/ (25)
☀	8 hrs	12 hrs	7 hrs	4 hrs
☂	62 mm	20 mm	82 mm	127 mm
month	Apr	Jul	Oct	Jan

Average monthly maximum temperature

Average monthly minimum temperature

Average daily hours of sunshine

Average monthly rainfall

ATHENS AND AROUND ATHENS

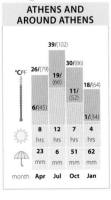

°C/°F		39/(102)	30/(86)	
	26/(79)	19/ (66)	11/ (52)	18/(64)
	6/(45)		7/(45)	1/(34)
☀	8 hrs	12 hrs	7 hrs	4 hrs
☂	23 mm	6 mm	51 mm	62 mm
month	Apr	Jul	Oct	Jan

Northern Greece

Central and Western Greece

Around Athens

Athens

The Peloponnese

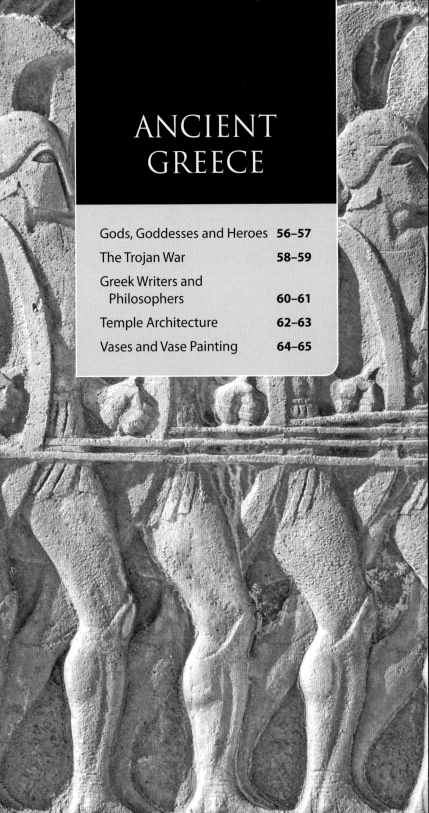

ANCIENT GREECE

Gods, Goddesses and Heroes

The Greek myths that tell the stories of the gods, goddesses and heroes date back to the Bronze Age when they were told aloud by poets. They were first written down in the early 6th century BC and have lived on in Western literature. Myths were closely bound up with Greek religion and gave meaning to the unpredictable workings of the natural world. They tell the story of the creation and the "golden age" of gods and mortals, as well as the age of semi-mythical heroes, such as Theseus and Herakles, whose exploits were an inspiration to ordinary men. The gods and goddesses were affected by human desires and failings and were part of a divine family presided over by Zeus. He had many offspring, both legitimate and illegitimate, each with a mythical role.

Hades and Persephone were king and queen of the Underworld (land of the dead). Persephone was abducted from her mother Demeter, goddess of the harvest, by Hades. She was then only permitted to return to her mother for three months each year.

Eris was the goddess of strife.

Zeus was the father of the gods and ruled over them and all mortals from Mount Olympos.

Clymene, a nymph and daughter of Helios, was mother of Prometheus, creator of mankind.

Poseidon, one of Zeus's brothers, was given control of the seas. The trident is his symbol of power, and he married the sea-goddess Amphitrite, to whom he was not entirely faithful. This statue is from the National Archaeological Museum in Athens *(see pp72–5)*.

Hera, sister and wife of Zeus, was famous for her jealousy.

Athena was born from Zeus's head in full armour.

Paris was asked to award the golden apple to the most beautiful goddess.

Paris's dog helped him herd cattle on Mount Ida where the prince grew up.

Dionysos, god of revelry and wine, was born from Zeus's thigh. In this 6th-century BC cup painted by Exekias, he reclines in a ship whose mast has become a vine.

A Divine Dispute

This vase painting shows the gods on Mount Ida, near Troy. Hera, Athena and Aphrodite, quarrelling over who was the most beautiful, were brought by Hermes to hear the judgment of a young herdsman, the Trojan prince, Paris. In choosing Aphrodite, he was rewarded with the love of Helen, the most beautiful woman in the world. Paris abducted her from her husband Menelaos, King of Sparta, and thus the Trojan War began (see pp58–9).

Artemis, the virgin goddess of the hunt, was the daughter of Zeus and sister of Apollo. She can be identified by her bow and arrows, hounds and group of nymphs with whom she lived in the forests. Although sworn to chastity, she was, in contrast, the goddess of childbirth.

Happiness, here personified by two goddesses, waits with gold laurel leaves to garland the winner. Wreaths were the prizes in Greek athletic and musical contests.

Helios, the sun god, drove his four-horse chariot (the sun) daily across the sky.

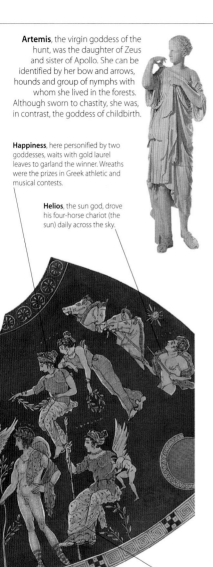

Hermes was the gods' messenger.

Aphrodite, the goddess of love, was born from the sea. Here, she has her son Eros (Cupid) with her.

Apollo, son of Zeus and brother of Artemis, was god of healing, plague and also music. Here he is depicted holding a lyre. He was also famous for his dazzling beauty.

The Labours of Herakles

Herakles (Hercules to the Romans) was the greatest of the Greek heroes, and the son of Zeus and Alkmene, a mortal woman. With superhuman strength, he achieved success, and immortality, against seemingly impossible odds in the "Twelve Labours" set by Eurystheus, King of Mycenae. For his first task, he killed the Nemean lion, and wore its hide ever after.

Killing the Lernaean hydra was the second labour of Herakles. The many heads of this venomous monster, raised by Hera, grew back as soon as they were chopped off. As in all his tasks, Herakles was helped by Athena.

The huge boar that ravaged Mount Erymanthus was captured next. Herakles brought it back alive to King Eurystheus who was so terrified that he hid in a storage jar.

Destroying the Stymfalían birds was the sixth labour. Herakles rid Lake Stymfalía of these man-eating birds, which had brass beaks, by stoning them with a sling, having first frightened them off with a pair of bronze castanets.

The Trojan War

The story of the Trojan War, first narrated in the *Iliad*, Homer's 8th-century BC epic poem, tells how the Greeks sought to avenge the capture of Helen, wife of Menelaos, King of Sparta, by the Trojan prince, Paris. The Roman writer Virgil takes up the story in the *Aeneid*, where he tells of the sack of Troy and the founding of Rome. Archaeological evidence of the remains of a city identified with ancient Troy in modern Turkey suggests that the myth may have a basis in fact. Many of the ancient sites in the Peloponnese, such as Mycenae and Pylos, are thought to be the cities of some of the heroes of the Trojan War.

Achilles binding up the battle wounds of his friend Patroklos

Gathering of the Heroes

When Paris *(see p56)* carries Helen back to Troy, her husband King Menelaos summons an army of Greek kings and heroes to avenge this crime. His brother, King Agamemnon of Mycenae, leads the force; its ranks include young Achilles, destined to die at Troy.

At Aulis, their departure is delayed by a contrary wind. Only the sacrifice to Artemis of Iphigéneia, the youngest of Agamemnon's daughters, allows the fleet to depart.

Fighting at Troy

The *Iliad* opens with the Greek army outside Troy, maintaining a siege that has already been in progress for nine years. Tired of fighting, yet still hoping for a decisive victory, the Greek camp is torn apart by the fury of Achilles over Agamemnon's removal of his slave girl Briseis. The hero takes to his tent and refuses adamantly to fight.

Deprived of their greatest warrior, the Greeks are driven back by the Trojans. In desperation, Patroklos persuades his friend Achilles to let him borrow his armour. Achilles agrees and Patroklos leads the Myrmidons, Achilles's troops, into battle. The tide is turned, but Patroklos is killed in the fighting by Hector, son of King Priam of Troy, who mistakes him for Achilles. Filled with remorse at the news of his friend's death, Achilles returns to battle, finds Hector, and kills him in revenge.

King Priam begging Achilles for the body of his son

Patroklos Avenged

Refusing Hector's dying wish to allow his body to be ransomed, Achilles instead hitches it up to his chariot by the ankles and drags it round the walls of Troy, then takes it back to the Greek camp. In contrast, Patroklos is given the most elaborate funeral possible with a huge pyre, sacrifices of animals and Trojan prisoners and funeral games. Still unsatisfied, for 12 days Achilles drags the corpse of Hector around Patroklos's funeral mound until the gods are forced to intervene over his callous behaviour.

Priam Visits Achilles

On the instructions of Zeus, Priam sets off for the Greek camp holding a ransom for the body of his dead son. With the help of the god Hermes, he reaches Achilles's tent undetected. Entering, he pleads with Achilles to think of his own father and to show mercy. Achilles relents and allows Hector to be taken back to Troy for a funeral and burial.

Although the Greek heroes were greater than mortals, they were portrayed as fallible beings with human emotions who had to face universal moral dilemmas.

Greeks and Trojans, in bronze armour, locked in combat

Achilles Kills the Amazon Queen

Penthesileia was the Queen of the Amazons, a tribe of warlike women reputed to cut off their right breasts to make it easier to wield their weapons. They come to the support of the Trojans. In the battle, Achilles finds himself face to face with Penthesileia and deals her a fatal blow. One version of the story has it that as their eyes meet at the moment of her death, they fall in love. The Greek idea of love and death would be explored 2,000 years later by the psychologists Jung and Freud.

An early image of the Horse of Troy, from a 7th-century BC clay vase

Achilles killing the Amazon Queen Penthesileia in battle

The Wooden Horse of Troy

As was foretold, Achilles is killed at Troy by an arrow in his heel from Paris's bow. With this weakening of their military strength, the Greeks resort to guile.

Before sailing away, they build a great wooden horse, in which they conceal some of their best fighters. The rumour is put out that this is a gift to the goddess Athena and that if the horse enters Troy, the city can never be taken. After some doubts, but swayed by supernatural omens, the Trojans drag the horse inside the walls. That night, the Greeks sail back, the soldiers creep out of the horse and Troy is put to the torch. Priam, with many others, is murdered. Among the Trojan survivors is

Aeneas who escapes to Italy and founds the race of Romans: a second Troy. The next part of the story (the *Odyssey*) tells of the heroes' adventures on their way home to Greece.

Death of Agamemnon

Klytemnestra, the wife of Agamemnon, had ruled Mycenae in the ten years that he had been away fighting in Troy. She was accompanied by Aigisthos, her lover. Intent on

vengeance for the death of her daughter Iphigéneia, Klytemnestra receives her husband with a triumphal welcome and then brutally murders him, with the help of Aigisthos. Agamemnon's fate was a result of a curse laid on his father, Atreus, which was finally expiated by the murder of both Klytemnestra and Aigisthos by her son Orestes and daughter Elektra. In these myths, the will of the gods shapes and overrides that of heroes and mortals.

Greek Myths in Western Art

From the Renaissance onwards, the Greek myths have been a powerful inspiration for artists and sculptors. Kings and queens have had themselves portrayed as gods and goddesses with their symbolic attributes of love or war. Myths have also been an inspiration for artists to paint the nude or Classically draped figure. This was true of the 19th-century artist Lord Leighton, whose depiction of the human body reflects the Classical ideals of beauty. His tragic figure of Elektra is shown here.

Elektra mourning the death of her father Agamemnon at his tomb

Greek Writers and Philosophers

The literature of Greece began with long epic poems, accounts of war and adventure, which established the relationship of the ancient Greeks to their gods. The tragedy and comedy, history and philosophical dialogues of the 5th and 4th centuries BC became the basis of Western literary culture. Much of our knowledge of the Greek world is derived from Greek literature. Pausanias's *Guide to Greece*, written in the Roman period and used by Roman tourists, is a key to the physical remains.

Hesiod with the nine Muses who inspired his poetry

Epic Poetry

As far back as the 2nd millennium BC, before even the building of the Mycenaean palaces, poets were reciting the stories of the Greek heroes and gods. Passed on from generation to generation, these poems, called *rhapsodes*, were never written down but were changed and embellished by successive poets. The oral tradition culminated in the *Iliad* and *Odyssey* (see pp58–9), composed around 700 BC. Both works are traditionally ascribed to the same poet, Homer, of whose life nothing reliable is known. Hesiod, whose most famous poems include the *Theogony*, a history of the gods, and the *Works and Days*, on how to live an honest life, also lived around 700 BC. Unlike Homer, Hesiod is thought to have written down his poems, although there is no firm evidence available to support this theory.

Passionate Poetry

For private occasions, and particularly to entertain guests at the cultivated drinking parties known as *symposia*, shorter poetic forms were developed. These poems were often full of passion, whether love or hatred, and could be personal or, often, highly political. Much of this poetry, by writers such as Archilochus, Alcaeus, Alcman, Hipponax and Sappho, survives only in quotations by later writers or on scraps of papyrus that have been preserved by chance from private libraries in Hellenistic and Roman Egypt. Through these fragments, we can gain glimpses of the life of a very competitive elite. Since *symposia* were an almost exclusively male domain, there is a strong element of misogyny in much of this poetry. In contrast, the fragments of poems discovered by the authoress Sappho, who lived on the island of Lésvos, are exceptional for showing a woman competing in a literary area in the male-dominated society of ancient Greece, and for describing with great intensity her passions for other women.

History

Until the 5th century BC, little Greek literature was composed in prose – even early philosophy was in verse. In the latter part of the 5th century, a new tradition of lengthy prose histories, looking at recent or current events, was established with Herodotus's account of the great war between Greece and Persia (490–479 BC). Herodotus put the clash between Greeks and Persians into a context, and included an ethnographic account of the vast Persian Empire. He attempted to record objectively what people said about the past. Thucydides took a narrower view in his account of the long years of the Peloponnesian War between Athens and Sparta (431–404 BC). He concentrated on the political history, and his aim was to work out the "truth" that lay behind the events of the war.

Herodotus, the historian of the Persian wars

The methods of Thucydides were adopted by later writers of Greek history, though few could match his acute insight into human nature.

An unusual vase-painting of a *symposion* for women only

The orator Demosthenes in a Staffordshire figurine of 1790

Oratory

Public argument was basic to Greek political life even in the Archaic period. In the later part of the 5th century BC, the techniques of persuasive speech began to be studied in their own right. From that time on, some orators began to publish their speeches. In particular, this included those wishing to advertise their skills in composing speeches for the law courts, such as Lysias and Demosthenes. The texts that survive give insights into both Athenian politics and the seamier side of Athenian private life. The verbal attacks on Philip of Macedon by Demosthenes, the 4th-century BC Athenian politician, became models for Roman politicians seeking to defeat their opponents. With the 18th-century European revival of interest in Classical times, Demosthenes again became a political role model.

Drama

Almost all the surviving tragedies come from the hands of the three great 5th-century BC Athenians: Aeschylus, Sophocles and Euripides. The latter two playwrights developed an interest in individual psychology (as in Euripides's *Medea*). While 5th-century comedy is full of direct references to contemporary life and dirty jokes, the "new" comedy developed in the 4th century BC is essentially situation comedy employing character types.

Vase painting of two costumed actors from around 370 BC

Greek Philosophers

The Athenian Socrates was recognized in the late 5th century BC as a moral arbiter. He wrote nothing himself but we know of his views through the "Socratic dialogues", written by his pupil, Plato, examining the concepts of justice, virtue and courage. Plato set up his academy in the suburbs of Athens. His pupil, Aristotle, founded the Lyceum, to teach subjects from biology to ethics, and helped to turn Athens into one of the first university cities. In 1508–11, Raphael painted this vision of Athens in the Vatican.

Plato saw "the seat of ideas" in heaven.

Aristotle, author of the *Ethics*, had a genius for scientific observation.

Euclid laid the rules of geometry in around 300 BC.

Epicurus advocated the pursuit of pleasure.

Socrates taught by debating his ideas.

Diogenes, the Cynic, lived like a beggar.

Temple Architecture

Temples were the most important public buildings in ancient Greece, largely because religion was a central part of everyday life. Often placed in prominent positions, temples were also statements about political and divine power. The earliest temples, in the 8th century BC, were built of wood and sun-dried bricks. Many of their features were copied in marble buildings from the 6th century BC onwards.

Pheidias, sculptor of the Parthenon, at work

Temple Construction

This drawing is of an idealized Doric temple, showing how it was built and used.

The cella, or inner sanctum, housed the cult statue.

The pediment, triangular in shape, often held sculpture.

The cult statue was of the god or goddess to whom the temple was dedicated.

Fluting on the columns was carved *in situ*, guided by that on the top and bottom drums.

A ramp led up to the temple entrance.

The stepped platform was built on a stone foundation.

The column drums were initially carved with bosses for lifting them into place.

700 BC	600 BC	500 BC	400 BC	300 BC
700 First temple of Poseidon, Ancient Isthmia (Archaic; *see p171*) and first Temple of Apollo, Corinth (Archaic; *see p166*)	**550** Second temple of Apollo, Corinth (Doric; *see p166*)	**520** Temple of Olympian Zeus, Athens, begun (Doric; completed Corinthian 2nd century AD; *see p115*)		
		6th century Temple of Artemis, Ancient Brauron (Doric; *see pp150–51*)		
		460 Temple of Zeus, Olympia (Doric; *see p175*)	**440–430** Temple of Poseidon, Soúnio (Doric; *see pp152–3*)	
7th century Temple of Hera, Olympia (Doric; *see p174*)		**447–405** Temples of the Acropolis, Athens: Athena Nike (Ionic), Parthenon (Doric), Erechtheion (Ionic) (*see pp98–103*)	**4th century** Temple of Apollo, Delphi (Doric; *see p233*); Temple of Athena Aléa, Tegéa (Doric and 1st Corinthian capital; *see p181*)	
		445–425 Temple of Apollo, Bassae (Doric with Ionic; *see p181*)		

Detail of the Parthenon pediment

The Development of Temple Architecture

Greek temple architecture is divided into three styles, which evolved chronologically, and are most easily distinguished by the column capitals.

The gable ends of the roof were surmounted by statues, known as *akroteria*, in this case of a Nike or "Winged Victory". Almost no upper portions of Greek temples survive.

The roof was supported on wooden beams and covered in rows of terracotta tiles, each ending in an upright *akroterion*.

Doric temples were surrounded by sturdy columns with plain capitals and no bases. As the earliest style of stone buildings, they recall wooden prototypes.

Triangular pediment filled with sculpture

Guttae imitated the pegs for fastening the wooden roof beams.

Triglyphs resembled the ends of cross beams.

Metopes could contain sculpture.

Doric capital

Ionic temples differed from Doric in their tendency to have more columns, of a different form. The capital has a pair of volutes, like rams' horns, front and back.

Akroteria, at the roof corners, could look Persian in style.

The frieze was a continuous band of decoration.

The Ionic architrave was subdivided into projecting bands.

The Ionic frieze took the place of Doric *triglyphs* and *metopes*.

Ionic capital

Stone blocks were smoothly fitted together and held by metal clamps and dowels: no mortar was used in the temple's construction.

The ground plan was derived from the megaron of the Mycenaean house: a rectangular hall with a front porch supported by columns.

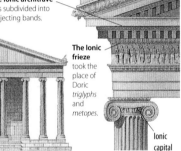

Corinthian temples in Greece were built under the Romans and only in Athens. They feature columns with slender shafts and elaborate capitals decorated with acanthus leaves.

The pediment was decorated with a variety of mouldings.

Akroterion in the shape of a griffin

The cella entrance was at the east end.

The entablature was everything above the capitals.

Acanthus leaf capital

Caryatids, or figures of women, were used instead of columns in the Erechtheion at Athens' Acropolis. In Athens' Agora (see pp94–5), tritons (half-fish, half-human creatures) were used.

Vases and Vase Painting

The history of Greek vase painting continued without a break from 1000 BC to Hellenistic times. The main centre of production was Athens, which was so successful that by the early 6th century BC it was sending its high-quality black- and red-figure wares to every part of the Greek world. The Athenian potters' quarter of Kerameikós can still be visited today *(see pp92–3)*. Beautiful works of art in their own right, the painted vases are the closest we can get to the vanished paintings with which ancient Greeks decorated the walls of their houses. Although vases could break during everyday use (for which they were intended), a huge number still survive intact or in reassembled pieces.

This 6th-century BC black-figure vase shows pots being used in an everyday situation. The vases depicted are *hydriai*. It was the women's task to fill them with water from springs or public fountains.

The white-ground lekythos was developed in the 5th century BC as an oil flask for grave offerings. They were usually decorated with funeral scenes, and this one, by the Achilles Painter, shows a woman placing flowers at a grave.

The naked woman holding a *kylix* is probably a flute-girl or prostitute.

The Symposion

These episodes of mostly male feasting and drinking were also occasions for playing the game of kottabos. On the exterior of this 5th-century BC kylix are depictions of men holding cups, ready to flick out the dregs at a target.

The Development of Painting Styles

Vase painting reached its peak in 6th- and 5th-century BC Athens. In the potter's workshop, a fired vase would be passed to a painter to be decorated. Archaeologists have been able to identify the varying styles of many individual painters of both black-figure and red-figure ware.

The body of the dead man is carried on a bier by mourners.

The geometric design is a prototype of the later "Greek-key" pattern.

Chariots and warriors form the funeral procession.

Geometric style characterizes the earliest Greek vases, from around 1000 to 700 BC, in which the decoration is in bands of figures and geometric patterns. This 8th-century BC vase, placed on a grave as a marker, is over 1 m (3 ft) high and depicts the bier and funeral rites of a dead man.

Eye cups were given an almost magical power by the painted eyes. The pointed base suggests that they were passed around during feasting.

This kylix is being held by one handle by another woman feaster, ready to flick out the dregs at a *kottabos* target.

The rhyton, such as this one in the shape of a ram's head, was a drinking vessel for watered-down wine. The scene of the *symposion* around the rim indicates when it would have been used.

This drinker holds aloft a branch of a vine, symbolic of Dionysos's presence at the party.

Striped cushions made reclining more comfortable.

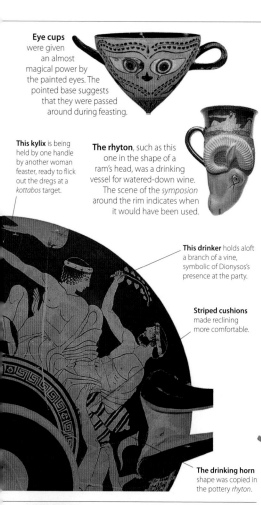

The drinking horn shape was copied in the pottery *rhyton*.

Black-figure style was first used in Athens around 630 BC. The figures were painted in black liquid clay on to the iron-rich clay of the vase which turned orange when fired. This vase is signed by the potter and painter Exekias.

Red-figure style was introduced in c.530 BC. The figures were left in the colour of the clay, silhouetted against a black glaze. Here, a woman pours from an *oinochoe* (wine jug).

Vase Shapes

Almost all Greek vases were made to be used; their shapes are closely related to their intended uses. Athenian potters had about 20 different forms to choose from. Below are some of the most commonly made shapes and their uses.

The amphora was a two-handled vessel used to store wine, olive oil and foods preserved in liquid such as olives. It also held dried foods.

This krater with curled handles or "volutes" is a wide-mouthed vase in which the Greeks mixed water with their wine before drinking it.

The hydria was used to carry water from the fountain. Of the three handles, one was vertical for holding and pouring, two horizontal for lifting.

The lekythos could vary in height from 3 cm (1 in) to nearly 1 m (3 ft). It was used to hold oil, both in the home and as a funerary gift to the dead.

The oinochoe, the standard wine jug, had a round or trefoil mouth for pouring, and just one handle.

The kylix, a two-handled drinking cup, was one shape that could take interior decoration.

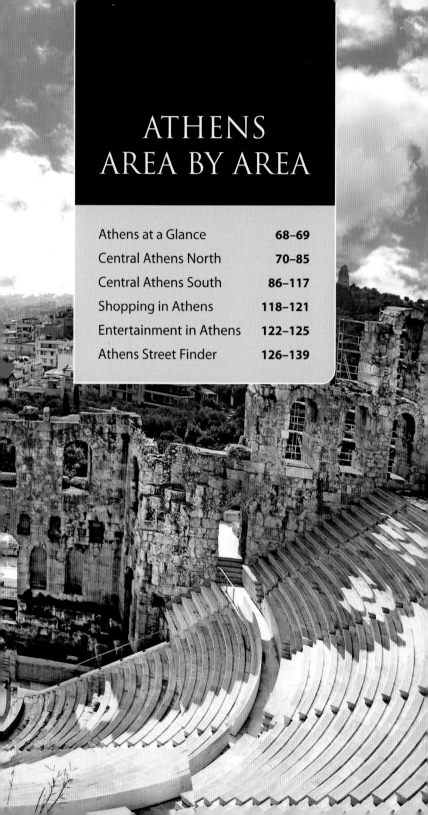

ATHENS
AREA BY AREA

Athens at a Glance

Athens has been a city for 3,500 years but its greatest glory was during the Classical period of ancient Greece from which so many buildings and artifacts still survive. The 5th century BC in particular was a golden age, when Perikles oversaw the building of the Acropolis. Within the Byzantine Empire and under Ottoman rule, Athens played only a minor role. It returned to prominence in 1834, when it became the capital of Greece. Today, it is a busy and modern metropolitan centre.

Locator Map

The Kerameikós quarter *(see pp92–3)* was once the potters' district of ancient Athens and site of the principal cemetery, whose grave monuments can still be seen. Tranquil and secluded, it lies off the main tourist track.

The Agora *(see pp94–5)*, or market place, was the ancient centre of commercial life. The Stoa of Attalos was reconstructed in 1953–6 on its original, 2nd-century BC foundations. It now houses the Agora Museum.

The Tower of the Winds *(see pp90–91)* stands beside the Roman forum, but this small, octagonal building is Hellenistic in style. The tower – built as a water clock, with a compass, sundials and weather vane – has a relief on each side depicting the wind from that direction.

| 0 metres | 500 |
| 0 yards | 500 |

The Acropolis *(see pp98–105)* has dominated Athens for over 2,000 years. From the scale of the Parthenon to the delicacy of the Erechtheion, it is an extraordinary achievement.

◀ Ancient theatre in Acropolis

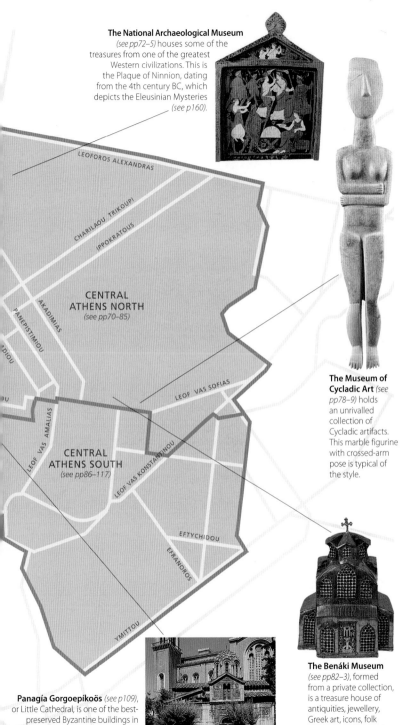

The National Archaeological Museum *(see pp72–5)* houses some of the treasures from one of the greatest Western civilizations. This is the Plaque of Ninnion, dating from the 4th century BC, which depicts the Eleusinian Mysteries *(see p160)*.

LEOFOROS ALEXANDRAS

CHARILAOU TRIKOUPI

IPPOKRATOUS

CENTRAL ATHENS NORTH *(see pp70–85)*

PANEPISTIMIOU

AKADIMIAS

DIOU

LEOF VAS SOFIAS

OU

LEOF VAS AMALIAS

CENTRAL ATHENS SOUTH *(see pp86–117)*

LEOF VAS KONSTANTINOU

EFTYCHIDOU

EFRANOROS

YMITTOU

The Museum of Cycladic Art *(see pp78–9)* holds an unrivalled collection of Cycladic artifacts. This marble figurine with crossed-arm pose is typical of the style.

The Benáki Museum *(see pp82–3)*, formed from a private collection, is a treasure house of antiquities, jewellery, Greek art, icons, folk costumes and Byzantine relics, such as this gold-plated incense holder.

Panagía Gorgoepíkoös *(see p109)*, or Little Cathedral, is one of the best-preserved Byzantine buildings in Athens. You can spot ancient carved reliefs reused in the walls of this tiny church.

CENTRAL ATHENS NORTH

Inhabited for 7,000 years, Athens was the birthplace of European civilization. It flourished in the 5th century BC when the Athenians controlled much of the eastern Mediterranean. The buildings from this era, including those in the ancient Agora and on the Acropolis, lie largely in the southern part of the city. The northern half has grown since the early 1800s when King Otto made Athens the new capital of Greece. When the king's architects planned the new, European-style city, they included wide, tree-lined avenues, such as Panepistimíou and Akadimías, that were soon home to many grand Neo-Classical public buildings and

mansion houses. Today, these edifices still provide elegant homes for all the major banks, embassies and public institutions, such as the University and the Library.

The chic residential area of Kolonáki is located in the north of the city centre, as is the cosmopolitan area around Patriárchou Ioakeím and Irodótou. These streets have excellent shopping and entertainment venues. Most of Athens' best museums, including the National Archaeological Museum, are also found in this area of the city. For information on getting around Athens, see pages 320–3.

Sights at a Glance

Museums and Galleries

1. National Archaeological Museum pp72–5
5. National Gallery of Art
6. War Museum
7. Byzantine Museum
8. Museum of Cycladic Art pp78–9
10. Benáki Museum pp82–3
11. Theatrical Museum
12. Museum of the City of Athens
13. National Historical Museum

Squares, Parks and Gardens

2. Exárcheia and Stréfi Hill
3. Lykavittós Hill
9. Plateía Kolonakíou

Churches

14. Kapnikaréa

Historic Buildings

4. Gennádeion

See also Street Finder maps pp126–139

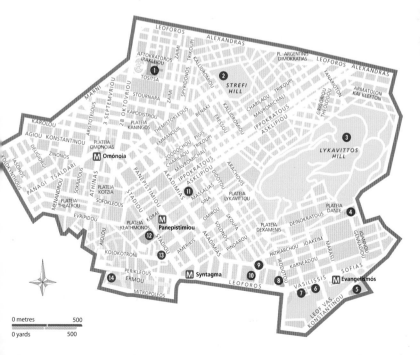

◀ The elegant façade of the Neo-Classical University building (see p85)

For keys to symbols see back flap

❶ National Archaeological Museum

Εθνικό Αρχαιολογικό Μουσείο

Opened in 1891, this superb museum, often known simply as the National Museum, brought together a collection that had previously been stored all over the city. Additional wings were added in 1939. The priceless collection was then dispersed and buried underground during World War II to protect it from possible damage. The museum reopened in 1946, but it took a further 50 years of renovation and reorganization finally to do justice to its formidable collection. With the combination of such unique exhibits as the Mycenaean gold, along with the unrivalled amount of sculpture, pottery and jewellery on display, this is without doubt one of the world's finest museums.

Neo-Classical entrance to the National Archaeological Museum on Patission

Bronze collection

Sculpture garden and café

Dipýlon Amphora
This huge Geometric vase was used to mark an 8th-century BC woman's burial and shows the dead body surrounded by mourning women. It is named after the location of its discovery near the Dipýlon Gate in Athens' Kerameikós *(see pp92–3)*.

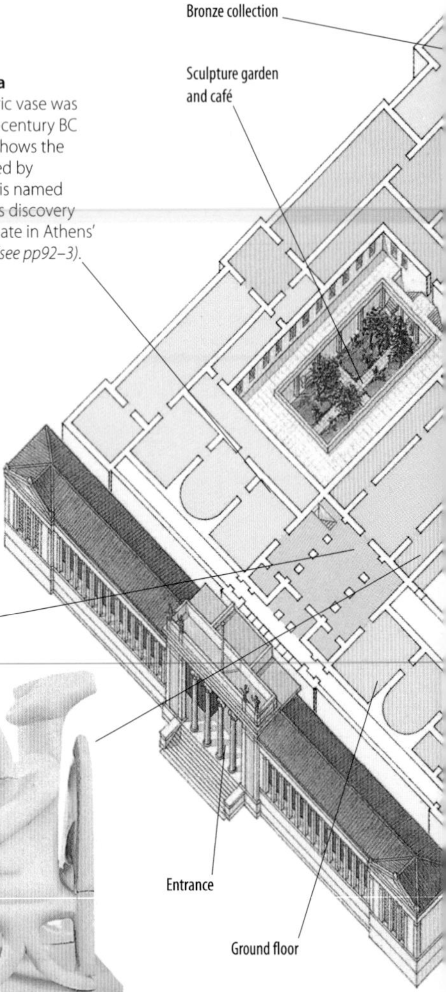

Main entrance hall

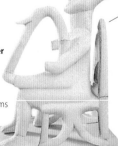

Harp Player
The minimalist Cycladic style of sculpture flourished in the 3rd millennium BC and originated in the Cyclades. The simple lines and bold forms of the marble figurines influenced many early 20th-century artists, including the British sculptor Henry Moore.

Entrance

Ground floor

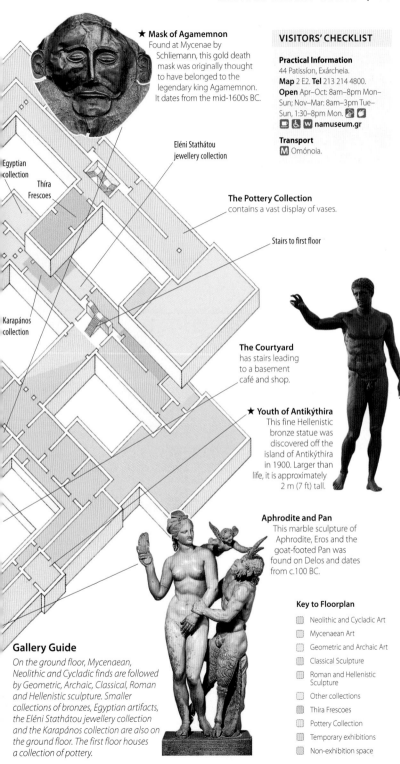

★ **Mask of Agamemnon**
Found at Mycenae by Schliemann, this gold death mask was originally thought to have belonged to the legendary king Agamemnon. It dates from the mid-1600s BC.

Eléni Stathátou jewellery collection

Egyptian collection

Thíra Frescoes

Karapános collection

The Pottery Collection
contains a vast display of vases.

Stairs to first floor

The Courtyard
has stairs leading to a basement café and shop.

★ **Youth of Antikýthira**
This fine Hellenistic bronze statue was discovered off the island of Antikýthira in 1900. Larger than life, it is approximately 2 m (7 ft) tall.

Aphrodite and Pan
This marble sculpture of Aphrodite, Eros and the goat-footed Pan was found on Delos and dates from c.100 BC.

VISITORS' CHECKLIST

Practical Information
44 Patission, Exárcheia.
Map 2 E2. **Tel** 213 214 4800.
Open Apr–Oct: 8am–8pm Mon–Sun; Nov–Mar: 8am–3pm Tue–Sun, 1:30–8pm Mon. 🅿️ 📷
📱 ♿ 🌐 namuseum.gr

Transport
Ⓜ Omónoia.

Key to Floorplan

▦ Neolithic and Cycladic Art
▦ Mycenaean Art
▦ Geometric and Archaic Art
▦ Classical Sculpture
▦ Roman and Hellenistic Sculpture
▦ Other collections
▦ Thíra Frescoes
▦ Pottery Collection
▦ Temporary exhibitions
▦ Non-exhibition space

Gallery Guide
On the ground floor, Mycenaean, Neolithic and Cycladic finds are followed by Geometric, Archaic, Classical, Roman and Hellenistic sculpture. Smaller collections of bronzes, Egyptian artifacts, the Eléni Stathátou jewellery collection and the Karapános collection are also on the ground floor. The first floor houses a collection of pottery.

Exploring the National Archaeological Museum's Collection

Displaying its treasures in chronological order, the museum presents an impressive and thorough overview of Greek art through the centuries. Beginning with early Cycladic figurines and continuing through the Greek Bronze Age, the exhibits end with the glories of Hellenistic period bronzes and a collection of busts of Roman emperors. High points in between include the numerous gold artifacts found at Mycenae, the elegant Archaic *koúroi* statues and the many examples of fine Classical sculpture.

Neolithic and Cycladic Art

The dawning of Greek civilization (3500–2900 BC) saw primitive decorative vases and figures. This collection also contains terracotta figurines, jewellery and a selection of weapons.

The vibrant fertility gods and goddesses, such as the *kourotróphos* (nursing mother) with child, are particularly well preserved. Of exceptional importance are the largest known Cycladic marble figurine, from Amorgós, and the earliest known figures of musicians – the *Flute Player* and *Harp Player*, both from Kéros. Later finds from Mílos, such as the painted vase with fishermen, reveal the changes in pot shapes and colour that took place in the late Cycladic Bronze Age.

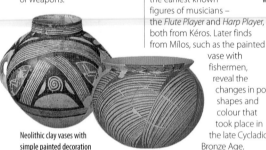

Neolithic clay vases with simple painted decoration

Mycenaean Art

It is not difficult to understand the allure of the museum's most popular attraction, the Hall of Mycenaean Antiquities, with its dazzling array of 16th-century BC gold treasures. Other exhibits in the collection include frescoes, ivory sculptures and seal rings made out of precious stones.

From the famous shaft graves (see p184) came a procession of daggers, cups, seals and rings as well as a number of regal death masks, including the justly famous *Mask of Agamemnon*. Two superb *rhytons*, or wine jugs, are also on display: one in the shape of a bull's head, made in silver with gold horns, and one in gold shaped like a lion's head. Equally rich finds from sites other than Mycenae have since been made. These include two gold bull cups found at Vafeió, in Crete, a gold phial entwined with dolphins and octopuses (excavated from a royal tomb at Déntra), clay tablets with the early Linear B script from the Palace of Nestor (see p205) and a magnificent sword from the Tomb of Stáfylos on the island of Skópelos.

Mycenaean bronze dagger, inlaid with gold

The Development of Greek Sculpture

Sculpture was one of the most sophisticated forms of Greek art. We are able to trace its development from the early *koúroi* to the great works of named sculptors such as Pheidias and Praxiteles in Classical times. Portraiture only began in the 5th century BC; even then, most Greek sculptures were of gods and goddesses, heroes and athletes and idealized men and women. These have had an enormous influence on Western art down the centuries.

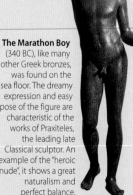

The Volomándra Koúros was discovered in Attica and dates from the mid-6th century BC. The highly stylized *koúroi* (statues of naked youths) first appear in the mid-7th century BC. Derived from Egyptian art, these figures share a common pose and proportions. Clothed *kórai* are the female counterpart.

The Marathon Boy (340 BC), like many other Greek bronzes, was found on the sea floor. The dreamy expression and easy pose of the figure are characteristic of the works of Praxiteles, the leading late Classical sculptor. An example of the "heroic nude", it shows a great naturalism and perfect balance.

Geometric and Archaic Art

Famed for its monumental burial vases, such as the *Dipýlon Amphora*, the Geometric period developed a more ornate style in the 7th century BC with the introduction of mythological and plant and animal motifs. By the 6th century BC, the full artistry of the black-figure vases had developed. Two rare examples from this period are a *lekythos* depicting Peleus, Achilles and the centaur Cheiron, and the sculptured heads known as *aryballoi*.

Warrior from Boiotia, early 7th century BC

Classical Sculpture

The collection of Classical sculpture contains both fine statues and a selection of grave monuments, mostly from the Kerameikós. These include the beautiful *stele* (c.410 BC) of Hegeso (*see p92*). Classical votive sculpture on display includes parts of a statue of the

This "valedictory stele" (mid-4th century BC) shows a seated woman bidding farewell to her family. The figures express a dignified suffering found in many Greek funerary reliefs.

goddess Hera, from the Argive Heraion in the Peloponnese, and many statues of the goddess Athena, including the Roman *Varvakeion Athena*, a reduced copy of the original ivory and gold statue from the Parthenon (*see p103*).

Roman and Hellenistic Sculpture

Although a large number of Greek bronzes were lost in antiquity, as metal was melted down in times of emergency for making weapons, the museum has some excellent pieces on display. These include the famous bronzes *Poseidon* and the *Horse with the Little Jockey*, both found at Cape Artemísion on Evvoia, and the *Youth of Antikýthira*, found in the sea off that island. Another of the best-known sculptures is the *Marathon Boy*.

Other Collections

The museum also houses several smaller collections, many donated by private in-dividuals. Among these is the glittering **Eléni Stathátou jewellery collection**, which covers the Bronze Age through to the Byzantine period. The **Karapános col-lection**, which is composed mainly from discoveries made at the site at Dodóni (*see p215*), contains many fine bronzes, including *Zeus Hurling a Thunderbolt*. Also on display are small decorative and votive pieces, and strips of lead inscribed with questions for the

oracle at Dodóni. Other collections include the **Egyptian collection** and the **Bronze collection**, which comprises many small pieces of statuary and decorative items discovered on the Acropolis.

Thíra Frescoes

Two of the famous frescoes discovered at Akrotíri on the island of Thíra (Santoríni) in 1967, and originally thought to be from the mythical city of Atlantis, are displayed in the museum. The rest are on Santoríni. Dating from 1500 BC, they confirm the sophistication of late Minoan civilization. The colourful, restored images depict boxer boys, and animals and flowers symbolizing spring time.

Pottery Collection

The strength of this vast collection lies not only in its size, but in the quality of specific works, repre-senting the flowering of Greek ceramic art. The real gems belong to the 5th century BC when red-figure vases and white-ground *lekythoi* became the established style (*see p64*) and were produced in vast numbers. Expressive painting styles and new designs characterize this period. The most poignant pieces are by the "Bosanquet Painter" and the "Achilles Painter" who portrayed young men by their graves.

Hellenistic bronze known as the *Horse with the Little Jockey*

Gold Hellenistic ring from the Eléni Stathátou collection

View northeast to Lykavittós Hill from the Acropolis

❷ Exárcheia and Stréfi Hill
Εξάρχεια Λόφος Στρέφη

Map 2 F2 & 3 A2. **Ⓜ** Omónoia.

Until recently, the area around Plateía Exarcheíon was renowned as a hotbed of anarchist activity. Prior to the invasion of students, Exárcheia was a very attractive area and the 19th-century Neo-Classical buildings still stand as testament to this. Today, the area is picking up again and although parts of it are still rather run-down, an influx of gentrification has brought many fashionable cafés, bars and *ouzerí* to the area. Themistokléous, which leads off the square down to Omónoia, is pleasant to wander along; the local food stores and small boutiques make a refreshing change from the noisy bars. Plateía Exarcheíon is especially lively at night when the outdoor cafés and the open-air cinema, the Riviera, in the streets that climb towards Stréfi, attract many visitors.

Every year, a demonstration takes place on 17 November, marking the date in 1973 when many students were killed by the Junta *(see p47)* during a sit-in.

The nearby park of Stréfi Hill, with its intriguing maze of paths, is quiet and peaceful by day but comes to life at night when its cafés are full. Stréfi Hill is one of the many green areas in Athens that provide welcome relief from the noise and grime of the city, particularly in the oppressive heat of summer.

The restaurant on Lykavittós Hill, overlooking Athens

❸ Lykavittós Hill
Λόφος Λυκαβηττού

Map 3 B4. **Funicular:** from Ploutárchou. **Open** 9am–2:30pm Mon–Sun.

The peak of Lykavittós (also known as Lycabettus) reaches 277 m (910 ft) above the city, and is its highest hill. It can be climbed on foot by various paths or by the easier, albeit vertiginous, ride in the funicular from the corner of Ploutárchou. On foot, it should take about 45 minutes. The hill may derive its name from a combination of the words *lýki* and *vaino*, meaning "path of light". The ancient belief was that this was the rock once destined to be the Acropolis citadel, accidentally dropped by the city's patron goddess, Athena. Although it is without doubt the most prominent hill in Athens, surprisingly little mention is made of Lykavittós in Classical literature; the exceptions are passing references in Aristophanes's *Frogs* and Plato's *Kritías*. This landmark is a favourite haunt for many Athenians, who come for the panoramic views of the city from the observation decks that rim the summit.

The small whitewashed chapel of **Agios Geórgios** crowns the top of the hill. It was built in the 19th century on the site of an older Byzantine church, dedicated to Profítis Ilías (the Prophet Elijah). Both saints are celebrated on their name days (Profítis Ilías on 20 July and Agios Geórgios on 23 April). On the eve of Easter Sunday, a spectacular candlelit procession winds down the peak's wooded slopes *(see p49)*.

Lykavittós Hill is also home to a summit restaurant and café and the open-air **Lykavittós Theatre**, where contemporary jazz, pop and dance performances are held annually during the Athens Festival *(see p50)*.

❹ Gennádeion

Γεννάδειον

American School of Classical Studies, Souidás 54, Kolonáki. **Map** 3 C4. **Tel** 210 723 6313. Ⓜ Evangelismós. 🚌 3, 7, 8, 13. **Open** 8:30am–9pm Mon–Fri, 9am–2pm Sat. **Closed** Aug, main public hols.

The Greek diplomat and bibliophile Ioánnis Gennádios (1844–1932) spent a lifetime accumulating rare first editions and illuminated manuscripts. In 1923, he donated his collection to the American School of Classical Studies. The Gennádeion building, named after him, was designed and built between 1923 and 1925 by the New York firm Van Pelt and Thompson to house the collection. Above its façade of Ionic columns is an inscription which translates as "They are called Greeks who share in our culture" – from Gennádios's dedication speech at the opening in 1926.

Researchers need special permission to gain access to over 70,000 rare books and manuscripts and no items are allowed to be removed from the library. Casual visitors may look at selected exhibits that are on show, and books, posters and postcards are for sale at the souvenir stall.

Exhibits in the main reading room include 192 Edward Lear sketches purchased in 1929. There is also an eclectic mix of Byron memorabilia, including the last known portrait of the poet made before his death in Greece in 1824 *(see p153)*.

The imposing Neo-Classical façade of the Gennádeion

❺ National Gallery of Art

Εθνική Πινακοθήκη

Vasiléos Konstantínou 50, Ilísia. **Map** 7 C1. **Tel** 210 723 5937. Ⓜ Evangelismós. 🚌 3, 13. **Open** 9am–3:30pm Mon & Thu–Sun, 2–9pm Wed. **Closed** for renovation and scheduled to reopen by 25 Dec 2015. ♿ 🚻 📶 **nationalgallery.gr**

Opened in 1976, the National Gallery of Art is housed in a modern low-rise building which contains a permanent collection of European and Greek art. The ground floor stages travelling exhibitions and opens out on to a sculpture garden. The first floor, with the exception of five impressive works by El Greco (1541–1614), is devoted to a minor collection of non-Greek, European art. Alongside works of the Dutch, Italian and Flemish schools, there are studies, engravings and paintings by Rembrandt, Dürer, Brueghel, Van Dyck, Watteau, Utrillo, Cézanne and Braque, among others. These include Caravaggio's *Singer* (1620), Eugène Delacroix's *Greek Warrior* (1856)

and Picasso's Cubist-period *Woman in a White Dress* (1939).

A changing display of Greek modern art from the 18th to the 20th century is featured on the second floor. The 19th century is represented mainly by numerous depictions of the War of Independence and seascapes, enlivened by portraits such as Nikólaos Gýzis's *The Loser of the Bet* (1878), *Waiting* (1900) by Nikifóros Lýtras and *The Straw Hat* (1925) by Nikólaos Lýtras. There are many fine works by major Greek artists including Chatzimicháïl, Chatzikyriákos-Gkíkas, Móralis and Tsaroúchis.

❻ War Museum

Πολεμικό Μουσείο

Corner of Vasilíssis Sofías & Rizári, Ilísia. **Map** 7 C1. **Tel** 210 725 2975. Ⓜ Evangelismós. 🚌 3, 7, 8, 13. **Open** May–Oct: 9am–7pm Tue–Sun; Nov–Apr: 9am–5pm Tue–Sun. **Closed** main public hols. ♿ 📶 **warmuseum.gr**

The War Museum was opened in 1975 after the fall of the military dictatorship *(see p47)*. The first nine galleries are chrono-logically ordered, and contain battle scenes, armour and plans from as far back as ancient Mycenaean times through to the more recent German occupation of 1941. Other galleries contain a miscellany of items, including a selection of different uniforms and Turkish weapons.

Spartan bronze helmet

There is a fine display of paintings and prints of leaders from the Greek War of Independence *(see pp44–5)*, such as General Theódoros Kolokotrónis (1770–1843). His death mask can also be seen in the museum. A sizeable collection of fine oils and sketches by the artists Flora-Karavía and Argyrós vividly captures the hardships of the two world wars.

Modern sculpture outside the National Gallery of Art

❽ Museum of Cycladic Art
Μουσείο Κυκλαδικής Τέχνης

Opened in 1986, this modern museum offers the world's finest collection of Cycladic art. It was initially assembled by Nicholaos and Dolly Goulandrís and has expanded with donations from other Greek collectors. The museum now has an excellent selection of ancient Greek and Cypriot art, the earliest from about 5,000 years ago. The Cycladic figurines, dating from the 3rd millennium BC, have never enjoyed quite the same level of popularity as Classical sculpture. However, the haunting simplicity of these marble statues has inspired many 20th-century artists and sculptors, including Picasso, Modigliani and Henry Moore.

Locator Map

Key

- Non-exhibition space
- Cycladic art
- Ancient Greek art
- Ancient Cypriot art
- Daily life in antiquity
- Temporary exhibitions

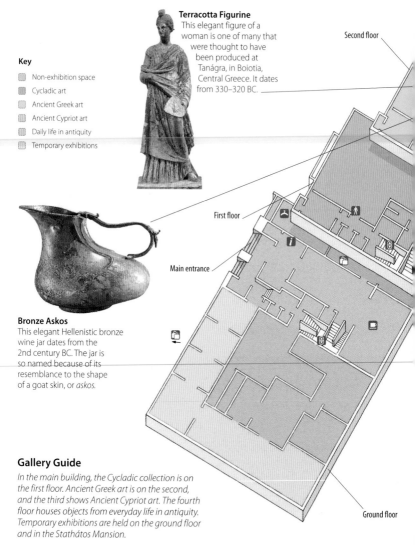

Terracotta Figurine
This elegant figure of a woman is one of many that were thought to have been produced at Tanágra, in Boiotia, Central Greece. It dates from 330–320 BC.

Second floor

First floor

Main entrance

Bronze Askos
This elegant Hellenistic bronze wine jar dates from the 2nd century BC. The jar is so named because of its resemblance to the shape of a goat skin, or *askos*.

Ground floor

Gallery Guide
In the main building, the Cycladic collection is on the first floor. Ancient Greek art is on the second, and the third shows Ancient Cypriot art. The fourth floor houses objects from everyday life in antiquity. Temporary exhibitions are held on the ground floor and in the Stathátos Mansion.

For hotels and restaurants see pp268–9 and pp282–5

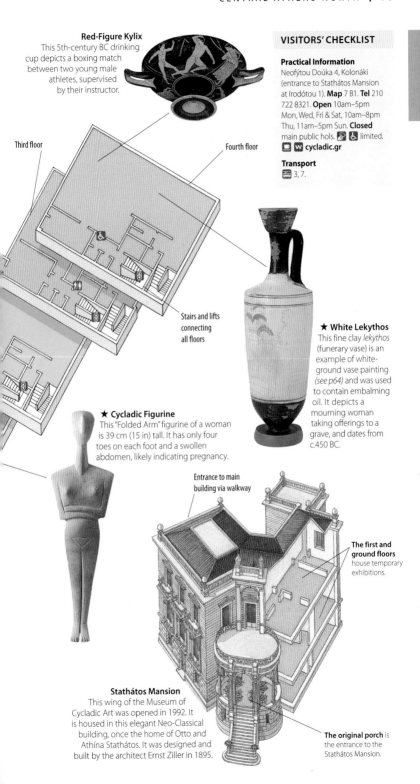

Red-Figure Kylix
This 5th-century BC drinking cup depicts a boxing match between two young male athletes, supervised by their instructor.

VISITORS' CHECKLIST

Practical Information
Neofýtou Doúka 4, Kolonáki (entrance to Stathátos Mansion at Irodótou 1). **Map** 7 B1. **Tel** 210 722 8321. **Open** 10am–5pm Mon, Wed, Fri & Sat, 10am–8pm Thu, 11am–5pm Sun. **Closed** main public hols. 🅿 ♿ limited. 🖥 🆆 cycladic.gr

Transport
🚌 3, 7.

Third floor

Fourth floor

Stairs and lifts connecting all floors

★ White Lekythos
This fine clay *lekythos* (funerary vase) is an example of white-ground vase painting (*see p64*) and was used to contain embalming oil. It depicts a mourning woman taking offerings to a grave, and dates from c.450 BC.

★ Cycladic Figurine
This "Folded Arm" figurine of a woman is 39 cm (15 in) tall. It has only four toes on each foot and a swollen abdomen, likely indicating pregnancy.

Entrance to main building via walkway

The first and ground floors house temporary exhibitions.

Stathátos Mansion
This wing of the Museum of Cycladic Art was opened in 1992. It is housed in this elegant Neo-Classical building, once the home of Otto and Athína Stathátos. It was designed and built by the architect Ernst Ziller in 1895.

The original porch is the entrance to the Stathátos Mansion.

A 14th-century icon of St Michael in the Byzantine Museum

❼ Byzantine Museum

Βυζαντινό Μουσείο

Vasilíssis Sofías 22, Plateía Rigíllis, Kolonáki. **Map** 7 B1. **Tel** 213 213 9500. Ⓜ Evangelismós. 🚌 3, 8, 7, 13. **Open** 8am–8pm Mon–Sun. **Closed** main public hols. ♿ ground floor only. 🅿 🌐 byzantinemuseum.gr

Originally called the Villa Ilissia, this elegant Florentine-style mansion was built between 1840 and 1848 by Stamátis Kleánthis for the Duchesse de Plaisance (1785–1854). This eccentric woman, wife of one of Napoleon's generals, was a key figure in Athens society during the mid-19th century and a dedicated philhellene.

Collector Geórgios Sotiríou converted the house into a museum in the 1930s with the help of architect Aristotélis Záchos. They transformed the entrance into a monastic court, incorporating a copy of a fountain from a 4th-century mosaic in Dafní *(see pp156–7)*.

Following extensive renovations, the museum reopened with a modern open-plan, split-level exhibition space built underground, below the courtyard. The museum's collection is now divided into two sections and laid out in chronological order: section one, *From the Ancient World to Byzantine*, traces the rise of Christianity, while section two, *The Byzantine World*, runs from the 6th century AD up until the fall of Constantinople in 1453.

Section one is dominated by fragments of ornamental stone carvings and mosaics taken from basilicas, sarcophagi, and early religious sculpture such as the *Shepherd Carrying a Lamb* and *Orpheus Playing a Lyre*, both of which illustrate

Funerary stele showing Orpheus with his lyre

the way in which the Christian church absorbed and adapted pagan symbols. Section two presents an array of icons, frescoes and precious ecclesiastical artifacts. Fine pieces to watch out for include the Treasury of Mytilene (a horde of 7th century gold and silver jewellery, coins and goblets discovered in a sunken ship), the Double-sided Icon of St George and the Mosaic Icon of the Virgin (both dating from the 13th century). There are also some magnificent frescoes that were rescued from the Church of the Episkopi and are cleverly displayed in the positions they would have been in the church, which was based on a cross in square plan with a dome and narthex. In summer, there are often concerts in the courtyard. Year-round, there are frequent guided tours free of charge. Call to find out what's on.

❽ Museum of Cycladic Art

See pp78–9.

Icons in the Orthodox Church

The *Episkepsis*, from the Byzantine Museum, depicting the Virgin and Child

The word icon simply means "image" and has come to signify a holy image through association with its religious use. Subjects range from popular saints such as St Andrew and St Nicholas to lesser-known martyrs, prophets and archangels. The image of the Virgin and Child is easily the most popular and exalted. Icons are a prominent feature in the Greek Orthodox religion and appear in many areas of Greek life. You will see them in taxis and buses, on boats and in restaurants, as well as in homes and churches. An icon can be in fresco, a mosaic, or made from bone or metal. The most common form is a portable painting, in wax-based paints applied to wooden boards treated with gesso. The figures are arranged so that the eyes are clearly depicted and appear to be looking directly at the viewer of the icon. These works, often of great artistic skill, are unsigned, undated and share a rigid conformity, right down to details of colour, dress, gesture and expression *(see pp24–5)*. The icon painter is careful to catch every detail of a tradition that stretches back hundreds of years.

Puppet Theatre from the Theatrical Museum

❾ Plateía Kolonakíou
Πλατεία Κολωνακίου

Kolonáki. **Map** 3 B5. 🚌 3, 7, 8, 13.

Kolonáki Square and its neighbouring side streets are the most chic and sophisticated part of Athens. The area is often missed by those who restrict themselves to the ancient sites and the popular flea markets of Monastiráki. Also known as Plateía Filikís Etaireías, the square is named after a small ancient column *(kolonáki)* found in the area. Celebrated for its designer boutiques and fashionable bars and cafés, smart antique shops and art galleries, sumptuous *zacharoplasteía* (pastry shops) and *ouzerí*, it revels in its status as the city's most fashionable quarter *(see p120)*. The lively pavement cafés around the square each attract a particular devoted clientele. At one, there may be rich kids drinking *frappé* (iced coffee) perched on their Harley Davidson motorbikes. Another, such as the *Lykóvrissi*, will be full of an older crowd of intellectuals sipping coffee and discussing the ever-popular subject of politics.

❿ Benáki Museum
See pp82–3.

⓫ Theatrical Museum
Μουσείο και Κέντρο Μελέτης του Ελληνικού Θεάτρου

Akadimias 50, Athens. **Map** 2 F4. **Tel** 210 362 9430. Ⓜ Panepistímio. 🚌 3, 8, 13. **Open** 10am–3pm Mon–Fri, 10am–1pm Sun. **Closed** Aug, 17 Nov, main public hols. ♿ limited. 📷

Housed in the basement of a fine Neo-Classical building, this small museum traces Greek theatrical history from Classical times to present day. There are displays of original posters, program-mes, costumes and designs from productions by influential directors such as Károlos Koun. There is also a colourful puppet theatre. The dressing rooms of famous Greek actresses such as Eléni Papadáki and Elli Lampéti have been recreated to give an insight into their lives.

Perikles, from the Theatrical Museum

⓬ Museum of the City of Athens
Μουσείο της Πόλεως των Αθηνών

Paparrigopoúlou 7, Plateía Klafthmónos, Sýntagma. **Map** 2 E5. **Tel** 210 323 1387. Ⓜ Panepistímio. 🚌 1, 2, 4, 5, 9, 11, 12, 15, 18. **Open** 9am–4pm Mon & Wed–Fri, 10am–3pm Sat–Sun. **Closed** main public hols. 📷

King Otto and Queen Amalía *(see p44)* lived here from 1831 until their new palace, today's Voulí parliament building *(see p116)*, was completed in 1838. It was joined to the neighbouring house to create what was known as the Old Palace.

The palace was restored in 1980 as a museum devoted to royal memorabilia, furniture and family portraits, maps and prints. It offers a delight-ful look at life during the early years of King Otto's reign. Exhibits include the manuscript of the 1843 Constitution, coats of arms from the Frankish (1205–1311) and Catalan (1311–88) rulers of Athens, and a scale model of the city as it was in 1842, made by architect Giánnis Travlós (1908–85). The museum also has a fine art collection, including Nikólaos Gýzis's *The Carnival in Athens* (1892) and a selection of water-colours by the English artists Edward Dodwell (1767–1832), Edward Lear (1812–88) and Thomas Hartley Cromek (1809–73).

Upstairs sitting room recreated in the Museum of the City of Athens

❿ Benáki Museum

Μουσείο Μπενάκη

This outstanding museum was founded in 1931 by Antónis Benákis (1873–1954), the son of Emmanouïl, a wealthy Greek who made his fortune in Egypt. Housed in an elegant Neo-Classical mansion, which was once the home of the Benákis family, the collection contains a diverse array of Greek arts and crafts, paintings and jewellery, local costumes and political memorabilia that spans over 5,000 years, from the Neolithic era to the 20th century.

Flag of Hydra
The imagery symbolizes the island of Hydra's supremacy in sea warfare as it was Greece's most powerful naval community.

Lecture hall

Bridal Cushion
This ornate embroidered cushion comes from Epirus and dates from the 18th century. It depicts a bridal procession, with ornamental flowers in the background.

Second floor

Roof garden

Auditorium

★ Detail of Wood Decoration
This intricately painted and carved piece of wooden panelling comes from the reception room of a mansion in Kozáni, in western Macedonia. It dates from the 18th century.

Atrium

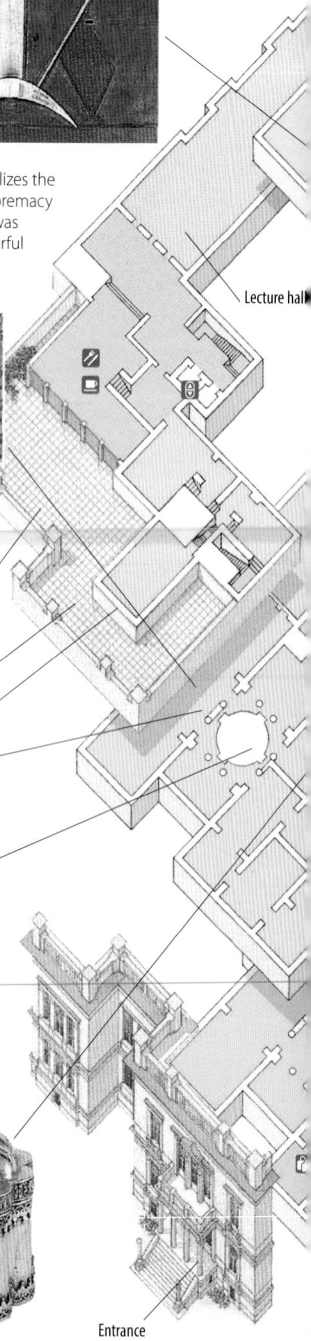

Silver Ciborium
Used to contain consecrated bread, this elegant piece of ecclesiastical silverware is dated 1667 and comes from Edirne, in Turkey.

Key to Floorplan

- ☐ Ground floor
- ☐ First floor
- ☐ Second floor
- ☐ Third floor
- ☐ Non-exhibition space

Entrance

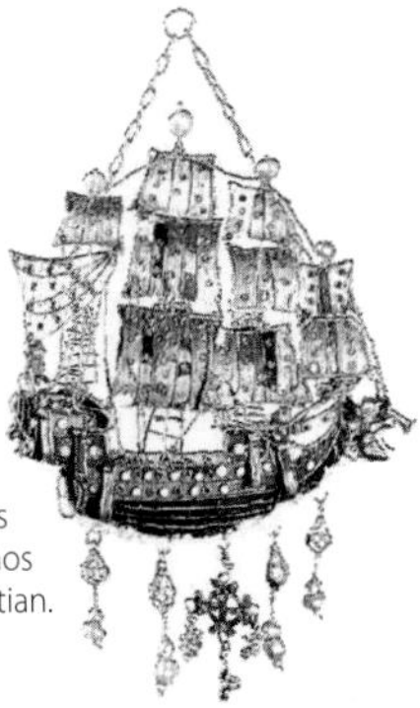

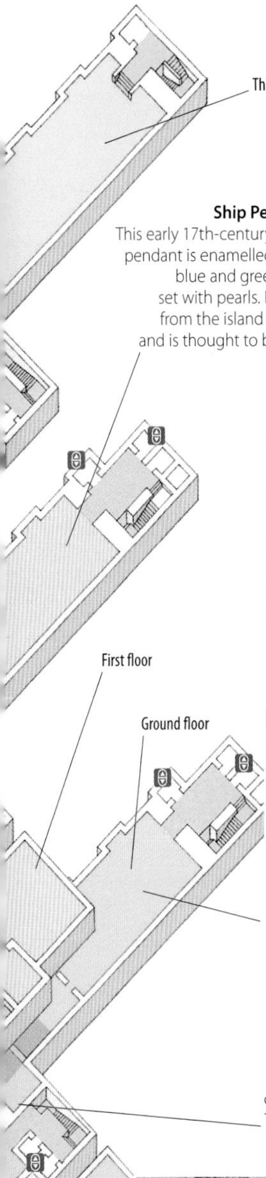

Third floor

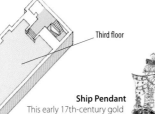

Ship Pendant
This early 17th-century gold
pendant is enamelled with
blue and green and
set with pearls. It comes
from the island of Pátmos
and is thought to be Venetian.

Gallery Guide

*The ground floor collection is arranged into different periods and ranges
from Neolithic to late-Byzantine art and Cretan icon painting. The first
floor exhibits are organized geographically and are from Asia Minor,
mainland Greece and the Greek islands. There is also a collection of
ecclesiastical silverware and jewellery. The second floor displays items
relating to Greek spiritual, economic and social life, and the third floor
concentrates on the Greek War of Independence (see pp44–5) and
modern political and cultural life.*

First floor

Ground floor

★ Icon of St Anne with the Virgin
A product of the Cretan School, this icon
of St Anne was painted in the 15th century.
St Anne is carrying the Virgin Mary as a child,
who is holding a white lily, symbol of purity.

Bowl from Paphos
Dating from the 13th century AD, this
colourful bowl originates from Cyprus.
The dancing figure is holding rattles.

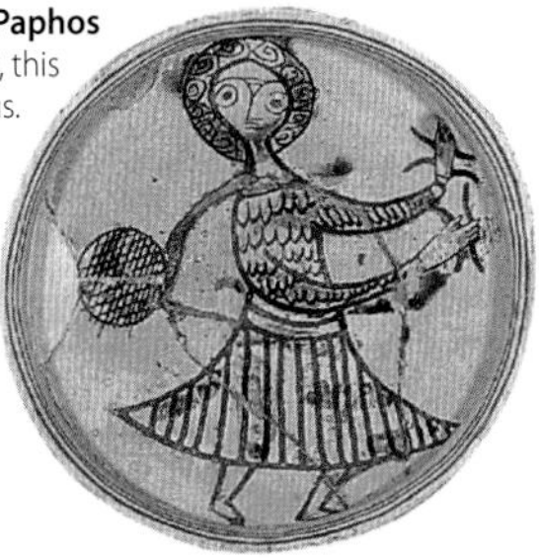

★ El Faiyûm Portrait
This Hellenistic portrait of a
man, painted on linen, dates
from the 3rd century AD.

Neo-Classical façade of the National Historical Museum

⓭ National Historical Museum

Εθνικό Ιστορικό Μουσείο

Stadíou 13, Sýntagma. **Map** 2 F5. **Tel** 210 323 7617. Ⓜ Sýntagma. 🚌 1, 2, 4, 5, 9, 10, 11, 18. **Open** 8:30am–2:30pm Tue–Sun. **Closed** main public hols. 🎫 free Sun. 🖥 **nhmuseum.gr**

Designed by French architect François Boulanger (1807–75), this museum was originally built as the first home of the Greek parliament. Queen Amalía laid the foundation stone in 1858, but it was 13 years later that it became the first permanent site of the Greek parliament. The country's most famous prime ministers have sat in the imposing chamber of the Old Parliament of the Hellenes, including Chárilaos Trikoúpis and Theódoros Deligiánnis, who was assassinated on the steps at the front of the building in 1905. The parliament moved to its present-day site in the Voulí building on Plateía Syntágmatos *(see p116)* after the Voulí was renovated in 1935.

In 1961, the building was opened as the National Historical Museum, owned by the Historical and Ethnological Society of Greece. Founded in 1882, the purpose of the society is to collect objects that illuminate the history of modern

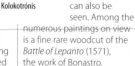

Statue of General Theódoros Kolokotrónis

Greece. The museum covers all the major events of Greek history from the Byzantine period to the 20th century in a chronological display. Venetian armour, traditional regional costumes and jewellery and figureheads from the warships used during the Revolution in 1821 are just some examples of the many exhibits on show.

The collection also focuses on major parliamentary figures, philhellenes and leaders in the War of Independence, displaying such items as Byron's sword, the weapons of Theódoros Kolokotrónis (1770–1843), King Otto's throne and the pen that was used by Elefthérios Venizélos to sign the Treaty of Sèvres in 1920. The revolutionary memoirs of General Makrigiánnis (1797–1864) can also be seen. Among the numerous paintings on view is a fine rare woodcut of the *Battle of Lepanto* (1571), the work of Bonastro.

Outside the building is a copy of Lázaros Sóchos's statue of Kolokotrónis on horseback, made in 1900, the original of which is in Náfplio *(see pp186–7)*, the former capital of Greece. A dedication on the statue reads (in Greek): "Theódoros Kolokotrónis 1821. Ride on, noble commander, through the centuries, showing the nations how slaves may become free men."

⓮ Kapnikaréa

Καπνικαρέα

Corner of Ermoú & Kalamiótou, Monastiráki. **Map** 6 D1. **Tel** 210 322 4462. Ⓜ Monastiráki. **Open** 9am–2pm Mon–Sun. **Closed** main public hols.

This charming 11th-century Byzantine church was rescued from demolition in 1834, thanks to the timely intervention of King Ludwig of Bavaria. Stranded in the middle of a square between Ermoú and Kapnikaréa streets, it is surrounded by the modern office blocks and shops of Athens' busy garment district.

Traditionally called the Church of the Princess, its foundation is attributed to Empress Irene, who ruled the Byzantine Empire from AD 797 to 802. She is revered as a saint in the Greek church for her efforts in restoring icons to the Empire's churches.

The true origins of the name "Kapnikaréa" are unknown, although according to some sources, the church was named after its founder, a "hearth-tax gatherer" *(kapnikaréas)*. Hearth tax was imposed on buildings by the Byzantines.

Restored in the 1950s, the dome of the church is supported by four Roman columns. Frescoes by Fótis Kóntoglou (1895–1965) were painted during the restoration, including one of the Virgin and Child. Much of Kóntoglou's work is also on display in the National Gallery of Art *(see p77)*.

The dome and main entrance of the Byzantine Kapnikaréa

Athenian Neo-Classical Architecture

Neo-Classicism flourished in the 19th century, when the architects who were commissioned by King Otto to build the capital in the 1830s turned to this popular European style. Among those commissioned were the Hansen brothers, Christian and Theophil, and also Ernst Ziller. As a result of their planning, within 50 years a modern city had emerged, with elegant administrative buildings, squares and tree-lined avenues. In its early days, Neo-Classicism had imitated the grace of the buildings of ancient Greece, using marble columns, sculptures and decorative detailing. In later years, it evolved into an original Greek style. Grand Neo-Classicism is seen at its best in the public buildings along Panepistimíou; its domestic adaptation can be seen in the houses of Pláka.

Schliemann's House (also known as Ilíou Mélathron, the Palace of Ilium, or Troy) was built in 1878 by Ziller. The interior is decorated with frescoes and mosaics of mythological subjects. It is now home to the Numismatic Museum (**Map** 2 F5).

The National Theatre was built between 1882 and 1890. Ernst Ziller used a Renaissance-style exterior with arches and Doric columns for George I's Royal Theatre. Inspired by the Public Theatre of Vienna, its interior was very modern for its time (**Map** 2 D3).

The National Library was designed by Danish architect Theophil Hansen in 1887 in the form of a Doric temple with two side wings. Built of Pentelic marble, it houses over half a million books, including many illuminated manuscripts and rare first editions (**Map** 2 F4).

The University of Athens was designed by Christian Hansen. This fine building, completed in 1864, has an Ionic colonnade and a portico frieze depicting the resurgence of arts and sciences under the reign of King Otto. A symbol of wisdom, the Sphinx is connected with Athens through the Oedipus legend (*see p225*). Oedipus, who solved the riddle of the Sphinx, later found sanctuary in enlightened Athens. Other statues on the façade include Patriarch Gregory V, a martyr of the War of Independence (**Map** 2 F4).

Athens Academy was designed by Theophil Hansen and built between 1859 and 1887. Statues of Apollo and Athena, and seated figures of Socrates and Plato, convey a Classical style, as do the Ionic capitals and columns. Inside the building, the Academy hall has beautiful frescoes that depict scenes from the myth of Prometheus (**Map** 2 F4).

CENTRAL ATHENS SOUTH

Southern Athens is dominated by the Acropolis and is home to the buildings that were at the heart of ancient Athens. Pláka and Monastiráki still revel in their historical roots as the oldest inhabited areas of the city, and are full of Byzantine churches and museums. Nestling among the restored Neo-Classical houses are grocery stores, icon painters and open-air tavernas. In the busy streets of Monastiráki's flea market, food vendors, gypsies and street musicians provide the atmosphere of a Middle Eastern bazaar. Southeast of Plateía Syntágmatos are the National Gardens, the city centre's tree-filled park. For information on getting around Athens, see pages 320–23.

Sights at a Glance

Museums and Galleries

1. Kyriazópoulos Folk Ceramic Museum
4. Municipal Art Gallery
8. Ilías Lalaoúnis Jewellery Museum
9. Kanellópoulos Museum
10. University of Athens Museum
11. Museum of Greek Popular Musical Instruments
17. Greek Folk Art Museum
18. Jewish Museum of Greece

Ancient Sites

2. *Tower of the Winds pp90–91*
5. *Kerameikós pp92–3*
6. *Ancient Agora pp94–5*
7. *Acropolis pp98–105*
19. Temple of Olympian Zeus

Churches

12. *Panagía Gorgoepíkoös p109*
13. Mitrópoli
14. Agios Nikólaos Ragavás
20. Russian Church of the Holy Trinity

Historic Districts

15. Anafiótika

Markets

3. Flea Market

Squares and Gardens

16. Plateía Lysikrátous
21. Plateía Syntágmatos
22. National Gardens

Historic Buildings and Monuments

23. Presidential Palace
24. Kallimármaro Stadium

Cemeteries

25. First Cemetery of Athens

See also Street Finder map pp126–39

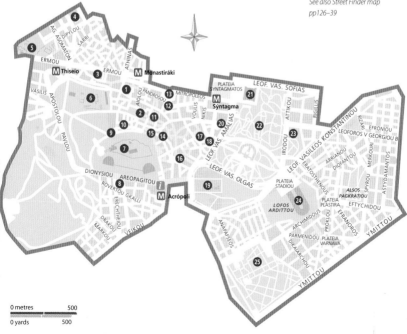

◀ Gateway to the magnificent Acropolis

For keys to symbols *see back flap*

Street-by-Street: Monastiráki

This old area of the city takes its name from the little sunken monastery in Plateía Monastirakíou. The former heart of Ottoman Athens, Monastiráki is still home to the bazaar and market stalls selling everything from junk to jewellery. The Fethiye Mosque and the Tzistarákis Mosque, home of the Kyriazópoulos Museum, stand as reminders of the area's Ottoman past. Roman influences are also strong in Monastiráki. The area borders the Roman Agora and includes the remains of Emperor Hadrian's library and the unique Tower of the Winds, a Hellenistic water clock. Monastiráki mixes the atmospheric surroundings of ancient ruins with the excitement of bargaining in the bazaar.

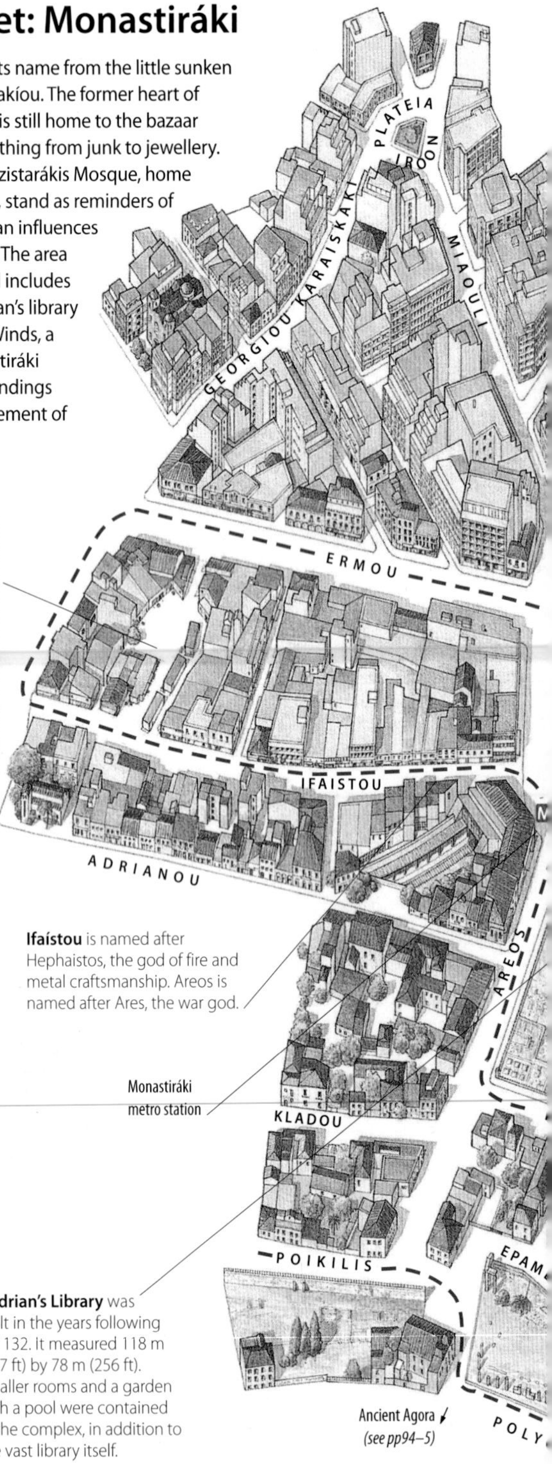

❸ Flea Market
Plateía Avissynías is the heart of the flea market, which extends through the surrounding streets. It is particularly popular on Sundays.

Key

━ Suggested route

```
0 metres        50
0 yards         50
```

Ifaístou is named after Hephaistos, the god of fire and metal craftsmanship. Areos is named after Ares, the war god.

Monastiráki metro station

Hadrian's Library was built in the years following AD 132. It measured 118 m (387 ft) by 78 m (256 ft). Smaller rooms and a garden with a pool were contained in the complex, in addition to the vast library itself.

Ancient Agora ✔
(see pp94–5)

Locator Map
See Athens Street Finder maps 2, 6

Pantánassa church belonged to the monastery (monastiráki) which gave the area its name. Also known as the church of the Dormition of the Virgin, it is thought to have been built in the 10th century. It is situated opposite the metro station, on the east side of Plateía Monastirakíou.

❶ **Kyriazópoulos Folk Ceramic Museum**
Housed in the old Tzistarákis Mosque, this museum is part of the Museum of Greek Folk Art. Originally opened in 1974, it contains around 800 fine ceramics originating from all over Greece.

Pláka *(see pp106–7)* ⟶

The Fethiye Mosque is situated in the corner of the Roman Agora. It was built by the Turks in the late 15th century to mark Mehmet the Conqueror's visit to Athens.

❷ ★ **Tower of the Winds**
This unusual, octagonal structure was built as a water clock and weather vane by the astronomer Andrónikos Kyrrestes in the 1st century BC.

❶ Kyriazópoulos Folk Ceramic Museum

Μουσείο Ελληνικής Λαϊκής Τέχνης, Συλλογή Κεραμικών Β. Κυριαζοπού-λου

Tzistarákis Mosque, Areos 1, Monastiráki. **Map** 6 D1. **Tel** 210 324 2066. **M** Monastiráki. **Open** 8am–3pm Mon & Wed–Sun. **Closed** main public hols. 🅿 **w** melt.gr

This colourful collection of ceramics was donated to the Greek Folk Art Museum in 1974 by Professor Vasíleios Kyriazópoulos. Now an annexe of the Folk Art Museum, the Kyriazópoulos Folk Ceramic Museum is housed in the imposing Tzistarákis Mosque (or the Mosque of the Lower Fountain). Of the hundreds of pieces on display, many are of the type still used today in a traditional Greek kitchen, such as terracotta water jugs from Aígina, earthenware oven dishes from Sífnos and storage jars from Thessaly and Chíos. There are also some ceramic figures and plates, based on mythological and folk stories, crafted by Minás Avramídis and Dimítrios Mygdalinós who came from Asia Minor in the 1920s.

The mosque itself is of as much interest as its contents. It was built in 1759 by the newly appointed Turkish *voivode* Tzistarákis. The *voivode* was the civil governor who

Ceramic of a young girl from Asia Minor

possessed complete powers over the law courts and the police. He collected taxes for his own account, but also had to pay for the sultan's harem and the treasury.

His workmen dynamited the 17th column of the Temple of Olympian Zeus *(see p115)* in order to make lime to be used for the stucco work on the mosque. Destruction of ancient monuments was forbidden by Turkish law and this act of vandalism was the downfall of Tzistarákis. He was exiled the same year. The mosque has been well restored after earthquake damage in 1981.

❷ Tower of the Winds

Αέρηδες

Within Roman Agora ruins, Pláka. **Map** 6 D1. **Tel** 210 324 5220. **M** Monastiráki. **Open** Apr–Oct: 8am–8pm daily; Nov–Mar: 8:30am–3pm daily. **Closed** main public hols. 🅿 ♿

The remarkable Tower of the Winds is set within the ruins of the Roman Agora. Constructed from marble in the 2nd century BC by the Syrian astronomer Andrónikos Kyrrestes, it was built as a combined weather vane and water clock. The name comes from the external friezes, personifying the eight winds. Sundials are etched into the walls beneath each relief.

The tower is well preserved, standing today at over 12 m (40 ft) high with a diameter of 8 m (26 ft). Still simply called Aérides ("the winds") by Greeks today, in the Middle Ages it was thought to be either the school or prison of Socrates, or even the tomb of Philip II of Macedon *(see p246)*. It was at last correctly identified as the Horologion (water clock) of Andrónikos in the 17th century. All that remains today of its elaborate water clock are the origins of a complex system of water pipes and a circular channel cut into the floor which can be seen inside the tower.

The west and southwest faces of the Tower of the Winds

The west- and north-facing sides each contain a hole which lets light into the otherwise dark interior of the tower.

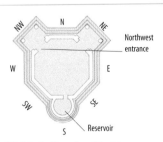

This interior floorplan of the tower shows the compass direction of the building's eight sides. External friezes personify each of the eight winds.

Northwest entrance

Reservoir

North

Northwest

West

Boreas blows the cold north wind through a large conch shell.

Skiron scatters glowing ashes from a bronze vessel.

Zephyros is a semi-naked youth scattering flowers.

❸ Flea Market
Παζάρι

From Plateía Monastirakíou to Plateía
Avyssinías, Monastiráki. **Map** 5 C1.
M Monastiráki. **Open** 8am–2pm Sun.

A banner welcomes visitors
to Athens' famous flea market,
past the ubiquitous tourist
trinket shops of Adrianoú and
Pandrósou streets. For the
locals, the true heart of
the market lies just west of
Plateía Monastirakíou, in Plateía
Avyssinías and its warren
of surrounding streets.

On Sunday mornings when
the shops are closed, the market
itself bursts into action. Traders
set out their bric-a-brac on
stalls and the pavement and
many bargains can be found,

Shoppers browsing in Athens' lively flea market

especially the colourful
handwoven woollen cloths
and the many bangles and
beads sold by hippies. More
expensive items are also on
sale, including brassware,
leatherware and silverware.

During the week, the shops
in the surrounding area are

open and filled with much
the same as the Sunday stalls.
Individual shops each have
their own specialities, so
hunt around before making a
purchase. You can buy almost
anything, from antiques and
old books to taverna chairs
and army surplus gear.

The southwest wind, Lips, heralds a swift
voyage. The reliefs show that each wind
was given a personality according to its
characteristics, and each promises different
conditions. Gentle Zephyros and chilly
Boreas, mentioned in Western literature
and represented in art and sculpture, are
the best known of these.

Whirling dervishes
used the tower as a
monastery in the mid-
18th century. The
dervishes were a Muslim
order of ascetics. The
tower's occupants
became a popular
attraction for Grand Tour
visitors who came
to witness the weekly
ritual of a frenzied
dance, which is
known as the *sema*.

Relief carving of
mythological figure

Metal rod
casting shadow

Lines of sundial
carved into wall
of tower

Southwest	South	Southeast	East	Northeast

Lips holds the
aphlaston (or stern
ornament) of a ship
as he steers.

Notos is the
bearer of rain,
emptying a
pitcher of water.

Euros is a bearded
old man, warmly
wrapped in
a cloak.

Apeliotes is a
young man
bringing fruits
and corn.

Kaïkias empties a
shield full of icy
hailstones on
those below.

Miss T K, by Giánnis Mitarákis, in the Municipal Art Gallery

❹ Municipal Art Gallery

Πινακοθήκη του Δήμου Αθηναίων

Peiraios 51, Plateía Koumoundoúrou, Omónoia. **Map** 1 C4. **Tel** 210 324 3022. Ⓜ Omónoia. **Open** 10am–9pm Tue, 10am–7pm Wed–Sat, 10am–3pm Sun. **Closed** 3 Oct, main public hols.

This little-visited museum has one of the finest archive collections of modern Greek art. Designed by architect Panagiótis Kálkos in 1872, the home of the museum is the old Neo-Classical Foundling Hospital. It was built to cope with the city's population explosion towards the end of the 19th century; unwanted babies were left outside the main entrance to be cared for by hospital staff.

The Municipality of Athens has been amassing the collection since 1923. It now offers a fine introduction to the diverse styles of modern Greek artists. Many paintings are passionate reflections on the Greek landscape, such as Dímos Mpraésas's (1878–1967) landscapes of the Cyclades, or Konstantínos Parthénis's (1882–1964) paintings of olive and cypress trees.

There are also portraits by Giánnis Mitarákis and still lifes by Theófrastos Triantafyllídis. Paintings such as Nikólaos Kartsonákis's *Street Market* (1939) also reveal the folk roots that are at the heart of much modern Greek art.

❺ Kerameikós

Κεραμεικός

This ancient cemetery has been a burial ground since the 12th century BC. The Sacred Way led from Eleusis *(see pp160–61)* to Kerameikós and the Panathenaic Way set out from the Dípylon Gate here to the Acropolis *(see pp98–101)*. Most of the graves remaining today are along the Street of the Tombs. The sculptures excavated in the early 1900s are in the National Archaeological Museum *(see pp72–5)* and the Oberlander Museum; however, plaster copies of the originals can be seen *in situ*.

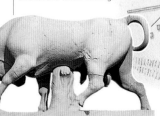

Grave Stele of Hegeso
This is from the family burial plot belonging to Koroibos of Melite. It shows his wife, Hegeso, admiring her jewels with a servant and dates from the late 5th century BC.

Precinct of Aristion

The Precinct of Lysimachides contains a marble dog, originally one of a pair.

The Sanctuary of Hekate was sacred to the ancient goddess of the underworld. It contained an altar and votive offerings.

Oberlander Museum

South terrace

★ **Tomb of Dionysios of Kollytos**
This fine tomb belongs to a rich treasurer. A bull often represents the god Dionysos.

Street of the Tombs

Most of the monuments in the Street of the Tombs date from the 4th century BC. The different styles, from the lavish stelae (relief sculptures) to the simple kioniskoi (small columns), all reveal the dignity that is typical of Greek funerary art.

Locator Map

Stele of Dexileos
Dexileos was a young man killed in 394 BC during the Corinthian War. The son of Lysanias, he is seen on the relief slaying an enemy.

🏛 **Oberlander Museum**

This museum is named after Gustav Oberlander (1867–1936), a German-American industrialist whose donations helped fund its construction in the 1930s. In Gallery 1, some large fragments from grave *stelae* found incorporated into the Dípylon and Sacred Gates are exhibited. These include a marble sphinx (c.550 BC) that

Winged sphinx from grave stele

once crowned a grave *stele*. Galleries 2 and 3 offer an array of huge Proto-geometric and Geometric amphorae and black-figure *lekythoi* (funerary vases). The most moving exhibits come from children's graves and include pottery toy horses and terracotta dolls. There are also examples of some of the 7,000 *ostraka* (voting tablets) *(see pp94–5)* found in the bed of the river Eridanos. Among the superb painted pottery, there is a red-figure *hydria* (water vase) of Helen of Troy and a *lekythos* of Dionysos with satyrs.

This tumulus was the burial place of an old Attic family dating from the 6th century BC.

Tomb of Hipparete

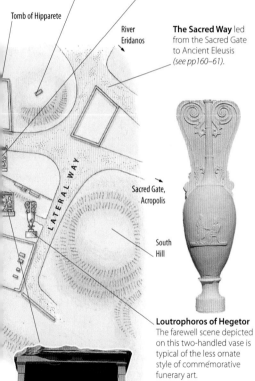

River Eridanos

The Sacred Way led from the Sacred Gate to Ancient Eleusis *(see pp160–61).*

Sacred Gate, Acropolis

South Hill

Loutrophoros of Hegetor
The farewell scene depicted on this two-handled vase is typical of the less ornate style of commémorative funerary art.

★ **Stele of Demetria and Pamphile**
This moving sculpture shows the seated Pamphile with her sister Demetria behind her. This was one of the last ornate stelae to be made in the late 4th century BC.

Geometric funerary amphora from the Oberlander Museum

❻ Ancient Agora
Αρχαία Αγορά

The Agora, or market–place, formed the political heart of ancient Athens from 600 BC. Democracy was practised in the *Bouleuterion* (Council) and the law courts, and in open meetings. Socrates was indicted and executed in the state prison here in 399 BC. The theatres, schools and stoas filled with shops also made this the centre of social and commercial life. Even the city mint that produced Athens' silver coins was here. The American School of Classical Studies began excavations of the Ancient Agora in the 1930s, and since then, the vast remains of a complex array of public buildings have been revealed.

Stoa of Attalos
This colonnaded building was reconstructed in the mid-20th century as a museum to house finds from the Ancient Agora site.

Odeion of Agrippa
This statue of a triton (half-god, half-fish) once adorned the façade of the Odeion of Agrippa. It dates from AD 150 and is now in the Agora museum.

KEY

① Hellenistic temple
② Stoa of Zeus Eleutherios
③ Altar of the twelve gods
④ Temple of Apollo Patroös
⑤ Temple of Ares
⑥ Triton statues
⑦ **The Panathenaic Way** was named after the Great Panathenaia festival which took place every four years.
⑧ Monopteros temple
⑨ Library of Pantainos
⑩ Southeast temple
⑪ **The middle stoa** housed shops.
⑫ Southwest temple
⑬ Heliaia
⑭ Southwest fountain
⑮ Latrines
⑯ **The Tholos** was the Council headquarters.
⑰ **Bouleuterion or Council chamber**
⑱ Arsenal
⑲ Metroön
⑳ Monument of the Eponymous Heroes
㉑ Altar of Zeus

Reconstruction of the Ancient Agora

This shows the Agora as it was in c.AD 200, viewed from the northwest. The main entrance to the Agora at this time was via the Panathenaic Way, which ran across the site from the Acropolis in the southeast to the Kerameikós in the northwest.

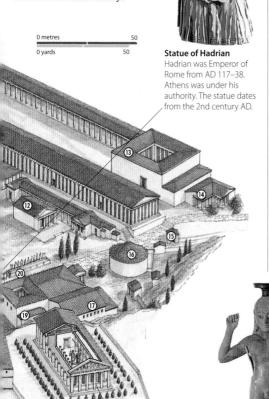

View across the Agora from the south showing the reconstructed Stoa of Attalos on the right

0 metres	50
0 yards	50

Statue of Hadrian
Hadrian was Emperor of Rome from AD 117–38. Athens was under his authority. The statue dates from the 2nd century AD.

Ostrakon condemning a man named Hippokrates to exile

🏛 Stoa of Attalos

This fine building was rebuilt between 1953 and 1956, helped by a huge donation from John D Rockefeller, Jr. An impressive two-storey stoa, or roofed arcade, founded by King Attalos of Pergamon (ruled 159–138 BC), it dominated the eastern quarter of the Agora until it was burnt down by the Heruli tribe in AD 267. Reconstructed using the original foundations and ancient materials, it now contains a museum whose exhibits reveal the great diversity and sophistication of ancient life. Artifacts include rules from the 2nd-century AD Library of Pantainos, the text of a law against tyranny from 337 BC, bronze and stone lots used for voting and a *klepsýdra* (water clock) used for timing speeches. *Ostraka* (voting tablets on which names were inscribed) bear such famous names as Themistokles and Aristeides the Just, the latter banished, or "ostracized", in 482 BC. More everyday items, such as terracotta toys and portable ovens, and hobnails and sandals found in a shoemaker's shop, are equally fascinating. Also on display are some beautiful black-figure vases and an unusual oil flask moulded into the shape of a kneeling boy.

Oil flask in the Archaic style

Hephaisteion
This temple, also known as the Theseion, is the best-preserved building on the site. It was built c.449–440 BC.

❼ Acropolis

Ακρόπολη

In the mid-5th century BC, Perikles persuaded the Athenians to begin a grand programme of new building work in Athens that has come to represent the political and cultural achievements of Greece. The work transformed the Acropolis with three contrasting temples and a monumental gateway. The Theatre of Dionysos on the south slope was developed further in the 4th century BC, and the Theatre of Herodes Atticus was added in the 2nd century AD.

Locator Map

★ Porch of the Caryatids
These statues of women were used in place of columns on the south porch of the Erechtheion. The originals, four of which can be seen in the Acropolis Museum (see p104), have been replaced by casts.

★ Temple of Athena Nike
This temple to Athena of Victory is on the west side of the Propylaia. It was built in 426–421 BC (see p100).

KEY

① **An olive tree** now grows where Athena first planted her tree in a competition against Poseidon.

② **The Propylaia** was built in 437–432 BC to form a new entrance to the Acropolis (see p100).

③ **The Beulé Gate** was the first entrance to the Acropolis (see p100).

④ **Pathway to Acropolis from ticket office**

⑤ **Two Corinthian columns** are the remains of choregic monuments erected by sponsors of successful dramatic performances (see p101).

⑥ **Panagía i Spiliótissa** is a chapel set up in a cave in the Acropolis rock (see p101).

⑦ **Sanctuary of Asklepios**

⑧ **The Acropolis rock** was an easily defended site. It has been in use for nearly 5,000 years.

⑨ **Stoa of Eumenes**

Theatre of Herodes Atticus
Also known as the Odeion of Herodes Atticus, this superb theatre was originally built in AD 161. It was restored in 1955 and is used today for outdoor concerts (see p101).

◀ The Caryatids in the Erechtheion temple ruins

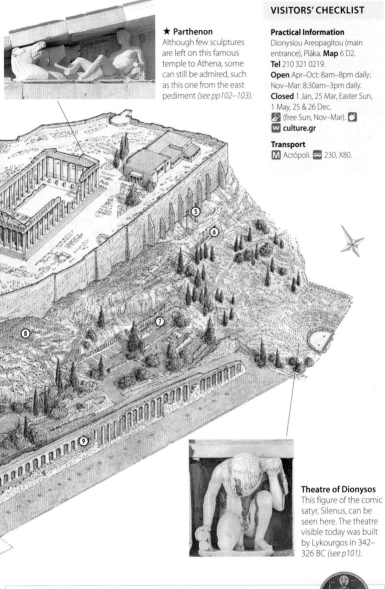

★ Parthenon
Although few sculptures are left on this famous temple to Athena, some can still be admired, such as this one from the east pediment *(see pp102–103).*

Theatre of Dionysos
This figure of the comic satyr, Silenus, can be seen here. The theatre visible today was built by Lykourgos in 342–326 BC *(see p101).*

3000 BC First settlement on the Acropolis during Neolithic period

AD 51 St Paul delivers sermon on Aeropagus Hill

480 BC All buildings of Archaic period destroyed by the Persians

AD 267 Germanic Heruli tribe destroy Acropolis

St Paul

| 3000 BC | 2000 BC | 1000 BC | AD 1 | AD 1000 |

1200 BC Cyclopean wall built to replace original ramparts

447–432 BC Construction of the Parthenon under Perikles

AD 1687 Parthenon damaged by Venetians

510 BC Delphic Oracle declares Acropolis a holy place of the gods, banning habitation by mortals

Perikles (495–429 BC)

AD 1987 Restoration of the Erechtheion completed

Exploring the Acropolis

Once through the first entrance, the Beulé Gate, straight ahead is the Propylaia, the grand entrance to the temple complex. Before going through here, it is worth exploring the Temple of Athena Nike, on the right. Beyond the Propylaia are the Erechtheion and the Parthenon *(see pp102–103)*, which dominate the top of the rock. There are also stunning views of Athens itself from the Acropolis. Access to all the temple precincts is banned to prevent damage. On the south slope of the Acropolis are the two theatres, once used for drama festivals in honour of the god Dionysos. The striking Acropolis Museum and the hills immediately to the west are covered on pages 104–105.

View of the Acropolis from the southwest

🏛 Beulé Gate

The gate is named after the French archaeologist Ernest Beulé who discovered it in 1852. It was built in AD 267 after the raid of the Heruli, a Germanic people, as part of the Roman Acropolis fortifications. It incorporates stones from the *choregic* monument *(see p113)* of Nikias that was situated near the Stoa of Eumenes. Parts of the original monument's dedication are still visible over the architrave. There is also an inscription identifying a Roman, Flavius Septimius Marcellinus, as donor of the gateway. In 1686, when the Turks destroyed the Temple of Athena Nike, they used the marble to build a bastion for artillery over the gate.

🏛 Temple of Athena Nike

This small temple was built in 426–421 BC to commemorate the Athenians' victories over the Persians. The temple frieze has representative scenes from the Battle of Plataéa (479 BC).

Designed by Kallikrates, the temple stands on a 9.5-m (31-ft) bastion. It has been used as both observation post and an ancient shrine to the goddess of Victory, Athena Nike, of whom there is a remarkable sculpture situated on the balustrade. Legend records the temple site as the place where King Aegeus stood waiting for his son Theseus to return from his mission to Crete to slay the Minotaur. Theseus had promised to swap his ships' black sails for white on his return, but in the melee of the victorious battle, had forgotten his promise. When King Aegeus saw the black sails, he presumed his son to be dead and threw himself into the sea. Built of Pentelic marble, the temple has four Ionic columns 4 m (13 ft) high at

each portico end. It was reconstructed in 1834–8, after being destroyed in 1686 by the Turks. On the point of collapse in 1935, it was again dismantled and reconstructed according to information resulting from more recent research.

🏛 Propylaia

Work began on this enormous entrance to the Acropolis in 437 BC. Although the outbreak of the Peloponnesian War in 432 BC curtailed its completion, its architect Mnesikles created a building admired throughout the ancient world. The Propylaia comprises a rectangular central building divided by a wall into two porticoes. These were punctuated by five entrance doors, rows of Ionic and Doric columns and a vestibule with a blue-coffered ceiling decorated with gold stars. Two wings flank the main building. The north wing was home to the pinakothíki, an art gallery.

During its chequered history – later as archbishop's residence, Frankish palace, and Turkish fortress and armoury – parts of the building have been accidentally destroyed; it even suffered the misfortune of being struck by lightning in 1645, and later the explosion of the Turkish gunpowder store *(see p102)*.

🏛 Erechtheion

Built between 421 and 406 BC, the Erechtheion is situated on the most sacred site of the Acropolis. It is said to be where Poseidon left his trident marks in a rock, and Athena's olive tree sprouted, in their battle for possession of the city. Named

The eastern end of the Erechtheion

The remains of the Theatre of Dionysos

after Erechtheus, one of the mythical kings of Athens, the temple was a sanctuary to both Athena Polias, and Erechtheus-Poseidon.

Famed for its elegant and extremely ornate Ionic architecture and caryatid columns in the shape of women, this extraordinary monument is built on different levels. The large rectangular cella was divided into three rooms. One contained the holy olive wood statue of Athena Polias. The cella was bounded by north, east and south porticoes. The south is the Porch of the Caryatids, the maiden statues which are now in the Acropolis Museum.

The Erechtheion complex has been used for a range of purposes, including a harem for the wives of the Turkish *disdar* (commander) in 1463. It was almost completely destroyed by a Turkish shell in 1827 during the War of Independence (*see pp44–5*). Restoration work here has caused heated disputes: holes have been filled with new marble, and copies have been made to replace original features that have been removed to the safety of the museum.

Theatre of Herodes Atticus

This small Roman theatre seats 5,000 spectators and is still in use today (*see p123*). Built by the Roman consul Herodes Atticus between AD 161 and 174, in memory of his wife, the shape was hollowed out of the rocks on the southern slope of the Acropolis. The semicircular

orchestra in front of the stage was repaved with alternating blue and white marble slabs in the 1950s. Behind the stage, its distinctive colonnade once contained statues of the nine Muses. The whole theatre was originally enclosed by a cedarwood roof that gave better acoustics and allowed for all-weather performances.

Theatre of Dionysos

D. Areopagitou, Makrygiánni.
Tel 210 322 4625.
Open Apr–Oct: 8am–8pm daily; Nov–Mar: 8:30am–3pm daily.

Throne from the Theatre of Dionysos

Cut into the southern cliff face of the Acropolis, the Theatre of Dionysos is the birthplace of Greek tragedy, and was the first theatre built of stone. Aeschylus, Sophocles, Euripides and Aristophanes all had their plays performed here, during the dramatic contests of the annual

City Dionysia festival, when it was little more than a humble wood-and-earth affair. The theatre was rebuilt in stone by the Athenian statesman Lykourgos between 342–326 BC, but the ruins that can be seen today are in part those of a much bigger structure, built by the Romans, which could seat 17,000. They used it as a gladiatorial arena, and added a marble balustrade with metal railings to protect spectators. In the 1st century AD, during Emperor Nero's reign, the orchestra was given its marble flooring, and in the 2nd century AD, the front of the stage was decorated with reliefs showing Dionysos's life. Above the theatre, there is a cave sacred to the goddess Artemis. This was converted into a chapel in the Byzantine era, dedicated to **Panagía i Spiliótissa** (Our Lady of the Cave), and was the place where mothers brought their sick children. Two large Corinthian columns nearby are the remains of choregic monuments erected to celebrate the benefactor's team winning a drama festival. The Sanctuary of Asklepios to the west, founded in 420 BC, was dedicated to the god of healing. Worshippers seeking a cure had to take part in purification rites before they could enter the temple precincts.

Interior of the Panagía i Spiliótissa chapel, above the Theatre of Dionysos

The Parthenon
Ο Παρθενώνας

One of the world's most famous buildings, this temple was begun in 447 BC. It was designed by the architects Kallikrates and Iktinos, primarily to house the 12-m (40-ft) high statue of Athena Parthenos (Maiden), sculpted by Pheidias. Taking nine years to complete, the temple was dedicated to the goddess in 438 BC. Over the centuries, it has been used as a church, a mosque and an arsenal, and has suffered severe damage. Built as an expression of the glory of ancient Athens, it remains the city's emblem to this day.

View of the Parthenon from the west

Parthenon Frieze
The frieze, designed by Pheidias, ran around the inner wall of the Parthenon. The metopes (sections of the frieze) depicted the Great Panathenaia festival, honouring Athena.

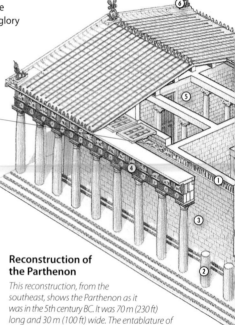

Reconstruction of the Parthenon

This reconstruction, from the southeast, shows the Parthenon as it was in the 5th century BC. It was 70 m (230 ft) long and 30 m (100 ft) wide. The entablature of this peripteral temple (with a single row of columns around the edge) was painted in blue, red and gold.

KEY

① **The Elgin Marbles** *(see p104)* were taken largely from the internal frieze.

② **Each column** was constructed from fluted drums of marble. The fluting was added once the columns were in place.

③ **Marble walls** concealed the cellas, or inner rooms.

④ **The external frieze** consisted of triglyphs and metopes.

⑤ **The west cella** was used as a treasury.

⑥ **Akroterion**

⑦ **The internal columns** were in two rows and Doric in style.

⑧ **The roof** was made from Pentelic marble tiles supported on wooden rafters.

⑨ **The steps** curved upwards slightly at the centre to make them appear level from a distance.

VEDUTA DEL CAST. D'ACROPOLIS DALLA PARTE DI TRAMONTANA

Explosion of 1687
During the Venetian siege of the Acropolis, General Francesco Morosini bombarded the Parthenon with cannon-fire. The Turks were using the temple as an arsenal at the time and the ensuing explosion demolished much of it, including the roof, the inner structure and 14 of the outer columns.

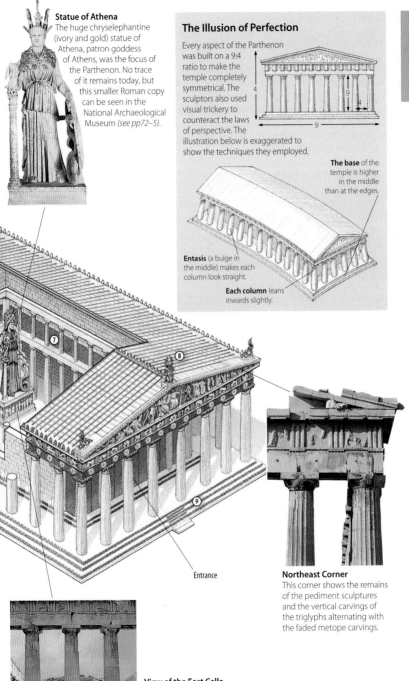

Statue of Athena
The huge chryselephantine (ivory and gold) statue of Athena, patron goddess of Athens, was the focus of the Parthenon. No trace of it remains today, but this smaller Roman copy can be seen in the National Archaeological Museum (see pp72–5).

The Illusion of Perfection

Every aspect of the Parthenon was built on a 9:4 ratio to make the temple completely symmetrical. The sculptors also used visual trickery to counteract the laws of perspective. The illustration below is exaggerated to show the techniques they employed.

The base of the temple is higher in the middle than at the edges.

Entasis (a bulge in the middle) makes each column look straight.

Each column leans inwards slightly.

Entrance

Northeast Corner
This corner shows the remains of the pediment sculptures and the vertical carvings of the triglyphs alternating with the faded metope carvings.

View of the East Cella
The cella was the inner room of the temple. In the case of the Parthenon, there were two – east and west. The east cella contained the enormous cult statue of Athena and the offerings bestowed upon it. The west cella was the back room, reserved for the priestess.

Around the Acropolis

The area around the Acropolis was the centre of public life in Athens. In addition to the Agora in the north *(see pp94–5)*, political life was largely centred on the Pnyx and the Areopagos, the hills lying to the west of the Acropolis; the Assembly met on the former and murder trials were heard by a council of ex-magistrates on the latter. Other ancient remains and the glittering Acropolis Museum, located at the foot of the Acropolis, provide a fascinating insight into what daily life was like in ancient Athens.

Excavation site at the Acropolis Museum

🏛 Acropolis Museum
Dionysiou Areopagitou 15, Acrópoli.
Tel 210 900 0900. Ⓜ Acrópoli.
Open Apr–Oct: 8am–4pm Mon,
8am–8pm Tue–Thu, Sat & Sun,
8am–10pm Fri; Nov–Mar: 9am–5pm
Tue–Thu, 9am–10pm Fri, 9am–8pm
Sat & Sun. 🎫 🚫 🖼 ♿
Ⓦ theacropolismuseum.gr

After decades of planning and delays, the Acropolis Museum opened in the historic Makrigiánni district, southeast of the Acropolis. The museum had been planned since the late 1970s to replace the old Acropolis Museum, situated next to the Parthenon, which was always considered too small and dilapidated to really do justice to the sculptures and architectural pieces found on the Acropolis hill. Today, the €130-million, multi-storey, all-glass showpiece designed by Bernad Tschumi, is undoubtedly a more fitting home for the hill's stunning treasures.

Tschumi had the added challenge of constructing the building over excavations of an early Christian settlement. Concrete pillars and a glass walkway allow the building to hover over the ruins, which are on view in the lobby near the entrance.

The rest of the collection is installed in chronological order and begins with finds from the slopes of the Acropolis. These include statues and reliefs from the Sanctuary of Asklepios.

The **Archaic Collection** is set out in a magnificent double-height gallery. Fragments of painted pedimental statues include mythological scenes of Herakles grappling with various monsters and the more peaceful votive statue of the *Moschophoros*, or Calf-Bearer, portraying a young man carrying a calf on his shoulders (c.570 BC).

The sky-lit **Parthenon Gallery** on the top floor is the highlight. Here, arranged around an indoor court and looking out on to the Parthenon, the remaining parts of the Parthenon frieze are displayed in the order in which they would have graced the Parthenon (there are significant blank spaces left for those held in London). The sculptures depict the Panathenaic procession, including the chariot and *apobates* (slaves riding chariot horses) and a sacrificial cow being led by youths.

On the level below, the **post-Parthenon Collection** comprises sculptures from the Temple of Athena Nike, and architectural features from the Propylaia and the Erechtheion, including the original four caryatids from the south porch.

The Elgin Marbles

These famous sculptures, also called the Parthenon Marbles, are held in the British Museum in London. They were acquired by Lord Elgin in 1801–3 from the occupying Turkish authorities. He sold them to the British nation for £35,000 in 1816. There is great controversy surrounding the Marbles. While some argue that they are more carefully preserved in the British Museum, the Greek government does not accept the legality of the sale and many believe they belong in Athens. A famous supporter of this cause was the Greek actress and politician, Melína Merkoúri, who died in 1994.

The newly arrived Elgin Marbles at the British Museum, in a painting by A Archer

🏛 Areopagus Hill

There is little left to see on this low hill today, apart from the rough-hewn, slippery steps and what are thought to be seats on its summit. The Areopagus was used by the Persians and Turks during their attacks on the Acropolis citadel, and played an important role as the home of the Supreme Judicial Court in the Classical period. It takes its name, meaning the "Hill of Ares", from a mythological trial that took place here when the god Ares was acquitted of murdering the son of Poseidon. The nearby **Cave of the Furies** inspired the playwright Aeschylus *(see p61)* to set Orestes's trial here in his play *Eumenides* (The Furies). The hill also achieved renown in AD 51, when St Paul delivered his sermon "On an unknown God" and gained his first convert, Dionysios the Areopagite, who subsequently became the patron saint of Athens.

🏛 Pnyx Hill

If Athens is the cradle of democracy, Pnyx Hill is its exact birthplace. During the 4th and 5th century BC, the *Ekklesia* (citizens' assembly) met here to discuss and vote upon all but the most important matters of state, until it lost its powers during Roman rule. In its heyday, 6,000 Athenians gathered 40 times a year to listen to speeches and take vital political decisions. Themistokles, Perikles and Demosthenes all spoke from the *bema* (speaker's platform) that is still visible today. Carved out of the rock face, it formed the top step of a platform that doubled as a primitive altar to the god Zeus. There are also the remains of the huge retaining wall which was built to support the semicircular terraces that placed citizens on a level with the speakers. It completely surrounded the auditorium, which was 110 m (358 ft) high.

🏛 Agios Dimítrios

Dionysíou Areopagítou, south slope of Acropolis. **Open** daily. 🚫 except Sun.

This Byzantine church is often called Agios Dimítrios Loumpardiáris, after an incident in 1656. The Turkish *disdar* (commander) at the time, Yusuf Aga, laid plans to fire a huge cannon called Loumpárda, situated by the Propylaia *(see p100)*, at worshippers in the church as they celebrated the feast day of Agios Dimítrios. However, the night before the feast, lightning struck the Propylaia, miraculously killing the commander and his family.

Cross from Agios Dimítrios church

🏛 Filopáppos Hill

The highest summit in the south of Athens, at 147 m (482 ft), offers spectacular views of the Acropolis. It has always played a decisive defensive role in Athens' history – the general Demetrios Poliorketes built an important fort here overlooking the strategic Piraeus road in 294 BC, and Francesco Morosini bombarded the Acropolis from here in 1687. Popularly called Filopáppos Hill after a monument still on its summit, it was also known

The Asteroskopeíon on the Hill of the Nymphs

to the ancient Greeks as the Hill of Muses or the Mouseion, because the tomb of Musaeus, a disciple of Orpheus, was traditionally held to be located here.

Built between AD 114–16, the Monument of Philopappus was raised by the Athenians in honour of Caius Julius Antiochus Philopappus, a Roman consul and philhellene. Its unusual concave marble façade, 12 m (40 ft) high, contains niches with statues of Philopappus and his grandfather, Antiochus IV. A frieze around the monument depicts the arrival of Philopappus by chariot for his inauguration as Roman consul in AD 100.

🏛 Hill of the Nymphs

This 103-m (340-ft) high tree-clad hill takes its name from dedications found carved on rocks in today's Observatory Garden. The Asteroskopeíon (Observatory), built in 1842 by the Danish architect Theophil Hansen, with funds from philanthropist Baron Sína, occupies the site of a sanctuary to nymphs associated with childbirth. The modern church of Agía Marína nearby has similar associations of childbirth; pregnant women used to slide effortlessly down a smooth rock near the church, in the hope of an equally easy labour.

The Monument of Philopappus, AD 114–116

Street-by-Street: Central Pláka

Pláka is the historic heart of Athens. Even though only a few houses date back further than the Ottoman period, it remains the oldest continuously inhabited area of the city. One explanation of its name comes from the word *pliaka* (old), which was used to describe the area by Albanian soldiers in the service of the Turks who settled here in the 16th century. Despite the crowds of tourists and the many Athenians who come to eat in the tavernas or browse in antique shops, it still retains the feel of a residential neighbourhood.

⑬ Mitrópoli
Athens' cathedral was built in the second half of the 19th century.

Thoukydídou
is named after the historian Thucydides (c.460–400 BC).

⑫ ★ Panagía Gorgoepíkoös
This tiny 12th-century church, also known as the Little Cathedral, has some beautiful carvings.

⑪ Museum of Greek Popular Musical Instruments
A range of folk instruments is displayed in this museum, which was opened in 1991.

Monastiráki
(see pp88–9)

Acropolis
(see pp98–105)

⑩ University of Athens Museum
Occupying the university's original home, this museum has memorabilia from the university's early days, including these old medical artifacts.

Ancient Agora
(see pp94–95)

⑨ Kanellópoulos Museum
Privately owned, this museum has exquisite works of art from all areas of the Hellenic world.

For hotels and restaurants see pp268–9 and pp282–5

Plateía Syntágmatos
(see p116)

⓱ Greek Folk Art Museum
Offering the best of Greek folk art, this has everything from shadow puppets to terracotta ornaments.

Locator Map
See Street Finder maps 5–6

CENTRAL ATHENS NORTH

CENTRAL ATHENS SOUTH

| 0 metres | 50 |
| 0 yards | 50 |

⓮ Agios Nikólaos Ragavás
This 11th-century, Byzantine chapel is a popular location for weddings.

⓰ Plateía Lysikrátous
Named after the monument in its centre, this square was a favourite haunt of the poet Byron.

Key
— Suggested route

⓯ Anafiótika
The whitewashed houses and winding streets resembling a Cycladic village were built in the 19th century by settlers from the island of Anáfi.

❽ Ilías Lalaoúnis Jewellery Museum

Μουσείο Κοσμήματος Ηλία Λαλαούνη

Karyatidon & P. Kallisperi 12, Acrópoli.
Map 6 D3. **Tel** 210 922 1044.
Ⓜ Acrópoli. **Open** 9am–3pm Wed–Sat, 11am–4pm Sun. **Closed** main public hols. 🅿 by prior written permission only. ♿ 📷
ⓦ lalaounis-jewelrymuseum.gr

Situated just below the Theatre of Dionysos, this small museum is a delight for anyone interested in decorative arts. The permanent collection comprises over 4,000 pieces spanning 60 years of jewellery making by designer Ilías Lalaoúnis, who is credited with the revival of Greek jewellery making in the 1950s.

❾ Kanellópoulos Museum

Μουσείο Κανελλοπούλου

Corner of Theorías & Pános 12, Pláka.
Map 6 D2. **Tel** 210 324 4447. Ⓜ Monastiráki. **Open** 8:30am–3pm Tue–Sun, noon–3pm Good Fri. **Closed** 1 Jan, 25 Mar, Easter Sun, 25, 26 Dec. 🅿
ⓦ pacanellopoulosfoundation.org

In an immaculately restored Neo-Classical town house, this museum has a varied collection of artifacts from all over the Hellenistic world. On display are 6th-century BC helmets, 5th-century BC gold Persian jewellery and Attic vases. Also on view are Cycladic figurines, some unusual terracotta figures of actors in their theatrical masks, and a fine 2nd-century AD El Faiyûm portrait of a woman.

A huge block of stone that fell from the walls of the Acropolis can still be seen as an exhibit on the ground floor.

Sculpture of a triton from the Kanellópoulos Museum

Rempétika musicians, Museum of Greek Popular Musical Instruments

❿ University of Athens Museum

Μουσείο Ιστορίας του Πανεπιστημίου Αθηνών

Thólou 5, Pláka. **Map** 6 D2.
Tel 210 368 9502. Ⓜ Monastiráki.
Open 9:30am–2:30pm Mon–Fri.
Closed Sat & Sun. ⓦ history-museum.uoa.gr

This three-storey house was the first home of the University of Athens. It opened on 3 May 1837 with 52 students and 33 professors in its first year. In November 1841, the University moved to its new quarters, and from 1922, the building was home to many immigrant families. While they were there, a taverna known as the "Old University" was opened on the ground floor.

In 1963, the building was declared a National Monument. Later reacquired by the university, the old building was opened as a museum in 1974. Today, the "Old University", as it is still known, has an eclectic collection of memorabilia such as corporeal body maps, anatomical models, scientific instruments and medicine jars.

⓫ Museum of Greek Popular Musical Instruments

Μουσείο Ελληνικών Λαϊκών Μουσικών Οργάνων

Diogénous 1–3, Pláka. **Map** 6 D1.
Tel 210 325 0198. Ⓜ Monastiráki.
Open 10am–2pm Tue–Sun, noon–6pm Wed. **Closed** 17 Nov, main public hols. ⓦ instruments-museum.gr

Cretan musicologist Phoebus Anogianákis donated over 1,200 musical instruments to the Greek State in 1978. In 1991, this study centre and museum was opened, devoted to the history of popular Greek music, including Anogianákis's collection. The museum traces the development of different styles of island music and the arrival of *rempétika* (Greek "blues") from Smyrna in 1922.

Instruments from all over Greece are displayed, with recordings and headphones. The basement contains church and livestock bells, as well as water whistles, wooden clappers and flutes. Elsewhere, there are wind instruments including *tsampoúna* (bagpipes made from goatskin) and string instruments such as the Cretan *lýra*.

⑫ Panagía Gorgoepíkoös
Παναγία η Γοργοεπήκοος

This domed cruciform church is built entirely from Pentelic marble, now weathered to a rich corn-coloured hue. Dating from the 12th century, it measures only 7.5 m (25 ft) long by 12 m (40 ft) wide. The size of the church is in scale with Athens when it was just a village in the 12th century. Adorned with friezes and bas-reliefs taken from earlier buildings, the exterior mixes the Classical and Byzantine styles. Although dedicated to Panagía Gorgoepíkoös (the Madonna who Swiftly Hears) and Agios Eleorthérios (the saint who protects women in childbirth), it is often affectionately known as the Mikrí Mitrópoli (Little Cathedral).

VISITORS' CHECKLIST

Practical Information
Plateía Mitropóleos, Pláka. **Map** 6
E1. **Open** 7am–7pm daily. 🚻

Transport
Ⓜ Monastiráki.

The south façade of the church, dwarfed by the giant Mitrópoli

Four brick pillars
replaced the original marble ones in 1834.

Allegorical Animals
This 12th-century bas-relief detail is one of a pair from the west façade.

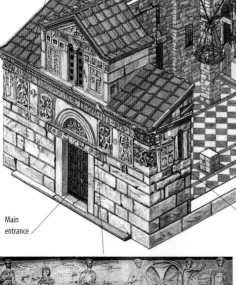

The floor is lower than ground level by about 30 cm (12 in).

Main entrance

Fragments of Classical buildings made from Pentelic marble were combined with Byzantine sections in the style of a Classical frieze.

Lintel Frieze
This relief depicting the months of the year dates from the 4th century BC. The central cross was added in the 12th century.

Modern mosaics above the main entrance to Athens' cathedral, Mitrópoli

⓭ Mitrópoli
Μητρόπολη

Plateía Mitropóleos, Pláka. **Map** 6 E1.
Tel 210 322 1308. Ⓜ Monastiráki.
Open 7am–7pm daily.

Work began in 1840 on this huge cathedral, using marble from 72 demolished churches for its walls. The cornerstone was laid in a ceremony by King Otto and Queen Amalía on Christmas Day 1842. It took another 20 years to finish the building, using three different architects (François Boulanger, Theophil Hansen and Dimítrios Zézos), which may account for its slightly ungainly appearance. On 21 May 1862, it was formally dedicated to Evangelismós Theotókou (the Annunciation of the Virgin) by the king and queen. At 40 m (130 ft) long, 20 m (65 ft) wide and 24 m (80 ft) high, it is the largest church in Athens.

The cathedral is the official seat of the Bishop of Athens, and remains a popular city landmark that has been used for ceremonial events from the coronations of kings to the weddings and funerals of the rich and famous.

Inside, there are the tombs of two saints murdered by the Ottoman Turks: Agía Filothéi and Gregory V. The bones of Agía Filothéi, who died in 1589, are still visible in a silver reliquary. Her charitable works included the ransoming of Greek women enslaved in Turkish harems. Gregory V, Patriarch of Constantinople, was hanged and thrown into the Bosphorus in 1821. His body was rescued by Greek sailors and taken to Odessa. It was eventually returned to Athens by Black Sea (Pontic) Greeks 50 years later.

⓮ Agios Nikólaos Ragavás
Άγιος Νικόλαος ο Ραγκαβάς

Corner of Tripodon & Prytaneíou 1,
Pláka. **Map** 6 E2. **Tel** 210 322 8193.
Ⓜ Monastiráki. 🚌 1, 2, 4, 5, 10, 11.
Open 8am–noon, 5–8pm daily.
♿ limited.

This typical 11th-century Byzantine church, rebuilt in the 18th century and restored to some of its former glory in the late 1970s, incorporates marble columns and other remains of ancient buildings in its external walls. It is one of the favourite parish churches of Pláka, frequently used for colourful Greek weddings which spill out on to the street at weekends. It was the first church in Athens to have a bell after the War of Independence (1821), and the first to ring out after the city's liberation from the Germans on 12 October 1944.

⓯ Anafiótika
Αναφιώτικα

Map 6 D2. Ⓜ Monastiráki.

Nestling beneath the northern slopes of the Acropolis, this area is one of the oldest settlements in Athens. Today, its white-washed houses, cramped streets, lazy cats and pots of basil on windowsills still give it the atmosphere of a typical Cycladic village. Its first residents

Looking down on Agios Nikólaos Ragavás church from Anafiótika

◀ Panoramic view of the Acropolis

were refugees from the Peloponnesian War *(see p34)*. By 1841, it had been colonized by workmen from Anáfi, in the Cyclades, who eventually gave the area its name. Part of the influx of island craftsmen, who helped to construct the new city following Independence, ignored an 1834 decree declaring the area an archaeological zone, and completed their houses overnight, installing their families by morning. By Ottoman law, this meant the authorities were powerless to knock the new houses down.

The area is bounded by two 17th-century churches: Agios Geórgios tou Vráchou to the east, which has a tiny courtyard filled with flowers, and Agios Symeón to the west, which contains a copy of a miraculous icon, originally brought from Anáfi.

Akrokérama, or terracotta sphinxes, on a roof in Anafiótika

⑯ Plateía Lysikrátous

Πλατεία Λυσικράτους

Lysikrátous, Sélley & Epimenídou, Pláka. **Map** 6 E2. 🚌 1, 5, 15.

Situated in the east of the Pláka district, this square is named after the monument of Lysikrates that dominates it. Despite Lord Elgin's attempts to remove it to England, the elegant structure is the city's only intact choregic monument. These monuments were built to commemorate the victors at the annual choral and dramatic festival at the Theatre of Dionysos *(see p101)*. They take their name from the rich sponsor *(choregos)* who produced the winning team. Built in 334 BC, this is the earliest known example where Corinthian capitals are used externally. Six columns rise in

a circle to a marble dome, decorated with an elegant finial of acanthus leaves which supported the winner's bronze trophy. It bears the inscription "Lysikrates of Kikynna, son of Lysitheides, was choregos; the tribe of Akamantis won the victory with a chorus of boys; Theon played the flute; Lysiades, an Athenian, trained the chorus; Evainetos was archon". The Athenians elected nine magistrates known as archons each year, and referred to the year by the name of one of them, the "eponymous archon." A frieze above this inscription, probably the theme of the winners' performance, depicts a battle between Dionysos, the god of theatre, and Tyrrhenian pirates. Surrounded by satyrs, the god transforms them into dolphins and their ship's mast into a sea serpent.

Capuchin friars converted the monument into a library. Grand tour travellers, such as Chateaubriand (1768–1848) and Byron *(see p153)*, stayed at their convent, which was founded on the site in 1669.

The monument of Lysikrates, named after the *choregos* of the winning team of actors

Byron was inspired while staying there and wrote some of his poem, *Childe Harold*, sitting in the monument during his final visit to Athens in 1810.

Not far from the monument is the beautifully restored 11th-century Byzantine church of Agía Aikateríni (St Catherine). In 1767, it was given to the monastery of St Catherine of Mount Sinai. It was renovated, but in 1882, the monastery was forced to exchange it for land elsewhere and it became a local parish church.

Icon Painters in Plaka

Pláka is littered with small artists' studios where icons are still painted using traditional methods. The best are situated just south of Plateía Mitropóleos, among the ecclesiastical shops selling vestments

and liturgical objects, on Agías Filothéis and Apóllonos streets. In some workshops, painters still use the Byzantine method of painting in egg-based tempera on specially treated wood. Customers of all religions can order the saint of their choice in a variety of different sizes. A medium-sized icon depicting a single saint, 25 cm by 15 cm (10 in by 6 in) and copied from a photograph, takes about one day to complete.

Ornate embroidery from Ioánnina, Epirus, on display in the Greek Folk Art Museum

⓱ Greek Folk Art Museum

Μουσείο Ελληνικής Λαϊκής Τέχνης

Kydathinaíon 17, Pláka. **Map** 6 E2.
Tel 210 321 3018. Ⓜ Acrópoli.
🚍 2, 4, 9, 10, 11, 12, 15. 🚊 1, 5.
Open 8am–3pm Tue–Sun.
Closed main public hols. 🅿
🅖 limited. 🆆 melt.gr

Greek folk art, including some embroidery and costumes from the mainland and Aegean islands, fills five floors in this fascinating museum. The collection also covers the renaissance of decorative crafts in the 18th and 19th centuries, to reveal a rich heritage of traditional techniques in skills such as weaving, woodcarving and metalwork.

The ground floor has an extensive collection of fine embroidery work, showing a wide range of techniques.

Displays on the mezzanine floor include ceramics, metalwork and woodcarving. The ceramics range from architectural works, such as chimneys, to decorative or practical pieces such as household pots. Made from terracotta and faïence, they include both glazed and

unglazed pieces. The metalwork on view includes examples made from copper, iron, bronze, steel and pewter. Many are covered with intricate decoration. The woodcarving products are equally impressive in their decoration, often being inlaid with mother-of-pearl, ivory or silver. The wood used varies widely, from walnut to fragrant cedar and wild olive.

Also on the mezzanine are disguise costumes. Their origin is thought to be in the ancient Greek drama festivals in honour of Dionysos, which made use of overtly expressive masks. The puppets from the Karagkiózis theatre (*see p155*) amused the audience by satirizing topical political and social life.

The first floor houses popular paintings, including works by Theófilos Chatzimichaïl (*see p222*). There is an excellent collection of silverware on the second floor of the museum, which displays of various ecclesiastical items such as chalices and crosses, as well as secular pieces, such as ornate weaponry and delicate jewellery. Examples of traditional weaving and stone-carving can be found on the third floor. The range of materials used for weaving includes lamb's wool, goat's hair, silk and plant fibres. Traditional costumes are also on show on this floor. The decorations and design, which are frequently elaborate, vary according to the geographical region. Costumes from many different areas are on display.

Decorative plate from Rhodes

⓲ Jewish Museum of Greece

Εβραϊκό Μουσείο της Ελλάδας

Níkis 39, Sýntagma. **Map** 6 F2.
Tel 210 322 5582. Ⓜ Sýntagma.
🚍 1, 2, 4, 5, 10, 11, 15.
Open 9am–2:30pm Mon–Fri,
10am–2pm Sun. **Closed** main public
hols & Jewish festivals. 🅖 📷
🆆 jewishmuseum.gr

This small museum traces the history of Greece's Jewish communities, which date back to the 3rd century BC. The exhibits present a revealing portrait of the Sephardic Jews, who fled Spain and Portugal in the 15th century, to settle throughout Greece in the religiously tolerant years of the Ottoman Empire.

Among the examples of traditional costumes and religious ceremonial instruments, one item of particular interest is the reconstruction of the *ehal*. This is the ark containing the Torah from the Pátra synagogue, which dates from the 1920s. It was rescued by Nikólaos Stavroulákis, founder of the museum, who has also written several books about the Greek Jews, on sale in the museum bookshop.

Moving displays of documentation record the German occupation of Greece during World War II, when 87 per cent of the Jewish population here was wiped out. Over 45,000 Greeks from Thessaloníki alone were sent to Auschwitz and other concentration camps during a period of five months in 1943.

Reconstruction of the ark from Pátra

Hadrian's Arch, next to the Temple of Olympian Zeus

🕙 Temple of Olympian Zeus
Ναός του Ολυμπίου Διός

Corner of Amalías & Vasilíssis Olgas, Pláka. **Map** 6 F3. **Tel** 210 922 6330.
Ⓜ Acrópoli. 🚌 2, 4, 11. **Open** 8am–8pm daily (Nov–Mar: to 3pm).
Closed main public hols. 🏛 (free Sun, Nov–Mar.) ♿ limited.

The temple of Olympian Zeus is the largest in Greece, exceeding even the Parthenon in size. Work began on this vast edifice in the 6th century BC, in the reign of the tyrant Peisistratos, who allegedly initiated the building work to gain public favour. Although there were several attempts over many years to finish the temple, it was not completed until 650 years later.

The Roman Emperor Hadrian dedicated the temple to Zeus Olympios during the Panhellenic festival of AD 132, on his second visit to Athens. He also set up a gold and ivory inlaid statue of the god inside the temple, a copy of the original by Pheidias at Olympia *(see pp174–6)*. Next to it, he placed a huge statue of himself. Both these statues have since been lost.

Only 15 of the original 104 Corinthian columns remain, each 17 m (56 ft) high – but enough to give a sense of the enormous size of this temple, which would have been approximately 96 m (315 ft) long and 40 m (130 ft) wide.

Corinthian capitals were added to the simple Doric columns by a Roman architect in 174 BC.

The temple is situated next to Hadrian's Arch, built in AD 131. It was positioned deliberately to mark the boundary between the ancient city and the new Athens of Hadrian.

The Russian Church of the Holy Trinity

🕙 Russian Church of the Holy Trinity
Ρωσική εκκλησία Αγίας Τριάδας

Fillelínon 21, Pláka. **Map** 6 F2. **Tel** 210 323 1090. Ⓜ Sýntagma. 🚌 1, 2, 4, 5, 9, 10, 11, 12, 15, 18. **Open** 7:30–10am Mon–Fri, 7–11am Sat & Sun.
Closed main public hols. ♿ limited.

Still in use by the Russian community, this was once the largest church in the city. Built in 1031 by the Lykodímou family (also called Nikodímou), it was ruined by an earthquake in 1701. In 1780, the Turkish governor, Hadji Ali Haseki, partly demolished the church to use its materials for the defensive wall that he built around the city. During the siege of the city in 1827, it received more damage from Greek shells fired from the Acropolis.

The church remained derelict until the Russian government restored it 20 years later. It was then reconsecrated as the Church of the Holy Trinity.

A large cruciform building, its most unusual feature is a wide dome, 10 m (33 ft) in diameter. Its interior was decorated by the Bavarian painter Ludwig Thiersch. The separate bell tower also dates from the 19th century, its bell a gift from Tsar Alexander II.

The Corinthian columns of the Temple of Olympian Zeus

The Tomb of the Unknown Soldier in Plateía Syntágmatos

❹ Plateía Syntágmatos

Πλατεία Συντάγματος

Sýntagma. **Map** 6 F1. 🚌 1, 5, 11, 12, 13, 15. Ⓜ Sýntagma.

This square (also known as Sýntagma Square) is home to the Greek parliament, in the Voulí building, and the Tomb of the Unknown Soldier, decorated with an evocative relief depicting a dying Greek hoplite warrior. Unveiled on 25 March 1932 (National Independence Day), the tomb is flanked by texts from Perikles's famous funeral oration. The other walls that enclose the square are covered in bronze shields celebrating military victories since 1821.

The National Guard (*évzones*) are on continuous patrol in front of the tomb, dressed in their famous uniform of kilt and pom-pom clogs. They are best seen at the changing of the guard, every Sunday at 11am.

❷ National Gardens

Εθνικός Κήπος

Borders Vasilíssis Sofías, Iródou Attikoú, Vasilíssis Olgas & Vasilíssis Amalías, Sýntagma. **Map** 7 A1. Ⓜ Sýntagma. 🚌 1, 3, 5, 7, 8, 10, 13, 18. **Open** dawn–dusk. Botanical Museum, zoo, cafés: **Open** 8am–until dusk daily (Nov–Mar: to 3pm).

Behind the Voulí parliament building, this 16-ha (40-acre) park, cherished by all Athenians and formerly known as the "Royal Gardens", was renamed the National Gardens by decree in 1923. Queen Amalía ordered the creation of the park in the 1840s; she even used the fledgling Greek navy to bring 15,000 seedlings from around the world. The gardens were landscaped by the Prussian horticulturalist Friedrich Schmidt, who travelled the world in search of rare plants.

Although the gardens have lost much of their original grandeur, they remain one of the most peaceful spots in the city. Shady paths meander past small squares, park benches and ponds filled with goldfish. A huge feral cat population is also resident in the park. Remains of Roman mosaics excavated in the park and an old aqueduct add atmosphere. Modern sculptures of writers, such as Dionýsios Solomós, Aristotélis Valaorítis and Jean Moreas, can be found throughout the park. There is also a small **Botanical Museum** to visit, a ramshackle zoo, and cafés. South of the park lies the **Záppeion** exhibition

hall, an impressive building in use today as a conference centre. It was donated by Evángelos and Konstantínos Záppas, cousins who made their fortunes in Romania. Built by Theophil Hansen, architect of the Athens Academy (*see p85*), between 1874 and 1888, it also has its own gardens. The elegant café next door to the Záppeion is a pleasant place to relax and refresh after a walk around these charming, peaceful gardens.

The tranquil and impressive National Gardens

❸ Presidential Palace

Προεδρικό Μέγαρο

Iródou Attikoú, Sýntagma. **Map** 7 A2. Ⓜ Sýntagma. 🚌 3, 7, 8, 13. **Closed** to the public.

This former royal palace was designed and built by Ernst Ziller (*see p85*) in c.1878. It was occupied by the Greek Royal Family from 1890 until the hasty departure of King Constantine in 1967. It is still guarded by the *évzones* whose barracks are at the top of the street. After the abolition of the monarchy, it became the official residence of the President of Greece and he still uses it today when hosting dignitaries. Its well-maintained gardens can just be seen through the iron railings.

Voulí parliament building in Plateía Syntágmatos, guarded by *évzones*

㉔ Kallimármaro Stadium

Καλλιμάρμαρο Στάδιο

Vasileos Konstantinou Avenue. **Map** 7 B3. **Tel** 210 752 2985. 3, 4, 11. **Open** 8am–7pm daily (Nov–Feb: to 5pm).

This huge marble structure set in a small valley by Ardittós Hill occupies the exact site of the original Panathenaic Stadium built by Lykourgos in 330–329 BC. It was first reconstructed for gladiatorial contests during Hadrian's reign (AD 117–138), then rebuilt in white marble by the wealthy Roman benefactor Herodes Atticus for the Panathenaic Games in AD 144. Neglected for many years, its marble was gradually quarried for use in new buildings.

In 1895, Geórgios Avéroff gave four million drachmas in gold for the restoration of the stadium in time for the start of the first modern Olympic Games on 5 April 1896. Designed by Anastásios Metaxás, the present structure is a faithful replica of Herodes Atticus's stadium, as described in the

Some of the ornate tombs in the First Cemetery of Athens

Guide to Greece by Pausanias (*see p60*). Built in white Pentelic marble, it is 204 m (669 ft) long and 83 m (272 ft) wide and seats up to 60,000. Between 1869 and 1879, architect Ernst Ziller excavated the site. His finds included a double-headed statue of Apollo and Dionysos, one of many used to divide the stadium's running track down its length. The statue is on show in the National Archaeological Museum (*see pp72–5*). During the 2004 Olympics, Kallimármaro hosted the marathon finish.

㉕ First Cemetery of Athens

Πρώτο Νεκροταφείο Αθηνών

Entrance in Anapáfseos, Méts. **Map** 7 A4. **Tel** 210 923 6118. 2, 4. **Open** 7am–sunset daily. limited.

Athens' municipal cemetery, which is not to be confused with the Kerameikós, the ancient cemetery (*see p92–3*), is a peaceful place, filled with pine and olive trees and the scent of incense burning at the well-kept tombs.

Fine examples of 19th-century funerary art range from the flamboyance of some of the marble mausoleums to the simplicity of the belle époque *Kimoméni* or *Sleeping Girl* (*see p46*). Created by Giannoúlis Chalepás, this beautiful tomb is found to the right of the main cemetery avenue where many of Greece's foremost families are buried.

Among the notable 19th- and 20th-century figures with tombs here are Theódoros Kolokotrónis (*see p84*), British philhellene historian George Finlay (1799–1875), German archaeologist Heinrich Schliemann (*see p184*), the Nobel Prize-winning poet Giórgos Seféris (1900–71) and the actress and politician Melína Merkoúri (1922–94).

In addition to the large number of tombs for famous people that are buried here, the cemetery contains a moving, single memorial to the 40,000 Athenians who perished through starvation during World War II.

A lone athlete exercising in the vast Kallimármaro Stadium

SHOPPING IN ATHENS

Shopping in Athens offers many delights. There are street markets, quiet arcades, traditional arts and crafts shops, and designer fashion boutiques to rival Paris and New York. Most Athenians go to the triangle which is formed by Omónoia, Sýntagma and Monastiráki squares to buy everyday household items, clothes and shoes. For leather goods, bargain hunters should head for Mitropóleos, Ermoú, Aiólou and nearby streets. Along the smarter Stadíou and Panepistimíou, there are world-class jewellers and large clothing stores. The maze of arcades in the centre also houses smart leather-goods shops, booksellers, cafés and *ouzerís*. The most stylish shopping is to be found in Kolonáki where some of the city's most expensive art galleries and antique shops are clustered among the foreign and Greek designer outlets selling the latest fashions. Around Athinás, Monastiráki and Pláka there is an eclectic mix of aromatic herb and spice stores, religious retailers selling icons and church candlesticks, second-hand bookshops with rare posters and prints, and catering stores packed with household goods such as pots and pans.

Opening Hours

Shops generally open from 9am–3pm, Monday to Saturday. On Tuesdays, Thursdays and Fridays, there is late shopping from 5:30–9pm. The exceptions are department stores, tourist shops, supermarkets, florists and *zacharoplasteía* (cake shops) which often open for longer. Many shops close every year throughout August, the time when many Greeks take their holidays.

Notos Galleries, one of the largest department stores in Athens

Department Stores and Supermarkets

The main stores are **Attica** and **Notos Galleries**. They stock a wide range of beauty products, clothes, gifts, and household goods. Attica is not as big as Notos Galleries but it is more exclusive. **Carrefour Marinopoulos** is a super-market chain as is **AB Vassilópoulos**, which is located in the city centre. Situated close to the Olympic Station, **The Mall Athens** and **Golden Hall** are two of the city's largest covered shopping complexes, filled with outlets and restaurants. The Mall Athens also has several cinemas.

Markets

Athens is famous for its flea markets. **Monastiráki** market starts early in the morning every Sunday, when dealers set out their wears along Adrianoú and neighbouring streets. Hawkers of *salépi* (a drink made from sesame seeds) and gypsy clarinet players weave through the crowds. The commercial tourist and antique shops of Pandrósou and Ifaístou, which collectively refer to themselves as "Monastiráki Flea Market", are open every day. Friday, Saturday and Sunday mornings are the best times to visit Plateía Avissynías. For food, the **Central Market** (Varvakios Agorá), which takes place every day except Sunday, is excellent, as are the popular *laïkés agorés* (street markets) selling fruit and vegetables, which occur daily in different areas. A centrally located *laïkí agorá* is the one on **Xenokrátous** in Kolonáki, and takes place each Friday.

Greeks buy in bulk and stallholders will find it strange if you buy small quantities of less than half a kilo (1 lb) of a fruit or vegetable. In most cases, you will be given a bag to serve yourself – do not be afraid to touch, smell and even taste.

Art and Antiques

As authentic Greek antiques become increasingly hard to find, many shops are forced to import furniture, glassware and porcelain from around the globe. Fortunately, however, there are still reasonable buys in old Greek jewellery, brass and copperware, carpets and embroidery, engravings and prints. Some can be found

Shoppers in Adrianoú at the centre of Monastiráki Flea Market

at **Antiqua**, just off Plateía Syntágmatos. Kolonáki is a prime area for small, exclusive stores around Sólonos, Skoufá and their side streets. Try the **Gallery Skoufa** for a selection of fine art pieces and temporary exhibitions, and **Serafinídis** for excellent antique kilims and carpets. Kolonáki is also the art centre with well-established galleries selling paintings and prints. The **Zoumpouláki Gallery** specializes in art and antiques.

Monastiráki also has many antique shops. Look out for **Skoutis** – a store selling 19th-century jewellery and costumes. Try **Martínos** for beautiful, ornate icons and silverware and the **Athens Gallery**, which specializes in fine art and sculpture.

Antique jewellery and ornaments for sale in Monastiráki

Traditional Folk Art and Crafts

Affordable popular folk art, crafts and souvenirs are plentiful in Monastiráki and Pláka. There are innumerable stores filled with ecclesiastical ephemera and cramped icon painters' studios. Many shops stock elegant wood carvings, rustic painted wooden trays and richly coloured *flokáti* rugs (see p213). **Amorgós** is packed with fine wood carvings and puppets, as seen in the Karagkiózis theatre in Maroúsi (see p155). Among the more unusual shops offering unique services is **Melissinós Art** in Psyrrí. This self-styled poet sandal-maker makes a wide variety of sturdy

The famous shoemaker and poet Stávros Melissinós

sandals and leather goods and is famous for handing out translations of his work as a parting gift.

Hellenic Art & Design sells a variety of affordable every-day objects designed by artists living in Greece. Beautiful carved shepherds' crooks from Epirus as well as a large variety of finely crafted ceramics can be found at the fascinating **Centre of Hellenic Tradition**.

Jewellery

Athens is justly famed for its jewellery stores. There is no shortage in Monastiráki and Pláka, which are full of small shops selling gold and silver. **Máris**, in Pláka, has a large selection of good-value classic and contemporary jewellery. Exclusive jewellers, such as **Anagnostópoulos**, can be found in Voukourestíou. Window displays also dazzle at the designer of world-class fame **Zolótas**, whose own pieces copy museum treasures. Another famous name is that of the designer Ilías Lalaoúnis, whose collections, inspired by Classical and other archaeological sources, such as the gold of Mycenae, are eagerly sought by the rich and famous. At the **Ilías Lalaoúnis Jewellery Museum**, over 3,000 of his designs are exhibited, and there is also a workshop where you can watch the craftsmen demonstrate the skills of the goldsmith and buy some of the jewellery.

Museum Copies

Museum shops provide some of the better buys in the city. Well-crafted, mostly tasteful copies draw on the wide range of ancient and Byzantine Greek art. They come in all shapes and sizes, from a life-size Classical statue to a simple Cycladic marble bowl. Many fine reproductions of the exhibits in the **Benáki Museum** (see pp82–3) can be bought from a collection of silverware, ceramics, embroidery and jewellery in the museum shop.

The **Museum of Cycladic Art** (see pp78–9) has some fine Tanagran and Cycladic figurines, bowls and vases for sale. There is a large selection of reproduction statues and pottery at the **National Archaeological Museum** (see pp72–5) souvenir shop. Apart from the museums, the Pláka shop **Orpheus** offers good quality marble and pottery copies of Classical Greek works as well as glittering Byzantine icons.

Display of reproduction red- and black-figure vases for sale

Periptero in Kolonáki selling English and Greek newspapers

Books, Newspapers and Magazines

All the *periptera* (kiosks) in the city centre sell foreign newspapers and magazines. English publications include the weekly *Athens News* and the monthly magazine *Odyssey (see p309)*. Athens' wealth of bookshops includes many selling foreign language publications. For foreign books, go to the huge branches of **Eleftheroudákis** or **Papasotiriou** on Panepistimíou, with specialist floors concentrating on English and Greek fiction, academic genres and children's books. Try **Politeia** for books on history, archaeology and classics, and **Libro** for fiction and non-fiction books and stationery.

One of the many designer stores to be found in Kolonáki

Clothes & Accessories

Although there are some famous Greek designers, such as **Parthénis**, whose hallmark is black and white minimalism, most fashion stores concentrate on imported clothes. However, there are plenty of high-quality clothes; every designer label can be found in the city's main fashion centre, Kolonáki. There are branches of such famous names as **Gucci**, **Ralph Lauren** and **Max Mara**. Such upmarket stores as **Sótris**, **Bettina**, **Free Shop**, **Paul & Shark** and **Luisa** typify the area's urban chic. For good-quality high-street fashion, there is the Spanish chain **Zara**.

Kitchenware

Cavernous catering stores in the side streets around the Central Market specialize in classic Greek kitchen-and-tableware. There are tiny white cups and copper saucepans used to make Greek coffee, long rolling pins for making filo pastry, and metal olive oil pourers. **Kotsóvolos** in Stadíou has a huge range of cheap and cheerful equipment, including traditional *kantária* (wine-measuring jugs), used to serve retsina in restaurants, round *tapsiá* (metal roasting dishes), and *saganákia* (two-handled pans) used for frying cheese. **Notos Home** in Omónoia stocks a good selection of kitchenware as well as furniture and other lifestyle products.

Food and Drink

There are myriad gourmet treats in Athens, including unusual *avgotáracho* (smoked cod roe preserved in bees-wax), herbs and spices, cheeses and wines. The bakeries and *zacharoplasteía* (patisseries) are irresistible, brimming with delicious breads and biscuits, home-made ice cream and yoghurt. **Aristokratikón**, off Plateía Syntágmatos, sells luxurious chocolates and marzipan. One of Athens' best patisseries, **Karavan**, is full of decadent *mpaklavás* and crystallized fruits. **Loumidis**, near Omónoia, is the best place to buy freshly ground coffee.

The Central Market on Athinás is one of the most enticing places for food shopping. It is surrounded by stores packed with cheeses, olives, pistachio nuts, dried fruits and pulses such as *fáva* (yellow split peas) and *gígantes* (butter beans). You will find a range of herbs and spices at **Bahar**, in particular dried savory and sage, lemon verbena and saffron. **Green Farm** is one of a new generation of organic supermarkets.

Two enterprising *cáves* (wine merchants), **The Winebox** in Xenokratous and **Cellier** in Kriezótou, offer a broad range of wines and spirits from various small Greek wineries. **Vrettós** in Pláka has an attractive and varied display of own-label spirits and liqueurs.

A crammed Athenian kitchenware store

DIRECTORY

Department Stores and Supermarkets

AB Vassilópoulos
Spýrou Merkouri 38,
Pagkrati. **Map** 7 C2.
Tel 210 725 8913. One
of several branches.

Attica
Panepistimíou 9,
Sýntagma. **Map** 2 F5.
Tel 211 180 2600.

Carrefour Marinopoulos
Kanari 9, Kolonáki. **Map** 3
A5. **Tel** 210 362 4907.

Golden Hall
Kifisías 37a, Maroúsi.
Tel 210 680 3450.

Notos Galleries
Stadíou and Aiólou,
Omónoia. **Map** 2 E4.
Tel 210 324 5811.

The Mall Athens
Andrea Papandreou 35,
Maroúsi.
Tel 210 630 0000.

Markets

Central Market (Varvakios Agorá)
Athinás, Omónoia.
Map 1 D4.

Monastiráki
Adrianoú & Pandrósou,
Pláka. **Map** 6 E1.

Xenokrátous
Xenokrátous, Kolonáki.
Map 3 C5.

Art and Antiques

Antiqua
Amaliás 2, Sýntagma.
Map 4 F2.
Tel 210 323 2220.

Athens Gallery
Pandrósou 14, Pláka.
Map 6 D1.
Tel 210 324 6942.

Gallery Skoufa
Skoufa 4, Kolonáki.
Map 3 A5.
Tel 210 360 3541.

Martínos
Pandrósou 50, Pláka.
Map 6 D1.
Tel 210 321 3110.

Serafetinídis
Pat. Ioakeim 21, Kolonáki.
Map 3 B5.
Tel 210 721 4186.

Skoutis
Dimokritou 10, Kolonáki.
Map 3 A5.
Tel 210 361 3557.

Zoumpouláki Gallery
Plateía Kolonakiou 20,
Kolonáki. **Map** 3 A5.
Tel 210 360 8278.

Traditional Folk Art and Crafts

Amorgós
Kódrou 3, Pláka.
Map 6 E1.
Tel 210 324 3836.

Centre of Hellenic Tradition
Mitropóleos 59 (Arcade) –
Pandrósou 36,
Monastiráki. **Map** 6 D1.
Tel 210 321 3023.

Hellenic Art & Design
Chairefontos 10, Pláka.
Map 6 E2.
Tel 210 322 3064.

Melissinós Art
Ag. Theklas 2, Psyrrí.
Map 2 D5.
Tel 210 321 9247.

Jewellery

Anagnostópoulos
Voukourestíou 8,
Kolonáki. **Map** 2 F5.
Tel 210 360 4426.

Ilías Lalaoúnis Jewellery Museum
Karyatidon & P. Kallisperi
12, Akropoli. **Map** 6 D3.
Tel 210 922 1044.

Máris
Ifaistou 5, Pláka.
Map 6 D1.
Tel 210 321 9082.

Zolótas
Stadiou 9, Kolonáki.
Map 2 F5.
Tel 210 322 1222.

Museum Copies

Orpheus
Pandrósou 28B, Pláka.
Map 6 D1.
Tel 210 324 5034.

Books, Newspapers and Magazines

Eleftheroudákis
Panepistimíou 15,
Athens.
Map 2 F5.
Tel 210 325 8440.

Libro
Pat. Ioakeim 8, Kolonáki.
Map 3 B5.
Tel 210 724 7116.

Papasotiriou
Panepistimiou 37,
Athensi.
Map 2 E4.
Tel 210 325 3232.

Politeia
Asklipiou 1–3 &
Akadímias, Pefkakia.
Map 2 F4.
Tel 210 360 0235.

Clothes & Accessories

Bettina
Anagnostopoúlou 29,
Kolonáki.
Map 3 A5.
Tel 210 339 2094.

Free Shop
Voukourestiou 50,
Kolonáki. **Map** 3 A5.
Tel 210 364 1500.

Gucci
Tsakálof 27, Kolonáki.
Map 3 A5.
Tel 210 360 2519.

Luisa
Skoufa 15. **Map** 3 A4.
Tel 210 363 5600.

Max Mara
Kanari 2, Kolonáki.
Map 3 A5.
Tel 210 360 7300.

Parthénis
Dimokrítou 20, Kolonáki.
Map 3 A5.
Tel 210 363 3158.

Paul & Shark
Anagnostopoulou 6,
Athens.
Map 3 B5.
Tel 210 339 2334.

Ralph Lauren
Voukourestíou 11,
Kolonáki. **Map** 3 A5.
Tel 210 361 1831.

Sótris
Anagnostopoúlou 30,
Kolonáki. **Map** 3 A4.
Tel 210 363 9281.
One of two branches.

Zara
Skoufa 22, Kolonáki.
Map 3 A5.
Tel 210 363 6340.
One of several branches.

Kitchenware

Kotsóvolos
Stadíou and
Dragatsaniou. **Map** 2 E4.
Tel 210 289 9999.

Notos Home
Plateía Kotzia, Omónoia.
Map 2 D4.
Tel 210 374 3000.

Food & Drink

Aristokratikón
Voulis 7, Sýntagma.
Map 2 E5.
Tel 210 322 0546.

Bahar
Evripídou 31, Omónoia.
Map 2 D4.
Tel 210 321 7225.

Cellier
Kriezótou 1, Kolonáki.
Map 3 A5.
Tel 210 361 0040.

Green Farm
Dimokrítou 13, Kolonáki.
Map 3 A5.
Tel 210 361 4001.

Karavan
Voukourestiou 11,
Kolonaki.
Map 2 F5.
Tel 210 364 1540.

Loumidis
Aiolou 106, Omónoia.
Map 2 E4.
Tel 210 321 4608.

The Winebox
Xenokrátous 25, Kolonáki.
Map 3 C5.
Tel 210 725 4710.

Vrettós
Kydathinaíon 41, Pláka.
Map 6 E2.
Tel 210 323 2110.

ENTERTAINMENT IN ATHENS

Athens excels in the sheer variety of its open-air summer entertainment. Visitors can go to outdoor showings of the latest film releases, spend lazy evenings in garden bars with the heady aroma of jasmine, or attend a concert in the atmospheric setting of the Herodes Atticus Theatre, which sits beneath the Acropolis.

The Mousikís Mégaron Concert Hall has given the city a first-class classical concert venue and draws some of the best names in the music world. For most Athenians,

however, entertainment means late-night dining in tavernas, followed by bar- and club-hopping until the early hours. There is also an enormous number of large discotheques, music halls and intimate *rempétika* clubs, playing traditional Greek music, throughout Athens. Whatever your musical taste, there is something for everyone in this lively city. Sports and outdoor facilities are also widely available, in particular watersports, which are within easy reach of Athens along the Attic coast.

Listings Magazines

The most comprehensive Greek weekly listings magazine is *Athinorama*, which is published on Thursdays. It lists events and concerts, and the latest bars and clubs. The English language publications, such as the weekly *Athens News* and the bimonthly *Odyssey*, also have listings sections. All publications are generally available at kiosks.

Booking Tickets

Although it is necessary to book tickets in advance for the summer Athens Festival *(see p50)* and for concerts at the Mégaron Concert Hall, most theatres and music clubs sell tickets at the door on the day of the performance. However, there is also a central ticket

office (Ticket Services, Panepistimiou 39, Tel: 210 723 4567), open daily from 10am to 4pm, where tickets can be purchased for the various events of the summer Athens Festival *(see p50)*.

Theatre and Dance

There are many fine theatres scattered around the city centre, often hidden in converted Neo-Classical mansion houses or arcades. Numerous popular revues that combine an entertaining mixture of contemporary political satire and comedy are regularly performed in theatres such as the **Lampéti**.

Some excellent productions of 19th-century Greek and European plays are staged at the **National Theatre**. Playhouses, such as the

The façade of National Theatre, Attica

Athinón, **Alfa** and **Vrettánia**, also mount Greek-language productions of works by well-known 19th- and 20th-century playwrights such as Ibsen.

The major classical venues, including the National Theatre, put on contemporary dance and ballet as well as plays and operas. The **Dóra Strátou Dance Theatre** on Filopáppos Hill performs traditional regional Greek dancing nightly between May and September.

The Dóra Strátou Dance Theatre performing traditional Greek dancing outdoors

The doorway to the outdoor Dexamení cinema

Cinema

Athenians love going to the cinema, especially from late May to September when the warm weather means that local open-air cinemas are open. All foreign-language films are subtitled, with the exception of children's films which are usually dubbed. The last showing is always at 11pm, which makes it possible to dine before seeing a movie.

The city centre has several excellent, large-screen cinemas showing the latest international releases. **Ideál**, **Elly** and **Village Cinemas Athens Metro Mall** are large, comfortable, indoor cinemas equipped with Dolby Stereo sound systems. The **Asti Cinema** tends to show a comprehensive range of art-house and cult movies.

Athenians like to hang out at the bars and tavernas next to open-air cinemas that are open in the summers from May to October, such as **Dexamení** in Kolonáki, the **Riviéra** in Exarcheía, **Cine Paris** in Pláka, **Cine Psyrri** in Psyrri or **Aegli Zappíou** in Zappío before catching the last performance. The acoustics are not always perfect but the relaxed atmosphere, in the evening warmth, with street noises, typically cats and cars, permeating the soundtrack, is an unforgettable experience. These cinemas seem more like clubs, with tables beside the seats for drinks and snacks. The outdoor **Thiseíon** cinema comes with the added attraction of a stunning view of the Acropolis.

Classical Music

The annual Athens Festival, held throughout the summer, attracts the major international ballet and opera companies, orchestras and theatrical troupes to the open-air **Herodes Atticus Theatre**, which seats 5,000 people, and to other venues around the city. This has always been the premier event of the classical music calendar. In 1991, the **Mousikís Mégaron Concert Hall** was inaugurated, providing a year-round venue for opera, ballet and classical music performances. This majestic marble building contains two recital halls with superlative acoustics, an exhibition space, a shop and a restaurant. The Olympia Theatre is home to the **Lyrikí Skiní** (National Opera), and stages excellent ballet productions as well as opera.

Details of concerts held at cultural centres such as the **French Institute** can be found in listings magazines and newspapers.

Traditional Greek Music

The lively Greek music scene thrives in a variety of venues throughout central Athens. The large music halls of Syngróu advertise on omnipresent billboards around the city. **Posidonio**, **Athinón Arena**, **Gyalino Mousiko Theatro** and **Stavros tou Notou** attract the top stars and their loyal fans. The more old-fashioned venues in Pláka, such as **Mostroú**, offers intimate surroundings for the haunting sounds of *rempétika* music, which draws its inspiration and defiant stance from the lives of the urban poor.

Rempétiki Istoría and **I Kali Zoi** are two of the places at which you can hear genuine bouzouki (Greek mandolin) music. Both bars have well-known bouzouki players, and reasonable prices.

Accordionist in Plateía Kolonakíou

Mpoémissa attracts a much younger crowd, more concerned with dancing the night away than with authenticity of the music.

A classical concert at the ancient Herodes Atticus Theatre

Rock and Jazz Music

International acts usually perform at large stadiums or the open-air **Lykavittós Theatre** as part of the annual Athens Festival. The **Gagarin 205 Live Music Space**, a successfully converted cinema, also attracts the very cream of foreign and Greek rock bands. Greek bands can be enjoyed at the **An Club**, which offers patrons the intriguing prospect of Greek rock-and-roll dinner dancing.

The city's premier jazz venue is the **Half Note Jazz Club**. The club is housed in a former stonemason's workshop and is located opposite the First Cemetery. The Half Note is a cosy and popular venue, presenting the best of foreign contemporary jazz.

Alternatively, **Six d.o.g.s** is a cultural centre featuring a project space, a bar, a café and an area for live music and theatrical performances by young Greek artists.

Live music in one of the city's popular rock clubs

Nightclubs

Athens is a hive of bars and nightclubs that come and go at an alarming rate. The up-and-coming areas of town are Gazi and the area around Sýntagma, where there are a number of trend-setting bar-restaurants: the best, such as **Gazarte** and **Boutique Club**, also have dance floors. Large clubs such as **B.e.d. Club** and **Villa Mercédes** offer special DJ nights and are good spots for dinner or for clubbing late at night.

Marathon runner in Athens retracing the path of his ancestors

Sport

Most taxi drivers will reel off their favourite football team to passengers before they have had a chance to mention their destination. Such is the Athenian passion for football that the two main rival teams, Panathenaïkós and Olympiakós, are always the subject of fervent debate. Each team is backed by a consortium of private companies, each of which also owns a basketball team of the same name. Football matches are played every Wednesday and Sunday during the September to May season. The basketball teams play weekly, in what is the latest popular national sport.

Lack of adequate parkland within the city means that joggers are a rare sight, despite the annual **Athens Open Marathon** every October. The athletes run from Marathon to the Kallimármaro Stadium in the centre of Athens *(see p117)*. The **Olympiakó Stadium** in Maroúsi seats 80,000 and was built in 1982. Its glass roof was designed by Spanish architect Santiago Calatrava for the 2004 Olympic Games. The Panathenaïkós football team are based here. It has excellent facilities for all sports and includes an indoor sports hall, swimming pools and tennis courts in its 100 ha (250 acres) of grounds. The **Karaïskáki Stadium** in Néo Fáliro is the home of the Olympiakós football team. There are also facilities there for many other sports including volleyball and basketball. Another famous event is the **Acropolis Rally**, a celebration of vintage cars, held around the Acropolis every spring. It attracts some 50 to 100 cars.

Outside the city centre, there are more facilities on offer, including bowling at the **Bowling Centre of Piraeus** and golf at the fine 18-hole **Glyfáda Golf Course**, which is located close to the airport. Tennis courts are available for hire at various places, including the **Politia Tennis Club**.

Proximity to the Attic coast means that a large variety of water sports is on offer. Windsurfing and water-skiing are widely available on most beaches. **Naftikos Omilos Vouliagmenis** offers water-skiing lessons for all ages and levels. One of the most renowned scuba-diving clubs is the **Athina Diving**, which has lessons for all levels.

Basketball, an increasingly popular national sport among the Greeks

DIRECTORY

Theatre and Dance

Alfa
Patisíon 37 & Stournári,
Exárcheia.
Map 2 E2.
Tel 210 523 8742.

Athinón
Voukourestíou 10,
Kolonáki. **Map** 2 E5.
Tel 210 331 2343.

Dóra Strátou Dance Theatre
Filopáppou Hill,
Filopáppou.
Map 5 B4.
Tel 210 324 4395.

Lampéti
Leof Alexándras 106,
Neapoli.
Map 4 D2.
Tel 210 645 7086.

National Theatre
Agíou Konstantínou 22,
Omónoia.
Map 1 D3.
Tel 210 528 8100.

Vrettánia
Panepistimíou 7,
Sýntagma. **Map** 2 E4.
Tel 210 322 1579.

Cinema

Aegli Zappiou
Garden of Zappio.
Map 7 A2.
Tel 210 336 9369.

Asti
Korai 4, Athens.
Map 2 E4.
Tel 210 322 1925.

Cine Paris
Kydathinaion 22, Pláka.
Map 6 E2.
Tel 210 322 2071.

Cine Psyrri
Sarri 40–44.
Map 1 C5.
Tel 210 324 7234.

Dexamení
Plateía Dexamenís,
Kolonáki.
Map 3 B5.
Tel 210 362 3942.

Elly
Akadimias 64, Omónoia.
Map 2 E3.
Tel 210 363 2789.

Ideál
Panepistimíou 46,
Omónoia.
Map 2 E4.
Tel 210 382 6720.

Riviéra
Valtetsioú 46, Exárcheia.
Map 2 F3.
Tel 210 384 4827.

Thiseíon
Apostólou Pávlou 7,
Thiseío.
Map 5 B2.
Tel 210 347 0980.

Village Cinemas Athens Metro Mall
Leoforos Vouliagmenis
276, Agios Dimitrios.
Tel 210 975 8300.
W village.gr

Classical Music

French Institute
Sína 31, Kolonáki.
Map 3 A4.
Tel 210 339 8600.

Herodes Atticus Theatre
Dionysíou Areopagítou,
Acropolis. **Map** 6 C2.
Tel 210 324 1807.

Lyrikí Skiní, Olympia Theatre
Akadimías 59, Omónoia.
Map 2 F4.
Tel 210 361 2461.
W nationalopera.gr

Mousikís Mégaron Concert Hall
V Sofías & Kókkali, Stégi
Patrídos.
Map 4 E4.
Tel 210 728 2333.
W megaron.gr

Traditional Greek Music

Athinón Arena
Peiraios 166, Gazi.
Map 1 A5.
Tel 210 347 1111.

Gyalino Mousiko Theatro
Leoforos Andrea Syngrou
143, Nea Smirni.
Map 1 A5.
Tel 210 931 5600.

I Kali Zoi
Thiseiou 12, Thiseio.
Map 1 C5.
Tel 211 408 3128

Mostroú
Mnisikléous 22, Pláka.
Map 6 D1.
Tel 210 322 5558.

Mpoémissa
Solomoú 13–15,
Exárcheia.
Map 2 D2.
Tel 210 383 8803.

Posidonio
Poseidónos 18, Ellinikó.
Tel 210 894 1033.

Rempétiki Istoría
Ippokrátous 181,
Neápoli.
Map 3 C2.
Tel 210 642 4937.

Stavros tou Notou
Frantzi & Tharipou 37,
Néos Kósmos.
Tel 210 922 6975.

Rock, Jazz and Ethnic music

An Club
Solomoú 13–15,
Exárcheia.
Map 2 E2.
Tel 210 330 5056.

Gagarin 205 Live Music Space
Liosíon 205, Athens.
Map 1 C1.
Tel 211 411 2500.

Half Note Jazz Club
Trivonianoú 17, Mets.
Map 6 F4.
Tel 210 921 3310.

Lykavittós Theatre
Lykavittós Hill.
Map 3 B4.
Tel 210 722 7209.

Six d.o.g.s
Avramiotou 6–8,
Monastiráki.
Map 2 D5.
Tel 210 321 0510.

Nightclubs

B.e.d Club
Poseidonos 58,
Glyfáda.
Tel 210 894 1620.

Boutique Club
.Filellinon 15, Athens.
Map 6 F1.
Tel 210 323 1351.

Gazarte
Voutadon 32–34, Gazi.
Map 1 A5.
Tel 210 346 0347.

Villa Mercédes
Andronikou and Tzaféri
11, Rouf.
Tel 210 342 2606.

Sport

Athina Diving
38 km Coastal Road,
Athens– Sounio,
Lagonissi.
Tel 229 102 5434.
W athinadiving.gr

Bowling Centre of Piraeus
Profitis Ilías, Kastélla.
Tel 210 412 7077.

Glyfáda Golf Course
Panopis 15 & Kypros,
Glyfáda.
Tel 210 894 6459.

Karaïskáki Stadium
Néo Fáliro.
Tel 210 480 0900.

Naftikos Omilos Vouliagmenis
Lemos Vouliagmenis.
Tel 210 896 2416.
W nov.gr

Olympiakó Stadium
Leof Kifisías 37, Maroúsi.
Tel 210 683 4060.
W oaka.com.gr

Politia Tennis Club
Aristotelous 18, Politia.
Tel 210 620 0003.
W politiatennisclub.gr

ATHENS STREET FINDER

Map references given for sights in Athens refer to the maps on the following pages. References are also given for Athens hotels (see pp268–9), Athens restaurants (see pp282–5) and for useful addresses in the Survival Guide section (see pp296–323). The first figure in the reference tells you which

Street Finder map to turn to, and the letter and number refer to the grid reference. The map below shows the area of Athens covered by the eight Street Finder maps (the map numbers are shown in black). The symbols used for sights and features are listed in the key below.

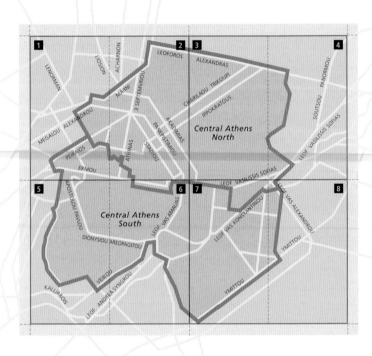

0 kilometres 1
0 miles 0.5

Key

- ▦ Major sight
- ▥ Place of interest
- ▦ Other building
- Ⓜ Metro station
- ▣ Railway station
- ▣ Main coach or bus station
- ▤ Trolleybus stop
- ▦ Tram stop
- ▣ Funicular
- ⓘ Tourist information
- ✚ Hospital with casualty unit
- ▣ Police station

- ✝ Church
- ✡ Synagogue
- ═ Railway line
- ▦ Pedestrianized street

Scale of Map Pages

0 metres 250
0 yards 250

Street Finder Index

Abbreviations

Ag	Agios, Agía (saint)
Leof	Leofóros (avenue)
Pl	Plateía (square)

Note Squares and avenues are indexed by their name followed by Plateía or Leofóros.

J

Jewish Museum	6 F2

K

Kairi	2 D5
Kaisareias	4 F3
Kaisareias	8 E5
Kakourgo Dikeiou	2 D5
Kalaischrou	6 E3
Kalamida	2 D5
Kalamiotou	2 E5
Kalchantos	8 F4
Kalkon	6 D5
Kallergi	1 C3
Kallidromiou	2 F1
Kalliga	3 B1
Kallikratous	3 A3
Kallimachou	7 C2
Kalimarmaro Stadium	7 B3
Kallirois	5 A4
Kallisperi	6 D3
Kallisthenous	5 A3
Kalogrioni	6 D1
Kaltezon	1 A2
Kalvou	3 B1
Kalypsous	1 A4
Kamaterou	2 D2
Kanari	3 A5
Kanari	8 D5
Kanellopoulos Museum	6 D2
Kaningos	2 E3
Kaningos, Plateia	2 E3
Kapetan Petroutsou	4 F2
Kaplanon	2 F4
Kapnikarea	6 E1
Kapnikareas	6 D1
Kapno	2 D2
Kapodistriou	2 E2
Kapsali	3 B5
Karachristos	4 D4
Karaiskaki	1 C5
Karaiskaki, Plateia	1 C3
Karatza	5 C4
Karea	6 F4
Karer	6 E4
Karitsi, Plateia	2 E5
Karneadou	3 C5
Karodistriou	5 A5
Karolou	1 C3
Karori	2 D5
Kartali	4 F4
Karyatidon	6 D3
Karydi	5 A1
Kassianis	3 C2
Katsantoni	3 A1
Katsikogianni	1 C5
Kavalotti	6 D3
Kedrinou	4 E1
Kekropos	6 E2
Kelsou	6 F5
Kennenty	8 E3
Kerameikos	1 B5
Kerameikou	1 A4
Kerameon	1 B2
Kerasountos	4 F4
Keratsiniou	1 A3
Kerkinis	4 E2
Kiafas	2 E3
Kilkis	1 A1
Kimonos	1 A2
Kiou Petzoglou	8 E2
Kioutacheias	8 E4
Kirras	4 F1
Kisamou	8 E5
Kitsiki Nikolaou, Plateia	3 C4
Klada	6 D5
Kladou	6 D1
Klathmonos, Plateia	2 E4

Kleanthi	7 B2
Kleious	1 A1
Kleisouras	8 E1
Kleisovis	2 E3
Kleisthenous	2 D4
Kleitomachou	7 A3
Kleitou	2 E4
Kleomenous	3 B4
Kleomvrotou	1 A4
Klepsydras	6 D2
Kodratou	1 B2
Kodrika	2 D5
Kodrou	6 E1
Koimiseos Theotokou	8 F3
Kokkali	4 E4
Kokkini	6 E4
Kolchidos	4 F1
Koletti	2 F3
Kolofontos	8 D2
Kolokotroni	2 E5
Kolokynthous	1 B3
Kolonaki, Pl	3 B5
Kolonou	1 B3
Komninon	3 B2
Koniari	4 D3
Kononos	8 D2
Konstantinou Lourou	4 E4
Konstantinou-poleos, Leof	1 A3
Kontogoni	3 C1
Kontoliou	8 D5
Korai	2 E4
Korai	7 C5
Kordeliou	8 E5
Korinis	1 C4
Korinthou	1 A1
Kornarou	6 E1
Koromila	5 C5
Koronaiou	4 F5
Koroneias	4 E2
Koronis	3 A3
Korytsas	8 F5
Koryzi	6 E4
Kosma Aitolou	4 D2
Kosma Melodou	3 B3
Kotopouli, M	2 D3
Kotyaiou	4 E3
Kotzia, Plateia	2 D4
Koukakiou, Plateia	5 C4
Kouma	3 A1
Koumanoudi	3 B1
Koumoundourou	2 D3
Koumpari	7 A1
Kountourioti, Plateia	5 B5
Kountouriotou	2 F2
Koutsikari	4 E1
Kraterou	4 F5
Kraterou	8 F1
Kratinou	2 D4
Kriezi	1 C5
Kriezotou	2 F5
Krinis	8 F5
Krisila	7 B4
Kritis	1 C1
Kritonos	8 D1
Kropias	1 B1
Krousovou	8 E1
Ktisiou	7 C2
Ktisiviou	7 B3
Kydantidon	5 A3
Kydathinaion	6 E2
Kymaion	5 A1
Kynaigeirou	1 B2
Kyniskas	7 A4
Kyprou, Leof	8 D5
Kyriazopoulos Folk Ceramic Museum	6 D1
Kyrillou Loukareos	4 D2
Kyrinis	3 C2
Kyvellis	2 E1

L

Lachitos	4 E4
Laertou	8 E4
Lakedaimonos	4 F1
Lamachou	6 F2
Lamias	4 F2
Lampardi	3 C2
Lampelet	1 B1
Lamprou Katsoni	3 C2
Lampsakou	4 E4
Laodikeias	4 F5
Larissa	1 B1
Larissis	1 B1
Larisis, Plateia	1 C1
Laskareos	3 B2
Laspa	3 B2
Lassani	6 D5
Lavragka	1 B2
Lazaion	5 C4
Lefkippou	8 D4
Lefkotheas	8 D4
Lekka	2 E5
Lempesi	6 E3
Lenorman	1 A1
Leocharous	2 E5
Leokoriou	1 C5
Leonida Drossi	3 C1
Leonidou	1 A4
Leonnatou	1 B3
Lepeniotou	1 C5
Leventi	3 B5
Levidou	8 E2
Limpona	2 D5
Liosion	1 C1
Litous	8 F5
Livini	4 D2
Livyis	4 F5
Lofos Ardittou	7 A3
Lofos Finopoulou	3 B1
Lomvardou	3 B1
Longinou	6 F4
Lontou	2 F3
Louizis Riankour	4 F2
Louka	1 C5
Loukianou	3 B5
Lydias	8 F3
Lykavittos Hill	3 B3
Lykavittou	3 A5
Lykavittou, Plateia	3 A4
Lykeiou	7 B1
Lykofronos	7 B5
Lykomidon	5 B1
Lykourgou	2 D4
Lysikratous	6 E2
Lysikratous, Pl	6 E2
Lysimachias	6 D5
Lysimachou	7 C5
Lysippou	7 B3

M

Madritis, Plateia	7 D1
Maiandrou	4 E5
Maiandroupoleos	4 F1
Mainemenis	4 F1
Makedonias	2 D1
Makedonon	4 E3
Makri	6 E3
Makris	8 E5
Makrygianni	6 E3
Makrynitsas	4 F1
Malamou	6 F4
Mamouri	1 C1
Manis	2 F3
Manoliasis	8 E2
Manou	8 D3
Mantineias	8 F5
Mantzakou	3 A2
Mantzarou	3 A4
Marasli	3 C5
Marathonos	1 B3
Marikas Iliadi	4 E3
Marinou Charvouri	6 F4
Markidi	4 F2

Markou Evgenikou	3 C2
Markou Mousourou	7 A3
Markou Mpotsari	5 C4
Marni	1 C3
Massalias	2 F4
Matrozou	5 B5
Mavili, Plateia	4 E3
Mavrikiou	3 B2
Mavrokordatou	2 E3
Mavrokordatou, Plateia	2 D2
Mavromataion	2 E1
Mavromichali	2 F3
Megalou Alexandrou	1 A4
Megalou Spilaiou	4 E2
Meintani	5 C5
Melanthiou	2 D5
Meleagrou	7 B2
Melidoni	1 B5
Melissou	7 C4
Menaichmou	6 E4
Menandrou	1 C4
Menedimou	1 B1
Menekratous	6 F5
Menonos	6 F5
Merkourie, M	4 D4
Merlie Oktaviou	3 A3
Merlin	3 A5
Mesogeion	8 D3
Mesolongiou	2 F3
Mesolongiou	8 E5
Mesolongiou, Plateia	8 D3
Messapiou	5 A4
Metagenous	6 E5
Metaxourgeiou, Plateia	1 B3
Meteoron	7 A5
Methonis	2 F2
Metonos	1 C4
Metsovou	2 F1
Mexi Ventiri	4 D5
Miaouli	2 D5
Michail Karaoli	8 F2
Michail Mela	4 D3
Michail Psellou	3 A1
Michail Voda	2 D1
Michalakopoulou	4 E5
Mikras Asias	4 F4
Mileon	4 F2
Milioni	3 A5
Miltiadou	2 D5
Mimnermou	7 B2
Miniati	7 A3
Mirtsiefsky	5 A4
Misaraliotou	6 D3
Misountos	8 E3
Misthou	8 D2
Mitromara	6 D3
Mitroou	6 D1
Mitropoleos	6 D1
Mitropoleos, Plateia	6 E1
Mitropoli	6 E1
Mitsaion	6 D3
Mnisikleous	6 D1
Momferratou	3 B1
Monastiraki	2 D5
Monastirakiou, Plateia	2 D5
Monastiriou	1 A3
Monemvasias	5 B5
Monis Asteriou	6 E2
Monis Petraki	4 D4
Monis Sekou	8 D2
Monument of Lysikrates	6 E2
Monument of Philopappus	5 C3
Moraiti, A	3 B3
Moreas, Z	5 C4
Morgkentaou	8 D5
Moschonision	8 F3
Mourouzi	7 B1

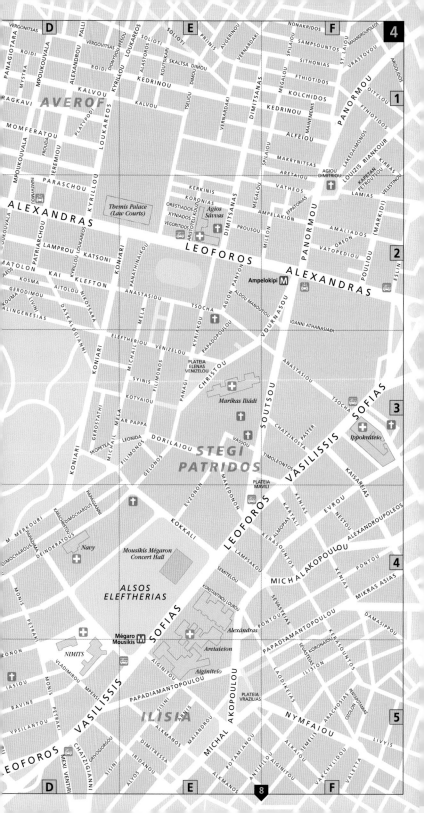

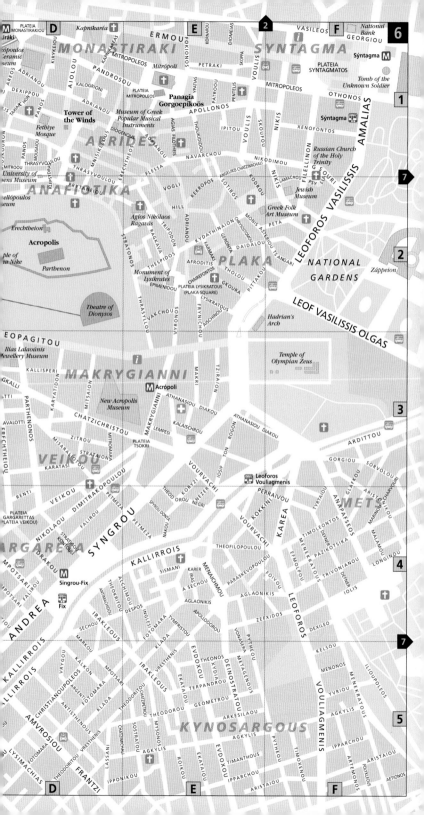

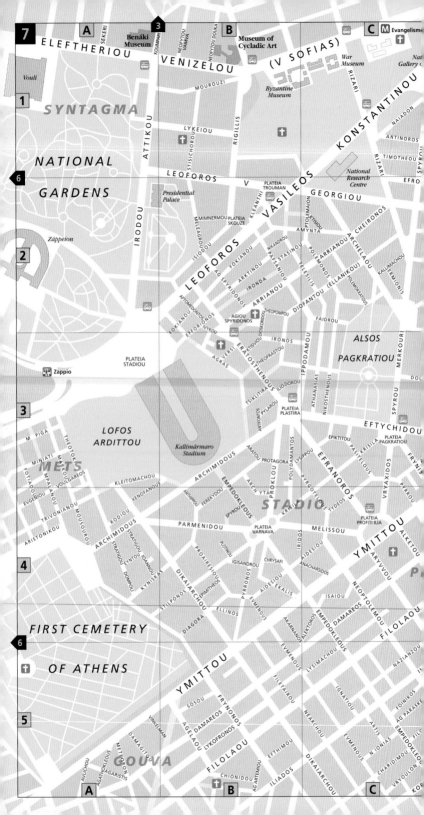

MAINLAND GREECE

Mainland Greece at a Glance

The unique attraction of the mainland lies in the wealth of ancient remains, set in landscapes of great natural beauty. Classical sites are most notable in the south, around Athens, and the coasts of Attica and the Peloponnese, while Macedonian remains can be seen in the temperate northeast. Byzantine monasteries and churches are found all over the country, particularly on the holy peninsula of Mount Athos which is governed by its 20 monasteries.

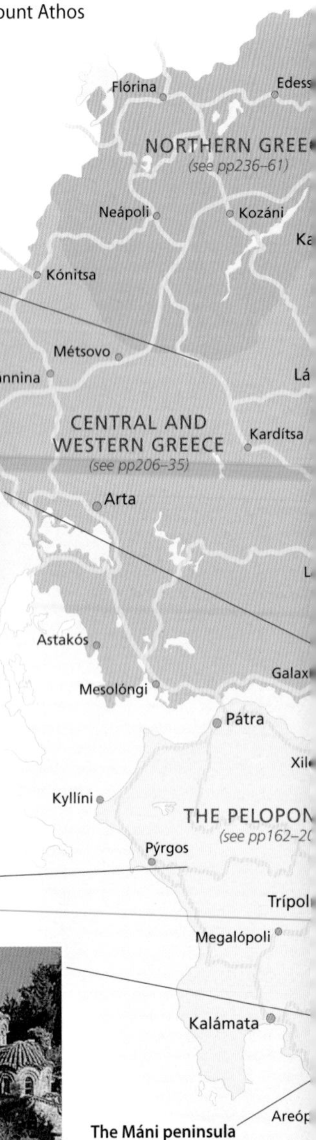

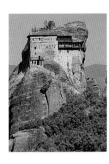

The Metéora area *(see pp220–21)* combines extraordinary sandstone pinnacles with some of the first medieval monasteries in Greece, perched on the rocky peaks.

Delphi *(see pp232–5)* is home to the evocative ruins of an ancient religious complex and theatre situated on Mount Parnassus.

Ancient Olympia *(see pp174–7)* was, from the 8th century BC to the 4th century AD, the site of the Panhellenic Games, forerunner of today's Olympics. One of the best-preserved buildings is the Temple of Hera *(left)*, dating from around the 6th century BC.

Mystrás *(see pp196–7)* is one of the best-preserved Byzantine complexes in Greece, exemplified by this church of Agía Sofía. It is a medieval city, and held out against the Ottomans until 1460.

The Máni peninsula *(see pp198–203)* is dotted with tower houses.

Flórina
Edess
NORTHERN GREE
(see pp236–61)
Neápoli
Kozáni
Ka
Kónitsa
Métsovo
Lá
Ioánnina
Igoumenítsa
CENTRAL AND
WESTERN GREECE
(see pp206–35)
Kardítsa
Arta
L
Astakós
Galax
Mesolóngi
Pátra
Xil
Kyllíni
THE PELOPON
(see pp162–2
Pýrgos
Trípol
Megalópoli
Kalámata
Areóp

0 kilometres   50
0 miles   25

◀ An aerial view of Marina Lávrio, southeast Attica

Thessaloníki's Archaeological Museum *(see pp250–51)* has spectacular gold finds from the tombs of the Macedonian kings, and this bronze head from around AD 235 of Alexander Severus.

Didymóteicho

Sidirókastro

Paranéstio

Dráma

Komotiní

Kavála

Alexandroúpoli

Thessaloníki

Néa Moudaniá

Osios Loúkas monastery *(see pp226–7)* is beautifully set in a flowering orchard. The octagonal design of the 11th-century dome was widely copied. Its plain exterior conceals the gold-ground mosaics inside.

Mount Athos has, since 1060, been entirely occupied by monks *(see pp256–8)*.

Vólos

Ancient Corinth *(see pp166–70)*, capital of the Roman province of Achaia, was renowned for its luxury and elegance, exemplified by this ornate capital.

The Monastery of Dafní *(see pp156–7)* is a famous work of Byzantine architecture with outstanding medieval mosaics decorating the interior of the church.

AROUND ATHENS *(see pp144–61)*

Corinth

Athens

Mycenae *(see pp182–4)*, one of Greece's oldest sites, dates back to 1550 BC; the Lion Gate was the entrance to the citadel. Mycenae was possibly ruled by Agamemnon.

Epidaurus *(see pp188–9)* has one of the best-preserved theatres in Greece.

anídi

Monemvasía *(see pp190–92)* means "one way in", a reference to the strategic advantage of this heavily fortified Byzantine seaport. Its former role as the main port of Byzantine Greece is reflected in the buildings of the old town.

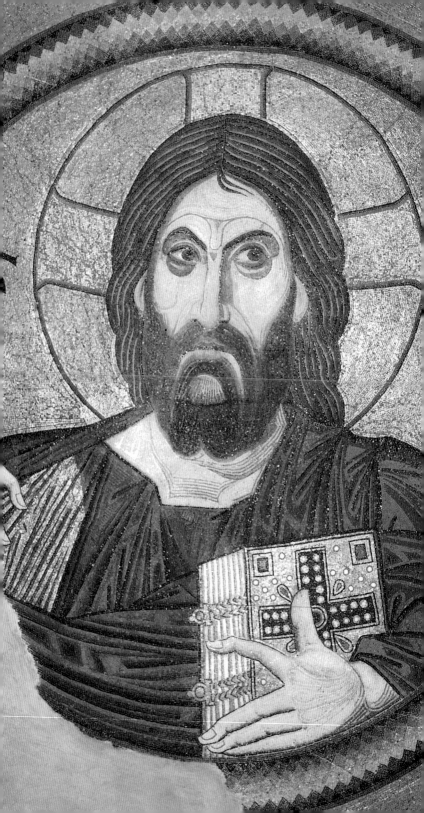

AROUND ATHENS

ATTICA

The area around Athens, known as Attica, is the spiritual heartland of ancient and modern Greece. Its archaeological sites have attracted generations of scholars and plunderers alike, and its mountains and coastline have provided important refuge in times of strife. Today, the golden beaches along the eastern coast attract those simply wishing to escape the bustle of modern Athens.

The land of Attica was the basis of Athenian wealth. The fine marble from the quarries on Mount Ymittós and Mount Pentéli was used for the temples and sculptures of ancient Athens. The silver from Lávrio financed their construction, and the produce from the local agricultural areas fed the population.

Attica has witnessed many significant historical events. The plain of Marathon was the site of one of the greatest battles in Greek history. Piraeus, now Greece's largest and busiest port, was also the port of ancient Athens. The Classical temples at less-known archaeological sites around the countryside, such as Eleusis, Ramnoús and Brauron, offer a rural retreat from the overcrowding and pollution of the city.

At Soúnio, the majestic, well-preserved Temple of Poseidon on the cape has been a beacon for mariners for centuries.

The Byzantine era also left a great legacy of fine architecture to the region. Two of the best examples of this are the imposing monasteries of Dafní and Kaisarianí, with their ornate mosaics and elegant stonework.

South of Athens, the summer heat of the Attic plain is ideal for growing crops. Grapes are a speciality in the Mesógeia (Midland) region, which produces some of the finest *retsina* in the country. North of Athens, the pine-forested Mount Párnitha provides interesting walks and offers superb views over the city from the summit.

The peaceful ruins of the Parthenon of the Bear Maidens at Ancient Brauron

◀ The Christ Pantokrátor figure in the dome of the *katholikón* of the Monastery of Dafní

Around Athens

Beyond the endless urban sprawl of Athens, the region around the city, known as Attica, offers the diversity of wild mountains, Byzantine monasteries and churches, evocative archaeological sites and sandy beaches. Not surprisingly, such easy accessibility to the coast and countryside has led to overcrowding in Athens' suburbs, and pollution around Piraeus and Ancient Eleusis. The hills of Mount Párnitha and Ymittós are rich in wildlife, with deserted trails, caves and icy spring water. In the summer months, Athenians move out to the Attic Coast, where the well-kept beaches have every kind of water sport facility, and there are bars and clubs. Towards the cape at Soúnio, there are countless fish tavernas by the sea and quiet rocky coves ideal for snorkelling.

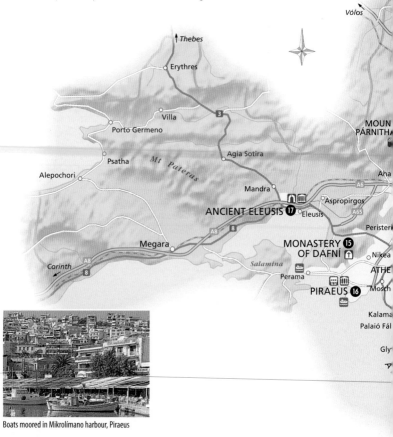

Boats moored in Mikrolímano harbour, Piraeus

Key

═══ Motorway

━━━ Major road

═══ Minor road

━━━ Scenic route

┅┅┅ Main railway

──── Minor railway

▬▬▬ Regional border

Getting Around

Athens' international airport, Elefthérios, serves the region. There are two routes out of Athens to southeast Attica: the popular coastal road from Piraeus to Soúnio, and the inland road, via Korópi and Markópoulo, to the east-coast towns of Pórto Ráfti and Lávrio. This is also the way for the turn-off to the port of Rafína, where there are ferry connections to Evvoia and the Cyclades. Frequent buses from Athens link all the towns in the area. Mount Párnitha and northern Attica are best reached by taking the 1 (E75) national road.

For hotels and restaurants see p270 and pp286–7

The Temple of Poseidon on the cape at Soúnio

Locator Map

Sights at a Glance

1 Ancient Oropós
2 Ramnoús
3 Marathónas
4 Rafína
5 *Ancient Brauron pp150–51*
6 Pórto Ráfti
7 Lávrio
8 Soúnio
9 Attic Coast
10 Paianía
11 Attica Zoological Park
12 Moní Kaisarianís
13 Kifisiá
14 Mount Párnitha
15 *Monastery of Dafní pp156–7*
16 *Piraeus pp158–9*
17 *Ancient Eleusis pp160–61*

0 kilometres   10
0 miles   5

ala Oropou
Aghii Apostoli
ENT ∙PÓS 1
Kalamos
81
RAMNOÚS 2
Kapandriti
Lake Marathónas
A1
Ag. Marina
MARATHÓNAS 3
TTICA
83
Ekali
Schinias
KIFISIÁ 13
aroussi
83
Nea Makri
Pendeli
Zoumberi
Máti
Pallini
83
RAFÍNA 4
54
MONÍ KAISARIANÍS
A6
85
ATTICA ZOOLOGICAL PARK
Loutsa
12
Spata
Ymittos
PAIANÍA 10
A62
ANCIENT BRAURON 5
89
Vravrona
ypoli
Koropi
PÓRTO RÁFTI 6
Markópoulo
Kaliva Thorikou
Kaki Thalassa
Vári
liagméni
Agia Marina
Keratea
árkiza
91
89
Lagonissi
COAST
Anávysos
Makrónisos
Palia Fokea
LÁVRIO 7
91
SOÚNIO 8

The *katholikón* of Moní Kaisarianís

For keys to symbols *see back flap*

View of the Enkoimitírion at Oropós

❶ Ancient Oropós

Ωρωπός

Kálamos, Attica. **Road map** D4.
Tel 22950 62144. 🚌 Kálamos.
Open daily. **Closed** main public hols.
♿

The peaceful sanctuary of
Oropós nestles on the left
bank of the Cheímarros, a
small river surrounded by
pine trees and wild thyme
bushes. It is dedicated to
Amphiáraos, a hero credited
with healing powers whom,
according to mythology,
Zeus rescued when he was
wounded in battle. It is said
that the earth swallowed up
Amphiáraos while he was
riding his chariot, and that he
then miraculously reappeared
through the sacred spring at
this site. In ancient times,
visitors would throw coins into
the spring in the hope of being
granted good health.

The Amphiaraion
sanctuary came to
prominence as a
healing centre in the
4th century BC, when
its Doric temple and
sacrificial altar were
built, attracting the
sick from all over
Greece. Houses
erected during the
Roman period, when
the area became a
popular spa centre,
are still visible on the
right bank of the river.
The Enkoimitírion
was the site's most
interesting building.
It was a long stoa, the remains
of which are still visible
today, where the patients
underwent treatment by
enkoimisis. This gruesome
ritual entailed the
sacrifice of a goat in
whose bloody hide
the patient would then
spend the night. The
next morning, priests
would prescribe
medicines based on
their interpretations
of the dreams of
the patient.

Marble throne from the
theatre at Oropós

Above the Enkoimitírion are
the remains of an impressive
theatre, which has a well-
preserved *proskenion* (stage)
and five sculpted marble
thrones, once reserved for the
use of priests and guests of
honour. On the right bank of
the valley, opposite the altar,
is a water clock dating from
the 4th century BC.

❷ Ramnoús

Ραμνούς

Attica. **Road map** D4. **Tel** 22940
63477. 🚌 **Open** daily (Sanctuary of
Nemesis only). **Closed** main public
hols. ♿ ♿

Ramnoús is a remote but
beautiful site, overlooking the
gulf of Evvoia. It is home to
the only Greek sanctuary
dedicated to the goddess
of vengeance, Nemesis. The
sanctuary was demolished
when the Byzantine Emperor
Arcadius decreed in AD 399 that
all temples left standing should
be destroyed. Thus only the
remains of this sanctuary can
be seen today. Within its
compound, two temples are
preserved side by side. The
smaller and older Temple
of Themis dates from the
6th century BC. Used
as a treasury and
storehouse in
ancient times, its
impressive poly-
gonal walls are
all that now survive.
Within the cella,
some important
statues of the
goddess and her priestess,
Aristonoë, were uncovered.
They can now be seen in the
National Archaeological
Museum (*see pp72–5*).

The larger Temple of Nemesis
dates from the mid-5th century
BC. It is very similar in design
to the Hephaisteion in Athens'
Agora (*see pp94–5*) and the
Temple of Poseidon at Soúnio
(*see p152*). Built in the Doric

The remains of the Temple of Nemesis at Ramnoús

style, the temple contained a statue of Nemesis by Agora-kritos, a disciple of Pheidias *(see p102)*. The statue has been partially reconstructed from fragments, and the head is now in the British Museum.

The quayside at the port of Rafína

❸ Marathónas
Μαραθώνας

Attica. **Road map** D4. **Tel** 22940 55155. Site & Museum: **Open** Tue–Sun. **Closed** main public hols.

The Marathon Plain is the site of the great Battle of Marathon, where the Athenians defeated the Persians. The burial mound of the Athenians lies 4 km (2 miles) from the modern town of Marathónas. This tumulus is 180 m (590 ft) in circumference and 10 m (32 ft) high. It contains the ashes of the 192 Athenian warriors who died in the battle. The spot was marked by a simple *stele* of a fallen warrior, Aristion, by the sculptor Aristocles. The original is now in the National Archaeological Museum *(see pp72–5)* in Athens. There is a copy at the site, inscribed with an epigram by the ancient poet Simonides: "The Athenians fought at the front of the Greeks at Marathon, defeating the gold-bearing Persians and stealing their power."

In 1970, the burial mound of the Plataians and royal Mycenaean tombs were found nearby in the village of Vraná. The Plataians were the only other Greeks who sent warriors in time to assist the Athenians already at the battle. The **Marathon Museum** displays archaeological finds from these local sites. There are also some beautiful Egyptian-

Plate discovered in the tomb of Plataians

style statues from the 2nd century AD, found on the estate of Herodes Atticus, on the Marathon Plain. This wealthy benefactor was born and bred in this area. He is known for erecting many public buildings in Athens, including the famous theatre located on the southern slope of the Acropolis *(see p104)* that was named in his honour.

Environs
Just 8 km (5 miles) west of Marathónas is **Lake Marathónas**, which is crossed by a narrow causeway. This vast expanse of water is man-made. The impressive dam, made from white Pentelic marble, was built in 1926. It created an artificial lake that was Athens' sole source of water until 1956. The lake is fed by the continuous streams of the Charádras and Varnávas, which flow down from Mount Párnitha *(see p155)* and makes a good setting for a picnic.

❹ Rafína
Ραφήνα

Attica. **Road map** D4. 8,600.

The charm of Rafína is its lively fishing port, packed with caïques and ferries. After Piraeus, it is the main port in Attica. Frequent buses from Athens bring passengers for the regular hydrofoil and ferry connections to the Cyclades and other Aegean islands.

One of the administrative *demes* (regions) of ancient Athens, Rafína is a long-established settlement. Although there is little of historical or archaeological interest, the town offers a selection of excellent fish restaurants and tavernas. Choose one by the waterside to sit and watch the hustle and bustle of this busy port.

Environs
North of Rafína, a winding road leads to the more picturesque resort of **Máti**. Once a quiet hamlet, it is packed today with trendy cafés and bars, apartment blocks and summer houses owned by Athenians.

The Battle of Marathon

When Darius of Persia arrived at the Bay of Marathon with his warships in 490 BC, it seemed impossible that the Greeks could defeat him. Heavily outnumbered, the 10,000 Greek hoplites had to engage 25,000 Persian warriors. Victory was due to the tactics of the commander Miltiades, who altered the usual battle phalanx by strengthening the wings with more men. The Persians were enclosed on all sides and driven back to the sea. Around 6,000 Persians died and only 192 Athenians. The origins of the marathon run also date from this battle. News of the victory was relayed by a runner who covered the 41 km (26 miles) back to Athens in full armour before dying of exhaustion.

Vase showing Greek hoplites fighting a Persian on horseback

❺ Ancient Brauron
Βραυρώνα

Situated near modern Vravrona, Brauron is one of the most evocative sites near Athens. Although little remains of its former architectural glory, finds in the museum reveal its importance as the centre of worship of Artemis, goddess of childbirth and protectress of animals *(see p57)*. Legend relates that it was founded by Orestes and Iphigéneia, the children of Agamemnon, who introduced the cult of Artemis into Greece. Evidence of Neolithic and Mycenaean remains have been found on the hill above the site, but the tyrant Peisistratos brought Brauron its fame in the 6th century BC when he made the worship of Artemis Athens' official state religion.

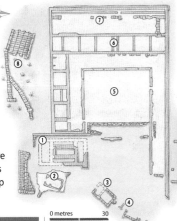

| 0 metres | 30 |
| 0 yards | 30 |

Key to the Sanctuary of Artemis

① Temple of Artemis
② Chapel of Agios Geórgios
③ Sacred House
④ Tomb of Iphigéneia
⑤ Parthenon of the Bear Maidens
⑥ Dormitories
⑦ Stoa
⑧ Stone Bridge

The Parthenon of the Bear Maidens at Brauron

Exploring Ancient Brauron

The centre of this compact site lies just north of the prehistoric acropolis. The 5th-century BC Doric **Temple of Artemis**, of which only the foundations remain, formed the focal point of the sanctuary to the goddess. Beside the temple stands a late Byzantine chapel, dedicated to **Agios Geórgios**.

From here, a path leads southeast to the oldest cult site in the sanctuary. This is said to be the **Tomb of Iphigéneia**, the high priestess of Artemis. Next to it are the foundations of the **Sacred House**, which was used as a home by the cult's priestesses. The most extensive remains at the site are to the northeast, at the **Parthenon of the Bear Maidens**. This courtyard may have been the place where young girls performed the bear dance. Surrounded by a late 5th-century BC **stoa**, the courtyard had rooms behind that were used as dining areas and **dormitories**. Only the foundations remain, but the stone sleeping couches and bases of statues can still be seen. There is also a 5th-century BC **stone bridge** to the west.

Brauronia Ceremony

Held every four years in the spring, the Brauronia festival was celebrated in atonement for the killing of one of Artemis's sacred pet bears. Although little is known about the mysterious rites today, Aristophanes mentions the "bear dance" that initiates had to perform in his play *Lysistrata*. Disguised as bears and adorned with saffron-coloured robes, young girls, aged between five and ten, performed a dance honouring this sacred animal.

Relief showing pilgrims approaching the altar of Artemis at the Brauronia ceremony

The small Byzantine chapel of Agios Geórgios

Mycenaean vase from the Brauron
Museum, 1200–1100 BC

Brauron Museum

This fascinating museum
has a wealth of finds from
the site. In Room 1, there are
cases filled with assorted
votive offerings such as
miniature vases and jewellery.
In Room 2 are the serene
statues of árktoi ("bear
maidens"). Room 3 has a
fine votive relief of the gods
Zeus, Leto, Apollo and
Artemis, and the remains
of an altar. Rooms 4 and 5
offer a variety of pre-historic
and Mycenaean finds,
including some ornate
Geometric vases.

Retsina

Although many Greeks prefer drinking whisky to wine these days,
retsina is still favoured by millions of tourists. Around 16 million
bottles were drunk in 1994, and 50 per cent of them
were exported around the world. The unique,
distinctive flavour comes from the Aleppo pine
resin which is added in small quantities to the
grape juice during fermentation. This method has
been used since antiquity to preserve and flavour
wine in Greece. Since entry into the EEC (now
called the EU) in 1981, traditional production
areas have had their own appellations.
Aficionados agree that some of the best retsina
comes from the Mesógeia appellation in Attica,
where the Savatiano grape is cultivated. Kourtákis,
the largest producers of retsina, have their
vineyards in Markópoulo and Koropí.

Collection of
pine resin

❻ Pórto Ráfti

Πόρτο Ράφτη

Attica. **Road map** D4. 3,300.

Pórto Ráfti takes its name from
Ráfti island which is visible just
off the headland. On the island
is a colossal marble statue of
a seated female, made in the
Roman period, known as "the
tailor" *(ráftis)*. It was most likely
built to be used as a beacon
for shipping and would have
lit up the harbour. Pórto Ráfti
has one of the best natural
harbours in Greece, although
the town itself has never
developed into an important
seafaring port. In April 1941,
during World War II, 6,000
New Zealand troops were
successfully evacuated
from the beach. Today, it is
primarily a pleasant holiday
resort, with tavernas and
bars. The area is rich in
archaeological history.

Many Mycenaean tombs have
been found south of the bay of
Pórto Ráfti, at Peratí, a port that
flourished in the 7th and 6th
centuries BC.

Environs

The remains of a fortress
that was built during the
Chremonidean War (268–
261 BC) between Egypt and
Macedon can be seen on the
southern **Koróni** headland.
The northern coastline of
Peratí is pockmarked with
unexplored caves, and attracts
many people who come to
swim in the clear water and
fish off the craggy rocks.
Markópoulo, a thriving
market town and viticultural
centre 8 km (5 miles) inland,
is famous for its tavernas.
Spicy sausages are for sale in
the butchers' shops and the
bakeries are fragrant with
the smell of fresh bread.

Pórto Ráfti harbour with Ráfti island in the background

One of the many 19th-century Neo-Classical buildings in Lávrio

❼ Lávrio

Λαύριο

Attica. **Road map** D4. 8,800. Thu.

Lávrio was famous for its silver mines in ancient times. They were used as a source of revenue for the Athenian state and financed Perikles's programme of grand public buildings in Athens in the 5th century BC *(see p34)*. They also enabled the general Themistokles to construct a fleet capable of beating the Persians at the Battle of Salamis in 480 BC. It was this excellent naval fleet which established Athens as a naval power. Before their final closure in the 20th century, the mines were also exploited by French and Greek companies for other minerals such as manganese and cadmium.

Originally worked by slaves, over 2,000 mine shafts have been discovered in the surrounding hills, and some are now open to visitors as the **Mineralogical Museum**. It is the only such museum in Greece. Traces of ore and minerals in the rock face can be seen on tours of the old mines. Since their closure, the area has suffered high unemployment. The old Neo-Classical houses and empty harbourfront warehouses indicate the former prosperity of the town. Makrónisos, the narrow island opposite the port, was used as a prison for political detainees during the Civil War *(see p46)*.

🏛 Mineralogical Museum

Leof Andréa Kordelá. **Tel** 22920 22817. **Open** 8am–3pm Tue–Sun.

❽ Soúnio

Σούνιο

9 km (5.5 miles) from Lávrio, Attica. **Road map** D4. **Tel** 22920 39363. to Lávrio. **Open** 8am–sunset daily.

The Temple of Poseidon, built on a site set back from sheer cliffs tumbling into the Aegean Sea at Soúnio (Cape Sounion), was ideally located for worship of the powerful god of the sea. Its brilliant white marble columns have been a landmark for ancient and modern mariners alike.

The present temple, built in 444 BC, stands on the site of older ruins. An Ionic frieze, made from 13 slabs of Parian marble, is located on the east side of the temple's main approach path. It is very eroded but is known to have depicted scenes from the mythological battle of the Lapiths and centaurs, and also the adventures of the hero

The Doric columns of the Temple of Poseidon

Theseus, who was thought to be the son of Poseidon, according to some legends.

Local marble, taken from quarries at nearby Agriléza, was used for the temple's 34 slender Doric columns, of which 15 survive today. The temple also

Ruins of the Temple of Poseidon

possesses a unique design feature which helps combat the effects of sea-spray erosion: the columns were cut with only 16 flutings instead of the usual 20, thus reducing the surface area exposed to the elements.

When Byron carved his name on one of the columns in 1810, he set a dangerous precedent for vandalism at the temple, which is now covered with scrawled signatures.

A waterside restaurant at Várkiza, along the Attic coast

⑨ Attic Coast

Παραλία Αττικής

Attica. **Road map** D4. 🚌

The coastal strip from Piraeus to Soúnio is often called the "Apollo Coast" after a small Temple of Apollo discovered at Vouliagméni. It is covered with beaches and resort towns that are always very busy at weekends, and particularly so in the summer holiday season.

One of the first places along the coast from Piraeus is the tiny seaside resort of **Palaió Fáliro,** which is home to the Phaleron War Cemetery. In this quiet spot is the Athens Memorial, erected in May 1961 to 2,800 British soldiers who died in World War II.

Noisy suburbs near Athens airport, like **Glyfáda** and **Álimos** (famous as the birthplace of the ancient historian Thucydides), are very commercialized with a large number of marinas, hotels and shopping malls.

At chic **Vouliagméni**, with its large yacht marina, luxury hotels line the promontory. A short

Byron in Greece

The British Romantic poet Lord Byron (1788–1824) first arrived in Greece in 1809 at the age of 21, and travelled around Epirus and Attica with his friend John Cam Hobhouse. In Athens, he wrote *The Maid of Athens,* inspired by his love for his landlady's daughter, and parts of *Childe Harold*. These publications made him an overnight sensation and, when back in London in 1812, he proclaimed: "If I am a poet it is the air of Greece which has made me one." He was received as a hero on his return to Greece in 1823, because of his desire to help fight the Turks in the War of Independence *(see pp44–5)*. However, on Easter Sunday 1824 in Mesolóngi, he died of a fever without seeing Greece liberated. Proving in his case that the pen is mightier than the sword, Byron is still venerated in Greece, where streets and babies are named after him.

Lord Byron, in traditional Greek costume, by T Phillips (1813)

walk northwards away from the coast, beside the main road, is the enchanting Vouliagméni Lake. This unusual freshwater lake lies beneath low, limestone cliffs. The stunning stretch of warm, sulphurous water has been used for years to bring relief to sufferers of rheumatism. There are changing rooms and a café close by.

At **Várkiza**, the wide bay is filled with windsurfers. By the main road there is a luxury club-restaurant, *Island*. Open throughout the summer season, it serves cocktails and Mediterranean cuisine and attracts a glamorous crowd. From Várkiza, a road snakes inland to **Vári**, renowned for its restaurants serving meat dishes.

The Vári cave is located about 2 km (1 mile) north of the village. Inside is a freshwater spring and some fine stalactites have developed. Some minor Classical ruins remain in the caves, although many have been removed.

There is unrestricted access and no admission charge.

From Várkiza to Soúnio, the coastal road is lined with quiet bathing coves, fish tavernas and luxury villas. **Anávysos** is a thriving market town surrounded by vineyards and fields. In its harbour, caïques sell locally caught fish every day, and there is a small street market every Saturday, with stalls piled high with seasonal fruit and vegetables.

Colourful stall of local produce in Anávysos

Sculpture in the gardens of the Vorrés Museum

❿ Paianía

Παιανία

Attica. **Road map** D4. 🚶 9,700. 🚌 🚍 Tue.

Just east of Athens, Paianía is a town of sleepy streets and cafés. In the main square, the church of **Zoödóchou Pigís** has some fine modern frescoes by the 20th-century artist Fótis Kóntoglou. The birthplace of the orator Demosthenes (384–322 BC), Paianía is more famous today for the **Vorrés Museum**. Set in beautiful gardens, this features private collector Ion Vorrés's eclectic array of ancient and modern art. The museum is divided into two sections, encompassing 3,000 years of Greek history and heritage. The first is housed in what was the collector's private home:

two traditional village houses filled with ancient sculptures, folk artifacts, ceramics, Byzantine icons, seascapes and furniture. The second section, housed in a specially built modern building, offers a unique overview of contemporary Greek art since the 1940s, with many excellent works by more than 300 different painters and sculptors, encompassing every major art movement from Photo-Realism to Pop Art.

🏛 **Vorrés Museum**
Diadóchou Konstantínou 1. **Tel** 210 664 4771. **Open** 10am–2pm Sat & Sun. **Closed** Aug & main public hols. 🅿 ♿ 🌐 vorresmuseum.gr

Environs
Above Paianía, the **Koutoúki Cave** is hidden in the foothills of Mount Ymittós. It was found in 1926 by a shepherd looking for a goat which had fallen into the 12,200 sq m (130,000 sq ft) cave. There are tours every half hour, with son et lumière effects lighting up the stalagmites and stalactites. The temperature inside is 17°C (62°F).

🕳 **Koutoúki Cave**
4 km (2.5 miles) W of Paianía. **Tel** 210 664 2108. **Closed** for renovation till end of 2015. 🅿

⓫ Attica Zoological Park

Αττικό Ζωολογικό Πάρκο

Yalou, Spata. **Road map** D4. **Tel** 210 663 4725. 🚌 319. **Open** 9am–sunset daily. 🅿 🍴 🌐 atticapark.com

Attica Zoological Park is an increasingly popular attraction just a short drive east of Athens. The zoo has over 300 species of animal, from white lions and tigers to yellow anacondas and pygmy hippos. It also has one of the largest bird collections in the world. In Cheetah Land, visitors can walk through a special tunnel within the cheetah enclosure.

⓬ Moní Kaisarianís

Μονή Καισαριανής

5 km (3 miles) E of Athens, Attica. **Road map** D4. **Tel** 210 723 6619. 🚌 to Kaisarianís. **Open** 8am–3pm Tue–Sun. **Closed** main public hols. 🅿

Moní Kaisarianís was founded in the 11th century. In 1458, when Sultan Mehmet II conquered Athens, the monastery was exempted from taxes in recognition of the abbot's gift to the sultan of the keys of the city. This led to great prosperity until 1792, when it lost these privileges and went into decline. The complex was used briefly as a convent after the War of Independence, until 1855. Its buildings were eventually restored in 1956.

The small *katholikón* is dedicated to the Presentation of the Virgin. All the frescoes

Moní Kaisarianís, hidden in the hills around Mount Ymittós

date from the 16th and 17th centuries.

Just above the monastery, the source of the River Ilissós has been visited since antiquity, its water is reputed to cure sterility. Before the Marathon dam was built *(see p149)*, the spring was Athens' main source of water.

⑬ Kifisiá
Κηφισιά

12 km (7.5 miles) NE of Athens, Attica. **Road map** D4. 👥 40,000. 🚌 Ⓜ Kifisiá.

Kifisiá has been a favourite summer retreat for many Athenians since Roman times. Once the exclusive domain of rich Greeks, it is congested today with apartment blocks and shopping malls. Traces of its former tranquillity can still be seen by taking a ride in a horse-drawn carriage. These wait by the metro station offering drives down shady streets lined with mansions and villas, built in a bizarre variety of hybrid styles such as Alpine chalet and Gothic Neo-Classicism.

The **Goulandrís Natural History Museum**, which opened in 1974, is housed in one of these villas. Its large collection covers all aspects of Greece's varied wildlife and minerals. There are 200,000 varieties of plants in the herbarium, and over 1,300 examples of taxidermy; the stuffed creatures are carefully displayed in their natural habitats.

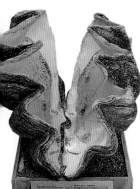

Clam shell outside the Goulandrís Natural History Museum, Kifisiá

The tiny chapel of Agía Triáda on the hillside of Mount Párnitha

🏛 Goulandrís Natural History Museum
Levídou 13. **Tel** 210 801 5870. **Open** 9am–2:30pm Tue–Fri, 9:30am–4pm Sat, 10am–4pm Sun. **Closed** main public hols. 📷

Environs
In Maroúsi, a suburb of Kifisiá, is the small **Spathári Museum of Shadow Theatre**, which is devoted to the fascinating history of the Karagkiózis puppet theatre. Shadow theatre came to Greece from the Far East, via players who used to travel throughout the Ottoman Empire performing for the aristocracy in the 18th century. It was soon transformed into a popular folk art by entertainers who would travel around Greece with their makeshift theatres. The name Karagkiózis refers to the indomitable and impoverished Greek character who is tormented by the other standard theatrical characters such as the rich Pasha and tough guy Stávrakas. The museum displays the history of two generations of the Spathári family, who were the leading exponents of this dying art, along with their home-made sets and puppets.

Puppet from the Museum of Shadow Theatre

🏛 Spathári Museum of Shadow Theatre
Mesogíon & Ípirou 27, Maroúsi. **Tel** 210 612 7245. **Open** 10am–2pm Mon–Sun. **Closed** main public hols.

⑭ Mount Párnitha
Όρος Πάρνηθα

Attica. **Road map** D4. 🚌 to Aharnés, Thrakomakedónes & Agía Triáda.

In ancient times, Mount Párnitha sheltered wild animals. Today, this rugged range, which extends nearly 25 km (16 miles) from east to west, is rich in less dangerous fauna. Tortoises can be seen in the undergrowth and birds of prey circle the summit of Karampóla at 1,413 m (4,635 ft). Wild flowers are abundant, particularly in autumn and spring when cyclamen and crocus carpet the mountain. There are spectacular views of alpine scenery, all within an hour's drive of the city. At the small town of **Acharnés**, a cable car ascends to a casino perched at over 900 m (3,000 ft). Still little used by hikers, the mountain has plenty of demanding trails. The most popular walk leads from Thrakomakedónes, in the foothills of the mountain, to the Báfi refuge. This uphill march takes about two hours, and offers superb views of the surrounding mountain scenery. Starting with thorny scrub typical of the Mediterranean *maquis*, it follows well-trodden paths to end among alpine firs and clear mountain air. Once at the Báfi refuge, it is worth walking on to the Flampoúri refuge, which has some dramatic views.

⓯ Monastery of Dafní
Μονή Δαφνίου

The monastery of Dafní was founded in the 5th century AD. Named after the laurels *(dáfnes)* that used to grow here, it was built with the remains of an ancient sanctuary of Apollo, which had occupied this site until it was destroyed in AD 395. In the early 13th century, Otto de la Roche, the first Frankish Duke of Athens, bequeathed it to Cistercian monks in Burgundy. Greek Orthodox monks took the site in the 16th century, erecting the elegant cloisters just south of the church. Following earthquake damage in 2000, the beautiful gold-leaf Byzantine mosaics in the *katholikón* (main church) have undergone major restoration.

Aerial view of the monastery complex

★ **Esonarthex Mosaics**
These mosaics include depictions of the *Last Supper* and the *Washing of the Feet*. The finest is the *Betrayal by Judas*. Christ stands unmoved as Judas kisses Him.

Entrance

Key to Mosaics in the Katholikon

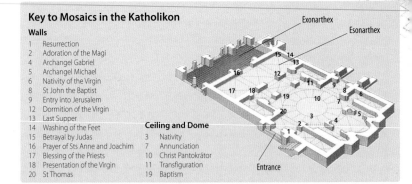

Walls

1 Resurrection
2 Adoration of the Magi
4 Archangel Gabriel
5 Archangel Michael
6 Nativity of the Virgin
8 St John the Baptist
9 Entry into Jerusalem
12 Dormition of the Virgin
13 Last Supper
14 Washing of the Feet
15 Betrayal by Judas
16 Prayer of Sts Anne and Joachim
17 Blessing of the Priests
18 Presentation of the Virgin
20 St Thomas

Ceiling and Dome

3 Nativity
7 Annunciation
10 Christ Pantokrátor
11 Transfiguration
19 Baptism

Exonarthex
Esonarthex
Entrance

★ **Christ Pantokrátor**
The Pantokrátor ("Almighty") gazes sternly down from the dome of the *katholikón*. Around the central figure are images of the 16 prophets.

VISITORS' CHECKLIST

Practical Information
Road Map D4.
Tel 210 581 1558.
10 km (6 miles) NW of Athens, Attica. **Open** 9am–2pm Tue & Fri.

Transport

The Transfiguration
This is in the northwest corner under the dome. Elijah and Moses are on either side of Christ and the apostles Peter, James and John are below.

The Windows
Elaborate three-tiered brickwork surrounds each of the windows.

KEY

① **The cloister** or a covered arcade, was built in the 16th century. On the other side of the courtyard, above a similar arcade, are the monks' cells.

② **The symmetry** of the design makes Dafní one of the most attractive examples of Byzantine architecture in Attica.

③ **The Gothic exonarthex** was built almost 30 years after the main church.

④ **The dome** is 8 m (26 ft) in diameter and 16 m (52 ft) high at the centre.

⑤ **Nave**

⑥ **Ticket office and museum**

⑯ Piraeus
Πειραιάς

One of the biggest Mediterranean ports, Piraeus is also one of the largest cities in Greece. It has been the port of Athens since ancient times. The Long Walls between Piraeus and Athens were started in 480 BC by Themistokles. However, Sulla destroyed the walls in 86 BC, and by the Middle Ages, Piraeus was little more than a fishing village. When Athens became the Greek capital in 1834, Piraeus was once again revitalized, with Neo-Classical buildings and factories. In 1923, 100,000 refugees came here from Asia Minor, bringing their culture and contributing to the cosmopolitan feel of this port city.

Small boats moored in peaceful Mikrólimano harbour

View across Kentrikó Limáni with ferries in the foreground

Exploring Piraeus

After the Junta (see p47) razed many irreplaceable public buildings in the town centre in the early 1970s, civic pride re-emerged with a vengeance. Beside the Municipal Theatre, there are elegant open-air restaurants and fountains in the shade of Neo-Classical façades. On the streets behind the main banks and ticket offices that rim the **Kentrikó Limáni** (the main ferry port), there are smart restaurants and shops, as well as some fine examples of Neo-Classical architecture, such as the **Town Hall**. For information on ferry departures from Kentrikó Limáni, see p319.

South of the railway station around Navarínou lies the lively market area, including fishmongers', fruit and vegetable stalls, ships' chandlers and hardware stores. On Sunday mornings, there is also a bustling flea market, which is centred on the antique shops around Plateía Ippodameías, and also on Alipédou and Skylítsi streets.

There are two harbours in Piraeus, situated east of Kentrikó Limáni. **Pasalimáni** (Pasha's Port, also known as Limáni Zéas) was once used to harbour the Ottoman fleet. Today, it is filled with luxurious yachts. Once known simply as Zéa, Pasalimáni used to be one of Themistokles's major naval ports, with dry docks for 196 triremes. Marína Zéas, the mouth of Pasalimáni, is a jetty used as a dock for hydrofoils to the Argo-Saronic islands. The second harbour, **Mikrolímano** (Little Harbour) houses many colourful fishing caïques. It is popular for its waterside fish restaurants and has a more relaxing ambience than the larger harbour.

On the coastal road between Pasalimáni and Mikrolímano, smart bars and clubs occupy the renovated Neo-Classical mansions in the gentrified **Kastélla** neighbourhood. Even traditionally working-class areas, such as Drapetsóna (the most important manufacturing centre in the country), are now popular for their late-night restaurants.

🎭 Municipal Theatre
Iroon Polytechneiou 32. **Tel** 210 414 3300. **Open** Tue–Sun.

The Neo-Classical façade of this imposing building is one of the delights of Piraeus. Designed by Ioánnis Lazarímos (1849–1913), who based his plans on the Opéra Comique in Paris, it has seating for 800, making it one of the largest modern theatres in Greece. It took nearly ten years to complete and was finally inaugurated on 9 April

Façade of the Municipal Theatre

1895. Today, it is the home of both the **Municipal Art Gallery** and also the **Pános Aravantinoú Museum of Stage Decor**. The Museum of Stage Decor has displays of set designs by the stage designer Pános Aravantinoú (who worked with the Berlin opera in the 1920s), as well as general ephemera from the Greek opera.

🏛 Archaeological Museum

Chariláou Trikoúpi 31.
Tel 210 452 1598.
Open 8am–3pm Tue–Sun.
Closed main public hols. 🎫 ♿

This museum is home to some stunning bronzes. Found by workmen in 1959, large statues of Artemis with her quiver, Athena with her helmet decorated with owls, and Apollo reveal the great expressiveness of Greek sculpture. The Piraeus *koúros* of Apollo, dating from 520 BC, is the earliest full-size bronze to be discovered. There is also a seated cult statue of the earth

Statue of Athena in the Archaeological Museum

goddess Cybele and a fine collection of Greek and Roman statues and grave stelae. Near the museum are the remains of the 2nd-century BC **Theatre of Zéa**; the remains include a well-preserved orchestra.

🏛 Hellenic Maritime Museum

Aktí Themistokléous, Freatýda. **Tel** 210 451 6264. **Open** 9am–2pm Tue–Sat. **Closed** main public hols, Aug. 🎫

On the quayside of Marína Zéas, an old submarine marks the entrance to this fascinating museum. Its first room is built around an original section of Themistokles's Long Walls. More than 2,000 exhibits, such as models of triremes, ephemera from naval battleships and paintings of Greek *trechantíri* (fishing caïques), explore the world of Greek seafaring. From early voyages around the Black Sea by trireme to 20th-century emigration to the New World by

transatlantic liner, the museum unravels the complexities of Greek maritime history. Exhibits include models of ships, maps, flags, uniforms and pictures. The War of Independence is well documented with information and memorabilia about the generals who served in it. The old naval ship *Averof*, which was the flagship of the Greek fleet until 1951, has been fully restored and is berthed nearby. As part of the museum, the ship is also open to visitors.

VISITORS' CHECKLIST

Practical Information
10 km (6 miles) SW of Athens, Attica. **Road map:** D4.
🚃 200,000. 🛈 EOT Athens (210 331 0392). 🛍 Sun (flea market). 🎭 theatre & music festival: May–Jul.

Transport
🚢 Kentrikó Limáni. 🚉 Kékropos (for Peloponnese), Kanári (for Northern Greece). Ⓜ Piraeus. 🚌 Plateía Koraï (for Athens), Plateía Karaïskáki (other destinations).

Piraeus City Centre

① Town Hall
② Municipal Theatre
③ Theatre of Zéa
④ Archaeological Museum
⑤ Pasalimáni
⑥ Hellenic Maritime Museum
⑦ Mikrolímano
⑧ Kastélla

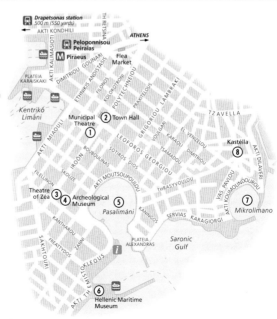

0 metres 500
0 yards 500

⑰ Ancient Eleusis

Αρχαία Ελευσίνα

Eleusis was an ancient centre of religious devotion that culminated in the annual Eleusinian Mysteries. These attracted thousands of people from around the Greek-speaking world, for whom the only initial requirement for becoming a *mystes* (or initiate) was to be neither a murderer nor a barbarian. Both men and women were freely admitted. Existing from Mycenaean times, the sanctuary was closed by the Roman Emperor Theodosius in AD 392, and was finally abandoned when Alaric, king of the Goths, invaded Greece in AD 396, bringing Christianity in his wake.

Anaktoron
This small rectangular stone edifice had a single entrance. It was considered the holiest part of the site. Meaning "palace", it existed long before the Telesterion, which was built around it.

Telesterion
Designed by Iktinos, this temple was built in the 5th century BC. It was constructed to hold several thousand people at a time.

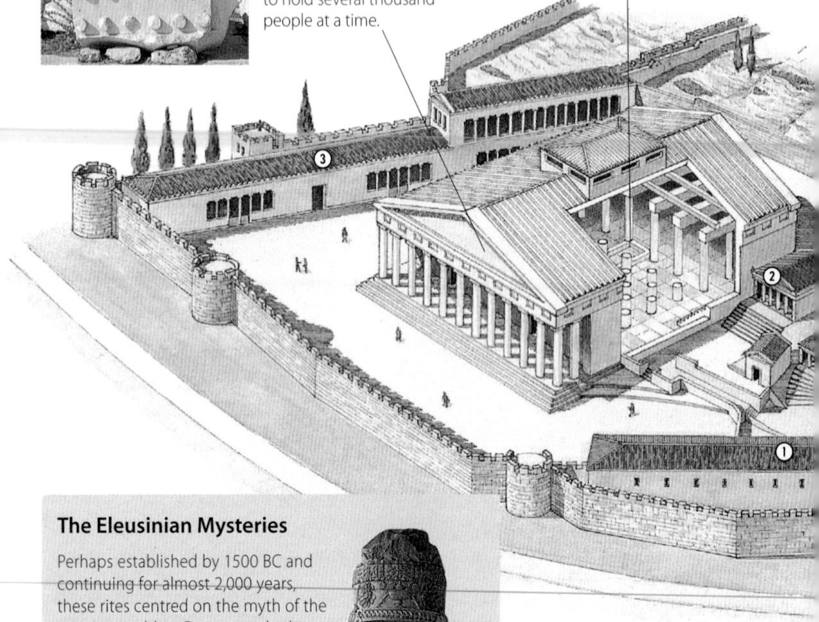

The Eleusinian Mysteries

Perhaps established by 1500 BC and continuing for almost 2,000 years, these rites centred on the myth of the grieving goddess Demeter, who lost her daughter Persephone (or Kore) to Hades, god of the Underworld, for nine months each year *(see p56)*. Participants were sworn to secrecy, but some evidence of the details of the ceremony does exist. Sacrifices were made before the procession from the Kerameikós *(see pp92–3)* to Eleusis. Here, the priestesses would reveal the vision of the holy night, thought to have been a fire symbolizing life after death for the initiates.

A priestess with a *kiste mystika* (basket)

KEY

① Roman houses

② Temple of Kore hewn out of rock

③ 4th-century BC shops and bouleuterion (council chamber)

④ One of a pair of triumphal arches

⑤ Temple of Artemis Propylaia

Ploutonion
This cave is said to be where Persephone was returned to earth. It was a sanctuary to Hades, god of the Underworld and the abductor of Persephone.

Greater Propylaia
Built from Pentelic marble in the 2nd century AD by the Roman Emperor Antoninus Pius, this was modelled on the Propylaia of Athens' Acropolis.

Well of Kallichoron
Demeter is believed to have grieved for Persephone here.

Relief from the Telesterion, now in the museum

Eleusis Museum
This small museum, south of the Telesterion, has five rooms. The entrance hall contains a copy of the famous relief from the Telesterion showing Triptólemos receiving grain from Demeter. Also in this room are a large 7th-century BC amphora and a copy of the Ninnion votive painting, one of the few remaining representations of the Eleusinian Mysteries. The other rooms are arranged on the left of the hall. In the first of these, there is an elegant 6th-century BC *koúros* and a 2nd-century BC Roman statue of Dionysos. In the second room, there are two models of the site. The third room has a Classical period terracotta sarcophagus and a large caryatid from the Lesser Propylaia carrying a *kiste mystika* basket on her head. The last room has a variety of pottery fragments, including examples of unusual terracotta containers that were used to carry foodstuffs in the annual *kernoforía* procession.

Fleeing maiden

Ancient Eleusis
This reconstruction is of Eleusis as it was in Roman times (c.AD 150) when the Mysteries were still flourishing. The view is from the east. Although there is little left today, it is still possible to sense the awe and mystery that the rites of Eleusis inspired.

Lesser Propylaia
This fragment shows sheaves of grain and poppies, which were used to make *kykeon*, the drink of the initiates.

THE PELOPONNESE

PELOPONNESE

One of the primary strongholds and battlefields of the 1821–31 Revolution, the Peloponnese is the kernel from which the modern Greek state grew. This enormous peninsula, which falls short of being an island by the mere 6-km (4-mile) width of the Corinth isthmus, also has some of the most spectacularly varied scenery and monuments on the mainland.

The name "Peloponnese" means "island of Pelops", who in legend was fed to the gods by Tantalos, his father. Resurrected, he went on to sire the Atreid line of kings, whose semi-mythical misadventures and brooding citadels were given substance by the discovery of remains at Mycenae. Today, the ancient and medieval sites of the Argolid region, to the south of Corinth, contrast with the elegantly Neo-Classical town of Náfplio.

In the west lies Ancient Olympia, the athletic and religious nexus of the ancient world and inspiration for the games' revival in modern times. The lush coastal plain of Ileía, heart of an early medieval Crusader principality, spawned Frankish-Byzantine architecture, most famously at Chlemoútsi. More purely Byzantine art adorns the churches of Mystrás, Geráki and the remote Máni region, whose warlike medieval inhabitants claimed to be descended from the warriors of ancient Sparta. Imposing Venetian fortifications at the beach-fringed capes of Methóni, Koróni and Monemvasía allowed the Venetians to play a role here after most of their other Aegean possessions were lost to the Ottomans.

In Arcadia, at the centre of the Peloponnese, lushly cultivated valleys rise to conifer-draped mountains and deep gorges such as the Loúsios; cliff-side monasteries and sombre hill-towns, like Stemnítsa, are a world apart from the popular Mediterranean image of Greece.

Restaurant terrace overlooking the sea, Monemvasía

◄ Outdoor tables line a flower-strewn street, Náfplio

Exploring the Peloponnese

Ancient and medieval ruins are abundant on the Peloponnese, and provide the main focus of sightseeing. Though there are few highly developed resorts away from the Argolid and Ileía, such areas as the Loúsios Gorge and Kalógria attract thousands of trekkers and naturalists. A rural economy is still paramount inland, with Pátra being the only large city. The landscape is dominated by forested mountains and the west coast, between Pátra and Methóni, boasts some of the finest beaches in the Mediterranean.

Karýtaina village, Loúsios Gorge

Key

— Motorway

= = Road under construction

— Major road

···· Minor road

— Scenic route

··-· Main railway

— Regional border

Getting Around

Major roads link Athens and Pátra via Corinth. Secondary roads are more interesting, if dangerously narrow. Buses link major towns with their surrounding villages, but it is not so easy to get from one major town to another. There is only one train line from Athens to the Peloponnese, and it goes as far as Kiato, north of Corinth; from there, you'll have to travel by bus to other destinations. The Rio-Antírio bridge crosses the Gulf of Corinth in the north to link the Peloponnese with mainland Greece. Ferries and hydrofoils *(see p319)* serve various points on the east coast, such as Monemvasía and Neápoli.

Gýtheio harbour, Inner Máni

For hotels and restaurants see p270–71 and pp287–8

Locator Map

0 kilometres 20
0 miles 20

Sights at a Glance

For keys to symbols see back flap

❶ Ancient Corinth

Αρχαία Κόρινθος

Ancient Corinth derived its prosperity from its position on a narrow isthmus between the Saronic and Corinthian gulfs. Transporting goods across this isthmus, even before the canal (see p171) was built, provided the shortest route from the eastern Mediterranean to the Adriatic and Italy. Founded in Neolithic times, the town was razed in 146 BC by the Romans, who rebuilt it a century later. Attaining a population of 750,000 under the patronage of the emperors, the town gained a reputation for licentious living, which St Paul attacked when he came here in AD 52. Excavations have revealed the vast extent of the city, destroyed by earthquakes in Byzantine times. The ruins constitute the largest Roman township in Greece.

Locator Map

★ **Lechaion Way**
This marble-paved road linked the port of Lechaion with the city, ending at a still-surviving stairway and an imposing *propylaion* (entrance).

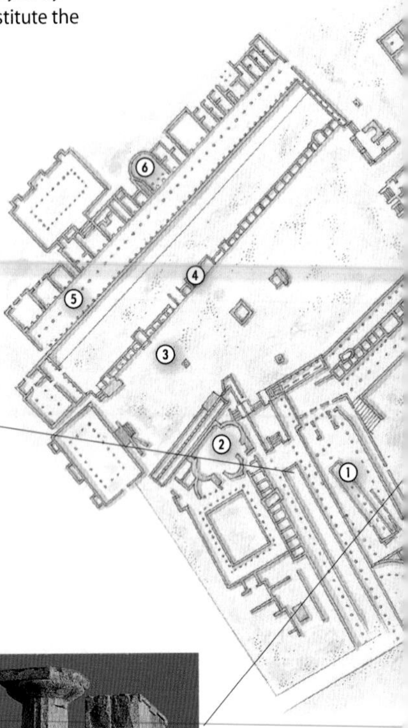

KEY

① **Basilica**

② **The Peirene fountain's** springs still supply the local modern village.

③ **The agora** was the hub of Roman civic life.

④ **The bema** (platform) was where St Paul was accused of sacrilege by the Jews of Corinth.

⑤ **South stoa**

⑥ **Bouleuterion**

⑦ **The northwest stoa** had two series of columns, the outer being Doric and the inner Ionic.

⑧ **The Glauke fountain's** four cisterns were hewn from a cubic monolith and filled by an aqueduct from the hills.

⑨ **The museum** contains artifacts from the site (see p170).

⑩ **The theatre** was modified in the 3rd century AD so water could be piped in and mock sea battles staged.

★ **Temple of Apollo**
The most striking structure of the lower city, this templ[e] was one of the few buildin[g] preserved by the Romans when they rebuilt the site in 46 BC. At the southeast corner, an ingenious stepped ramp leads to the temple terrace.

Temple of Octavia
These three ornate Corinthian columns, topped by a restored architrave, are all that remain of a temple, standing on a platform, dedicated to the sister of the Emperor Augustus.

VISITORS' CHECKLIST

Practical Information
7 km (4 miles) SW of modern Corinth, Peloponnese.
Road map C4. **Tel** 27410 31207.
Open Apr–Oct: 8am–8pm daily; Nov–Mar: 8:30am–3pm daily.
Closed 1 Jan, 25 Mar, Good Fri am, Easter Sun, 1 May, 25, 26 Dec.
limited. Acrocorinth: 4 km (2.5 miles) S of Ancient Corinth.
Tel 27410 31266. **Open** 8am–8pm daily (to 3pm Nov–Mar).

Transport
Site & Museum.

Acrocorinth
(see p170)

Odeion
This was one of several buildings endowed by Herodes Atticus, the wealthy Athenian and good friend of the Emperor Hadrian.

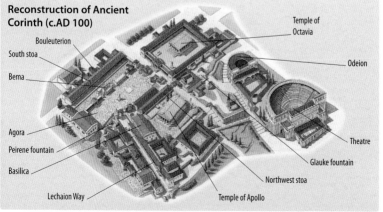

Reconstruction of Ancient Corinth (c.AD 100)

Bouleuterion
South stoa
Bema
Agora
Peirene fountain
Basilica
Lechaion Way
Temple of Apollo
Northwest stoa
Glauke fountain
Theatre
Odeion
Temple of Octavia

Exploring Acrocorinth and the Museum

Excavations of recent years have yielded numerous artifacts now on view in the museum, and have revealed the vast extent of the ancient city, which included the summit of Acrocorinth. Altogether, the ruins constitute the largest Roman township in Greece, since few earlier structures were restored after the Romans destroyed the town in 146 BC. Acrocorinth became one of medieval Greece's most important fortresses and can now be reached by a road which climbs the western face of the hill from the lower town.

🏛 Acrocorinth

Acrocorinth, 4 km (2 miles) above the main city, has been held and refortified by every occupying power in Greece since Roman times. Entry is on the west, where the peak's natural defences are weakest, through three successive gateways from different eras. The lowest is mostly Turkish; the middle, Frankish; and the third and highest, Byzantine, though it and two adjacent towers incorporate abundant ancient masonry. Beyond sprawls a 24-ha (60-acre) terraced wilderness of minaret stumps, Muslim tombs, and lonely mosques or chapels – all that remains of the town abandoned almost two hundred years ago, when its last defenders, the Turks, were defeated.

The lower elevation at the southwest corner of the 5-km (3-mile) circuit of walls sports a Venetian tower, while the true, northeast summit bears the scant foundations of an Aphrodite temple, attended in

Mosaic of Bacchus (Dionysos), 2nd century AD, in the museum

antiquity by 1,000 sacred prostitutes. It was against such practices that St Paul wrote his two "letters to the Corinthians". Today, its attraction is one of the most sweeping views in the whole of Greece, up to 60 km (37 miles) in all directions from the Geráneia range in the northeast to the peaks of Zíria in the southwest. Towards Zíria, a prominent nearby hill, Penteskoúfi, was fortified by the Franks during the 13th century.

Acrocorinth could withstand lengthy sieges owing to the presence of the upper Peirene

spring, on the southeast side of the ramparts. A stairway descends to a vaulted, subterranean chamber pool; in dry seasons, the water recedes to expose a column supporting an ornate Hellenistic pediment.

🏛 Museum

The site museum, just south of the odeion, ranks among Greece's best provincial collections. All periods of the ancient town's history are represented, though the Roman gallery in the west wing is particularly rich. Here, pride of place goes to 2nd-century AD mosaics lifted from the floors of nearby villas: a head of Bacchus (Dionysos) set in a circular geometric pattern, a nude shepherd playing his flute to three cows, and a goat napping under a tree. The north doorway is flanked by two columns in the shape of Phrygian prisoners, shown with their arms crossed, their tunics and long hair seeming to prefigure medieval art. Also housed in the west wing are some of the 274 objects stolen from the museum in 1990 and recovered nine years later in Miami. The east gallery features older artifacts. Attic ware from the 5th century BC (*see pp64–5*), including the famous "Owl" vase, is rarer than the 7th- and 6th-century BC pottery, some painted with fantastic beasts, for which Corinth was noted.

At the shrine of Asklepios, just within the northern boundary of the ancient city walls, votive offerings in the shape of afflicted body parts were found and are on display in a back room, the precursors of the *támmata* or metal *ex votos* left in modern Orthodox churches. Other oddities include a 6th-century marble sphinx and Hellenistic pediments with lion-head spouts.

Stone reliefs in the central courtyard include depictions of the Labours of Herakles (*see p57*), one of which was performed nearby at the sanctuary of Neméa.

The entrance to Acrocorinth, with its three gateways

Ships passing through the Corinth Canal with the road bridge overhead

❷ Corinth Canal
Διώρυγα της Κορίνθου

Peloponnese. **Road map** C4.
Loutráki.

Stormy Cape Matapan, or Taínaro *(see p203)*, the southernmost point of the Peloponnese, was one of the dreaded capes of antiquity; rather than risk sailing around it, boats would be unloaded on one shore of this isthmus, dragged the 6 km (4 miles) across on the *díolkos* (paved slipway), and then refloated.

The traffic enriched Corinth and inspired plans for a canal. Emperor Nero began construction, but the project was only completed between 1882 and 1893. The 23-m (75-ft) wide canal is obsolete in an age of giant container ships which easily weather the cape, but small freighters squeezing through are regularly seen from the road bridge above.

Environs
Near the southern end of the canal is the site of **Ancient Isthmia**, once the major local religious centre (devoted to

View of the Sanctuary of Hera at Perachóra, Cape Melangávi

Poseidon) and location of the biennial Isthmian Games. Today, only foundations of Poseidon's temple (7th century BC) and the remains of a starting gate for track events in the adjacent, vanished stadium are traceable.

The site museum stresses finds from Kechriés, Corinth's eastern port; unique exhibits include panels of painted glass or stone embedded in a resin matrix. They were intended to decorate an Isis temple but were never used owing to an earthquake in AD 375.

🏛 Ancient Isthmia
Southern end of Corinth Canal.
Site & Museum: **Tel** 27410 37244.
Open 8am–3pm Tue–Sun.
Closed main public hols. 🚻 ♿

❸ Heraion of Perachóra
Ηραίον της Περαχώρας

13 km (8 miles) W of Loutráki, Peloponnese. **Road map** C4.

Probably founded during the 8th century BC, the Heraion of Perachóra (a nearby village) was primarily a religious centre. Only foundations and column stumps remain of the Archaic temple of Hera Limenia, plus an altar and a Classical stoa, but the site has an incomparable setting, above a tiny cove on the south shore of Cape Melangávi, close to a 19th-century lighthouse.

Scenic Vouliagméni Lake, 3 km (2 miles) east, is fringed by Aleppo pines, with the best swimming and a selection of tavernas at its west end.

❹ Ancient Neméa
Αρχαία Νεμέα

5 km (3 miles) NE of Neméa, Peloponnese. **Road map** C4.
Tel 27460 22739.
Site: **Open** 8:30am–3pm Mon–Fri.
Museum: **Open** 8:30am–3pm Tue–Sun. **Closed** main public hols. 🚻 ♿

Evocatively occupying an isolated rural valley, the site of Ancient Neméa is a local landmark, with the Doric columns of its 4th-century Zeus temple plainly visible from afar. Below them lie the broken remains of column drums toppled by vandals between the 4th and 13th centuries AD. At the west end of the temple's complete floor, the deep *adyton* (underground crypt) has been exposed.

A short walk to the southwest, under a giant modern shelter, is a Hellenistic bathhouse, which is now open to the public after extensive excavations. The digs revealed the plunge-pool and feed system and also uncovered the Byzantine village, which took root here in the 4th century, including graves, kilns and a basilica built above the ancient pilgrims' inn.

The **museum** has interesting reconstructions and old engravings. The Hellenistic stadium, 400 m (1,300 ft) to the southeast, has the earliest known vaulted entrance tunnel.

Three Doric columns of the Temple of Zeus, Ancient Neméa

Stalactites and stalagmites at the Cave of Lakes

❺ Mount Chelmós
Ορος Χελμός

Peloponnese. **Road map** C4. 🚌 to Kalávryta.

Rising to 2,355 m (7,729 ft), Mount Chelmós is the third highest point of the Peloponnese, its foothills cloaked in extensive forests and divided by deep gorges. The most famous of these is Mavronéri, where the waterfall cascading from the remote north face of the summit is claimed to be the source of the mythical river Styx.

Overlooking the wooded Feneoú valley, on the south-eastern slopes, stands the remote monastery of **Agíou Georgíou Feneoú**, originally founded in 1693, though mostly dating to the mid-18th century. The *katholikón*, with its high dome and transept, offers unusual frescoes. A stairway leads to a "secret" school, which functioned during the Ottoman years.

Moní Agías Lávras, 6 km (4 miles) from Kalávryta, played a pivotal role in the Greek Revolution. The Archbishop of Pátra raised the standard of revolt here on 25 March 1821, the banner now being the centrepiece of a nationalist shrine in the upstairs treasury (*see pp44–5*).

Founded in 961, Agías Lávras has been rebuilt after its destruction by the Germans in 1943. On the day before their arrival, the Germans had set fire to the town of Kalávryta, where they perpetrated one of their worst occupation atrocities, massacring 1,436 men and boys in reprisal for local resistance. The cathedral clock is permanently stopped at the time the killing began.

The **Cave of the Lakes**, near Kastriá, was known in ancient times but was lost until its rediscovery in 1964. Groups can visit the first 350 m (1,150 ft) of the cave, down to the second of 15 lakes. The massive stalactite-hung caverns were formed by an underground river, which still flows during the winter.

🦇 Cave of the Lakes
16 km (10 miles) S of Kalávryta. **Tel** 26920 31633. **Open** 9am–4:30pm daily (to 5:30pm Sat & Sun). 🅿️

Old steam locomotive at Diakoftó

❻ Kalávryta-Diakoftó Railway
Οδοντωτός Σιδηρόδρομος Καλαβρύτων–Διακοφτού

Peloponnese. **Road map** C4. **Tel** 26920 22245. 🚉 several daily (9am–4pm) Kalávryta–Diakoftó–Kalávryta. 🚉 **W** odontotos.com

The most enjoyable narrow-gauge railway in Greece was engineered between 1889 and 1896 by an Italian company to bring ore down from the Kalávryta area. Over 22 km (14 miles) of track were laid, over 6 km (4 miles) of which relies on a third rail (a "rack and pinion" system), engaged where grades are up to one in seven. Two of the original steam locomotives, replaced in 1959, are displayed at Diakoftó. For a good view of the mechanism, travel by the driver.

En route there are 14 tunnels and many bridges over the Vouraïkós Gorge. The single station of Méga Spílaio, with two modest hotels, is roughly halfway. The station is the start of a 45-minute trail up to **Moní Méga Spílaio**, which is believed to be the oldest monastery in Greece.

⑦ Pátra

Πάτρα

Peloponnese. **Road map** C4.
🏔 231,000. 🚉 🚌 🚍
ℹ️ Filopimenos 26 (2610 620353).
Open 8am–3pm daily.

Greece's third largest city and second port is no beauty. Tower blocks dominate the few elegantly arcaded streets of this planned Neo-Classical town. Where Pátra excels is in its celebration of carnival – the best in Greece – for which the city's large gay community and student body both turn out in force.

On the ancient acropolis, the originally Byzantine *kástro* bears marks of every subsequent era. The vast bailey, filled with gardens and orchards, often hosts public events, as does the nearby brick Roman odeion.

At the southwest edge of town, the mock-Byzantine basilica of **Agios Andréas** stands where St Andrew was supposedly martyred, and houses his skull and a fragment of his cross.

Environs

Founded in 1861, the **Achaïa Clauss Winery** was Greece's first commercial winery and is now one of the largest vintners in Greece. It produces 30 million litres (7 million gallons) a year, with grapes gathered from across the country. Tours include a visit to the Imperial Cellar, where Mavrodaphne, a fortified dessert wine, can be tasted.

🍷 **Achaïa Clauss Winery**
Petroto, 6 km (4 miles) SE of Pátra.
Tel 2610 580100. **Open** 10:30am–
6:30pm daily. **Closed** main pub hols.
♿ 📷 🌐 clauss.gr

⑧ Kalógria

Καλόγρια

Peloponnese. **Road map** B4. 🚌 to
Lápas. ℹ️ Lápas town hall (26930
31868).

The entire lagoon-speckled coast, from the Araxos river mouth to the Kotýchi lagoon, ranks as one of the largest wetlands in Europe. Incorporating the Strofiliá marsh and a 2,000-ha (5,000-acre)

Sandy beaches of Kalógria

umbrella pine dune-forest, the area enjoys limited protection as a reserve. Development is confined to a zone between the Prokópos lagoon and the excellent, 7-km (4-mile) beach of Kalogriá. The dunes also support Aleppo pines and valonea oaks, while bass, eels and water snakes swim in the marsh channels.

Migratory populations of ducks, including pintails and coots, live at Kotýchi, while marsh harriers, owls, kestrels and falcons can be seen all year round. A **Visitor Centre** at Lápas runs nature trails through the dunes nearby.

ℹ️ **Visitor Centre**
Kotýchion Strofiliás. **Tel** 26233 60814.
Open 9am–3pm Mon–Fri.
Closed main public hols. ♿ 📷

⑨ Chlemoútsi Castle

Χλεμούτσι

Kástro, Peloponnese. **Road map** B4.
Open daily.

The most famous Frankish castle in Greece, known also as "Castel Tornesi" after the gold *tournois* coin minted here in medieval times, was erected between 1219 and 1223 to defend thriving Glaréntza port (Kyllíni) and the principality capital of Andreville (Andravída). To bolster the weak natural defences, exceptionally thick walls and a massive gate were built; much of the rampart catwalk can still be followed. The magnificent hexagonal keep has echoing, vaulted halls; a plaque by the entry commemorates the 1428–32 residence of Konstantínos Palaiológos, the last Byzantine emperor, while he was governor of Ileía.

Steps lead to a roof for views over the Ionian islands and the coastal plain. Chlemoútsi is now being reconstructed, with the enormous fan-shaped courtyard already used for summer concerts.

The modern Byzantine-style basilica of Agios Andréas, Pátra

⓾ Ancient Olympia
Ολυμπία

At the confluence of the rivers Alfeiós and Kládeos, the Sanctuary of Olympia enjoyed over 1,000 years of esteem as a religious and athletics centre. Though the sanctuary flourished in Mycenaean times *(see pp30–31)*, its historic importance dates to the coming of the Dorians and their worship of Zeus, after whose abode on Mount Olympos the site was named. More elaborate temples and secular buildings were erected as the sanctuary acquired a more Hellenic character, a process completed by 300 BC. By the end of the reign of Roman Emperor Hadrian (AD 117–38), the sanctuary had begun to have less religious and political significance.

Aerial view south over the Olympia site today

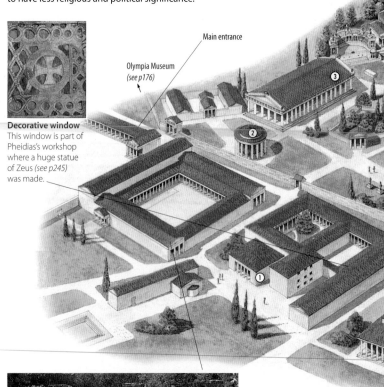

Decorative window
This window is part of Pheidias's workshop where a huge statue of Zeus *(see p245)* was made.

Main entrance

Olympia Museum
(see p176)

Palaestra
This was a training centre for wrestlers, boxers and long-jumpers. Much of the colonnade which surrounded the central court has been reconstructed.

0 metres 50
0 yards 50

Stadium Entrance
Late in the 3rd century BC, the stadium entrance acquired a vaulted ceiling, part of which survives. The existing stadium was the third laid out at Olympia.

Reconstruction of Olympia (AD 100)

This shows Olympia as it was under the Romans. At that time, the worship of Zeus predominated; the games were dedicated to him, and his temple (containing a huge statue of the god) was at the heart of the Olympian enclosure.

KEY

① **The Heroön** housed an altar dedicated to an unknown hero.

② **The Philippeion**, commissioned by Philip II, honours the dynasty of Macedonian kings.

③ **The Temple of Hera**, begun in the 7th century BC, is one of the oldest temples in Greece.

④ **The Treasuries**, which stored votive offerings from their donor city-states, looked like miniature temples.

⑤ **The Metroön** was a Doric shrine to the pre-Olympian goddess Rhea.

⑥ **South Hall**

⑦ **Altar of Oaths**

⑧ **The Bouleuterion**, or council house, was the seat of the Olympic Senate.

⑨ **Sanctuary entrance**

⑩ **The Leonidaion**, with its clover-shaped water-garden, accommodated distinguished guests.

Temple of Zeus
Though only column bases and tumbled sections remain, they clearly indicate the grandeur of this 5th-century BC Doric temple.

Exploring the Olympia Archaeological Museum

The Olympia Archaeological Museum, built opposite the excavation site to display its many treasures, officially opened in 1982 and is one of the richest museums in Greece. Except for the central hall, devoted solely to the pediment and metope sculptures from the Zeus temple, and the corner room dedicated to the games, the exhibits are arranged chronologically over 12 rooms, proceeding clockwise from the entrance hall from pre-history, through the Classical period, to the Romans.

Prehistoric, Geometric and Archaic Galleries

To the left of the entrance hall, room 1 contains finds from the Prehistoric period including pottery and 7th-century BC bronze reliefs. There is also a model of the early Helladic Pelopian Tumulus. Exhibits in room 2 include a bronze tripod cauldron, elongated male figures upholding cauldron handles and griffin-headed cauldron ornaments, popular in the 7th century BC. There are also bronze votive animals from the Geometric period, found in the area surrounding the altar of Zeus. Room 3 has lavishly painted terracotta architectural members from various buildings in the sanctuary.

Zeus and Ganymede, in terracotta

Classical Galleries

Weapons and helmets made by pilgrims and athletes at Olympia were favourite offerings to Zeus. Two famous helmets used in the Persian Wars *(see p33)* are shown in room 4: an Assyrian helmet, and that of Miltiades, victor at the Battle of Marathon *(see p149)*. This room also contains a 5th-century BC Corinthian terracotta of *Zeus and Ganymede*, the most humanized of the portrayals of Zeus.

The central hall houses surviving relief statuary from the Temple of Zeus. Unusually, both pediments survive, their compositions carefully balanced though not precisely symmetrical. The more static east pediment tells of the chariot race between local king Oinomaos and Pelops, suitor for the hand of the king's daughter Hippodameia. Zeus stands between the two contestants; a soothsayer on his left foresees Oinomaos's defeat. The two local rivers are personified in the corners. The western pediment, a metaphor for the tension between barbarism and civilization, portrays the mythological *Battle of the Lapiths and the Centaurs*. The centaurs, invited to the wedding of Lapith king Peirithous, attempt, while drunk, to abduct the Lapith women. Apollo, god of reason, is central, laying a reassuring hand on

Peirithous's shoulder as the latter rescues his bride from the clutches of the centaur chief. Theseus is seen to the left of Apollo preparing to dispatch another centaur, while the Lapith women watch from the safety of the corners. The interior metopes, far less intact, depict the *Twelve Labours of Herakles*, a hero mythically associated with the sanctuary.

In its own niche, the fragmentary 5th-century BC *Nike* (room 6), by the sculptor Paionios, was a thanks-offering from Messene and Náfpaktos, following their victory over Sparta during the Peloponnesian War *(see p34)*. A plaster reconstruction allows visualization of the winged goddess on the back of an eagle as she descends from heaven to proclaim victory.

The more complete *Hermes*, by Praxiteles, also has a room to itself (room 8), and shows the nude god carrying the infant Dionysos to safety, away from jealous Hera. The arm holding the newborn deity rests on a tree-trunk hung with Hermes'

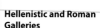

Statue of Hermes by Praxiteles

cape; Dionysos reaches for a bunch of grapes in the elder god's now-vanished right hand. Room 7 is devoted to Pheidias's workshop and the tools and materials used to create his gold and ivory statue of Zeus.

Hellenistic and Roman Galleries

Room 9 contains late-Classical and Hellenistic finds including the terracotta sima of the Leonidaion. Rooms 10 and 11 are devoted to a series of statues of Roman emperors and generals and a marble bull dedicated by Regilla, wife of Herodes Atticus. Displays in room 12 include glass from the late-Roman cemetery at Frangonisi, Miraka, in which athletes and sanctuary officials were buried.

The Origins of the Olympic Games

The establishment of the Olympic Games in 776 BC is traditionally treated as the first certain event in Greek history. Originally, men's sprinting was the only event and competitors were local; the first recorded victor was Koroivos, a cook from nearby Elis. During the 8th and 7th centuries BC, wrestling, boxing, equestrian events and boys' competitions were added. The elite of many cities came to compete and provided victory trophies, although, until the Romans took charge in 146 BC, entry was restricted to Greeks. Local cities disputed control of the games, but a sacred truce guaranteed safe conduct to spectators and competitors. Part of a pagan festival, the Christians did not approve of the games and they were banned by Theodosius I in AD 393.

The ancient pentathlon consisted of sprinting, wrestling, javelin- and discus-throwing and the long jump (assisted by swinging weights). From 720 BC, athletes competed naked and women were excluded from spectating.

Wrestling and boxing are depicted on this 6th-century BC amphora. The boxers are shown wearing *himantes*, an early type of boxing glove made of leather straps wrapped around the hands and wrists.

The Olympic revival came in 1896, when the first modern games were held in Athens *(see p117)*. They were organized by the Frenchman Baron Pierre de Coubertin.

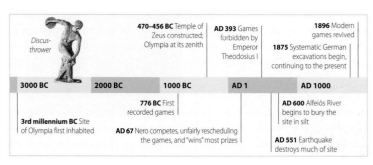

3000 BC	2000 BC	1000 BC	AD 1	AD 1000

Discus-thrower

470–456 BC Temple of Zeus constructed; Olympia at its zenith

AD 393 Games forbidden by Emperor Theodosius I

1896 Modern games revived

1875 Systematic German excavations begin, continuing to the present

3rd millennium BC Site of Olympia first inhabited

776 BC First recorded games

AD 67 Nero competes, unfairly rescheduling the games, and "wins" most prizes

AD 600 Alfeiós River begins to bury the site in silt

AD 551 Earthquake destroys much of site

⓫ Loúsios Gorge
Φαράγγι του Λούσιου

Although merely a tributary of the Alfeiós River, the Loúsios stream in its upper reaches boasts one of the most impressive canyons in Greece. Scarcely 5 km (3 miles) long, the Loúsios Gorge is nearly 300 m (985 ft) deep at the narrowest, most spectacular portion. Because of its remote mountain setting near the very centre of the Peloponnese, the Loúsios region was one of the strongholds of the revolutionaries during the Greek War of Independence *(see pp44–5)*. Medieval monasteries and churches cling to the steep cliffs of the gorge, and hiking trails have been marked, connecting some of the area's highlights. The picturesque villages *(see p180)* of the canyon's east bank make suitable touring bases.

Néa Moní Filosófou
Situated on the west bank amid the narrows, this 17th-century monastery was renovated and restaffed by a caretaker monk. Frescoes in the church date from 1693 and illustrate many seldom-depicted biblical episodes, such as the *Gadarene Swine*.

★ Ancient Gortys
The Asklepieíon, or therapeutic centre, of Ancient Gortys occupies a sunken excavation on the west bank. It includes the foundations of a 4th-century BC temple to Asklepios, the god of healing.

KEY

① **Agios Andréas,** an 11th-century chapel, stands just below the Loúsios.

② **Paleá Moní Filosófou,** dating to 960, is the oldest monastery of the area. It is now in ruins.

③ **Dimitsána** is the best place to join the path.

④ **Stemnítsa** *(see p180)* is a charming village and a good place to hike out to, having passed through the gorge.

Kókkoras Bridge
This restored medieval bridge once carried the age-old road linking the regions of Arcadia and Ileía. Anglers fish for trout here in the icy river water.

For hotels and restaurants see pp270–71 and pp287–8

Wooded flanks of the Loúsios Gorge, viewed from the south

VISITORS' CHECKLIST

Practical Information
Peloponnese. **Road map** C4.
All monasteries: **Open** dawn–
dusk (often closed for
1–2 hours at midday).
Moní Aimyalón: **Open** daily.
Néa Moní Filosófou: **Open** daily.
Ancient Gortys: **Open** daily.
Closed main public hols.
Trekking: Take walking shoes
and maps; paths are not always
robust or clearly marked. Do not
enter the gorge after heavy rain.

Transport
🚌 Dimitsána.

Zigovisti

0 kilometres   1
0 miles   0.5

Tripoli

★ **Moní Aimyalón**
Founded in 1605, Moní Aimyalón is
tucked into a side canyon, above
garden plots. A passage partly hewn
through the rock leads to its barrel-
vaulted church with excellent frescoes
from 1608.

Elliniko

★ **Moní Agíou Ioánnou
Prodrómou**
Wedged into a palisade on
the canyon's east flank,
this 12th-century monastery is
the most spectacular sight of the
Loúsios. There is room for only a
dozen monks in the tiny, frescoed
church whose shape is dictated
by the cliff face.

Key
═══ Minor road
- - Footpath

For keys to symbols *see back flap*

Exploring Around the Loúsios Gorge

Overlooking the gorge are some of the most beautiful hill-towns in the Arcadia region, making good bases for exploring the area. The best-marked trail is between Néa Moní Filosófou and Moní Prodrómou (take water and food). Dimitsána has one bus service daily to Trípoli, while two weekday buses between Andrítsaina and Trípoli can be picked up below Karýtaina. Getting around by car is best, though taxis are available. Winters can be chilly and wet, with snow chains required.

Bridge over the Alfeiós River, below Karýtaina, complete with chapel

The narrow streets of Dimitsána

Dimitsána

Spread along an airy ridge with the River Loúsios on three sides and glorious views down the valley, Dimitsána stands on the Classical site of ancient Teuthis. The town boasts four belfries; that of **Agía Kyriakí** is illuminated at night, while the three-level **Pyrsogiannítiko** bell tower was erected by skilled Epirot masons in 1888.

Two clerics involved in the 1821 revolution against Turkish rule *(see pp44–5)* were born here. The birthplace of Archbishop Germanós of Pátra, who helped instigate the revolution, is marked by a plaque near the summit of westerly Kástro hill. A plaque dedicated to Patriarch Gregory V stands in the market; he was hanged in Istanbul when news of the revolt reached the sultan.

Dimitsána's mansions date from its heyday as a trade centre in the 18th century. There were 14 powder factories here during

the War of Independence – the town's **Water Mill Museum** has exhibits on powdermaking.

🏛 **Water Mill Museum**
Dimitsána. **Tel** 27950 31630.
Open 10am–6pm Wed–Mon.
Closed main public hols.

Stemnítsa

Situated in a large hollow, the village of Stemnítsa forms a naturally hidden fortress. In medieval times, Stemnítsa was one of Greece's main metalworking centres. Today, it boasts a well-respected school for gold- and silversmiths. A **Folk Museum** re-creates workshops of indigenous craftsmen and local house interiors, and hosts a gallery of weaponry, textiles and ceramics belonging to the Savvopoúlou family.

Among a number of magnificent medieval churches, those of **Treís Ierárches**, near the Folk Museum, and 10th-century **Profítis Ilías**, up on Kástro hill, have frescoes in excellent condition. The 12th-century **Panagía Mpaféro** has an unusual portico, while the **Moní**

Zoödóchou Pigís was where the revolutionary chieftains held their first convention during the War of Independence; it is for this reason that Stemnítsa was called the first capital of Greece.

🏛 **Folk Museum**
Stemnítsa. **Tel** 27950 81252.
Open Oct–Jun:10am–1pm Mon & Wed–Fri, 10am–2pm Sat & Sun; Jul–Sep: 10am–1pm Mon & Sun, 10am–1pm & 5–8pm Wed, Thu & Sat, 5–8pm Fri. **Closed** Tue (Oct–Jun), main public hols. 🆆 stemnitsamuseum.com

Karýtaina

In a strategic position on a bend of the Alfeiós, Karýtaina is now a virtual ghost town of less than 200 inhabitants. It has a 13th-century **Kástro**, dating to the time when the town was the seat of a Frankish barony. The castle was the hideout of Theódoros Kolokotrónis, who survived a long Turkish siege here in 1826. The **Panagía tou Kástrou** boasts restored 11th-century column capitals with intricate reliefs.

Environs

East of Karýtaina, a bridge over the Alfeiós dates to 1439; four of six original arches survive, with a tiny chapel built into one pier.

The town of Dimitsána, seen from the east

For hotels and restaurants see pp270–71 and pp287–8

⑫ Andrítsaina
Ανδρίτσαινα

Peloponnese. **Road map** C4.
🏛 900. 🚌

Despite its current role as the gateway to the Temple of Bassae, the sleepy town of Andrítsaina is hardly touched by tourism. Tavernas and shops around its central square, home to a lively morning produce market, make few concessions to modernity in either their cuisine or their vivid displays. These are echoes of the 18th century, when this was a major market centre. Downhill from the 18th-century fountain of Traní, a **Folk Museum** features local rag-rugs, traditional dress and metalware.

🏛 Folk Museum
Andrítsaina. **Open** daily. **Closed** main public hols.

Environs
The 5th-century BC **Temple of Bassae** graces a commanding knoll, occupying the most remote site of any major ancient sanctuary. Today, it hides under an enormous tent, until 50 million euros (£33 million) can be raised to reinstall the architraves. Without them, winter frost damages the temple's colonnades, now reinforced by scaffolding.

Below Bassae lies the modern village of Figaleía, named after the ancient town to the west. The citizens of Ancient Figaleía built the temple in thanks to Apollo Epikourios for stopping a plague. A path descends to the gorge of the Nédas river.

🏛 Temple of Bassae
14 km (9 miles) S of Andrítsaina.
Tel 26260 22275. **Open** Apr–Oct: 8:30am–sunset daily (to 3pm Nov–Mar). 🚫 ♿

⑬ Ancient Tegéa
Τεγέα

Peloponnese. **Road map** C4. **Tel** 27150 56540. 🚌 Site: **Open** daily.
Museum: **Open** 8:30am–3pm Tue–Sun. **Closed** main public hols. ♿
🌐 tegamuseum.gr

South of modern Trípoli, the remains of the ancient city of

Typical street-café scene at the traditional town of Andrítsaina

Tegéa lie near the village of Aléa. The most impressive ruin is the 4th-century BC Doric temple of Athena Aléa, with its massive column drums, the second largest temple in the Peloponnese after Olympia's Temple of Zeus *(see p175)*. The site **museum** has sculpture from the city, including a number of fragments of the temple pediment.

⑭ Argos
Άργος

Peloponnese. **Road map** C4.
🏛 20,000. 🚌

One of the oldest settlements in Greece, modern Argos is a busy, rather shabby market town, with its open-air fairground next to a restored Neo-Classical marketplace. To the east of the central square, the **Archaeological Museum** exhibits local finds from all eras. Highlights include a bronze helmet and breastplate, and an Archaic pottery fragment showing Odysseus blinding Polyphimos, as well as a *krater* (bowl) from the 7th century BC.

The most visible traces of Ancient Argos lie on the way to Trípoli, where Roman baths and an amphitheatre are dwarfed by the size of one of the largest and most steeply raked theatres in the Greek world. From here, a path climbs Lárisa hill, one of Argos's two ancient acropoleis.

🏛 Archaeological Museum
E of Plateía Agíou Pétrou. **Tel** 27510 68819. **Open** 8:30am–3pm Tue–Sun. **Closed** main public hols. 🚫 ♿

Environs
Heading south of Ancient Argos, past the theatre, a minor road leads to the village of **Ellinikó** on the outskirts of which stands an intact pyramidal building. Dating from the 4th century BC, the structure is thought to have been a fort guarding the road to Arcadia.

Lérna, further south, is a 2200-BC palace dubbed the "House of the Tiles" for its original terracotta roofing. It now shelters under a modern protective canopy. Adjacent Neolithic house foundations and two Mycenaean graves, inside the palace foundations, suggest two millennia of habitation. Settlers were attracted by springs which powered watermills and still feed a deep seaside pond. This was the home of the legendary nine-headed serpent Hydra, which Herakles killed as one of his Labours *(see p57)*.

Seating in the ancient theatre of Argos, seen from the stage

⑮ Mycenae

Μυκήναι

The fortified palace complex of Mycenae, uncovered by the archaeologist Heinrich Schliemann (see p184) in 1874, is one of the earliest examples of sophisticated citadel architecture. The term "Mycenaean", more properly late Bronze Age, applies to an entire culture spanning the years 1700–1100 BC. Only the ruling class inhabited this hilltop palace, with artisans and merchants living just outside the city walls. It was abandoned in 1100 BC after a period of great disruption in the region.

Secret Stairway
A flight of 99 steps drops to a cistern deep beneath the citadel. A torch is needed to see your way down the steps. Linked to a spring outside, the cistern provided water in times of siege.

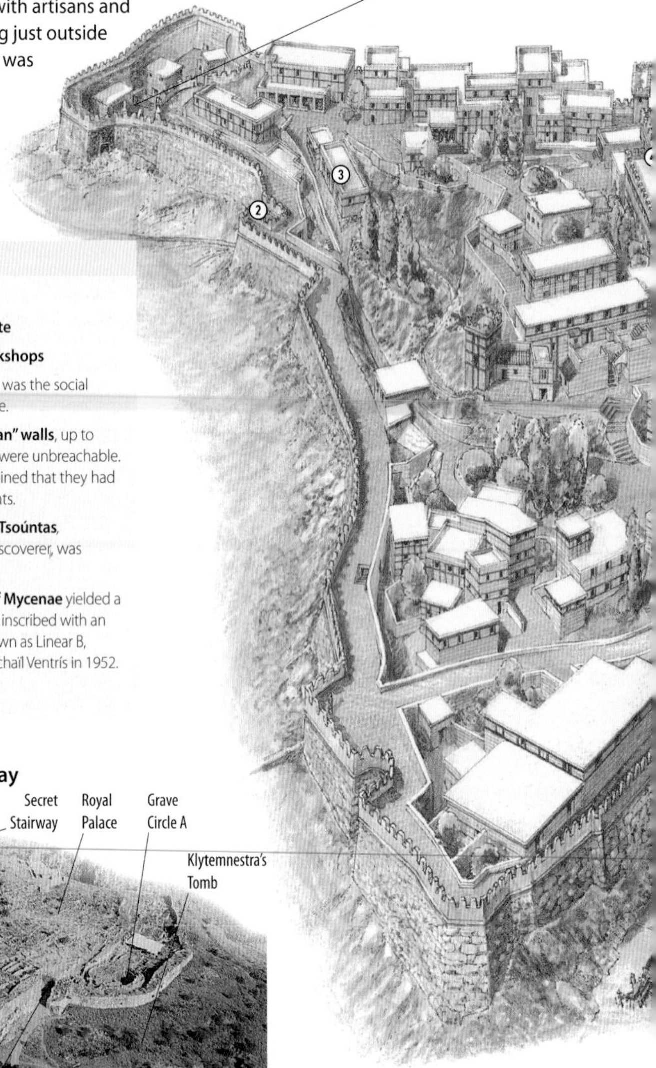

KEY

① **Bastion**

② **Northeast gate**

③ **Artisans' workshops**

④ **The megaron** was the social heart of the palace.

⑤ **The "Cyclopean" walls**, up to 14 m (46 ft) wide, were unbreachable. Later Greeks imagined that they had been built by giants.

⑥ **The House of Tsoúntas**, named after its discoverer, was a minor palace.

⑦ **The houses of Mycenae** yielded a number of tablets inscribed with an archaic script, known as Linear B, deciphered by Michaïl Ventrís in 1952.

⑧ **Great ramp**

Mycenae Today

Secret Stairway — Royal Palace — Grave Circle A

Klytemnestra's Tomb

Lion Gate — Path to the Treasury of Atreus — Grave Circle B

Reconstruction of Mycenae

This illustration shows Mycenae as it was in the time of the House of Atreus and the 1250 BC Trojan War (see pp58–9). Most tombs lie outside the walls (see p184).

Royal Palace
Situated at the acropolis summit, only the floors remain of this central structure. Burn-marks dating to its destruction in 1200 BC are still visible on the stone.

Grave Circle A
This contained six royal family shaft graves containing 19 bodies. The 14 kg (31 lb) of gold funerary goods are on display in Athens *(see p74)*.

VISITORS' CHECKLIST

Practical Information
2 km (1 mile) N of Mykínes, Peloponnese. **Road map** C4.
Tel 27510 76585 **Open** Apr–Oct: 8am–8pm daily; Nov–Mar: 8am–3pm daily. Museum: **Open** Apr–Oct: 8am–8pm daily; Nov–Mar: 8am–3pm daily. **Closed** 1 Jan, 25 Mar, Good Fri am, Easter Sun, 1 May, 25, 26 Dec. Treasury of Atreus & Museum.

Transport
to Mykínes.

Klytemnestra, after murdering her husband, Agamemnon

The Curse of the House of Atreus

King Atreus slaughtered his brother Thyestes's children and fed them to him; for this outrage, the gods laid a curse on Atreus and his descendants *(see p184)*. Thyestes's surviving daughter, Pelopia, bore her own father a son, Aigisthos, who murdered Atreus and restored Thyestes to the throne of Mycenae. But Atreus also had an heir, the energetic Agamemnon, who seized power.

Agamemnon raised a fleet to punish the Trojan Paris, who had stolen his brother's wife, Helen. He sacrificed his daughter to obtain a favourable wind. When he returned, he was murdered by his wife, Klytemnestra, and her lover – none other than Aigisthos. The murderous pair were in turn disposed of by Agamemnon's children, Orestes and Elektra.

Lion Gate
The Lion Gate was erected in the 13th century BC, when the walls were realigned to enclose Grave Circle A. It takes its name from the lions carved above the lintel.

Exploring the Tombs of Mycenae

Mycenae's nobles were entombed in shaft graves, such as Grave Circle A *(see p183)* or, later, in *tholos* ("beehive") tombs. The *tholos* tombs, found outside the palace walls, were built using successive circles of masonry, each level nudged steadily inward to narrow the diameter until the top could be closed with a single stone. The entire structure was then buried, save for an entrance approached by a *dromos* or open-air corridor.

The entrance to the Treasury of Atreus, with a gap over its lintel

the bones from previous burials. A 9-m (30-ft) long lintel stone stands over the entrance; weighing almost 120 tonnes (264,550 lb), it is still not known how it was hoisted into place, and is a tribute to Mycenaean building skills.

The treasury is also known as the Tomb of Agamemnon. However, the legendary king and commander of the Trojan expedition *(see pp58–9)* could not have been buried here, as the construction of the tomb predates the estimated period of the Trojan War by more than 100 years.

Treasury of Atreus

The Treasury of Atreus *(see p183)* is the most outstanding of the *tholos* tombs. Situated at the southern end of the site, the tomb dates from the 14th century BC and is one of only two double-chambered tombs in Greece. It has a 36-m (120-ft) *dromos* flanked by dressed stone and a small ossuary (the second chamber) which held

Tomb of Klytemnestra

Of the other *tholos* tombs, only the so-called Tomb of Klytemnestra, which is situated just west of the Lion Gate, is as well preserved as that of Atreus. It is a small, single-chambered sepulchre with narrower and more steeply inclined walls, but the finely masoned *dromos* and similar

Heinrich Schliemann

Born in Mecklenburg, Germany, Heinrich Schliemann (1822–90) was self-educated and by the age of 47 had become a millionaire, expressly to fund his archaeological digs. Having discovered Troy and demonstrated the factual basis of Homer's epics, he came to Mycenae in 1874 and commenced digging in Grave Circle A. On discovering a gold death mask which had preserved the skin of a royal skull, he proclaimed: "I have gazed upon the face of Agamemnon!" Although archaeologists have since dated the mask to 300 years earlier than any historical Trojan warrior, the discovery corroborated Homer's description of "well-built Mycenae, rich in gold".

triangular air hole over the entrance (which also relieved pressure on the lintel) date it to the same period.

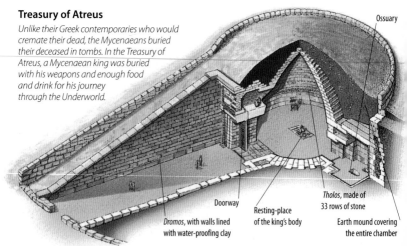

Treasury of Atreus

Unlike their Greek contemporaries who would cremate their dead, the Mycenaeans buried their deceased in tombs. In the Treasury of Atreus, a Mycenaean king was buried with his weapons and enough food and drink for his journey through the Underworld.

Ossuary

Doorway

Resting-place of the king's body

Dromos, with walls lined with water-proofing clay

Tholos, made of 33 rows of stone

Earth mound covering the entire chamber

⑯ Ancient Tiryns
Τίρυνθα

4 km (2 miles) NW of Náfplio, Pelo-ponnese. **Road map** C4. **Tel** 27520 22657. 🚌 **Open** Apr–Oct: 8am–8pm Mon–Fri, 8am–3pm Sat & Sun; Nov–Mar: 8am–3pm daily. 🅿

The 13th-century BC citadel of Tiryns confirms Homer's epithet "mighty-walled". A 700-m (2,300-ft) circuit of Cyclopean walls (named after the giants who could be imagined manoeuvering the huge blocks into place) attains a thickness of 8 m (26 ft). The fortifications, over double their present height, were necessarily stronger than those of Mycenae since Tiryns was not on a naturally strong site. The bluff on which it stood was only 18 m (59 ft) higher than the surrounding plain which, in ancient times, was a salt marsh.

An inclined ramp to the east, designed with sharp turns to expose attackers' unshielded sides, leads to the massive middle gate, the lintel of which has long been missing. At the southern end of the complex, beyond and beneath the vanished inner gate, a gallery with a pointed corbel ceiling has had its walls polished by the fleeces of sheep which have sheltered here for centuries. On the west side, a stone stairway between inner and outer walls, leading to a postern gate, has been completely preserved. The lower, northern acropolis was the last to be enclosed and was used to protect commoners, animals and (as at Mycenae) a water supply.

Environs
The early 13th-century Byzantine church of the Panagías rears up startlingly in the cemetery at **Agía Triáda**, a village which is 5 km (3 miles) north of Tiryns. The walls are constructed of

The remnants of the Tower of Theseus, Ancient Troezen

ancient masonry to shoulder height; above that, at the southeast corner of the building, the builders have inserted an entire Classical grave *stele*.

Further north, the **Argive Heraion** was the Archaic and Classical religious centre of the Argolid. The most impressive remains are those of a late 5th-century BC temple. Home to the priestesses of Hera, and a huge ivory-and-gold cult statue of the goddess, the temple was flanked by stoas, identifiable by remaining column stumps. Above the temple is the ledge where the Achaian leaders swore loyalty to Agamemnon before sailing for Troy. To the west, complete with drain-gutter,

stands the "Peristyle Building" where *symposia* were hosted.

🏛 Argive Heraion
10 km (6 miles) N of Tiryns. **Open** 8am–3pm daily.

⑰ Náfplio
See pp186–7.

⑱ Epidaurus
See pp188–9.

⑲ Ancient Troezen
Τροιζήνα

60 km (37 miles) E of Náfplio, Peloponnese. **Road map** D4. **Open** unrestricted access.

Near the modern village of Troizína are the sparse ruins of ancient Troezen, the legendary birthplace of the hero Theseus and the setting for Euripides' incestuous tragedy *Hippolytus*. Remains from many eras are scattered over a wide area; most conspicuous are three Byzantine chapels known as *Episkopí*, from the time when this was the seat of the Bishops of Damála.

The town was built on a high bluff isolated by two ravines; the westerly Damála Gorge is sheer, and half an hour's walk up it, a natural rock arch called the "Devil's Bridge" spans the canyon. Near the lower end of the gorge stands the "Tower of Theseus", Hellenistic at its base, medieval higher up.

Foundations of the Argive Heraion, seen at dawn

⑰ Náfplio

Ναύπλιο

With its marble pavements, looming castles and remarkably homogenous architecture, Náfplio is the most elegant town in mainland Greece. It emerged from obscurity in the 13th century and endured many sieges during the struggles between Venice and Turkey for the ports of the Peloponnese. The medieval quarter, to the west, is mostly a product of the second Venetian occupation (1686–1715). From 1829 until 1834, the town was the first capital of liberated Greece.

View over Náfplio from the stairway to the Palamídi fortress

Exploring Náfplio

Defended to the south by the Akronafplía and Palamídi fortresses and to the north by Boúrtzi castle, Náfplio occupies the northern side of a peninsula at the head of the Argolic Gulf. Since the Venetian period, **Plateía Syntágmatos** has been the hub of public life, and still looks much as it did three centuries ago when a couple of mosques were erected by the victorious Ottomans. One stands at the east end of the square and now houses a cinema; Vouleftikó Mosque, to the south, was where the Greek parliament *(voulí)* first met. West of the bus station, **Agios Geórgios** cathedral was built as a mosque during the first Ottoman occupation (1540–1686). Also converted is the **Catholic church**, another early mosque near the top of Potamiánou, which contains a

President Kapodístrias

monument honouring fallen philhellenes, including George Washington's nephew. Four Turkish fountains survive from the second Turkish occupation (1715–1822). The most famous are the scroll-arched one behind the "Cinema" Mosque and another opposite **Agios Spyrídon** on Kapodistríou; this is near where President Kapodístrias was assassinated on 9 October 1831. There are less elaborate Ottoman fountains up the steps at number 9 Tertsétou, and

at the corner of Potamiánou and Kapodistríou.

🏛 Archaeological Museum

Plateía Syntágmatos. **Tel** 27520 27502. **Open** 8am–3pm Tue–Sun. ♿

Exhibits here largely centre on Mycenaean artifacts from various local sites, including Tiryns *(see p185)*. Noteworthy are a Neolithic *thylastro* (baby-bottle), a late Helladic octopus vase, a full set of bronze Mycenaean armour and a complete Mycenaean boar's tusk helmet. There is also a large selection of Prehistoric, Archaic and Classical pottery.

🏛 Folk Art Museum

Vas. Alexandrou 1. **Tel** 27520 28947. **Open** 9am–3pm Wed–Mon. 📷 ♿ 🌐 pli.gr

This award-winning museum, established in a former mansion by the Peloponnesian Folklore Foundation, focuses on textiles. Regional costumes are exhibited across two floors with Queen Olga's stunning blue and white wedding gown taking pride of place on the first floor. Also on the first floor are paintings by major Greek artists Giánnis Tsaroúchis and Theófilos Chatzimichaïl *(see p222)*. On the second floor are guns and an impressive grandfather clock decorated with revolutionary scenes.

🏰 Boúrtzi

NW of harbour.

This island fortress acquired its appearance during the second Venetian occupation, and until 1930, had the dubious distinction of being the local executioner's

The fortified isle of Boúrtzi, north of Náfplio harbour

residence. It defended the only navigable passage in the bay; the channel could be closed off by a chain extending from the fortress to the town.

Akronafplía

W of Palamídi. **Open** unrestricted access.

Akronafplía, also known as Its Kale ("Inner Castle" in Turkish), was the site of the Byzantine and early medieval town, and contains four Venetian castles built in sequence from west to east. The most interesting relic is the Venetian Lion of St Mark relief over the 15th-century gate just above the Catholic church. The westernmost "Castle of the Greeks" was Náfplio's ancient acropolis, now home to the clock tower, a major landmark.

Palamídi

Polyzoïdou. **Tel** 27520 28036. **Open** Apr–Oct: 8am–8pm; Nov–Mar: 8am–3pm daily. **Closed** main public hols.

Palamídi, named after the Homeric hero Palamedes, the son of Náfplios and

Palamídi fortress seen from the isle of Boúrtzi

Kliméni, is a huge Venetian citadel built between 1711 and 1714. It was designed to withstand all contemporary artillery, though it fell to the Ottomans in 1715 after a mere one-week siege, and to the Greek rebels led by Stáïkos Staïkópoulos on 30 November 1822, after an 18-month campaign.

The largest such complex in Greece, Palamídi consists of a single curtain wall enclosing seven self-sufficient forts, now named after Greek heroes; the gun slits are aimed at each other as well as outward, in case an enemy managed to penetrate the defences. Fort Andréas was the Venetian

VISITORS' CHECKLIST

Practical Information
Peloponnese. **Road map** C4.
👤 12,000. ℹ️ Ikostíspémptis Martíou 24 (27520 24444).
Open 9am–1pm & 4–8pm daily.
🎭 Náfplio Cultural Festival: Jul.

Transport
🚌 corner of Polyzoïdou.
🚍 Syngroú.

headquarters, with a Lion of St Mark in relief over its entrance. The Piazza d'Armi, from where Náfplio assumes toy-town dimensions below you, offers arguably the best views in the country. At the summit, an eighth fort, built by the Ottomans, looks south towards Karathóna beach.

Environs
The 12th-century convent of **Agía Moní** nestles 4 km (2 miles) outside Náfplio; the octagonal dome-drum rests on four columns with Corinthian capitals. Just outside the walls, in an orchard, the Kánathos fountain still springs from a niche decorated with animal reliefs; this was ancient Amymone, where the goddess Hera bathed each year to renew her virginity.

Náfplio Town Centre

1. Archaeological Museum
2. Plateía Syntágmatos
3. Folk Art Museum
4. Agios Geórgios
5. Agios Spyrídon
6. Catholic Church
7. Akronafplía

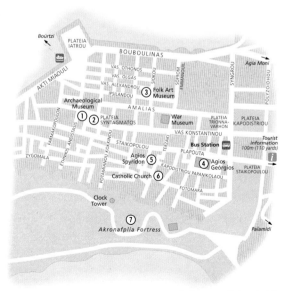

⑱ Epidaurus
Επίδαυρος

Though most renowned for its magnificent theatre, the Sanctuary of Epidaurus was an extensive therapeutic and religious centre, dedicated to the healing god Asklepios. A mortal physician deified by Zeus after his death for retrieving a patient from the underworld, Asklepios was depicted in his temple here clutching a staff and flanked by a dog and a serpent – common symbols of natural wisdom. This sanctuary was active from the 6th century BC until at least the 2nd century AD, when the traveller-historian Pausanias recorded a visit.

Dusk over Epidaurus during a modern production at the theatre

The Theatre

Designed by Polykleitos the Younger late in the 4th century BC, the theatre is well known for its near-perfect acoustics which are endlessly demonstrated by tour group leaders. Owing to the sanctuary's relative remoteness, its masonry was never pilfered, and it remained undiscovered until the 1970s. It has the only circular *orchestra* (stage) to have survived from antiquity, though the altar that once stood in the centre has now gone. Two side corridors, or *paradoi*, gave the actors access to the stage; each had a monumental gateway whose pillars have now been

Foundations of the *tholos* building in the Asklepieion

re-erected. Behind the *orchestra* and facing the auditorium stand the remains of the *skene*, the main reception hall, and the *proskenion* which was used by performers as an extension of the stage. Today, the theatre is still the venue for a popular summer festival of ancient drama.

The Asklepieion

Most of the Asklepieion, or Sanctuary of Asklepios, is being re-excavated and many of its monuments are off-limits. One of the accessible sites is the *propylaia*, or monumental gateway, at the north edge of the sanctuary, its original entrance. Also preserved are a ramp and some buckled pavement from the Sacred Way which led north from the gateway to the coastal town of ancient Epidaurus. At the northwestern end of the

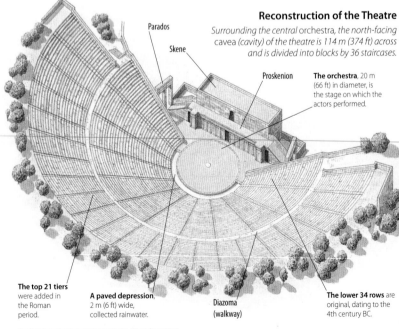

Reconstruction of the Theatre

Surrounding the central orchestra, *the north-facing* cavea (cavity) *of the theatre is 114 m (374 ft) across and is divided into blocks by 36 staircases.*

Parados

Skene

Proskenion

The orchestra, 20 m (66 ft) in diameter, is the stage on which the actors performed.

The top 21 tiers were added in the Roman period.

A paved depression, 2 m (6 ft) wide, collected rainwater.

Diazoma (walkway)

The lower 34 rows are original, dating to the 4th century BC.

Overview of today's site showing the stadium at the bottom (west)

sanctuary stand the remains of the *tholos* (a circular building of uncertain function, also designed by Polykleitos), whose concentric passages are thought to have been used either as a pit for sacred serpents, or possibly as the locale for rites by the cult's priests. Patients slept in the *enkoimitírion* – a hall north of the *tholos* where they would await a diagnostic dream or a visit from the harmless serpents. Therapeutic mineral springs, which are still on tap beside the museum, also played a part in the curing of patients who were brought here. Only the foundations of Asklepios's temple have survived, lying to the east of the *tholos*.

Another undisturbed point is the late Classical stadium south of the *tholos*. With intact rows of stone benches and a starting line still visible, this was used during the quadrennial festival in honour of Asklepios. The Romans built an odeion inside the Hellenistic gymnasium, to host the festival's musical contests.

Environs
The adjacent village of Lygourió reflects the importance of the region during Byzantine times. There are three Byzantine churches, the most distinguished being the 14th-century **Koímisis tis Theotókou**, which has superb early medieval frescoes.

The Origins of Greek Drama

Greek drama developed from ritual role-play at festivals of Dionysos *(see p56)*. First came group dancing – 6th-century BC Athenian vases show groups elaborately costumed, often as animals. In the late 6th century BC, the first Greek theatres appeared: rectangular (later round) spaces with seats on three sides. Singing and dancing choruses were joined by individual actors, whose masks made visible at a distance the various character roles, all played by just three male actors. The depiction of animal choruses on vases suggests humorous presentation, but the earliest plays in Athens were tragedies, staged in sets of three by a single writer *(see p61)*, in which episodes from epic poems and mythology were acted out. Historical events were rarely dramatized as they were politically sensitive. Comedy became part of the dramatic festival at Athens only in the 480s BC. Theatre was mass entertainment and had to cater for large numbers – during the Roman period, the theatre at Epidaurus could hold 13,000 people – but it is uncertain whether women were permitted to attend the performances.

Masks were worn by actors to express the personality of the characters they played.

Souvenir statuettes, such as this terracotta figurine of a sinister character from one of the later comedies, could be bought as mementos after performances.

The chorus, though chiefly an impersonal commentator, often spoke directly to the characters, questioning them on the wisdom of their actions.

⑳ Monemvasía
Μονεμβασία

A fortified town built on two levels on a rock rearing 350 m (1,150 ft) above the sea, Monemvasía well deserves its nickname, "the Gibraltar of Greece". A town of 50,000 in its 15th-century prime, Monemvasía enjoyed centuries of existence as a semi-autonomous city-state, living off the commercial acumen (and occasional piracy) of its fleets and its strategic position astride the sea lanes from Italy to the Black Sea. Exceptionally well defended, it was never taken by force but fell only through protracted siege *(see p192)*. Though the upper town is in ruins, most of the lower town is restored.

Pathway to Upper Town
A paved stair-street zigzags up the cliff face from the lower town to the tower gate of the upper town *(see p192)*.

★ Agía Sofía
Standing at the summit of Monemvasía, this beautiful 13th-century church is the only intact remnant of the upper town *(see p192)*.

Panagía Myrtidiótissa
The façade of this 18th-century church sports a Byzantine inscription and a double-headed eagle from an earlier Byzantine church.

"The Gibraltar of Greece"
Monemvasía was severed from the mainland by an earthquake in AD 375, remaining an island until the causeway was built in the 6th century.

VISITORS' CHECKLIST

Practical Information
Peloponnese. **Road map** C5.
🏛 800. ℹ 27320 61210
(number for the tourist police, available during summer).
Mosque Museum: **Tel** 27320 61403. **Open** 8am–3pm Tue–Sun.
Closed Mon & main public hols.

Transport
🚌 Main square. 🚌 Géfira.

Christós Elkómenos
Restored in 1697, this 13th-century cathedral with its Venetian belfry is stark inside; the only decoration is the plaque of two peacocks above the door.

★ Walls
The 16th-century walls are 900 m (2,953 ft) long and up to 30 m (98 ft) high. Much of the parapet can be walked.

KEY

① **The mosque** has been refurbished as a museum to display local finds, including some fine marble works.

② **Western gate**

③ **The birthplace** of prominent poet and communist Giánnis Rítsos (1909–90) is marked by a plaque and a bust near the front gate of his house.

④ **Agios Nikólaos**, begun in 1703, resembles Myrtidiótissa in its masonry, cruciform plan and cement-covered dome.

⑤ **The east gate** opens on to a former burial ground known as Lípsoma.

⑥ **Panagía Chrysafítissa** has its bell hanging from a cypress tree.

⑦ **The sea gate** gave access to the sea when the main port was threatened.

The cliff-top church of Agía Sofía, at dawn, Monemvasía upper town

The Siege of Monemvasía

The siege of Monemvasía by the Greeks, early in the War of Independence *(see pp44–5)*, began on 28 March 1821. Due to a Greek ruse, the town's Turkish garrison was badly supplied with food, and reinforcements failed to arrive. By late June, both Christians and Muslims were forced to eat weeds, cats and mice, some even resorting to cannibalism. Turkish civilians in the lower town urged surrender, but the garrison of the upper town refused. The besiegers also seemed set to give up, but one night, the Greek commander inside the town convinced three messengers to swim from the Portello Gate to the revolutionary forces on the mainland, giving them word to persevere. They did, and on 1 August, the Turks surrendered, handing over the keys of the city to the Greek Prince Kantakouzinós.

The taking of Monemvasía by Prince Kantakouzinós

Exploring the Upper Town

First fortified in the 6th century as a refuge from raiding Avars, the upper town is the oldest part of Monemvasía. Largely in ruins, the area is now under the protection of the Greek archaeological service. Though in medieval times it was the most densely populated part of

Ruins of Monemvasía's 13th-century fortress

the peninsula, the upper town is deserted today, the last resident having departed in 1911.

A path climbs the cliff face above the town's northwestern corner, leading to an entrance gate which still has its iron slats. Directly ahead, a track leads to the summit's best-preserved building, the church of **Agía Sofía**. It was founded by Emperor Andronikos II (1282–1328) in emulation of Dafní monastery *(see pp156–7)* near Athens. With its 16-sided dome, the church perches on the brink of the northerly cliff and is visible from a considerable distance inland. The west portico is Venetian, while the niche on the south wall dates from its use as a mosque. A few frescoes surviving from the early 14th century are badly faded, but the *Ancient of Days* can be discerned in the sanctuary's vault, as can the *Birth of John the Baptist* in the north vault. Carved ornamentation has fared

better, such as the marble capitals flanking the south windows, depicting mythical monsters and a richly dressed woman.

To the west are the remains of a 13th-century **fortress**, amid the debris of former barracks, guardrooms and a gunpowder magazine from the Venetian period. A vast **cistern** recalls the times of siege when great quantities of water had to be stored. Food supplies, entirely imported, were more of a problem, as was demonstrated by the siege of 1821.

Agía Paraskeví, viewed from Byzantine Geráki

㉑ Geráki
Γεράκι

Peloponnese. **Road map** C5.
🚗 2,000. 🚌

Occupying a spur of Mount Párnonas, Geráki is like a miniature Mystrás with its *kástro* overlooking the frescoed Byzantine churches on the slopes below. The polygonal **kástro** was built in 1254–5 by the Frank, Jean de Nivelet, though it was ceded in 1262 to the Byzantines, together with Monemvasía and Mystrás. Inside, 13th-century **Agios Geórgios** is a hybrid Franko-

Byzantine church, the third aisle and narthex added after 1262; a carved marble screen and varied frescoes decorate its interior. Below the west gate, 13th-century **Zoödóchou Pigís** sports a complete Gothic door and south window, while inside, later frescoes include *Christ on the Road to Calvary*. At the base of the hill, the domeless, 14th-century church of **Agía Paraskeví** has a fine *Nativity* in its cross vault, plus a painting of the donor family on the west wall.

Environs
Four more churches stand a short drive to the west in **Geráki** village. Both 12th-century Agios Athanásios and 13th-century Agios Sózon share a cross-in-square plan, with a high dome on four piers. Market edicts of the Roman Emperor Diocletian, inscribed on stone, flank the doorway of barrel-vaulted, 14th-century Agios Ioánnis Chrysóstomos, covered inside with scenes from the life of Christ and the Virgin. Tiny Evangelístria has a Pantokrátor fresco in its dome.

7th-century BC clay head of a woman, from Spárti acropolis

㉒ Spárti
Σπάρτη

Peloponnese. **Road map** C5.
🚗 20,000. 🚌

Though one of the most powerful of the Greek city-states, ancient Sparta was unfortified and has few ruins dating to its heyday. The acropolis lies 700 m (2,300 ft) northwest of the modern town centre. On the western side of the acropolis is the cavity of the Roman theatre, its masonry largely pilfered to build Mystrás, while directly east stands the long, arcaded stoa which once held shops. Of the Artemis Orthia sanctuary just east of town, where Spartan youths were flogged to prove their manhood, only some Roman seating remains. The most interesting finds are on display in the museum.

The highlight of the rich **Archaeological Museum** is the fine collection of Roman mosaics, including two lions rampant over a vase, Arion riding his dolphin, Achilles disguised as a woman on Skýros, and a portrait of Alkibiades. A Classical marble head of a warrior, possibly Leonidas I *(see p228)*, was found on the acropolis, while bas-reliefs of Underworld serpent-deities hail from a sanctuary of Apollo at Amyklés, 8 km (5 miles) south of Spárti. Bizarre ceramic masks are smaller replicas of those used in dances at the Artemis Orthia sanctuary.

🏛 **Archaeological Museum**
Agíou Níkonos & Likourgou. **Tel** 27310 28575. **Open** 8am–3pm Tue–Sun. **Closed** main public hols. 🅿 ♿

Life in Ancient Sparta

Rising to prominence around 700 BC, Sparta became one of the most powerful city-states of ancient Greece. Its power was based on rigid social and military discipline, as well as hatred of foreigners, which eventually led to its downfall as it had no allies. The "city" was made up of five villages, where the male citizens lived communally in constant readiness for war. Warriors were selected at the age of seven and subjected to rigorous training – whipping contests, with young boys as the victims, were held in the sanctuary of Artemis Orthia. Sparta was able to support its citizens as professional soldiers because it had conquered neighbouring Messenia, and the enslaved population provided all the food required. Sparta led the Greek forces against the Persians, but ceased to be a major power after defeat by Thebes in 371 BC.

5th-century BC bronze figurine of a Spartan warrior

㉓ Mystrás
Μυστράς

Majestic Mystrás occupies a panoramic site on a spur of the severe Taÿgetos range. Founded by the Franks in 1249, it soon passed to the Byzantines, under whom it became a town of 20,000 and, after 1348, the seat of the Despots of Morea. The despotate acted semi-independently and had become the last major Byzantine cultural centre by the 15th century, attracting scholars and artists from Italy and Serbia as well as Constantinople. One result was the uniquely cosmopolitan decoration of the Mystrás churches – their pastel-coloured frescoes, crowded with detail, reflect Italian Renaissance influence.

Plan of Mystrás

0 metres 100
0 yards 100

KASTRO

UPPER TOWN

LOWER TOWN

Spárti & Néos Mystrás

Key to Plan

① Lower town entrance
② Mitrópoli
③ Moní Perivléptou
④ Moní Pantánassas
⑤ Vrontóchion
⑥ Monemvasía Gate
⑦ Despots' Palace
⑧ Agía Sofía
⑨ Upper town entrance
⑩ Kástro

Exploring Mystrás

Now in ruins, Mystrás consists of a lower and upper town, linked by the Monemvasía Gate. The site can be entered from the castle at the top of the upper town or from the base of the lower town. Allow half a day for exploring the monasteries, churches, palaces and houses which line the narrow, winding streets. An unusual northwest-to-southeast alignment of the

churches is dictated by the site's steep topography.

🏛 Mitrópoli
The Mitrópoli, situated by the lower town entrance, is

The 14th-century fresco of the *Nativity* in the south vault of Moní Perivléptou

VISITORS' CHECKLIST

Practical Information
5 km (3 miles) W of Spárti, Peloponnese. **Road map** C5.
Tel 27310 83377. **Open** May–Sep: 8am–8pm daily; Oct–Apr: 8am–3pm daily. **Closed** 1 Jan, 25 Mar, Good Fri, Easter Sun, 1 May, 25 & 26 Dec.

Transport
🚌 to Néos Mystrás.

the oldest church in Mystrás. It is approached through a double courtyard. Like many Balkan cathedrals, it began life in 1291 as a barrel-vaulted nave flanked by two aisles. The domes were added early in the 1400s in a clumsy attempt to equal the architecture of the Pantánassas and Afentikó churches. Frescoes, mostly early 14th century, show the martyrdom of the church's patron (Agios Dimítrios) in the northeast vaulting, while Christ's miracles begin next to these with the *Healing of the Lepers* and continue on the southwest aisle in such scenes as the *Wedding at Cana*. In the narthex is the *Preparation of the Throne of Judgment*, flanked by angels, a theme repeated in the southwest diaconicon (sacristy). The last Byzantine emperor, Konstantínos Palaiológos, was crowned here in 1449; a double-eagle plaque marks the spot.

🏛 Moní Perivléptou
Squeezed against the rock face, the 14th-century monastery of Perivléptou has a compact, three-aisled church. Its small dome retains a fresco of the Pantokrátor, flanked by the Virgin and prophets, arranged in diminishing order of importance. The 14th-century frescoes, the most refined in Mystrás, focus on the 12 major church feasts. They include a vivid *Nativity* and *Baptism* in the south

The hillside with remains of Byzantine Mystrás, seen from the south

vault, the *Transfiguration* and *Entry into Jerusalem*, complete with playing children, in the west aisle, and *Doubting Thomas* and the *Pentecost* in the north vault, decorating the wall over the entrance.

🏠 Moní Pantánassas

Dating to 1428, Pantánassas was the last church built at Mystrás. With its decorated apses and the brickwork of its arcaded belfry it imitates Afentikó in the Vrontóchion as an eclectic architectural experiment. The highest frescoes, from 1430, are of most merit, particularly a vivid *Raising of Lazarus* in the northeast vault. Both the *Nativity* and the *Annunciation* in the southwest vault feature animals. The southeast aisle displays the *Descent into Hell*, in which Christ raises Adam and Eve from their coffins, opposite a lively *Entry into Jerusalem*.

🏠 Vrontóchion

A 13th-century monastic complex built by Abbot Pachómios, the Vrontóchion

was the cultural centre of medieval Mystrás – in the 15th century, the Neo-Platonist philosopher Geórgios Gemistós, or Plethon, (1355–1452) taught here. It has two churches; the earliest, Agioi Theódoroi, dates from 1295 and has the largest dome at Mystrás, supported on eight arches. Few frescoes survive. The early 14th-century Afentikó (or Panagía Odigítria) is richly frescoed, with six domes. The galleries and two north-side chapels are shut, but in the west gallery dome, a *Virgin Orans* (praying) and *Prophets* are visible; in the south vault, a crowded *Baptism* includes water monsters. Above the altar, apostles gesticulate towards the aura of the rising Christ in the *Ascension*. The best-preserved frescoes can be found in the north bay of the narthex.

🏛 Despots' Palace

The Despots' Palace consists of two wings which are currently being reconstructed. The northeast wing was begun by the

Franks; the northwest hall, erected after 1348 and a rare example of Byzantine civic architecture, has the throne room of the rulers of the Cantacuzene and Palaiológos dynasties. The square was a venue for public events under the despots and a marketplace under the Ottomans.

The ruins of the Despots' Palace, viewed from the south

🏠 Kástro

Flanked by sheer ravines to the south and west, and crowning the summit of the upper town, the kástro is reached by a path leading from the upper entrance which stands above the church of Agía Sofía. Built by Guillaume de Villehardouin in 1249, the Kástro retains its original Frankish design, though it was greatly altered by the Byzantines and Turks. A double circuit of curtain walls encloses two baileys, and a walkway can be taken around most of the structure, affording panoramic views over the lower town.

It was here that the German writer Goethe, in Part Two of *Faust*, set the meeting of Faust and Helen of Troy, revived after 3,000 years.

Afentikó church, part of the Vrontóchion complex

For hotels and restaurants see pp270–71 and pp287–8

㉔ Outer Máni
Έξω Μάνη

A harsh, remote region, bounded by mountains to the north, the rocky Máni was the last part of Greece to embrace Christianity, doing so in the 9th century with an enthusiasm borne out by dozens of surviving Byzantine chapels. Though well defended against invaders, the area has a history of internal feuding which led to the building of its many tower houses. A ravine at Oítylo divides Inner Máni, to the south *(see pp202–3)*, from the more fertile Outer, or Messenian, Máni which boasts some of the finest country in the Mediterranean.

VISITORS' CHECKLIST

Practical Information
Peloponnese. **Road map** C5.

Transport
🚆 🚌 Kalamáta.

Oítylo

Though administratively within the region of Lakonía, by tradition the village of Oítylo (pronounced "Itilo") belongs to the Outer Máni. It affords superb panoramic views over Limeníou Bay and across a flanking ravine, traditionally the border between the Inner and Outer Máni, to Kelefá Castle *(see p202)*. Its relatively good water supply fosters a lush setting around and below the village, with cypresses and a variety of orchard trees. Unlike most Mániot villages, Oítylo is not in economic decline. Its many fine houses include graceful 19th-century mansions. The village was capital of the Máni between the 16th and 18th centuries, and was the area's most infamous slave-trading centre; both Venetians and Turks were sold to each other here. A plaque in the square, written in French and Greek, commemorates the flight, in 1675, of 730 Oítylots to Corsica – 430 of whom were from the Stefanópoulos clan. Seeking refuge from the Turks, the Oítylots were granted passage by the Genoese and, once in Corsica, founded the villages of Paomia and Cargèse. These towns account for the stories of Napoleon's part-Mániot origins.

Environs

From the southwestern corner of Oítylo, a broad path descends west to **Moní Dekoúlou**, nestled in its own little oasis. The 18th-century church features an ornate *témblon* (wooden altar screen) and vivid original frescoes; though they have been preserved by the darkness, a torch is required to see them now. The monastery is only open in the evenings or by prior arrangement with the resident caretakers.

The village of **Néo Oítylo** stands 4 km (2 miles) south of the monastery. Quietly secluded, the village has a pebble beach with fine views.

The Mániot Feuds

By the 15th century, a number of refugee Byzantine families had settled in the Máni, the most powerful forming a local aristocracy known as the Nyklians. Feuding between clans over the inadequate land was rife, though only Nyklians had the right to construct stone towers, which attained four or five storeys and came to dominate nearly every Mániot village.

Once commenced, blood feuds could last months, even years, with periodic truces to tend to the crops. Clansmen fired at each other from facing towers, raising them in order to be able to catapult rocks on to opponents' roofs. The hostilities ended only with the total destruction or submission of the losing clan. Historically, the most important clans were those of Mavromichális at Areópoli, Grigorákis at Gýtheio and Troupákis at Kardamýli, whose members boasted of never having been completely subjugated by any foreign power. The Ottomans wisely refrained from ruling the Máni directly, but instead quietly encouraged the clans to feud in order to weaken potential rebellions, and appointed a Nyklian chieftain as *bey* (regional lord) to represent the sultan locally. Under the final *bey*, Pétros Mavromichális, the clans finally united, instigating the Greek Independence uprising on 17 March 1821 *(see pp44–5)*.

Pétros Mavromichális

Oítylo viewed from the northwest, looking towards Kelefá Castle

Agios Spyrídon south window, framed with marble reliefs

Kardamýli

Kardamýli was the lair of the Troupákis family, important rivals of the Mavromichális clan. Nicknamed Moúrtzinos, or "Bulldogs", for their tenacity in battle, they claimed to be descended from the Byzantine dynasty of Palaiológi. Olive oil *(see p279)* used to be the chief source of income for Kardamýli, but this has now been superseded by tourism.

Inland rises the ancient and medieval acropolis, heralded by twin Mycenaean chamber tombs. In Old Kardamýli (sign posted) are Troupákis-built towers, which stand alongside the 18th-century church of **Agios Spyrídon**. This building is made of Hellenistic masonry and graced by a pointed, four-storey belfry; the south window and doorway are framed by intricate marble reliefs.

Environs

Two paths lead from Kardamýli, one upstream along the **Vyrós Gorge** where two monasteries shelter beneath the cliffs; the other to the villages of Gourniés and Exochóri. A short drive to the south, **Stoúpa** is popular for its two sandy bays; novelist Níkos Kazantzákis (1883–1957) lived here briefly and partly based his Zorba the Greek character on a foreman who worked nearby. The village of **Agios Nikólaos**, a short walk to the south, curls around Outer Máni's most photogenic harbour. It has four tavernas and the closest beach is at Agios Dimítrios, 3 km (2 miles) further south.

Mount Taÿgetos

The distinctive pyramidal summit and knife-edged ridge of Mount Taÿgetos, standing at 2,404 m (7,885 ft), divides the regions of Messinía and Lakonía. Formed of limestone and densely clad in black pine and fir, the range is the watershed of the region and

Taÿgetos, seen through the Vyrós Gorge

offers several days of wilderness trekking to experienced, well-equipped mountaineers.

Anavrytí and Palaiopanagiá, on the east, and Pigádia and Kardamýli, on the west, are the usual trailhead villages. Various traverses can be made by using the Vyrós and Ríntomo gorges which drain west from the main ridge; an unstaffed alpine refuge at Varvára-Deréki, above Palaiopanagiá, is the best starting point for those wanting to head straight for the summit.

The ridge of Mount Taÿgetos with an olive grove in the foreground

㉕ Inner Máni
Μέσα Μάνη

Inner, or Lakonian, Máni is divided into two regions – the "Shadowed", western flank and the "Sunward", eastern shore. The former is famous for its numerous caves and churches, the latter for its villages which perch dramatically on crags overlooking the sea. With its era of martial glory over (*see p194*), Inner Máni is severely depopulated, its only future being as a holiday venue. Retired Athenians of Mániot descent have restored the famous towers as hunting lodges for the brief autumn shoot of quail and turtle dove.

VISITORS' CHECKLIST

Practical Information
Peloponnese. **Road map** C5.
ℹ Gýtheio (27330 29032).
Museum of the Máni: Marathonísi Islet. **Tel** 27330 22676.
Open 9am–3pm daily.
Pýrgos Diroú Caves: 12 km (7 miles) S of Areópoli. **Tel** 27330 52223. **Open** 8am–3pm daily (Jun–Sep: 9am–6pm daily).

Transport
🚌 Gýtheio. 🚌 Areópoli.

Gýtheio
The lively town of Gýtheio is the gateway to the Máni peninsula and one of the most attractive coastal towns in the southern Peloponnese. It was once the naval base of ancient Sparta (*see p193*), though the main ancient relic is a Roman theatre to the north. The town was wealthy in Roman times, when it exported the purple molluscs used for colouring imperial togas. Until World War II, Gýtheio exported acorns used in leather-tanning, gathered by women and children from nearby valleys.

The town's heart is Plateía Mavromicháli, with the quay extending to either side lined by tiled, 19th-century houses. The east-facing town enjoys sunrises over Cape Maléas and the Lakonian Gulf while snowy Mount Taÿgetos looms beyond a low ridge to the north.

In the bay, and linked to the waterfront by a causeway, lies the islet of Marathonísi, thought to be Homer's Kranaï islet. It was here that Paris of Troy and Helen spent their first night together (*see p56*). It is dominated by the Tzanetakis tower, a crenellated 18th-century fortress which now houses the **Museum of the Máni**. The subject of the exploration of the Máni in medieval times is covered on the ground floor, while the exhibits of the upper storey place the tower houses in their social context.

Environs
Standing 12 km (7 miles) to the southwest, the **Castle of Passavá** was built in 1254 by the Frankish de Neuilly clan to guard a defile between Kelefá and Oítylo. Its name stems from *passe avant*, the clan's motto, though the present building is an 18th-century Turkish construction. The Turks left the castle in 1780 after Tzanetbey Grigorákis avenged the murder of his uncle by massacring 1,000 Muslim villagers inside. Today's overgrown ruins are best approached from the southwest.

Areópoli
The Mavromichális (*see p198*) stronghold of Tsímova was renamed Areópoli, "the city of Ares" (god of war), for its role in the War of Independence (*see p44*); it was here that the Mániot uprising against the Turks was proclaimed by Pétros Mavromichális. Now the main town of the Máni, its central old quarter features two 18th-century churches: **Taxiarchón** boasts the highest bell tower in the Máni, as well as zodiacal apse reliefs, while **Agios Ioánnis**, adorned with naïve frescoes, was the chapel of the Mavromichális.

Environs
Ottoman **Kelefá Castle**, standing 10 km (6 miles) north of Areópoli, is the second castle guarding the Máni. It was built in 1670 to command the bays of Oítylo and Liméni and counter the impending Venetian invasion (*see p42*). The bastions of the pentagonal curtain walls are preserved. The castle can be

19th-century houses lining the harbour of Gýtheio

◀ Semi-ruined tower houses of Vátheia village, the architectural jewel of the Máni reached from the Areópoli–Gýtheio road (signposted) and from a footpath from Oítylo.

Pýrgos Diroú Caves

This cave system is one of the largest and most colourful in Greece. During summer, crowds take a 30-minute punt ride along the underground stream which passes through Glyfáda cavern, reflecting the overhanging stalactites. A 15-minute walk then leads to the exit. A nearby chamber, called Alepótrypa cave, is drier and just as spectacular with waterfalls and a lake. Until an earthquake closed the entrance, the cave was home to Neolithic people, and a separate **museum** chronicles their life and death.

The Shadowed Coast

Between Pýrgos Diroú and Geroliménas lies the 17-km (11-mile) shore of the Shadowed Coast. Once one of the most densely populated regions of the Máni, it is famous for its numerous Byzantine churches built between the 10th and 14th centuries. The ruins of many Mániot tower houses can also be found.

Among the finest churches is 11th-century **Taxiarchón**, at Charoúda, with its interior covered by vivid 18th-century frescoes. Heading south, the road continues to **Agios Theódoros**, at Vámvaka, where the dome is supported by

Corner turret of Ottoman Kelefá Castle, near Areópoli

carved beams; birds bearing grapes adorn its marble lintel.

Káto Gardenítsa boasts the 12th-century **Agía Soteíra**, with its frescoed iconostasis and domed narthex, while 12th-century **Episkopí**, near Stavrí, has a complete cycle of 18th-century frescoes.

Near Ano Mpoulárioi village, doorless **Agios Panteleímon** offers 10th-century frescoes (the earliest and the most primitive

in the Máni), while in the village, the 11th-century **Agios Stratigós** bears a set of 12th- and 13th-century frescoes – the *Acts of Christ* is the most distinguished.

Vátheia, 10 km (6 miles) east of Geroliménas, is one of the most dramatically located of the villages; overlooking the sea and Cape Taínaro, its bristling tower houses constitute a showpiece of local architectural history.

Tower houses of Vátheia village, viewed from the southeast

㉖ Koróni

Κορώνη

Peloponnese. **Road map** C5.
 1,400.

One of the "eyes of Venice" (along with Methóni), Koróni surveys the shipping lanes between the Adriatic and Crete. It stands at the foot of a Venetian castle, begun in 1206, whose walls now shelter the huge **Timíou Prodrómou** convent. A Byzantine chapel and foundations of an Artemis temple stand by the gate of the convent whose cells and chapels command fine views.

The town, lying beneath the castle and divided by stepped streets, dates to 1830. Little has changed here and many houses retain elaborate wrought-iron balconies, horizontal-slat shutters and tile "beaks" on the undulating roofs. A lively seafront is the sole concession to tourism.

Battle of Navarino

An unexpected naval engagement which decided the War of Independence *(see pp44–5)*, the Battle of Navaríno took place on 20 October 1827. Victory here by the French, Russian and English allies over the Ottoman fleet broke the Greek-Ottoman deadlock and resolved the problem of the sultan's refusal of an armistice. The allied fleet of 27 ships, commanded by admirals Codrington, de Rigny and Heyden, entered Navaríno Bay where Ibrahim Pasha's armada of 89 lay anchored. The outnumbered allies merely intended to intimidate Ibrahim into leaving the bay, but were fired upon, and a full-scale battle ensued. By nightfall, three-quarters of the Ottoman fleet was sunk, with negligible allied casualties; Greek independence was now inevitable. The admirals are honoured by an obelisk in their namesake square in Pýlos.

The dramatic *Battle of Navaríno*, painted by Louis Ambroise Garneray (1783–1857)

㉗ Methóni

Μεθώνη

Peloponnese. **Road map** B5.
 1,300.

Methóni, a key Venetian port, controlled the lucrative pilgrim trade to Palestine after 1209. With the sea on three sides, its rambling **castle** is defended on its landward side by a Venetian moat, bridged by the French in 1828. The structure combines Venetian, Ottoman and even French military architecture. The remains within the walls include two ruined *hammams* (baths), a Venetian church, minaret bases and the main street. Boúrtzi, an islet fortified by the Turks, stands beyond the Venetian sea-gate.

Castle
Open 8am–3pm daily.
Tel 27230 28759.

㉘ Pýlos

Πύλος

Peloponnese. **Road map** C5.
 2,500.

The town of Pýlos, originally known as Avaríno (later Navaríno) after the Avar tribes which invaded the area in the 6th century, is French in design, like Methóni. Life is confined to Plateía Trión Navárchon and the seafront on either side.

To the west, the castle of **Niókastro**, Ottoman and Venetian in origin, was extensively repaired by the French after 1828; their barracks are now a gallery of antiquarian engravings by the artist René Puaux (1878–1938). An institute of underwater archaeology is situated in the former dungeons of the hexagonal keep. The roof gives views over the outer bailey, immense Navaríno Bay and Sfaktiría island, site of a memorable Athenian victory over the Spartans.

The fortified islet of Boúrtzi, off the coast at Methóni, with its 16th-century octagonal tower

The arcaded former mosque, now Sotíras church, Pýlos

The perimeter walls are dilapidated, but it is possible to walk along the parapet, starting from the imposing west bastion overlooking the mouth of the bay, and finishing above the east gate. The domed and arcaded church of **Sotíras**, once a mosque, is the only medieval survival in the outer bailey.

🏛 Niókastro

Town centre. **Tel** 27230 22010. **Open** 8am–3pm Tue–Sun. **Closed** main public hols. 🖼 🔣 limited.

Environs

Boat tours visit a number of memorials on and around **Sfaktiría**, which commemorate those sailors lost in the Battle of Navaríno, foreign philhellenes and revolutionary heroes.

The north end of Navaríno Bay, 11 km (7 miles) north of Pýlos, has excellent beaches, especially **Voïdokoiliá** lagoon, where Telemachos, Odysseus's son, disembarked to seek news of his father from King Nestor. You can walk up the dunes to **Spiliá tou Néstora**, an impressively large cave, which may have been the inspiration for Homer's cave in which Nestor and Neleus kept their cows. A more strenuous path continues to Palaiókastro, the ancient acropolis and Franco Venetian castle, built on Mycenaean foundations.

🏛 Nestor's Palace
Ανάκτορο του Νέστορα

16 km (10 miles) NE of Pýlos, Peloponnese. **Road map** B5. 🚌 Site: **Tel** 27630 31437. **Closed** for renovation; may open in 2015. Museum **Tel** 27630 31358. **Open** 8:30am–3pm Tue–Sun. **Closed** public hols. 🖼 🔣 limited.

Discovered in 1939, the 13th-century BC palace of Mycenaean King Nestor was excavated by Carl Blegen from 1952. Hundreds of tablets in the ancient Linear B script were found, as well as a bathtub and olive oil jugs (the contents of which fuelled the devastating fire of 1200 BC). Today, only waist-high walls and column bases suggest the typical Mycenaean plan of a two-storey complex around a central hall. The **museum**, 3 km (2 miles) away in Chóra, has frescoes from the palace.

🏛 Ancient Messene
Αρχαία Μεσσήνη

34 km (21 miles) NW of Kalamáta, Peloponnese. **Road map** C5. **Tel** 27240 51201. 🚌 Site: **Open** 8am–8pm daily. Museum: **Open** 9am–4pm daily. **Closed** main public hols. 🖼

Ancient Messene is now confusingly known as Ithómi – named after the mountain that sits overhead. It is an underrated, intriguing site, still undergoing excavation. The city walls are 9 km (6 miles) long and date from the 4th century BC. They enclose a vast area that incorporates the foundations of a Zeus temple, and the acropolis on Mount Ithómi to the northeast. The massive, double Arcadia Gate situated on the north side is flanked by square towers.

The archaeological zone includes the picturesque village of Mavrommáti, whose water is still supplied by the ancient Klepsýdra fountain at the heart of the site. Below the village, you will find an odeion (amphitheatre), a *bouleuterion* (council hall), stoas and a monumental stairway, all of which surround the foundations of an Asklepios temple. Just a little way further down the hill from here lies a well-preserved stadium.

Remains of the Arcadia Gate, with its fallen lintel, Ancient Messene

CENTRAL AND WESTERN GREECE

EPIRUS · THESSALY · STEREÁELLÁDA

Central and Western Greece encompasses many of the lesser-known regions of mainland Greece and is, therefore, little touched by tourism. Though Epirus has produced a distinctive and largely autonomous culture, Stereá Elláda has always been of strategic importance, with the pass at Thermopylae and the Vale of Tempe providing invasion routes into the very heart of Greece.

This region of Greece is dominated by the central plain of Thessaly (the former bed of an inland sea) and the sights of interest lie largely on the periphery. Isolated by the Píndos mountains, the Epirus region, to the west, has the strongest of regional identities, having played a minor role in ancient Greece and maintained a large degree of autonomy under the Turks. The regional capital, Ioánnina, is thus a fascinating mixture of Turkish architecture and the local traditions of silversmithing and woodcarving.

To the east, the grand Katára Pass, guarded in Ottoman times by the town of Métsovo, cuts through the mountains, providing access to the Byzantine Metéora

monasteries which soar on the summits of the area's steeply eroded peaks.

In Stereá Elláda, one of the country's most important ancient sights, the ruins of the Delphic Oracle, stands only a short drive away from the Monastery of Osios Loúkas, perhaps the finest of late Byzantine buildings, decorated with some of the period's greatest mosaics.

While the Gulf of Corinth has many popular resorts, the towns of Lamía, Arta, Tríkala, and Mesolóngi (where the British poet Lord Byron died) make few concessions to tourism and so offer a more accurate picture of life in Greece today: its markets, tavernas, church-going and the evening *vólta*.

Megálo Pápigko, one of the many remote, once-isolated villages of Zagória in the Epirus region

◀ The 18th-century Misíus bridge over Voïdomátis river in the Víkos Gorge, Epirus

Exploring Central and Western Greece

Stretching from Attica in the south to Macedonia in the north, the vast expanse of Central and Western Greece has a little of everything, from excellent beaches to the venerable towns of Ioánnina and Métsovo with their craftsmen's guilds and Ottoman heritage. The Pílio offers the best combination of scenery and coastal resorts, while no one should miss the two prime attractions of Ancient Delphi, site of the oracle of Apollo, and the Byzantine splendour of the monasteries of Metéora. Walkers should head north where, in addition to the Víkos Gorge, the Píndos Mountains have several of Greece's highest peaks. The flora and fauna are both splendid here, especially in spring, but wildlife enthusiasts should not miss the wonderful wetlands around Mesolóngi and the beautiful Amvrakikós Gulf, near Arta.

Key

═══ Motorway
═ ═ Road under construction
─── Major road
······ Minor road
─── Scenic route
─··─ Main railway
▬▬ National border
▬▬ Regional border

Agíou Nikoláou, one of Metéora's soaring monasteries

Sights at a Glance

1. Píndos Mountains
2. Zagória
4. Métsovo
5. Ioánnina
6. Dodóni
7. Párga
8. Kassópi
9. Préveza
10. Arta
11. *Metéora pp220–21*
12. Trikala
13. Vale of Tempe
14. *Pílio pp222–4*
15. *Thebes*
16. *Monastery of Osios Loúkas pp226–7*
17. Mount Parnassus
18. Lamía and Thermopylae
19. *Ancient Delphi pp232–5*
20. Gulf of Corinth
21. Mesolóngi

Walks

3. Víkos Gorge

For hotels and restaurants see pp271–2 and pp288–90

Doric columns of the Temple of Apollo, Delphi

Locator Map

Getting Around

There are domestic airports at Préveza, which receives European charter flights in summer, Larisa and Ioánnina. Internal flights are fairly inexpensive if travelling from another part of Greece, but within the region, a car is by far the best way to travel. Central Greece's main roads are generally good, though twisting mountain routes can make journeys longer than they seem on the map. The E55 is a good, fast road, as are the other major E roads which circle the region. Trains serve only a small part of the eastern side of the area, though bus connections are good between major towns, with services to smaller villages.

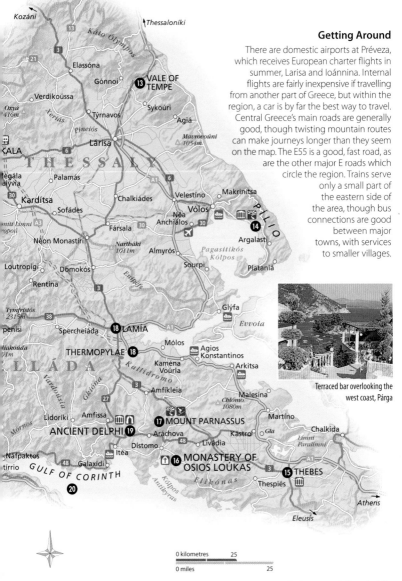

Terraced bar overlooking the west coast, Párga

0 kilometres   25

0 miles   25

Lake Drakolímni, behind the sheer cliffs of Astráka

❶ Píndos Mountains

Οροσειρά Πίνδου

Epirus. **Road map** B2. ✈ 🚌 Ioánnina. 🛈 Dodónis 39, Ioánnina (26510 41868). **Open** 8am–3pm Mon–Fri.

The Píndos is a vast range stretching from the Greek border with Albania south beyond Métsovo. It extends east into Macedonia, and west towards the Ionian Sea, incorporating two national parks, Greece's second longest gorge and its second highest mountain, Oros Smólikas, standing at 2,640 m (8,660 ft). The Píndos National Park lies just inside western Macedonia, between Métsovo and Vovoúsa, while the Víkos-Aóos National Park is a boot-shaped area encompassing the Víkos Gorge (*see p212*) and the Aóos River.

The peaks are snow-covered from October until May, when the melting snows water the ground, producing swathes of lilac crocus, gentians, grass-of-Parnassus and many species of orchid (*see p27*). The protection offered by the parks provides the visitor with an increased chance of seeing roe deer, wild boar and the European wild cat, all of which exist in small numbers.

Smólikas is accessible during summertime for those who are well equipped and prepared for camping or staying in mountain huts. Slightly easier to reach from the fascinating Zagorian villages by the Víkos Gorge are Gamíla 2,500 m (8,200 ft) and Astráka 2,440 m (8,000 ft), while the two mountain lakes both called Drakolímni are each worth the effort it takes to get to them. One is below Gamíla, near a sheer drop to the Aóos River, while the other stands beneath Smólikas.

Although there are good walking guides and maps of the area, with mountain huts to stay in and accommodation in some of the larger villages, visitors should not venture into the mountains unless they are experienced walkers. The weather can change quickly, and in many places you will be a long way from any kind of settlement – though this is one of the main attractions of the Píndos Mountains. They show the rugged side of Greece, offering remote valleys and routes where few visitors venture.

Wildlife of the Píndos Mountains

Visitors to the coastal lowlands are often sceptical when told that wolves and bears still survive in Greece. However, despite the severe erosion of their natural habitat over the last 20 years, both European wolves and European brown bears can be found. The Píndos mountains, and particularly the northern regions towards Albania, continue to harbour the greatest numbers of these endangered and now protected creatures. They are extremely wary of man, having been persecuted by farmers and goatherds down the centuries. Therefore, visitors should consider themselves very fortunate if they see a bear. Wolves are just as hard to see but more evident, as they can often be heard howling at dawn and dusk, and will even respond to imitations of their howls. They pose no real threat to visitors.

The silver European wolf, a native of the region

One of the 80 European brown bears of the northern Píndos

❷ Zagória

Zayópia

Epirus. **Road map** B2.

Some of Europe's most spectacular scenery can be found only 25 km (15 miles) north of Ioánnina *(see p214)*, in the area known as Zagória. Though the soil is largely uncultivable, on the forested hillsides, some 45 traditional Epirot villages still survive; many of them boast imposing *archontiká* (mansions) dating to prosperous 18th- and 19th-century Ottoman times when Zagória was granted autonomy.

Vlach and Sarakatsan shepherds *(see p213)* make up most of the settled population. Over the winter months, the shepherds used to turn to crafts, forming into guilds of itinerant masons and wood-carvers, who would travel the Balkans selling their trades. This hard and ancient way of life is under threat, as the villagers, and especially the younger generation, prefer to earn their living from tourism.

A series of arched packhorse bridges are among the most memorable monuments to the skills of the local people and are unique features of the region.

Vítsa village, by the Víkos Gorge

Two especially fine examples can be seen at either end of the village of **Kípoi**. Southwestern Zagória is the busiest area, with a bus from Ioánnina to Monodéndri bringing in walkers and climbers. Some of the villages in the east of the region, such as **Vrysochóri**, were refuges for guerrillas during World War II and therefore burnt by the Germans; they have recovered only slowly.

Near the almost deserted village of **Vradéto**, a 15th-century muletrack zigzags its way up a steep rockface beyond which the path leads to a stunning view of the spectacular Víkos Gorge *(see p212)*. **Monodéndri**, opposite Vradéto, is the usual starting point for the gorge trail, though another path can be taken from **Vítsa**. Nearby are the two villages of **Megálo Pápigko** and **Mikró Pápigko**. They are 4 km (2 miles) apart and their names reflect their sizes, but even "big" Pápigko is no more than a scattering of houses around cobbled streets, with a choice of restaurants, and rooms available in renovated mansions.

Further south, though still surrounded by mountains, is the relatively thriving village of **Tsepélovo**. It has a bus service to Ioánnina and a restored mansion which provides accommodation, as well as a number of *pensions* and tavernas. Its cobbled streets and slate-roofed houses provide a perfect portrait of a Zagórian village.

Packhorse bridge near the village of Kípoi

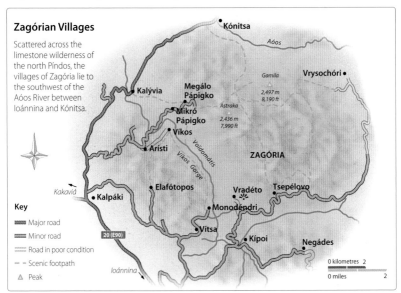

Zagórian Villages

Scattered across the limestone wilderness of the north Píndos, the villages of Zagória lie to the southwest of the Aóos River between Ioánnina and Kónitsa.

Kónitsa

Aóos

Gamila
Vrysochóri

Kalývia

Megálo Pápigko

2,497 m
8,190 ft

Astraka

Mikró Pápigko

2,436 m
7,990 ft

Víkos

Arísti

Voïdomátis

Víkos Gorge

ZAGÓRIA

Elafótopos

Vradéto

Tsepélovo

Kakaviá

Kalpáki

Monodéndri

Vítsa

20 (E90)

Kípoi

Negádes

Ioánnina

Key

▦ Major road

▬ Minor road

═ Road in poor condition

- - Scenic footpath

△ Peak

0 kilometres   2

0 miles   2

❾ Víkos Gorge Walk

To trek the length of the Víkos Gorge is to undertake what is arguably the greatest walk in Greece. Carved by the Voïdomátis River, the deeply eroded limestone walls rise to 915 m (3,000 ft). The gorge cuts through the Víkos-Aóos National Park, established in 1975. Cairns and waymarks define the route which snakes through the boulder-strewn ravine bed and continues up through stands of beech, chestnut and maple to the higher ground. Egyptian vultures, are commonly seen circling in the thermals, and lizards and tortoises abound. The walk begins at Monodéndri, but landslides and lack of maintenance make the route challenging, and should only be attempted by experienced hikers. There is a shorter 4-km (2-mile) walk between the northern villages of Mikró Pápigko and Víkos.

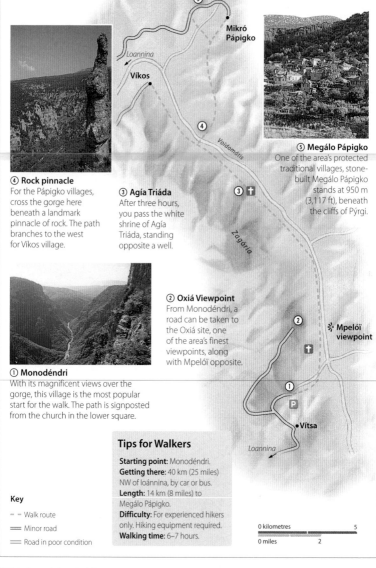

④ Rock pinnacle
For the Pápigko villages, cross the gorge here beneath a landmark pinnacle of rock. The path branches to the west for Víkos village.

③ Agía Triáda
After three hours, you pass the white shrine of Agía Triáda, standing opposite a well.

⑤ Megálo Pápigko
One of the area's protected traditional villages, stone-built Megálo Pápigko stands at 950 m (3,117 ft), beneath the cliffs of Pýrgi.

② Oxiá Viewpoint
From Monodéndri, a road can be taken to the Oxiá site, one of the area's finest viewpoints, along with Mpelói opposite.

※ **Mpelói viewpoint**

① Monodéndri
With its magnificent views over the gorge, this village is the most popular start for the walk. The path is signposted from the church in the lower square.

Tips for Walkers

Starting point: Monodéndri.
Getting there: 40 km (25 miles) NW of Ioánnina, by car or bus.
Length: 14 km (8 miles) to Megálo Pápigko.
Difficulty: For experienced hikers only. Hiking equipment required.
Walking time: 6–7 hours.

Key

‐ ‐ Walk route

═ Minor road

═ Road in poor condition

0 kilometres ___ 5
0 miles ___ 2

For keys to symbols *see back flap*

❹ Métsovo

Μέτσοβο

Epirus. Road map: B2. 🏔 3,500. 🚌
ℹ️ 26560 41233.

Situated close by the Katára
Pass (the route crossing the
Píndos Mountains), Métsovo
has a vitality unique among
Greek mountain towns. It
was originally a small village
inhabited by Vlach shepherds,
but it became one of the
region's most important
commercial centres after being
granted tax privileges in return
for guarding the pass during
Ottoman times *(see pp42–3)*.
Local merchant families
invested their new wealth
in the town and continue
to do so today by providing
endowments and grants to
encourage industry among
the local craftspeople.

One such family was the
Tosítsas, and some idea of
the size of their wealth can be
gained by touring the rebuilt
18th-century **Archontikó
Tosítsa**, which has been
preserved as a museum. Rising
to three floors, the mansion
contains an armoury and
washroom on the ground floor,
with huge wood-panelled
reception rooms and bedrooms
upstairs, carpeted with
beautiful, locally woven *kilim*

Shepherds' crooks, rugs and silverware in a souvenir shop in Métsovo

rugs. Intricate gold- and
silverware are on display, as
well as collections of Epirot
costumes and embroidery.
Would-be visitors must wait
outside for the half-hourly
guided tour.

Another of Métsovo's
benefactors was the writer and
politician Evángelos Avéroff
(1910–90), who founded the
Avéroff Museum. The core of
the gallery is Avéroff's own
collection of some 200

Interior of the Archontikó Tosítsa, Métsovo

paintings and sculptures he
acquired over the years, always
with the ambition of opening a
museum of modern Greek art in
his home town. His collection
has been expanded to show
the work of several dozen
Greek artists from the 19th
and 20th centuries.

Ancient traditions have
survived in the area, from
the simple craft of carving
shepherds' crooks (from the
town's sheep farming days)
to embroidery and wine- and
cheese-making. Some of the
older men (and a few women)
still wear traditional costumes;
you can see them, dressed in
black, sitting in the shelters and
cafés around the town square.
The shelters are needed during
winter when the town, at 1,156
m (3,793 ft), becomes a popular
ski resort. The rugs on sale in the
souvenir shops also reflect this
alpine character.

🏛 **Archontikó Tosítsa**
Off main thoroughfare. **Tel** 26560
41084. **Open** 9am–1pm & 4–5:30pm
Fri–Wed. 🈲

🏛 **Avéroff Museum**
Off central square. **Tel** 26560 41210.
Open 10am–4pm Wed–Mon. 🈲
🌐 averoffmuseum.gr

Environs

Fifteen minutes' walk south,
signposted from the centre
of town, stands the small and
charming 14th-century **Moní
Agíou Nikoláou**. Today, it is
inhabited only by caretakers
who are more than happy to
show visitors the church's vivid
post-Byzantine frescoes, the
monks' living quarters and their
own supplies of flowers, fruit
and vegetables.

Vlach Shepherds

Of unknown origin, the nomadic Vlach shepherds are today centred
in the Píndos Mountains, particularly in and around Métsovo. Their
language, which has no written form, is a dialect of Latin origin,
and it is thought that they might be descended
from Roman settlers who moved through Illyria
into the northern Balkans. Traditionally, their
way of life has been transhumant – spending
summers in the mountains before moving down
to the plains of Thessaly with their sheep
for six months to avoid the worst of the
winter snows. It is a hard way of life
which is gradually disappearing, and
the shepherds who remain can be
found in such villages as Métsovo
and Vovoúsa in Epirus, and Avdélla,
Samarína and Smíxi in western
Macedonia – their traditional
summer settlements. Their
winter homes lie mainly around
Kastoriá *(see p244)*.

Zagorian Vlach shepherd

❺ Ioánnina
Ιωάννινα

The capital of the Epirus region, Ioánnina prospered during Ottoman times (see pp42–3) when its famous craftsmen's guilds, including the silversmiths', were formed. The Turkish influence is most visible in the fortress area which extends on a small headland into Lake Pamvótis (it was once moated on its landward side). Though dating to the 13th century, the area was rebuilt in 1815 by Ali Pasha, the Turkish tyrant most closely associated with it. Inside the fortress precinct, a village-like peace reigns, though the bustle of the bazaar and the modern area is a reminder that this is still the region's busiest city.

Aslan Pasha Mosque, housing the Popular Art Museum

Ioánnina and the isle of Nisí, seen from the north

from the 5th century BC, statuettes of young children and lead tablets inscribed with questions for the oracle.

🏛 Popular Art Museum
Michaíl Angélou 42. Tel 26510 20515. **Open** 9am–2pm Tue & Thu–Sun (5:30–8pm Mon & Wed). **Closed** main public hols. 🐾

Housed in a mansion, this museum has a collection of local crafts. As well as silverwork and traditional costumes, there are woven textiles made by the nomadic, tent-dwelling Sarakatsans who number less than the Vlach tribe (see p213).

🏛 Municipal Museum
Aslan Pasha Mosque. **Tel** 26510 26356. **Open:** 8:30am–4pm daily. **Closed** main public hols. 🐾

At the northern corner of the fortress, this small museum is housed within the Aslan Pasha Mosque, built by Aslan Pasha in 1618. While the mosque itself, which retains original decoration on its dome, makes a visit worthwhile, the weapons and costumes on display tell something of Ioánnina's recent past. Turkish furniture inlaid with mother-of-pearl can also be found, alongside Jewish rugs and tapestries.

🏛 Byzantine Museum
Inner Fortress. **Tel** 26510 25989. **Open** Jun–Sep: 8am–8pm Tue–Sun, 1:30–8pm Mon; Oct–May: 8am–5pm. **Closed** main public hols. 🐾

This modern museum contains a few items from local archaeological excavations, but the core is an imaginative display of icons from the 16th to the 19th centuries. Silverware, for which the town is renowned, is displayed in a separate annexe, once the treasury, with a reconstruction of a typical silversmith's workshop.

🏛 Archaeological Museum
Plateía 25 Martíou 6. **Tel** 26510 01051. **Open** 8am–3pm Tue–Sun. 🐾 ♿

Set in a small park, this museum displays various artifacts that include items from the site of Dodóni. Among these is a bronze eagle

Ali Pasha

Ali Pasha was born in Albania in 1741 and, in 1788, was installed at Ioánnina by the Turks as Pasha of Epirus. Though a murderer, he was a great administrator who made the town one of the wealthiest in Greece. His aim was to gain independence from his overlords and by 1820, he had an empire stretching from Albania to the Peloponnese. When news spread of his intention to create a Greco-Albanian state, Sultan Mahmud II of Turkey dispatched troops to put him to death. After a long siege within the fortress at Ioánnina, Ali Pasha agreed to meet the Turkish commander on the island of Nisí where, on 24 January 1822, he was hunted down, trapped and killed.

Tapestry of Ali Pasha (centre), Moní Agíou Panteleímonos, Nisí

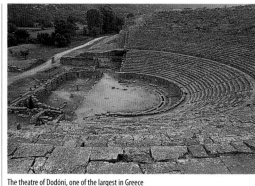

The theatre of Dodóni, one of the largest in Greece

🌿 Nisí

15 minutes by boat NE from fortress.
Though its first inhabitants
were the monks who came here
in the early years of the 13th
century, the single village on
the isle of Nisí owes its existence
to 17th-century refugees from
Mániot feuds (see p198). Its
main building is Moní Agíou
Panteleímonos, where the
reconstructed room in which Ali
Pasha was shot can be visited,
the bullet holes still visible in
the floor. Other rooms contain
a few of his possessions, some
costumes and period prints.

Stalactites in the Pérama Caves

Environs

Greece's largest cave network,
the **Pérama Caves**, are near the
village of Pérama, 4 km (2 miles)
north of Ioánnina. They were
discovered in 1940 by a
shepherd hiding from the
Germans, but only fully explored
years later. Now, there are
regular guided tours taking
visitors along the 1,700 m
(5,600 ft) of passages, where
multicoloured lights pick out
the stalactites and stalagmites.

🌿 Pérama Caves

Pérama. **Tel** 26510 81521.
Open 9am–7pm daily. 📷

❻ Dodóni
Δωδώνη

Epirus. **Road map** B2. **Tel** 26510
82287. 🚌 **Open** 8am–8pm daily (to
3pm Nov–Mar). **Closed** main public
hols. 📷 free on Sun. ♿

Dating to at least 1,000 BC,
the Oracle of Zeus at Dodóni
is the oldest in Greece and was
second in status only to the
one at Delphi (see pp232–5).
The site is located 22 km
(14 miles) southwest of
Ioánnina in a placid green
valley on the eastern slopes
of Mount Tómaros.

The oracle focused on a sacred
oak tree ringed with tripods
which held a number of bronze
cauldrons placed so that they
touched each other. Prophecies
were divined from the sound
these made, in harmony with
the rustling of the oak leaves,
when one of the cauldrons was
struck. Petitioners would inscribe
their questions on lead
tablets for the
priestess to read
to Zeus; some of
these have been
found on the
site and can be
seen in the
Archaeological
Museum in
Ioánnina. The
reputed power of
the oak tree was
such that Jason, on
his quest for the Golden Fleece
(see p224), travelled across from
the Pílio to acquire one of its
branches to attach to his ship,
the Argo. By the 3rd century BC,
a colonnaded courtyard was

Justinian, the last Roman Emperor
to visit Dodóni

built around the tree for
protection; it contained a
small temple of which only
foundations remain. The tree
was uprooted in AD 393 on the
orders of the Roman Emperor
Theodosios (ruled 379–395) in
accordance with his policy of
stamping out pagan practices.
He also believed that buried
treasure might be found
beneath the site.

The main feature of Dodóni
today is the theatre, which, with
its capacity for 17,000 spectators,
is one of the largest in Greece. Its
walls rise to 21 m (69 ft) and are
supported by solid towers where
kestrels now nest. Used by the
ancient Greeks for dramatic
performances, the theatre was
later converted by the Romans
into an arena for animal fights;
bulls and big cats would have
been kept in the two triangular
pens on either side of the
stage. The whole structure of
the theatre was restored
in the early 1960s and
is now used for
performances
in summer.
Dodóni also
includes the
ruins of a stadium,
acropolis and
Byzantine basilica –
all reminders of
the time when
this valley was the
location of a
flourishing market town.

Dodóni fell into ruin in the 6th
century AD, when the Roman
Emperor Justinian decided to
found the new and more easily
defendable city of Ioánnina.

The tiered, amphitheatre-shaped town of Párga, seen across Párga Bay

❼ Párga

Πάργα

Epirus. **Road map** B3. 🏔 2,000.
🚌 ⛴ Tue.

Párga, the main beach resort of Epirus, is a busy holiday town whose charms are often overwhelmed by the number of summer visitors. The Venetian fortress dominating the west side of the harbour was built in the late 16th century on the site of a building destroyed in 1537 during a brief period of Turkish rule. The Ottomans later returned under the command of Ali Pasha *(see p214)*, who bought the town from the British in 1819. After this, many of Párga's inhabitants left for Corfu, though it was regained by the Greeks in 1913.

There are two small beaches within walking distance of the town centre and two larger ones about 2 km (1 mile) away: Váltos, the biggest, is to the north and Lychnos to the southwest. Fish restaurants line Párga's waterfront, affording fine views across the harbour to a group of small islands.

Environs

37 km (23 miles) south of Párga is the **Necromanteion of Efyra** (Oracle of the Dead), the mythological gateway to Hades. Steps descend to the vaults where, in the 4th century BC, drugs and mechanisms may have heightened the sensation of entering the Underworld for visitors who sought advice from the dead.

🏛 **Necromanteion of Efyra**
Open 8:30am–3pm daily. 🚫

❽ Kassópi

Κασσώπη

Zálongo, Epirus. **Road map** B3. 🚌
Open daily.

The Kassopians were a tribe which lived in this region in the 4th century BC. The remains of their capital city stand on a hillside plateau overlooking the Ionian Sea, from where the island of Paxoí is plainly visible. Kassópi is reached by a pleasant walk through pine groves from the village of Kamarína.

Greek Orthodox priests in Párga

A site plan illustrates the layout of the once-great city, now the home of birds and lizards.

Just above it is **Moní Zalóngou**, with its monument commemorating the women of Soúli, who threw themselves from the cliffs in 1806 rather than be captured by Turkish-Albanian troops.

The remains of the city of Kassópi

❾ Préveza

Πρέβεζα

Epirus. **Road map** B3. 🏔 13,000. ✈
🚌 🚍 ℹ Eleftheríou Venizélou (26820 21078). ⛴ daily (fish).

Often seen as a transit point, the charming town of Préveza repays a longer visit, particularly for the lively atmosphere among its waterfront cafés and tavernas. It is picturesquely situated on the northern shore of the narrow "Channel of Cleopatra", at the mouth of the Amvrakikós Gulf. It was here that the naval Battle of Actium was fought in 31 BC *(see p38)*.

Two ruined forts, on either side of the straits, recall the town's Venetian occupation in 1499, though in 1798 it passed, via the French, into the hands of Ali Pasha *(see p214)*.

Environs
Seven km (4 miles) north of Préveza stand the ruins of **Nikópoli** ("Victory City"), built by the Roman Emperor Octavian to celebrate his victory at Actium. The city was founded on the site where the emperor's army was camped. Later sacked by the Goths, it was finally destroyed by the Bulgars in 1034. The remains are dominated by the city walls and the theatre. A museum displays artifacts from the site, which is quite overgrown.

Nikópoli
Tel 26820 89892. **Open** 8:30am–3pm daily. **Closed** main public hols. (museum only).

❿ Arta
`Άρτα`

Epirus. **Road map** B3. 33,000.
Krystalli Sq (26810 78551).
Open 7am–3pm Mon–Fri.
Mon–Sat (veg).

Though it is the second largest town in Epirus, after Ioánnina, Arta remains largely untouched by tourism. This traditional Greek market town has a lively, bazaar-like area, established by the Turks who occupied Arta from 1449 to 1881. The **fortress** dates from the 13th century, when the city was the capital of the despotate of Epirus. Stretching from Thessaloníki to Corfu, this was an independent Byzantine state set up after the fall of Constantinople in 1204 *(see p41)*. It lasted until the start of the Turkish occupation. Some

Timber-framed houses in the Old Quarter of Tríkala

of the town's many 13th- and 14th-century Byzantine churches can be found in the streets near the fortress. The most striking is the **Panagía Parigorítissa**. Built between 1283 and 1296, it is a three-tier building topped with towers and domes. **Agía Theódora**, on Pýrrou, contains the marble tomb of the saintly wife of 13th-century Epirot ruler Michael II.

Approaching from the west, the main road into town crosses the river Arachthos by a 17th-century stone **bridge**. According to local folklore, the builder of the bridge, frustrated by each day's work being ruined by the river at night, was advised by a bird that the problem could be solved by putting his wife in the bridge's foundations. This he did, burying her alive, after which the bridge was successfully completed.

⓫ Metéora
See pp220–21.

⓬ Tríkala
Τρίκαλα

Thessaly. **Road map** C2. 68,000.
Mon–Sat.

Tríkala was the home of Asklepios, the god of healing, and today is the market centre for the very fertile plain of Thessaly. As such, it is a thriving town with a number of remains from its Turkish past. One is the **market** near the main square, another the **Koursoúm Tzamí**, a graceful mosque built in 1550 on the south side of the River Lithaíos. Surrounding the **fortress** is the Old Quarter of Varósi, with a number of Byzantine churches *(see pp24–5)*. The fortress stands on the site of the ancient acropolis, which was built in the 4th century BC. It is situated in beautiful grounds overlooking the river.

⓭ Vale of Tempe
Κοιλάδα των Τεμπών

Thessaly. **Road map** C2.

As the E75 approaches Macedonia, it follows the river Pineíos through the Vale of Tempe – the fertile valley where Apollo was said to have purified himself after slaying the serpent Python. Close to the **Wolf's Jaws** or **Lykostómio** (the narrowest point of the gorge) is the **Spring of Daphne**, where a bridge leads to the chapel of **Agía Paraskeví**, carved out of the rock. The **Kástro Gónnon** at the northern end of the Vale was built by Perséas, leader of the Macedonians during the war with Rome *(see pp36–7)*, to control what has long been a vital route between Central and Northern Greece.

The arched packhorse bridge of Arta, leading into town from the west

⓫ Metéora
Μετέωρα

The natural sandstone towers of Metéora (or "suspended rocks") were first used as a religious retreat when, in AD 985, a hermit named Barnabas occupied a cave here. In the mid-14th century, Neílos, the Prior of Stagai convent, built a small church. Then, in 1382, the monk Athanásios, from Mount Athos, founded the huge monastery of Megálo Metéoro on one of the many pinnacles. Twenty-three monasteries followed, though most had fallen into ruin by the 19th century. In the 1920s, stairs were cut to make the remaining six monasteries more accessible, and today, a religious revival has seen the return of monks and nuns.

Location of Monasteries of Metéora

Rousánou
Moní Rousánou, perched precariously on the very tip of a narrow spire of rock, is the most spectacularly located of all the monasteries. Its church of the Metamórfosis (1545) is renowned for its harrowing frescoes, painted in 1560 by the iconographers of the Cretan school.

KEY

① **Outer walls**

② **Monastic cells**

③ **The refectory** contains a small icon museum.

④ **Ascent Tower**, made in 1536, was used to winch up goods and people by a windlass mechanism.

⑤ **Net descending from tower**

Megálo Metéoro
Also known as the Great Meteoron, this was the first and, at 623 m (2,045 ft), highest monastery to be founded. By the entrance is a cave in which Athanásios first lived. His body is buried in the main church.

◀ Towering sandstone towers with a monastery in the foreground, Metéora

Katholikón
Dedicated to Agioi Pántes (All Saints), the church is adorned with frescoes, including one of Theofánis (right) and Nektários, its founders.

VISITORS' CHECKLIST

Practical Information
Thessaly. **Road map** B2.
i Efthymiiou Vlahava 1
(24323 50274). Megálo Metéoro:
Open Apr–Oct: 9am–5pm Wed–Mon; Nov–Mar: 9am–4pm Thu–Mon. Varlaám: **Open** Apr–Oct: 9am–4pm Sat–Thu; Nov–Mar: 9am–3pm Sat–Wed. Agios Nikólaos: **Open** 9am–2pm Sat–Thu (Nov–Mar: 9am–1pm). Rousánou: **Open** Apr–Oct: 9am–6pm Thu–Tue; Nov–Mar: 9am–2pm Thu–Tue. Agía Triáda: **Open** Apr–Oct: 9am–5pm Fri–Wed; Nov–Mar: 10am–4pm Fri–Tue. ✝ Agios Stéfános: **Open** Apr–Oct: 9am–1:30pm & 3:30–5:30pm Tue–Sun; Nov–Mar: 9:30am–1pm & 3–5pm Tue–Sun. ✝ 🎨 all monasteries.

Transport
🚌

Varlaám

Founded in 1518, the monastery of Varlaám is named after the first hermit to live on this rock in 1350. The katholikón was built in 1542 and contains some frescoes by the Theban iconographer Frágkos Katelános.

— Entrance

The Building of the Monasteries

Though it is unknown how the first hermits reached the tops of these often vertical rock faces, it is likely that they hammered pegs into tiny gaps in the rock and hauled building materials to the summits. Another theory is that kites were flown over the tops, carrying strings attached to thicker ropes which were made into the first rope ladders.

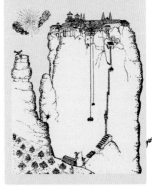

⑭ Pílio
Πήλιο

The mythological home of the forest-loving centaurs, the Pílio peninsula, with its woods of chestnut, oak and beech, is one of the most beautiful regions of the mainland. The mountain air is sweet with the scent of herbs which, in ancient times, were renowned for their healing powers. The area became populated in the 13th century by Greeks retreating from the Ottomans *(see pp42–3)*, under whose rule they were taxed onerously. Most villages were built close to mountain monasteries, though the thick stone walls and narrow windows of a typical Pílio house indicate how uncertain their freedom really was. After centuries of protecting their culture, this is now one of the few areas of Greece to have a strong local cuisine.

Makrinítsa
Cars are banned from the steep cobbled streets of this traditional village *(see p224)*.

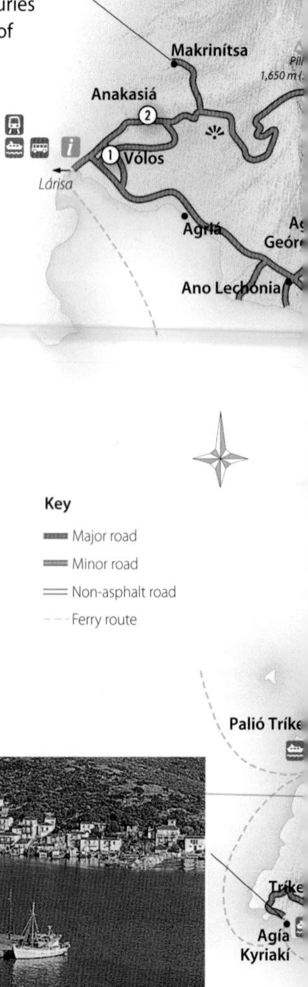

Makrinítsa

Anakasiá

Pílio
1,650 m (

② ① Vólos

Lárisa

Agriá

A
Geór

Ano Lechónia

Theófilos Chatzimichaíl

Born on Lésvos in 1873, Theófilos came to the Pílio in 1894 after reportedly killing a Turk in Smyrna. His favoured medium was the mural, though he also painted ceramics and the sides of fishing boats, *kafeneío* counters or horse carts when the mood struck him. He executed numerous mural commissions in the Pílio, notably at the Kontós mansion in Anakasiá. Though unhappily isolated, and mocked by the locals for his strange habits (he dressed in the costumes of his heroes, including Alexander the Great), he had a passion for all things Greek. After Lésvos's unification with Greece in 1912, he returned home destitute and ill. His fortunes changed after meeting his future patron Stratís Eleftheriádis, who provided for the painter's needs until Theófilos's death in 1934.

Konstantínos Palaiológos mural (1899) by Theófilos

Key

━━ Major road

━━ Minor road

═══ Non-asphalt road

---- Ferry route

Palió Tríke

KEY

① **Vólos** is the capital of the region, straddling the only route into the peninsula. It has an excellent Archaeological Museum *(see p224)*.

② **Anakasiá**, now little more than a suburb of Vólos, has a museum to the Greek painter Theófilos Chatzimicháïl.

③ **Agios Ioánnis** has one of the Pílio's most popular beaches.

④ **Tsagkaráda** is a delightful mountain village on wooded slopes. In its central square is the largest and oldest (1,000 years) plane tree in Greece.

Tríke

Agía
Kyriakí

Agía Kyriakí
Overlooked by the isolated hilltop village of Tríkeri, this small fishing port lacks a beach and hotels but has a working boatyard and good, simple fish tavernas for those very few visitors who take the trouble to travel here.

For hotels and restaurants see pp271–2 and pp288–90

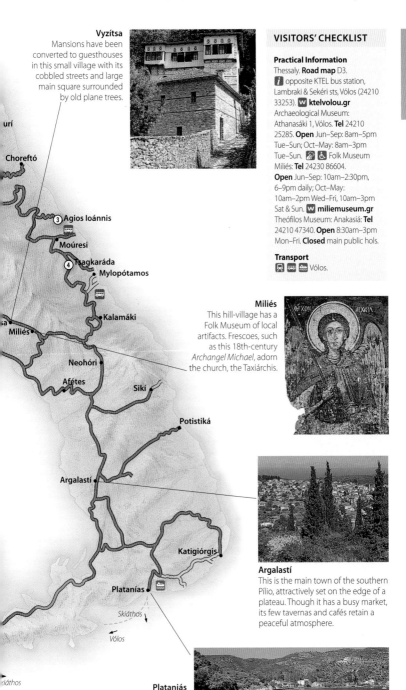

Vyzítsa
Mansions have been converted to guesthouses in this small village with its cobbled streets and large main square surrounded by old plane trees.

VISITORS' CHECKLIST

Practical Information
Thessaly. **Road map** D3.
ℹ️ opposite KTEL bus station, Lambraki & Sekéri sts, Vólos (24210 33253). **W** **ktelvolou.gr**
Archaeological Museum: Athanasáki 1, Vólos. **Tel** 24210 25285. **Open** Jun–Sep: 8am–5pm Tue–Sun; Oct–May: 8am–3pm Tue–Sun. 🎭 ♿ Folk Museum Miliés: **Tel** 24230 86604. **Open** Jun–Sep: 10am–2:30pm, 6–9pm daily; Oct–May: 10am–2pm Wed–Fri, 10am–3pm Sat & Sun. **W** **miliemuseum.gr**
Theófilos Museum: Anakasiá: **Tel** 24210 47340. **Open** 8:30am–3pm Mon–Fri. **Closed** main public hols.

Transport
🚉 🚌 🚍 Vólos.

Miliés
This hill-village has a Folk Museum of local artifacts. Frescoes, such as this 18th-century *Archangel Michael*, adorn the church, the Taxiárchis.

Argalastí
This is the main town of the southern Pílio, attractively set on the edge of a plateau. Though it has a busy market, its few tavernas and cafés retain a peaceful atmosphere.

Plataniás
With its fine beach and boats travelling back to Vólos and to Skiáthos island, Plataniás is popular with Greek tourists. A number of fish tavernas provide excellent seafood.

For keys to symbols *see back flap*

Exploring the Pílio

Travelling by car, a circular tour of the northern villages can be made in a day following the road southeast from Vólos to Afétes, via Tsagkaráda. The hills in this region rise to 1,650 m (5,415 ft) at the summit of Mount Pílio, and in addition to dense woodlands, the area produces a large number of apples, pears, peaches and olives. While less dramatic, the southern Pílio is still hilly enough to ensure that many villages are at the end of single "dead end" roads, making travel here time consuming.

Restored traditional mansions on the hillside of Makrinítsa

Vólos

Vólos is one of Greece's fastest growing industrial centres and, since it was devastated by earthquakes in the 1950s, it is difficult to imagine its mythological past. Once the site of ancient Iolkós, the home of Jason, who went in search of the Golden Fleece, Vólos's history is illustrated by what can be found in the excellent **Archaeological Museum**. The museum contains an extensive collection of painted funerary stelae from the 3rd century BC, found at Dimitriás on the far side of the Gulf of Vólos. Collections of Neolithic pottery from the nearby sites of Sésklo and Dimíni can also be found, and there is a room dedicated to the Ancient games held in Thessaly, many of which involved horses.

Northern Villages

From Vólos, the road leads southeast, past Ano Lechónia, through the "Vólos Riviera", providing a circular route of the mountainous northern Pílio. On weekends during summer, a traditional Pilion train runs from Káto Lechónia to Miliés. From the popular inland resorts of **Miliés** and **Vyzítsa** (the latter preserved as a "traditional settlement" by the government), the road turns north past Tsagkaráda to **Agios Ioánnis**. This is the main resort of the east coast; the beaches of Papá Neró and Pláka are particularly fine and are both within easy walking distance. Some of the Pílio's best restaurants can be found in nearby **Moúresi**.

Returning towards Vólos, take the turning to **Makrinítsa** – a traditional mountain village, regarded as the most important destination for any traveller of the area. Founded in the 13th century by refugees from the first sacking of Constantinople (see p41), the village has beautiful churches, the most impressive being Agios Ioánnis, and the Moní Theotókou. Several traditional mansions also survive, some functioning as guesthouses. Close to Agios Ioánnis, there is a café with an interior decorated with frescoes painted by the artist Theófilos (see p222).

Anakasiá is the last village before Vólos and home to the delightful Theófilos Museum.

Jason and the Argonauts

According to legend, the Golden Fleece came from a winged ram sent by Hermes, the gods' messenger, to protect two children, Helle and Phrixus, from their evil stepmother. Though Helle drowned, Phrixus was reared in Kolchis, in present-day Georgia, where the ram was sacrificed and its fleece given to the king, Aeëtes. Years later, Jason, Phrixus's cousin, set sail from the kingdom of Iolkós (now Vólos) after his half-brother usurped the throne. Jason was in search of the Fleece, which made its wearer invincible. With a crew of 50, Jason came to Kolchis where King Aeëtes set several tasks before relinquishing the Fleece. After falling in love with the king's daughter, Medea, Jason achieved his tasks and the Argonauts carried the Fleece back to Iolkós in triumph.

Detail from *The Golden Fleece* (c.1905) by Herbert Draper (1864–1920)

Fisherman with his nets at the waterfront, Vólos

For hotels and restaurants see pp271–2 and pp288–90

Sarcophagus detail outside the Thebes Archaeological Museum

⓯ Thebes

Θήβα

Stereá Elláda. **Road map** D4.
🏛 20,000. 🚌 🚃

Although it was briefly the most powerful city of Greece, in the 4th century BC, the Thebes of today is little more than a quiet provincial town. It played an important role in the power struggles of Classical Greece, until defeated by Philip II of Macedon. Thebes' original acropolis has been built over through the years, but excavations have unearthed Mycenaean walls as well as jewellery, pottery and important tablets of Linear B script which are now in the **Archaeological Museum**. One of the highlights of the museum is the collection of Mycenaean sarcophagi, similar to those found on Crete. The museum's courtyard and well-tended garden stand alongside a 13th-century Frankish tower, all that remains of a castle ruined in 1311 by the Catalans.

A bridge over the river bed, a short walk eastwards from the museum, marks the traditional site of the Fountain of Oedipus,

The Legend of Oedipus

According to legend, Oedipus was the ill-fated son of Laius and Jocasta, the king and queen of Thebes. Even before his birth, the Delphic Oracle (*see p232*) had foretold that he would kill his father and become his mother's husband. To defy the prophecy, Laius abandoned Oedipus, though the child was rescued and reared by the king and queen of Corinth whom Oedipus believed to be his real parents. Years later, when he heard of the prophecy, Oedipus fled to Thebes, killing a man on his way, unaware that he was King Laius. On reaching Thebes, he found the city gates barred by the Sphinx which he vanquished by solving one of its riddles. The Thebans made him their king and he married the widowed Jocasta. When the truth about his past was revealed, Oedipus blinded himself and spent his final days as an outcast.

Oedipus and the Sphinx, from a 5th-century BC cup

where the legendary King Oedipus is said to have washed blood from his hands after unwittingly killing his father on his way to the city.

🏛 **Archaeological Museum**
Plateía Threpsiádou 1. **Tel** 22620 27913. **Closed** until 2015. ♿ ⓑ

Environs

Ten km (6 miles) north lie the ruins of **Gla**, once a Mycenaean stronghold (*see pp182–4*). Its walls are 3 km (2 miles) long and up to 5 m (16 ft) high, surrounding a hill where the ruins of a palace and agora can be found.

⓰ Monastery of Osios Loúkas

See pp226–7.

⓱ Mount Parnassus

Όρος Παρνασσός

Stereá Elláda. **Road map** C3.
🚌 Delfoí. ⓘ Vasiléon Pávlou & Freideríkis 44, Delfoí (22650 82900). **Open** 7:30am–2:30pm daily.

Rising to a height of 2,457 m (8,061 ft), the limestone mass of Mount Parnassus dominates the eastern region of Stereá Elláda. The lower slopes are covered with Cephalonian fir, and beneath them, in summer, the wildflower meadows burst into colour. Vultures and golden eagles are common, as are wolves which come down from the Píndos Mountains (*see p210*) in winter.

The village of **Aráchova** is the best base for exploring the area and is renowned for its wine, cheese and sheepskin rugs. There are many mountain trails for summer hikes, though a detailed walking map is recommended. Reaching the top of Liákoura, the highest peak, involves a long hike and camping overnight on the mountain.

From Aráchova, the two ski centres at **Fterólaka** and **Kelaria** are only 26 km (16 miles) away. Open from January to March, they provide a chair lift to 1,900 m (6,250 ft); from here, a ski lift can be taken up to the ski slopes. In summer, Fterólaka and Kelaria function as excursion centres.

Fir-covered foothills beneath the ridge of Mount Parnassus

⓰ Monastery of Osios Loúkas
Μονή Οσίου Λουκά

Dedicated to a local hermit and healer, Holy Luke, Osios Loúkas monastery was architecturally one of medieval Greece's most important buildings. It was built by Emperor Romanós in c.1011 who extended an earlier church dating from AD 944. The octagonal style of the main church became a hallmark of late Byzantine church design *(see pp24–5)*, while the mosaics inside lifted Byzantine art into its final great period. During the time of the Ottoman Empire *(see pp42–3)*, Osios Loúkas witnessed a great deal of fighting, as the cannons in the courtyard testify. Here, in 1821, Bishop Isaias declared his support for the Greek freedom fighters.

The monastery seen from the west with the slopes of Mount Elikónas in the background

KEY

① **The narthex** is the western entrance hall; it contains a number of mosaics of Christ's Passion.

② **West portal**

③ **The exterior** is a mixture of dressed Póros stone and red brick.

④ **The monastic cells** are small with arched roofs.

⑤ **The north transept** contains medallion-shaped mosaics of saints.

⑥ **The Theotókos**, built in the early 11th century, is a smaller church dedicated to the Mother of God; its name means "god- bearing".

⑦ **The apse** has a mosaic of the Virgin and Child pre-dating a devastating earthquake in 1659.

⑧ **The katholikón**, or main church, dates to 1011 and is built in the octagonal style.

⑨ **The southwest chapel** has early 11th-century frescoes.

⑩ **The refectory** was used as a workshop as well as for meals; it now contains a museum of Byzantine sculpture.

★ **Washing of the Apostles' Feet**
Based on a style dating to the 6th century, this 11th-century work is the finest of the narthex mosaics. Set on a gold background, it depicts Christ teaching his apostles humility.

For hotels and restaurants see pp271–2 and pp288–90

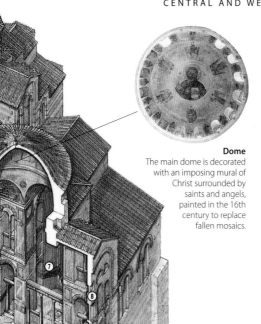

Dome

The main dome is decorated with an imposing mural of Christ surrounded by saints and angels, painted in the 16th century to replace fallen mosaics.

VISITORS' CHECKLIST

Practical Information
8 km (5 miles) E of Dístomo.
Road map C4. **Tel** 22670 22797.
Site & Museum: **Open** May–
Sep: 9am–6pm daily; Oct–Apr:
8am–5pm daily.

Transport

★ Crypt

This 10th-century shrine, from the original site, contains the sarcophagus of Holy Luke, and such frescoes as this *Descent from the Cross*.

Holy Luke

Born in Aegina in 906, Osios Loúkas ("Holy Luke") is known to have been a spiritual child who, in his early teens, left home to seek isolation in central Greece and developed a reputation as a healer. In around 940, he arrived at this spot on the western slopes of Mount Elikónas, with its glorious view over a peaceful valley of cornfields and groves of almond and olive trees. Here, he settled with some disciples, adding the gift of prophecy to his healing powers. He died in 953, by which time the first monastic cells and the site's first small church had been constructed.

The waterfront houses of Galaxídi in the Gulf of Corinth

⓲ Lamía and Thermopylae

Λαμία καί Θερμοπύλαι

Stereá Elláda. **Road map** C3.
🚂 68,000. 🚌 ℹ️ Leof. Kalivion 14,
(22310 32289). 🛍️ Sat.

Set in the valley between two wooded hills, Lamía is typical of many medium-sized Greek towns; though it is little known, it has much to offer, with a lively Saturday market. A 14th-century Catalan **kástro**, built on the site of the town's ancient acropolis, provides excellent views over the roofs to the surrounding countryside.

Lamía is chiefly associated with the Lamian War (323–322 BC), when Athens tried to throw off Macedonian rule after the death of Alexander the Great *(see pp36–7)*. This is recalled at the **Lamía Museum**, which also has displays of architectural remains from Delphi *(see pp232–35)*.

A short drive east of Lamía, the Athens road crosses the **Pass of Thermopylae**. It was here, in 480 BC, that an army of

some 7,000 soldiers, under the command of Leonidas I of Sparta, met an overwhelming force from Persia whose numbers Herodotus *(see p60)* cites as 2,641,610. Though Leonidas held the pass for a number of days, the Persians forced a path through and attacked the Greeks from the rear. Only two Greek soldiers survived the ordeal, after which all of central Greece, including Athens, fell to the Persians. The Persian land forces were eventually defeated by Athens and her allies at the Battle of Plataiai in 479 BC *(see p33)*.

An impressive bronze statue of King Leonidas, cast in 1955, stands at the roadside opposite the burial mound of the soldiers who died here. Just to the left of the mound are the famous

Statue of King Leonidas at the Pass of Thermopylae

sulphur springs from which Thermopylae was given its name, which means the "Hot Gates".

The present landscape has changed considerably from the narrow gorge of old; the coastline to the north has been extended by the silt brought down by the River Spercheiós, pushing the sea back over 5 km (3 miles).

🏛️ **Lamía Museum**
Kástro. **Tel** 22310 29992.
Open 8:30am–2:30pm Tue–Sun.
Closed main public hols. 🅿️ ♿

⓳ Ancient Delphi

See pp232–5.

⓴ Gulf of Corinth

Κορινθιακός Κόλπος

Stereá Elláda. 🚌 to Náfpaktos.

The northern coast of the Gulf of Corinth contains several well-known resorts as well as many tiny coastal villages far removed from the usual tourist route. All are served by major roads which, like the resorts, offer fine views across the gulf to the mountains of the Peloponnese.

From Delphi, the main road leads southwards through the largest olive grove in Greece, passing **Itéa**, a busy port. The church of Agios Nikólaos, 17 km (11 miles) west, stands on a hill surrounded by the old stone buildings of **Galaxídi**. The history of the town is told in the **Nautical Museum**, while the 19th-century mansions at the waterfront are reminders of the great wealth brought by the town's shipbuilding industry. Though the industry cleared the region of trees, a reforestation scheme begun early in the 20th century has successfully restored the area to its former beauty. The next major town is **Náfpaktos**. Though perhaps less attractive than Galaxídi, it still possesses plenty of charm and character.

A Venetian fortress stands above the town, its ramparts running down as far as the beach, almost enclosing the harbour. The Venetian name for the town was Lepanto. In 1571, the famous naval Battle of Lepanto *(see p42)*, in which the Venetians, Spanish and Genoese defeated the Ottomans, was fought here. A popular story to emerge from the battle purports that the Spanish author Miguel de Cervantes (1547–1616) lost an arm in the conflict, though in fact only his left hand was maimed.

At **Antírrio**, the coast comes closest to the Peloponnese, and from here, a new suspension bridge and regular car ferry cross the stretch of water known as the "Little Dardanelles" to Río, on the southern shore. Beside the harbour stands the originally Frankish and Venetian Kástro Roúmelis. Another castle can be seen across the water on the Peloponnese.

🏛 Nautical Museum

Mouseíou 4, Galaxídi. **Tel** 22650 41558. **Open** 8:30am–3:30pm Tue–Sun. **Closed** main public hols. 🔊

㉑ Mesolóngi

Μεσολόγγι

Stereá Elláda. **Road map** B3.
🚌 12,000. 🚍 🚌 Tue & Sat.

Meaning "amid the lagoons", Mesolóngi is a town perfectly located for fishing, though the industry is now in decline. In 1821, the town became a centre of resistance to the Turks during the War of Independence *(see pp44–5)*, when a leader, Aléxandros Mavrokordátos, set up his headquarters here. In January 1824, Lord Byron *(see p153)* came to fight for the liberation of Greece, but died of a fever in April. His heart lies beneath his statue in the Garden of Heroes.

Nearby, the Gate of the Exodus is a tribute to those who fought the Turks in 1826. Nine thousand Greeks were killed in battle here and those that survived detonated their explosives as they were taken prisoner by the enemy. This self-sacrifice led to the Turks surrendering Mesolóngi in 1828 without firing a shot. A small museum charts the history of the town.

Statue of Lord Byron at Mesolóngi

Saltpan Birdlife

With its importance for food preservation, the production of salt is a major enterprise in the Mediterranean, the most extensive areas in Greece being around Mesolóngi and the Amvrakikós Gulf. Seawater is channelled into large artificial lakes, or saltpans, which, with their high concentrations of salt, attract a large amount of wildlife. Brine shrimps thrive, providing food for a wide variety of birds. Two of the most striking waders are the avocet and the great egret, though also common is the black-winged stilt with its long red legs. The area is also home to Kentish plovers, stone curlews, and the short-toed lark.

Avocet

Great egret

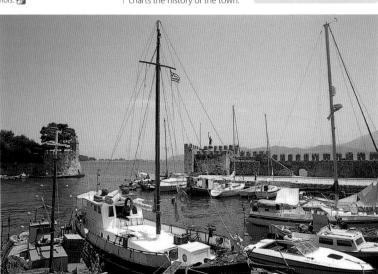

The fortified harbour of Náfpaktos in the Gulf of Corinth

⑩ Ancient Delphi
Δελφοί

According to legend, when Zeus released two eagles from opposite ends of the world, their paths crossed in the sky above Delphi, establishing the site as the centre of the earth. Renowned as a dwelling place of Apollo, from the end of the 8th century BC, individuals from all over the ancient world visited Delphi to consult the god on what course of action to take, in both public and private life. With the political rise of Delphi in the 6th century BC and the reorganization of the Pythian Games *(see p234)*, the sanctuary entered a golden age which lasted until the Romans came in 191 BC. The oracle was abolished in AD 393 with the Christianization of the Byzantine Empire under Theodosius.

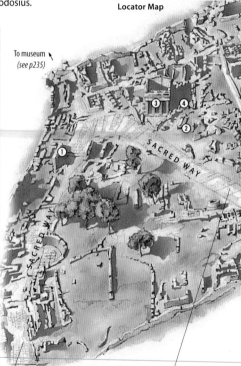

Locator Map

To museum ▸
(see p235)

The Oracle of Delphi

The Delphic Oracle was the means through which worshippers could hear the words of the god Apollo, spoken through a priestess, or *Pythia*, over the age of 50. Questioners paid a levy called a *pelanos* and sacrificed an animal on the altar. The question was then put to the *Pythia* by a male priest. The *Pythia* would answer in a trance, perhaps induced by vapours from a crack in the ground over which she sat on a tripod. Her incantations were interpreted by the priest, though the answers were often ambiguous. King Croesus of Lydia (r.560–546 BC) came to ask if he should make war against Cyrus the Great of Persia and was told that if he crossed a river, then he would destroy a great empire. In marching on Cyrus, his troops crossed the River Halys and he did destroy an empire, though it turned out to be his own.

The main entrance was once a market place (agora) where religious objects could be bought.

The Sanctuary of Apollo

Also known as the Sacred Precinct, this is at the heart of a complex that also included a stadium and a sacred spring (see pp234–5). It is entered through an agora from which the Sacred Way winds through the ruins of memorials and treasuries.

★ **Sacred Way**
Leading to the Temple of Apollo, this path was lined with up to 3,000 statues and treasuries, built by city-states to house their people's offerings.

◀ Ruins of the ancient city of Delphi

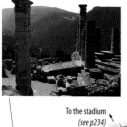

★ Temple of Apollo
A temple has stood on this site since the 6th century BC, but the remains visible today date from the 4th century BC. Some reconstruction work has been done since French archaeologists uncovered the foundations in 1892, to give an impression of its original grandeur.

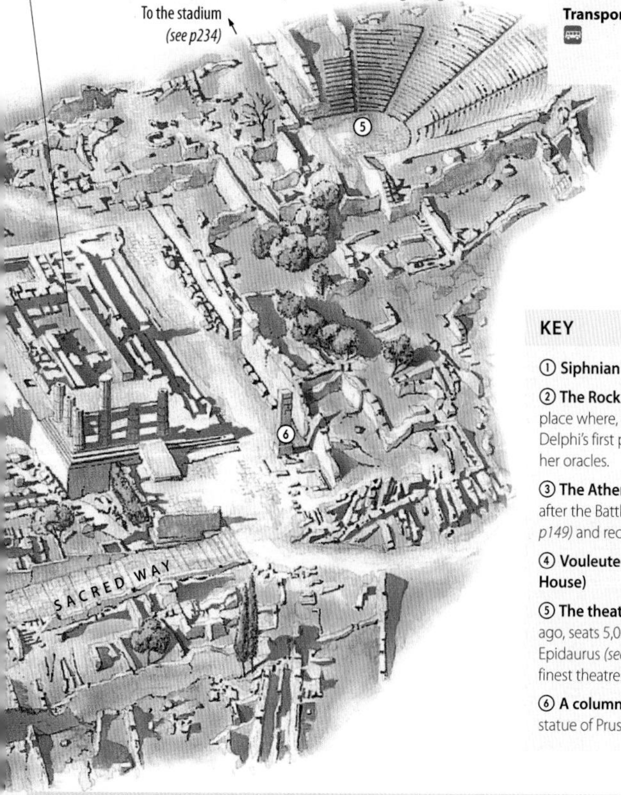

To the stadium
(see p234)
5
6
SACRED WAY

VISITORS' CHECKLIST

Practical Information
Mount Parnassus, Stereá Elláda.
Road map C3. **Tel** 22650 82312.
Site & Museum: **Open** 8am–8pm daily (to 3pm Nov–Mar).
Closed main public hols.

Transport

KEY

① **Siphnian Treasury**

② **The Rock of the Sibyl** marks the place where, according to legend, Delphi's first prophetess pronounced her oracles.

③ **The Athenian Treasury** was built after the Battle of Marathon *(see p149)* and reconstructed in 1906.

④ **Vouleuterion (Delphic Council House)**

⑤ **The theatre**, built 2,500 years ago, seats 5,000 people. It rivals Epidaurus *(see pp188–9)* as one of the finest theatres in Greece.

⑥ **A column** once supported a statue of Prusias, King of Bithynia.

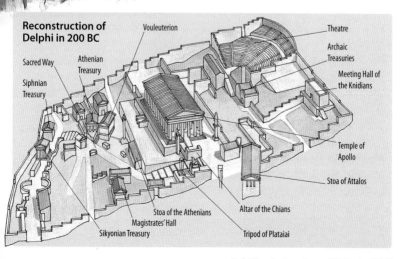

Reconstruction of Delphi in 200 BC

Vouleuterion
Theatre
Archaic Treasuries
Meeting Hall of the Knidians
Sacred Way
Athenian Treasury
Siphnian Treasury
Temple of Apollo
Stoa of Attalos
Altar of the Chians
Stoa of the Athenians
Magistrates' Hall
Sikyonian Treasury
Tripod of Plataiai

Exploring Delphi

The first excavations at Delphi began in 1892, uncovering a much larger area than is apparent now. Though it is most famous for the Sanctuary of Apollo, Delphi also had a sanctuary dedicated to the goddess Athena, whose temple, along with a structure known as the *tholos*, can be seen in a second enclosure to the south. North of the theatre is the stadium where the Pythian Games were held. These, after the Olympic Games *(see p177)*, were the most important sporting event in the Greek calendar, providing an opportunity for strengthening the ethnic bond of the Greek nation which was otherwise divided into predominantly rival city-states.

The Stadium, viewed from the remains of the entrance archway

🔊 Marmaria Precinct
Southeast of the Temple of Apollo, a path leads to the Marmaria Precinct, or "marble quarry", where the Sanctuary of Athena Pronaia can be found. At the sanctuary's entrance stand the ruins of a 4th-century BC temple dedicated to Athena. At the far end of the sanctuary are the remains of an earlier temple to the goddess, which was built around 510 BC. Between the two temples stands the Marmaria's most remarkable, and most photographed, monument: the circular *tholos*. The purpose of this structure is still unknown. The rotunda dates from the start of the 4th century BC, and was originally surrounded by 20 columns. Three of these columns were re-erected in 1938. They stand to provide some hint of the building's former beauty.

🔊 Stadium
This is one of the very best-preserved stadia in the country. Almost 200 m (655 ft) long and partly hewn out of the rocks above the main sanctuary, it held 7,000 spectators who gathered for the field and track events every four years during the Pythian Games. The games grew out of a musical festival, held in the theatre every eight years, to celebrate Apollo's mythical slaying of the serpent Python. Though poetry and musical recitals remained central to the occasion, from 582 BC, athletic events in the stadium were added and the festival became known as the Pythian Games. All prizes in these tournaments were purely honorary; each winner was awarded the traditional laurel wreath and the right to have his statue in the sanctuary.

Made entirely of limestone from Mount Parnassus, the present structure dates from Roman times and most of the seating is still intact. The best-preserved seats are the backed benches on the north side, made for the presidents of the games and honoured guests.

🔊 Castalian Spring
Before entering the Sacred Precinct, it is believed that everyone visiting Delphi for religious purposes, including athletes, was required to purify themselves in the clear but icy waters of the Castalian Spring – this process principally involved

The *tholos* beside the Sanctuary of Athena Pronaia, Marmaria Precinct

the washing of their hair. The Oracle *Pythia (see p232)* would also wash here before making her pronouncements. The visible remains of the fountain date either from the late Hellenistic or the early Roman period. A number of niches in the surrounding rock once held the votive offerings left for the nymph Castalia, to whom the spring was dedicated.

It is said that the British romantic poet Lord Byron *(see p153)* once plunged into the spring, inspired by the belief that the waters would enhance the poetic spirit.

The niches of the Castalian Spring

🔘 Gymnasium

Water from the Castalian Spring ran down to this area to provide cold baths (until the Romans added hot baths in the 2nd century AD) for athletes training for the Pythian Games. The original cold baths, which can be seen in a square courtyard, are some 9 m (30 ft) in diameter. East of the baths lies the Palaestra, or training area, surrounded by the remains of what once were changing rooms and training quarters. As well as an outdoor running track, a covered track 180 m (590 ft) in length was used in bad weather. The gymnasium was built on many levels due to the sloping terrain and was also used for intellectual pursuits – Delphi's poets and philosophers taught here.

🔘 Delphi Museum

The museum at Delphi contains a collection of sculptures and architectural remains of an importance second only to those of the Athenian Acropolis *(see pp98–105)*.

There are 13 rooms of exhibits, all on the ground floor. In one of the rooms, there is a scale model that reconstructs the Sanctuary of Apollo in a triumph of limestone whites, blue marble, gold and terracotta. The sanctuary is surrounded by friezes and statues and its size and former beauty is represented vividly.

Votive chapels, or "treasuries", lined the Sacred Way *(see p232)* and contained offerings of thanks, in the form of money or works of art, from towns grateful for good fortune following a favourable prophecy from the Oracle. The Theban Treasury, for example, was established after the victory of Thebes at the Battle of Leuktra in 371 BC. There are two rooms dedicated to the surviving sculpture from the Siphnian and Athenian treasuries, the wealth of the former illustrated by an outstanding frieze depicting the Greek heroes waging war on the giants. The colossal Naxian Sphinx was presented by the wealthy citizens of Náxos in 560 BC; it stands 2.3 m (7.5 ft) high and once had its place atop a column reaching over 10 m (33 ft) in height. The most famous of the museum's exhibits is a life-size bronze statue, the *Charioteer*.

The statue was commissioned by a Sicilian tyrant named Polyzalos to commemorate a chariot victory in the Pythian Games in 478 BC. Another notable exhibit is the sculpture of *Three Dancing Girls* grouped around a column. The column is believed to have supported a tripod of the kind sat on by the *Pythia* as she went into her oracular trances. The girls are thought to be celebrating the feast of the god Dionysos *(see p56)*, who also resided in the sanctuary. His presence was honoured in the winter months when Apollo was resting or away elsewhere. Don't miss the Omphalos, or "navel" stone. This is a Hellenistic or Roman copy of the stone that was believed to have marked the place above which Zeus's eagles met, establishing the sanctuary of Delphi as the centre of the earth *(see p232)*.

The bronze *Charioteer*

Detail from the frieze of the Siphnian Treasury on display in the Delphi Museum

NORTHERN GREECE

MACEDONIA · THRACE

Macedonia is Greece's largest prefecture and contains the country's second city, Thessaloníki. It is the homeland of Alexander the Great, and the heart of the ancient Hellenistic Empire. In contrast, Thrace has been largely influenced by Turkish culture but, like Macedonia, it is an area of comparatively unexplored natural beauty, with many mountain ranges and rivers.

The name Macedonia derives from the Makednoi, one of the tribes who first inhabited the region in the late 4th century BC. The legacy of the Macedonian Empire is evident in the many ancient sites, including Vergína, the location of King Philip II of Macedon's tomb; Pélla, the birthplace of Alexander; and Díon, Philip's city in the foothills of Mount Olympos. During the reign of the Roman Emperor Galerius in the 3rd century AD, many fine monuments were built, including the landmark arch in Thessaloníki. The Byzantine era also left an outstanding legacy of architecture, seen in the many churches throughout Northern Greece. Muslim influences remain strong, particularly in Thrace,

where eastern-style bazaars and minarets can still be seen. Macedonia and Thrace have a cooler, damper climate than much of Greece and hence a flourishing flora. Bordering Central Greece is the country's highest mountain, Olympos, and in the northwest lie the beautiful Préspa Lakes. Local produce includes tobacco from Thrace, and wine from Náousa.

In contrast to the busy beaches on its western side, the Chalkidikí peninsula in Macedonia has the holy Mount Athos to the east. After a purported visit from the Virgin Mary, the Byzantine Emperor Monomáchos banished women and children from the site. This decree is still valid today.

Villagers at a taverna in the Néstos Valley

◄ One of the monasteries by the sea, Mount Athos

Exploring Northern Greece

Northern Greece offers varied pleasures. The bustle of modern Thessaloníki can be combined with a beach holiday in Chalkidikí, or with an exploration of some of the ancient Macedonian sites. Lovers of natural history will appreciate the National Park around the Préspa Lakes on the border with Albania, and the Dadiá Forest and Evros River Delta to the east near Turkey. Walkers will want to explore the paths of Mount Olympos. Kastoriá and Kavála, two relatively little-known Greek towns, both reward a lengthy visit as well as making excellent bases for travelling further afield. Kavála offers access to the fascinating but little-visited region of Thrace. This region's three main towns – Xánthi, Komotiní and Alexandroúpoli – all offer the attractive combination of Greek and Turkish influence. Alexandroúpoli is also ideal as a family holiday resort with its beaches and seafront cafés.

A typical stall at the fruit and vegetable market in Xánthi, selling local produce

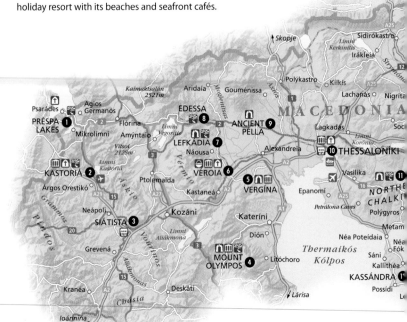

Reedbeds by the Mikrí Préspa lake

For hotels and restaurants see pp272–3 and pp290–91

Sights at a Glance

Getting Around

Thessaloníki's airport serves both international and domestic routes. Airports at Kastoriá, Kozáni and Alexandroúpoli are for domestic flights only. Ferry connections link Thessaloníki with the Sporades, and Kavála and Alexandroúpoli with the northern Aegean islands. Fast trains travel south from Thessaloníki to Athens, and east into Thrace. The main E75 highway runs south to Athens, while the E90 highway joins Thessaloníki to Thrace. Buses go from Thessaloníki to Alexandroúpoli and Kastoriá.

Locator Map

Kastaniés

Orestiáda

Rodópi

Káto Nevrokópi

Néstos

Didymóteicho

alakió

Paranéstio

NÉSTOS VALLEY

Echínos

Soufli

áni

Drama

Stavroúpoli

THRACE

Sapka

Dadiá

DADIÁ FOREST

Alistráti

XÁNTHI

Iasmos

KOMOTINÍ

Limni vistonida

Sápes

Istanbul

Pangaío

KAVÁLA

Eleftheroúpoli

Néstos

Xylaganí

AVDIRA

MARÓNEIA

Féres

mfípoli

Keramotí

ALEXANDROÚPOLI

Thasos

Thracian Sea

Evros

ós

jeira

lerissós

Ouranoúpoli

urvouroú

MOUNT ATHOS

SITHONIÁ

Áthos 2033m

Sárti

órto Karrás

to

Kalamítsi

ó

0 kilometres 50

0 miles 20

Key

— Motorway

— Major road

····· Minor road

— Scenic route

·-·- Main railway

▬ International border

▬ Regional border

The harbour of Kavála, in eastern Macedonia

For keys to symbols *see back flap*

Beautiful landscape of the Préspa Lakes

❶ Préspa Lakes
Εθνικός Δρυμός Πρεσπών

Macedonia. **Road map** B1.
to Flórina. Agios Germanós
(23850 51211).

This is the only national park
in Greece which is made up
largely of water. It is one of the
mainland's most beautiful and
unspoilt places and was little
visited in the past because of its

rather inaccessible location.
The border with Albania runs
through the southwest corner
of the Megáli Préspa lake,
joining the border of the
Former Yugoslav Republic of
Macedonia. The Greek area
of the lake, together with the
smaller Mikrí Préspa lake and
surrounding countryside, make
up the 255 sq km (100 sq miles)
of national park, established in

1974. The area is so important
for wildlife that Mikrí Préspa and
the reed beds that fringe it form
a park within a park, a core of
some 49 sq km (19 sq miles)
regarded as a complete
protection area. The boundary
of the core area is clearly
indicated by signs to
prevent accidental trespass.

Over 1,300 species of plant
can be found here, including
the endemic *Centaurea
prespana*, which has small daisy-
like flowers. There are over
40 species of mammal, such as
bears, wolves, otters, roe deer,
wild boar and wild cats. The area
is also one of the last remaining
breeding refuges in Europe for
the Dalmatian pelican, whose
numbers are down to less than
1,000 pairs worldwide, with
about 150 of these nesting in
the Préspa Lakes. Other birds
more frequently seen include

Wetland Wildlife

In contrast to the dry and stony terrain found in
much of Greece, the north has some outstanding
wetlands with a range of different habitats.
Reed-fringed lake margins hold large colonies
of breeding birds and amphibians, while the
open water is home to numerous fish and aquatic
insects. The marshes are rich in flowers and full of
songbirds; the man-made habitats such as saltpans
and lagoons offer sanctuary to nesting waders.

Lake Korónia is easy to view from
nearby villages, most of which have
their own colonies of white storks.
In spring, terrapins and frogs gather
in the shallow margins of the lake.

Kentish plovers nest on
the margins of wetlands,
such as the Préspa Lakes.

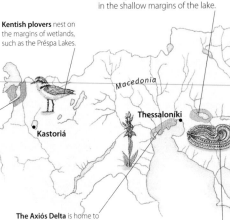

Thessaloníki

Macedonia

Kastoriá

The Préspa Lakes support
colonies of rare Dalmatian
pelicans. When nesting, they
need the peace and quiet this
protected area provides.

The Axiós Delta is home to
dragonflies and, on the
margins, a wealth of spring
flowers and bee orchids.

Whipsnakes are common in
northern Greece, particularly
around Lake Korónia.

herons, cormorants, egrets, storks, golden eagles and goosanders.

Scattered around the lakes are several small villages. One of these, on the shore of Megáli Préspa, is **Psarádes**, a picturesque village where fishermen provide a boat service on to the lake. From the boat, you can see

Psarádes village on the banks of Megáli Préspa

hermitages, icons painted on the rocks by the shore, and two churches: the 15th-century **Panagía Eleoúsa** and the 13th-century **Metamórfosi**. To the east of Mikrí Préspa is **Mikrolímni**. The village has wet meadows to the north that are rich in birdlife. Southwest of Mikrolímni, a path leads to the Ellinikí Etaireía Biological Station, used as a base by research scientists who want to stay in the area while studying.

Fresco from Metamórfosi church

In summer, the beaches of fine, pale sand that stretch alongside Megáli Préspa can be enjoyed along with a dip in the blue, but rather cold, waters of the lake.

Environs

Northeast of the park lies the village of **Agios Germanós**, which has an 11th-century Byzantine church and a number of traditional houses, built in the local architectural style. The village is also home to the **Préspa Information Centre,** which has a permanent exhibition explaining the ecological importance of the Préspa National Park. Guides are available to show visitors around the park, but this must be arranged in advance.

Just out of the village, a road leads up to the summits of Kaló Neró, at 2,160 m (7,090 ft), and Mázi, at 2,060 m (6,760 ft), which give superb views across the lakes below.

Glossy ibises have one of their last remaining European strongholds in the wetlands of northern Greece. Seen in good light, their feathers have a metallic sheen.

The Evros Delta lies close to the border with Turkey and access to many of the best areas can be difficult. Numerous water birds, including little egrets, nest and feed in easily viewed locations.

Purple herons nest in the reedbeds of the Evros Delta.

Pórto Lágos's lagoons, pools and marshes are a haven for ruddy shelducks.

Xánthi

Kavála

Thrace

Alexandroúpoli

Key

- Préspa Lakes
- Axiós Delta
- Lake Korónia
- Néstos Delta
- Pórto Lágos
- Evros Delta
- — National boundary

The Néstos Delta is one of the finest wetlands in Greece. Many species of birds inhabit the extensive reedbanks and clumps of trees, in particular large breeding colonies of herons and egrets.

| 0 kilometres | 50 |
| 0 miles | 50 |

Ancient Monastery of Símonos Pétras ▶

❷ Kastoriá
Καστοριά

Macedonia. **Road map** B2. 🏔 17,000.
✈ 10 km (6 miles) S of Kastoriá. 🚌
ℹ Plateía Olympiakí Flóga (24670
29630). 🛍 Wed.

Kastoriá is the Greek for "place of beavers". These animals used to live in Lake Kastoriá (also known as Lake Orestiáda) by which the town stands, one of the loveliest settings in Greece. Evidence of a prehistoric settlement was unearthed here in 1940. In 200 BC, the Romans captured the town, then known as Keletron. The beavers first brought the furriers here in the 17th century and, despite the fact that the animals were extinct in the area by the 19th century, trading continued. By then, the furriers were also importing unwanted fur scraps, including mink castoffs, and making desirable garments out of them. The fur trade exists today, with the craftsmen still making the fur coats that can be bought in shops here, in Thessaloníki and Athens.

The town prospered as a result of the fur trade, as its several remaining 17th- and 18th-century mansions testify. Most of these are found in the southeast quarter of the town. The elegant Skoutári and Nanzí mansions have interior courtyards and three floors. The ground floor in each case is built of stone; the upper two are made of wood. They have fine timbered rooms fitted with cupboards, hearths and raised platforms. The lower stone floor is used for storage, while the living quarters are in the wooden upper floor which juts out over the street.

The town's **Folk Museum** is housed in the Aïvazí mansion. Built in the 15th century, it was lived in until as recently as 1972. It now has an eloquent display of the lifestyle of the wealthy fur

The Skoutári mansion in Kastoriá, built in the 18th century

traders. There is typically elaborate woodwork in the salon on the upper floor. The kitchens beneath and the wine cellar have also been restored.

Another notable feature of the town are its many Byzantine churches. Fifty-four survive, and most are listed as ancient monuments, including the 11th-century **Panagía Koumbelídiki**, situated towards the south end of Mitropóleos. The church is named after its unusually tall dome (or *kubbe*, in Turkish). Some of the churches are tiny and hidden away in Kastoriá's labyrinth of streets, as they were originally private chapels. Many are closed to the public, with some of their icons removed, most of which are now on display in the **Byzantine Museum**, which is also sometimes referred to as the Archaeological Museum. The small collection

Apse and cupola of Panagía Koumbelídiki

has exquisite pieces on display, including some fine icons.

🏛 Folk Museum
Kapetán Lázou 10. **Tel** 24670 28603.
Open 10am–5pm Tue–Sat,
11am–5pm Sun. **Closed** main
public hols. ♿

🏛 Byzantine Museum
Plateía Dexamenís. **Tel** 24670 26781.
Open 8:30am–3pm Tue–Sun.
Closed main public hols.

❸ Siátista
Σιάτιστα

Macedonia. **Road map** B2. 🏔 5,000.
ℹ Plateía Tsistopoúlou (24650
21280).

Siátista was founded in the 1430s, after the Turkish conquest of Thessaloníki. Like Kastoriá, the town flourished as a result of the fur trade despite the lack of local fur. Sable and martin remnants were brought in, mainly from Russia, made up into garments, and then traded or sold in Western Europe.

The wealth that this created in the 18th century went into the building of many fine mansion houses. The Ottoman influence in their decoration is strong. The **Nerantzopoúlou** mansion is one of several in the town that can be visited. Keys and directions to the other mansions, including the **Manoúsi** and **Poulkídou**, can also be obtained here.

🏛 Nerantzopoúlou Mansion
Plateía Chorí. **Tel** 24650 22254. **Open**
Tue–Sun. **Closed** main public hols.

View across Siátista, in the Mount Askion range, western Macedonia

View of the Mount Olympos mountain range, Litóchoro

❹ Mount Olympos

Όλυμπος

17 km (10 miles) W of Litóchoro, Macedonia. **Road map** C2.
🚌 Litóchoro. 🛈 Town Hall: Agios Nikoláou 17, Litóchoro (23523 50100).

The name Mount Olympos refers to the whole range of mountains, 20 km (12 miles) across. The highest peak in the range, at 2,917 m (9,571 ft), is Mýtikas. The whole area constitutes the Olympos National Park.

Over 1,700 plant species are found here, many of them endemic to the park. Chamois, boars and roe deer also live in this area.

The base for walkers is the village of **Litóchoro**, a lively place with several hotels and tavernas. Walking maps are available and a marked trail leads up into the national park. Mýtikas can be reached in a demanding walk of at least six hours. It is imperative to camp out overnight or stay in one of the two mountain refuges, rather than attempt to get up and down in a day.

Environs

About 10 km (6 miles) north of Litóchoro is the village of Díon, which has an excellent museum showing finds from **Ancient Díon**. This site is near the

Roman mosaic from Ancient Díon

modern village and splendidly set between the coast and the Olympian peaks, its very name deriving from *Díos*, or "of Zeus". To the Macedonians, it was a holy city, and in the 4th century BC, some 15,000 people lived here. The flat plains were used as a military camp and rallying point by King Philip II of Macedon *(see pp36–7)*. Although Díon was a military camp, rather than a civilian city, there was a temple to Zeus, a theatre and a stadium at the site. Later, the Romans built a city here. The ruins visible today date mainly from that era, and include fine mosaics from the 2nd century AD and well-preserved Roman baths. There is also a theatre and the remnants of a sanctuary dedicated to the Egyptian

goddess Isis. She was worshipped by the Romans as a foreign deity, along with many others that were similarly "adopted" into the pantheon. A second temple, dedicated to Zeus, has also been unearthed here.

The bright and modern **Díon Museum** in the village shows films of the excavations, and it is worth seeing before visiting the site. Also on display are toys, kitchen utensils and jewellery, all finds from the sanctuary of Isis. Together, they give a vivid picture of life in Ancient Díon.

🏛 Ancient Díon
E of Díon. **Tel** 23510 53484.
Open 8am–7pm daily (to 3pm Tue–Sun in winter). **Closed** main public hols. 🅿 🔲 ancientdion.org

🏛 Díon Museum
Díon. **Tel** 23510 53206. **Open** 8am–7pm Tue–Sun (8:30am–3pm Tue–Sun in winter). **Closed** main public hols. 🅿

The Home of Zeus

Zeus, chief and most powerful of the ancient Greek gods, lived on Mount Olympos along with the other immortals and was thought to be responsible for the destinies of men. He was also god of weather and thunderstorms. Many of the myths tell of Zeus's amorous liaisons and his numerous children, some of whom were gods or goddesses and some heroes *(see pp56–7)*. He was worshipped at Olympia and at Dodóni in Epirus, site of the oldest oracle in Greece.

❺ Vergína
Βεργίνα

12 km (7 miles) SE of Véroia, Macedonia.
Road map C2. 🚌 Museum:
Tel 23310 92347. **Open** May–Oct:
8am–8pm daily; Nov–Apr:
8:30am–3pm Tue–Sat (to 7pm Sun).
🎫 (tickets also valid for Royal Tombs).

Outside the village of Vergína,
during excavations in 1977,
archaeologist Professor Manólis
Andrónikos found an entrance to
a tomb. The bones inside
included a skull with one eye
socket damaged, evidence that
the tomb belonged to King Philip
II of Macedon, who received such
a wound in the siege of Methóni.
The bones were discovered in
a stunning gold funerary box,
embellished with the symbol
of the Macedonian Sun. The
discovery confirmed that this
area was the site of Aigai, the first
capital of Macedon. The finds
from this tomb, as well as finds
from several other **Royal Tombs**
nearby, are now on display
in the museum here and are
considered the most important
in Greece since Schliemann's
discoveries at Mycenae
(see pp182–4).
 A short walk further along
the road from Philip's tomb are
some earlier discoveries, known
as the **Macedonian Tombs**. The
dark interior hides splendid

Terracotta head of a young man, from the Museum at Véroia

solid marble doors and a
beautiful marble throne.
 The **Palace of Palatítsia**
stands beyond on a mound.
It is thought to have been first
occupied in about 1000 BC,
though the building itself dates
from the 3rd century BC.
Today, only low foundations
remain, along with the ruins of
a theatre 100 m (330 ft) below,
thought to be the site of
Philip II's assassination.

🏛 **Royal Tombs, Macedonian
Tombs, Palace of Palatítsia**
Tel 23310 92394. **Open** Apr–Oct:
8am–7:30pm Tue–Sun, 1:30–7:30pm
Mon; Nov–Mar: 8:30am–3pm
Tue–Sun. **Closed** main public
hols. 🎫

The Macedonian Royal Family

The gold burial casket found at Vergína is emblazoned with the
Macedonian Sun, the symbol of the king. Philip II was from a
long line of Macedonian kings that began in about 640 BC
with Perdiccas I. Philip was the first ruler to unite the whole of
Greece as it existed at that time. Also incorrectly known as the
Macedonian Star, the Sun is often seen on flags within the
region. Much of Greece's pride in the symbol lies in the fact that
Alexander the Great used it throughout his empire *(see pp36–7)*.
He was just 20 when his father was assassinated at Aigai in
336 BC. He inherited his father's already large empire and also
his ambition to conquer
the Persians. In 334 BC,
Alexander crossed the
Dardanelles with 40,000
men and defeated the
Persians in three different
battles, advancing as far
as the Indus Valley before
he died at the age of
33. With his death, the
Macedonian Empire divided.

Burial casket featuring the Macedonian Sun

❻ Véroia
Βέροια

Macedonia. **Road map** C2. 🏔 48,000.
🚌 🚆 🚊 Tue.

The largest town in the region,
Véroia is interesting mainly for
its 50 or so barnlike churches,
which have survived from the
17th and 18th centuries.
 The town's **Archaeological
Museum** has a good selection
of exhibits, discovered locally,
and the bazaar area bustles on
market days, as Véroia is the
centre of the local peach-
growing industry.

🏛 **Archaeological Museum**
Anoixéos 47. **Tel** 23310 24972.
Open May–Oct: 8am–8pm daily;
Nov–Apr: 8am–5pm Tue–Sun.
Closed main public hols. 🎫

Chília Déndra park at Náousa, near Lefkádia

❼ Lefkádia
Λευκάδια

Macedonia. **Road map** C2. **Tel** 23320
41121. 🚌 **Open** 7am–3pm Tue–Fri,
10am–6pm Sat & Sun. **Closed** main
public hols.

The four Macedonian Tombs
of Lefkádia are set in a quiet
agricultural area. The caretaker
is usually at one of the two
tombs that are signposted.
The first of these is the **Tomb
of the Judges**, or Great Tomb.
This, the largest tomb, with a
chamber 9 m (30 ft) square and
a frescoed façade portraying
Aiakos and Rhadamanthys,
the Judges of Hades, has
been restored. Beyond is the
Anthemíon Tomb, or Tomb of

Pebble mosaic of the Lion Hunt from the House of the Lion Hunt at Ancient Pélla

the Flowers, with well-preserved flower paintings on the roof. The key to the **Tomb of Lyson and Kallikles** is sometimes available from the caretaker. The entrance is through a metal grate in the roof. The fourth tomb, called the **Tomb of Kinch** after its Danish discoverer, or the **Tomb of Niafsta** after its one-time occupant, is closed to visitors.

Environs

Renowned for the large park of Chília Déndra (1,000 trees), also known as Agios Nikólaos, **Náousa** is the home of the Boutari wine-making family. It is situated on the edge of the hills above the plain that extends east to Thessaloníki. Like Edessa, Náousa has waters flowing through it. Riverside tavernas in the park offer fresh trout as well as the good local wine.

❽ Edessa

Έδεσσα

Macedonia. **Road map** C1. 🏛 16,000. 🚌 🚉 *i* Parko Katarrákton (23810 20300). **Open** 10am–4pm Mon–Fri, 10am–6pm Sat & Sun. 🛒 Thu.

Edessa is the capital of the modern Pélla region and a popular summer resort. It is renowned for its waterfalls, which plunge down a ravine from the town to the valley floor below. The largest fall is the **Káranos**, at 24 m (79 ft), which has a cave behind it. The surrounding gardens and park are pleasant, with cafés and restaurants.

❾ Ancient Pélla

Πέλλα

38 km (24 miles) NW of Thessaloníki, Macedonia. **Road map** C1. 🚌 **Tel** 23820 31160. Site: **Open** Nov–Apr: 11am–6pm Mon, 8am–8pm Tue–Sun; May–Oct: 8am–3pm. Museum: **Open** same hours as the site. **Closed** main public hols. 🅿 ♿

This small site, which straddles the main road, was once the

Káranos waterfall at Edessa

flourishing capital of Macedon. The court was moved here from Aigai (near modern Vergína) in 410 BC by King Archelaos, who ruled from 413 to 399 BC. It is here that Alexander the Great was born in 356 BC, and later tutored by the philosopher Aristotle. Some sense of the existence of a city can be gained from a plan of the site, which shows where the main street and shops were located. King Archelaos's Palace is believed to have been north of the main site. The site has some of the best-preserved and most beautiful pebble mosaics in Greece. The stones are uncut and have been carefully picked not only for their size, but also for their warm, subtle colouring. Dating from about 300 BC, the mosaics include vivid hunting scenes. One of the most famous is of Dionysos riding a panther. The mosaic is protected from the weather in the now-covered House of the Lion Hunt. This was built at the end of the 4th century BC and originally comprised 12 rooms around three open courtyards, the whole structure being 90 m (295 ft) long by 50 m (165 ft) wide.

⑩ Thessaloníki
Θεσσαλονίκη

Thessaloniki, also known as Salonica, is Greece's second city, founded by King Kassandros in 315 BC. The Romans made it capital of their province of Macedonia Prima in 146 BC, and in AD 395, it became part of the Byzantine Empire. In 1430, it was captured by the Turks who held it until 1912. Today, Thessaloníki is a bustling cosmopolitan city. It has a flourishing cultural life and is a major religious centre, with an array of splendid churches *(see p252)*, such as Agía Sofía and Agios Dimítrios, which is the largest church in Greece.

Cafés and fountains in the park near Plateía Chánth

Exploring Thessaloníki

Furniture shop in the back streets

Greece's second city is also a very busy port, which adds to the bustle and the wealth of this fascinating metropolis. Situated on the Thermaic Gulf, it has an attractive waterfront promenade, known as the *paralía*, and a pleasant leafy park. It also boasts a large number of beautiful Byzantine churches *(see p252)*. In recent years, Thessaloníki has developed its international exhibition facilities and become a major trade fair centre. The city has many museums, including the Archaeological Museum *(see pp250–51)*.

The Great Fire of August in 1917 destroyed nearly half the buildings within the medieval walls, including the entire Jewish quarter. Some, however, survived, and many from the original Ottoman bazaar have been restored. One such building is the **Bezesténi**, once a hall for valuables and now home to plush shops. The **Modiáno**, a covered meat and produce hall, is named after the Jewish family who once owned it. West of Modiáno are some of the best *ouzerí* bars, and **Plateía Aristotélous** is home to many posh cafés.

🏛 Arch of Galerius
Egnatía.

The principal architectural legacy of Roman rule is found at the eastern end of the long main street, Egnatía, which was itself a Roman construction, known as Via Egnatia. Here stands the Arch of Galerius, built in AD 303 by Galerius (then Caesar of the East, or deputy emperor) to celebrate his victory over the Persians in AD 297. Its carvings show scenes from the battle. There was once a double arch here, with a palace to the south. Some of its remains can be seen in Plateía Navarínou.

Section of carving from the Arch of Galerius

🏯 White Tower and Paralía
On the waterfront. **Tel** 2310 267832. **Open** 8am–8pm daily. 🔊

Probably Thessaloníki's most famous sight is the White Tower on the *paralía*. Built in 1430, the Turks added three such towers to the 8-km (5-mile) city walls. Today, it houses rotating exhibitions on several floors of small circular rooms. The original stone steps climb up to a roof with lovely views of the *paralía*.

🏯 Rotónda
Filíppou.

Standing north of the Arch of Galerius is the Rotónda. It is thought that this impressive building was constructed as a mausoleum for Galerius, emperor of the eastern Roman Empire AD 305–311. Today, it is closed, but it has been used in the past both as a church – it is also known as Agios Geórgios – and as a mosque. The minaret nearby is now the only one in Thessaloníki.

🏛 Museum of Byzantine Culture
Leofórou Stratoú 2. **Tel** 2310 306400. **Open** 8am–8pm daily. **Closed** main public hols. 🔊 ♿
W mbp.gr

Situated behind the Archaeological Museum *(see pp250–51),* this small, modern museum was opened in 1995. On display are Byzantine icons that date from the 15th to the 19th centuries, and fine jewellery. All of the items are beautifully displayed and there are plans to expand the collection.

White Tower on the seafront

weapons, documents and personal items tell the story well. Vivid tableaux depict the struggle and its effect on ordinary people. In one, a Turk with a rifle bursts violently into a schoolroom while a Greek freedom fighter hides under the floorboards. This was the celebrated Pávlos Melás, who fought to free Macedonia from the Turks. Also on display in the museum are his gun and dagger.

🏛 Museum of the Macedonian Struggle

Proxénou Koromilá 23. **Tel** 2310 229778. **Open** 9am–2pm Tue–Fri, 10am–2pm Sat. **Closed** main public hols. 🌐 imma.edu.gr

This is situated in a late 19th-century mansion which originally housed the Greek Consulate when Thessaloníki was under Turkish rule. Photographs, newspapers,

🏛 Folklife and Ethnological Museum

Vasilíssis Olgas 68. **Tel** 2310 830591. **Open** 9am–3:30pm Fri–Tue, 9am–9:30pm Wed. 🌐 lemmth.gr

This museum is a 20-minute walk from the Archaeological Museum. There are displays of folk costumes, and detailed small models showing rural activities such as ploughing, winnowing, threshing, and children playing. The gruelling

life of the nomadic Sarakatsan shepherds is well documented, and a vivid display shows the incredible events at the annual fire-walking ceremony in Lagkadás, a village 20 km (12 miles) northeast of Thessaloníki. The museum also hosts several temporary exhibitions throughout the year and has an extensive archive of fascinating period photography showing the reality of life during the early 20th century.

Thessaloníki Town Centre

① Rotónda
② Arch of Galerius
③ Agía Sofía
④ Plateía Aristotélous
⑤ Museum of the Macedonian Struggle
⑥ White Tower and Paralía
⑦ Archaeological Museum
⑧ Museum of Byzantine Culture

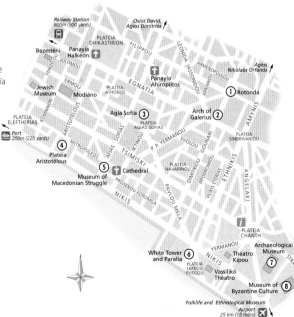

0 metres 400
0 yards 400

For keys to symbols see back flap

Thessaloníki Archaeological Museum
Αρχαιολογικό Μουσείο Θεσσαλονίκης

This modern museum, opened in 1963, contains a host of treasures. It concentrates on the finds made within the city and at the many sites in Macedonia. The displays progress chronologically through the ages, giving a clear picture of the area's history. The inner rooms surrounding the courtyard house a number of fabulous gold items from ancient Macedon, including the treasures discovered during excavations at Macedonian cemeteries. The annexe basement contains a small exhibition on the prehistory of Thessaloníki.

Faïence Vase
Found in a 2nd-century BC grave in Thessaloníki, this ornate vase is from Ptolemaic Egypt and is the only such faïence vase in Greece.

Field House
Garden Grave

★ Floor Mosaics from a Thessaloníki House
These detailed mosaics depicting marine-world mythology are Roman. This mosaic shows a nereid (sea nymph) and a dolphin.

Main entrance

Gallery Guide

An outer circle of rooms surrounds a block of inner rooms housing a collection of Macedonian gold. The outer rooms contain treasures from the first centuries of Thessaloníki and the kingdom of Macedon. The basement of the annexe holds a display of prehistoric antiquities and temporary exhibitions.

Outdoor courtyard with Roman floor mosaic

Marble Sarcophagus
This 2nd- or 3rd-century Roman sarcophagus is decorated with a vivid relief depicting an Amazon battle. The Amazons, a mythical warrior tribe of women, were a favourite subject for artists *(see p59)*.

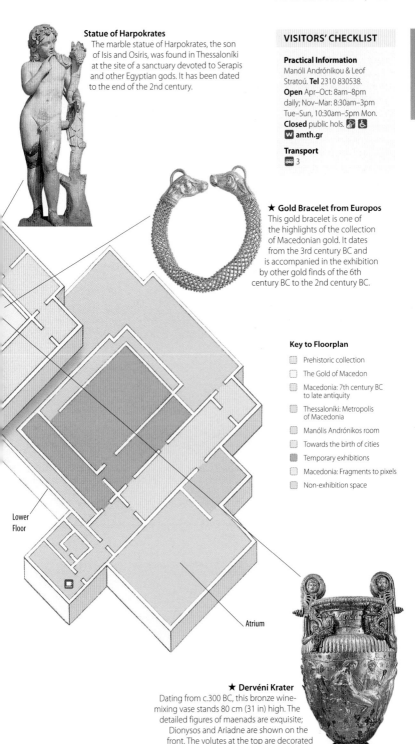

Statue of Harpokrates
The marble statue of Harpokrates, the son of Isis and Osiris, was found in Thessaloníki at the site of a sanctuary devoted to Serapis and other Egyptian gods. It has been dated to the end of the 2nd century.

VISITORS' CHECKLIST

Practical Information
Manóli Andrónikou & Leof Stratoú. **Tel** 2310 830538.
Open Apr–Oct: 8am–8pm daily; Nov–Mar: 8:30am–3pm Tue–Sun, 10:30am–5pm Mon.
Closed public hols. 🅿 ♿
🅦 amth.gr

Transport
🚌 3

★ Gold Bracelet from Europos
This gold bracelet is one of the highlights of the collection of Macedonian gold. It dates from the 3rd century BC and is accompanied in the exhibition by other gold finds of the 6th century BC to the 2nd century BC.

Key to Floorplan

- Prehistoric collection
- The Gold of Macedon
- Macedonia: 7th century BC to late antiquity
- Thessaloníki: Metropolis of Macedonia
- Manólis Andrónikos room
- Towards the birth of cities
- Temporary exhibitions
- Macedonia: Fragments to pixels
- Non-exhibition space

Lower Floor

Atrium

★ Dervéni Krater
Dating from c.300 BC, this bronze wine-mixing vase stands 80 cm (31 in) high. The detailed figures of maenads are exquisite; Dionysos and Ariadne are shown on the front. The volutes at the top are decorated with the head of Herakles.

Exploring Thessaloníki's Churches

Thessaloníki has the richest collection of Byzantine churches in Greece. Of the hundreds of 5th-century basilicas that once stood across the country, only two remain. Both of these, Agios Dimítrios and Acheiropoítos, are in Thessaloníki. The 8th-century Agía Sofía is a very significant Byzantine building, both for its mosaics and its role in influencing future architectural development. Three different 14th-century churches – Agios Nikólaos Orfanós, Agioi Apóstoloi and Agía Aikateríni – give an insight into what was a period of architectural innovation.

Agía Sofía church

The mosaic of Ezekiel's vision in Osios Davíd

🏛 Agios Dimítrios

Agíou Dimitríou 97. **Open** 6am–10pm daily. 🛗 Crypt **Open** 10:30am–8pm Sun, 12:30–7pm Mon, 8am–8pm Tue–Sat.

This, the largest church in Greece, was entirely rebuilt after the fire of 1917, which destroyed the 7th- and 13th-century fabric of the basilica. The oldest, 3rd-century AD portion is the crypt. Originally a Roman bath, this, according to legend, is the site of the imprisonment, torture and murder in 305 AD of the city's patron saint Dimítrios – a Roman soldier converted to Christianity and martyred on the orders of Emperor Galerius. Six small 5th–7th-century mosaics are found both on the piers flanking the altar and high up on the west side of the church. These mosaics rank among the finest in Greece and include depictions of Dimítrios with young children, or in the company of the church's builders.

🏛 Osios Davíd

Kástro. **Open** daily.

This delightful small chapel was founded some time in the late 5th century. Behind the altar is an original vivid mosaic of the *Vision of Ezekiel*, rare in that it depicts Christ without a beard. In marvellous condition, it owes its freshness to having been concealed beneath plaster and only discovered in 1921. There are also some frescoes from the 12th century, including a fine *Baptism* and *Nativity*. Although the church is usually locked, there is a caretaker who greets visitors and will unbolt the doors.

🏛 Agía Sofía

Plateía Agías Sofías. **Open** 8:30am–2pm, 5:30–8pm daily.

The church of Agía Sofía is dedicated to the Holy Wisdom (Sofiá) of God, just like the mosque of the same name in Istanbul. It was built in the mid-8th century. In 1585, it became a mosque, but was reconsecrated as a church in 1912. It contains many mosaics and frescoes dating back to the 9th and 10th centuries, including a fine *Ascension* scene in the 30-m (100-ft) high dome. The entrance formerly had a portico, which was obliterated during an Italian air raid in 1941. The imposing nature of the building is emphasized by its location in a partially sunken garden.

🏛 Agios Nikólaos Orfanós

Kástro. **Open** 8am–2:45pm Tue–Sun; key available from warden at Irodhotou 17, opposite the church. 🛗

Situated in a garden plot amongst the lanes of the ancient Kástra district, or upper town, this small, triple-apsed 14th-century church began life as a dependency of the larger Moni Vlatádon, further up the hill. Today, Agios Nikólaos Orfanós retains the richest and best-preserved collection of late Byzantine frescoes in the city. Distributed over the central cella and both aisles, they show rare scenes from the Passion, including Christ mounting the Cross, and Pilate seated in judgment.

Agios Dimítrios, the largest church in Greece

The stretch of sandy beach at Kallithéa on Kassándra

⓫ Northern Chalkidikí
Βόρεια Χαλκιδική

Macedonia. **Road map** D2.
🚌 to Polýgyros.

The north of Chalkidikí is a quiet and delightful hilly region, often overlooked by those whose main interests are the beaches to the south. A glimpse of the hidden interior is given when visiting the **Petrálona Caves**, situated on the edge of Mount Katsíka, 55 km (34 miles) southeast of Thessaloníki. It was in these red-rock caverns in 1960, the year after the caves were discovered by local villagers, that a skull was found. It was believed to be that of a young woman, aged about 25 when she died. A complete skeleton was subsequently discovered, and these are the oldest bones yet to be found in Greece, dating back at least 250,000 years, and possibly even 700,000. Amid the stalactites and stalagmites, reconstructions of the cave dwellers have been arranged in the caves, along with the bones, teeth and tools that were also found here.

In the northeast of the area is the small village of **Stágeira**, the birthplace of Aristotle (384–322 BC). On a hilltop, just outside the village, is a huge white marble statue of the philosopher, and there are sweeping views over the surrounding countryside.

🏛 Petrálona Caves
Mount Katsíka, 55 km (34 miles) SE of Thessaloníki. **Tel** 23730 73365.
Open May–Oct: 9am–7pm Tue–Sun; Nov–Apr: 9am–3pm Tue–Sun.
Closed main public hols. 🅿

⓬ Kassándra
Κασσάνδρα

Statue of Aristotle, Stágeira

Southern Chalkidikí, Macedonia.
Road map D2.
🚌 to Kassándreia.

Much of this area's population was killed in the War of Independence in 1821, and the numbers never really recovered. Little was left on the promontory of Kassándra other than a few fishing villages. However, over the last 30 years, many resorts have sprung up.

Néa Poteídaia marks the start of Kassándra proper and straddles the narrow neck of the peninsula, with a good sandy beach, a marina and an attractive town square. On the west coast, **Sáni** has excellent beaches and a luxury resort complex. There are quiet bays around the village of **Possídi**, on a promontory halfway down the west coast. On the east coast, **Néa Fókaia** still functions as a fishing village in spite of the steady invasion of tourism, whereas **Kallithéa**, to the south, is the largest resort on Kassándra.

⓭ Sithonía
Σιθωνία

Southern Chalkidikí, Macedonia.
Road map D2. 🚌 to Agios Nikólaos.

While the peninsula of Sithonía is only marginally larger than Kassándra, it has fewer resorts and a thickly wooded interior. The peninsula begins at **Metamórfosi**, which has a sandy beach shaded by pine trees. **Vourvouroú** is one of the first villages you come to on the north side. A collection of villas spreads along the coast, with a few hotels and a selection of eating places.

To the south of this area is a long undeveloped stretch of coast, with several unspoilt beaches, until you reach the large resort of **Sárti**. At the tip of Sithonía is **Kalamítsi**, little more than a sandy beach and a few bars, while **Pórto Koufó** at the end of the west coast is still a pleasant fishing village set on a bay amid wooded hills. The **Pórto Karrás** resort, halfway down the west coast, was set up by the Karrás wine family. It has three hotels, a marina, a shopping centre, water sports, horse riding, a golf course and tennis.

Boats docked at Pórto Koufó on Sithonía

Mount Athos
Άγιον Όρος

To the Greeks, this is the Holy Mountain, which at 2,030 m (6,660 ft), is the highest point of Chalkidikí's most easterly peninsula. Unique in Greece, Athos is an autonomous republic ruled by the 1,700 monks who live in its 20 monasteries. Only adult males may visit the peninsula, but it is possible to see many of the monasteries from a boat trip along the coast. Together, they include some fine examples of Byzantine architecture and provide an insight into monastic life.

Kólpos Agíou Orous

- Ierissós
- Ouranoúpoli
- Metóchi Chourmítsas
- Chelandaríou
- Esfigmenou
- Zográfou
- Vatopediou
- Kastamonítou
- Skiti Agíou
- Pantokratora
- Docheláriou
- Andréa
- Stavronikíta
- Xenofontos
- Karyés
- Koutloumousíou
- Agiou Panteleímonos
- Iviron
- Xiropotamoú
- Filotheou
- Dáfni
- Karakallou
- Simonos Petras
- Grigoríou
- Megistis Lávras
- Agíou Dionysíou
- Mt Athos
- Agíou Pávlou
- Néa Skíti
- Skíti Timíou
- Skiti Agías Annas
- Pródromou

The Monasteries of Athos

--- Ferry route

Mount Athos from the West

This illustration shows the view seen when travelling by boat along the west of Athos. The most northerly monastery on this coast is Zográfou and the most southerly is Agíou Pávlou. The eastern monasteries are covered on p258

Agíou Panteleímonos
Also known as Rosikón (of the Russians), this 11th-century monastery's imposing walls hide many colourful onion-domed churches, evidence of the Russian Orthodox influence on Athos.

0 kilometres		15
0 miles		10

To Ouranoúpoli

① ② ③

Docheiaríou
This 10th-century monastery houses a fragment of the True Cross and an icon of the Virgin with healing powers.

◄ Coastline of the city of Kavála

Visiting Mount Athos

Only ten non-Orthodox men per day are allowed to visit Mount Athos, with a stay of four nights. To apply, send a fax request with your preferred start date to visit, together with a copy of your passport, to the Ministery of Macedonia and Thrace at +2310 270092. Apply well in advance. Once confirmed, you must book the monasteries you wish to visit; the Ministery has the monastery telephone numbers. On the day of your visit, be at the Ouranópolis Pilgrims' Bureau by 8am to collect your *Diamenterion* (official permit); bring your confirmation and passport. Boats leave daily at 9:45am for the monasteries. For more information, contact the Pilgrims Bureau, 109 Egnatia Street, 54622 Thessaloníki, Greece (tel: +2310 833733).

Vatopedíou refectory

Ouranoúpoli
The main town on Athos is where boat trips
around the peninsula start.

Agíou Pávlou
This monastery houses 90 monks,
many from Zákynthos and Kefalloniá,
and has some 13,000 books and
manuscripts in its library.

Grigoríou
Founded in the 14th century,
this monastery was totally
rebuilt after a disastrous fire in
1761, which destroyed all but a
few holy relics. About 40 monks
live here today.

KEY

① **Zográfou** was founded in
AD 971, but the present buildings
are 18th– and 19th-century.

② **Kastamonítou** was founded
in the 11th century by a hermit
from Asia Minor.

③ **Xenofóntos** was founded
in the late 10th century. A
second chapel was built in
1837, using some 14th-century
mosaic panels.

④ **Xiropotámou** was founded
in the 10th century, but the
present buildings date from
the 18th century.

⑤ **Dáfni** is Athos's port and has a
population of 16. A bus goes

from here to the capital, Karyés,
15 minutes away.

⑥ **Símonos Pétras** was named
after Saint Simon who founded
the monastery in the 14th
century AD after seeing a
strange light burning on
this remote ridge one
Christmas night.

⑦ **Agíou Dionysíou** is perched
80 m (260 ft) above the
sea. Its walls conceal
the 16th-century church of
Agios Ioánnis Pródromos.

⑧ **Néa Skíti** belongs to Agíou
Pávlou.

⑨ **Mount Athos**

For hotels and restaurants see pp272–3 and pp290–91

Exploring Mount Athos

Not all of the 20 monasteries on Athos can be seen from the popular boat trips from Ouranoúpoli, although some boats do go round the whole peninsula. A few are hidden in the mountains and others cling to the eastern coast of the peninsula. In addition to the Greek Orthodox monasteries on Mount Athos, there is one Russian (Agíou Panteleímonos), one Bulgarian (Zográfou) and one Serbian (Chelandaríou). Remote hermitages and monastic villages in the hills of the peninsula are preferred by some monks, as a quieter alternative to the relatively busy monastery life.

Orthodox Life on Mount Athos

The monks grow their own fruit and vegetables

The East Coast Monasteries

The first monastery to be founded on Athos was the **Megístis Lávras** (Great Lavra). It is situated at the southeastern end of the peninsula, on a rocky outcrop (see pp40–41). It was founded in AD 963 by Athanásios the Athonite, and is the only one of the monasteries never to have suffered from fire. It also has the largest font of all the monasteries, which is outside, shaded by a cypress tree said to have been planted over 1,000 years ago by Athanásios himself.

Halfway along the eastern coast stand the monasteries of Ivíron and Stavronikíta. **Moní Ivíron** was founded in the late 10th century by a monk from Iberia (modern Georgia), hence its name. Its church was built in the early 11th century and restored in 1513. The monastery's main courtyard contains another 16 chapels, one housing a miraculous icon of the Virgin Mary.

Stavronikíta, to the north, stands on top of a rocky headland. It was first mentioned in a document dated AD 1012.

Moní Vatopedíou, one of the largest monasteries on Athos, is sited on a small promontory at the northern end of the east coast. It was founded in the latter half of the 10th century, and a notable feature is its *katholikón*, or main church, also built in the 10th century. It contains icons dating from the 14th century, though they have been retouched over the years. A wealthy monastery, it is among the best preserved on Mount Athos.

Painting in Megístis Lávras

Under the Byzantine time system operating on Athos, midnight is at dawn, and morning services begin about an hour before – around 3 or 4am, Greek time. A monk walks around striking a small wooden *símandro* (a carved plank) with a mallet to wake the other monks and call them to prayer. The monks eat two meals a day, consisting mostly of food they grow themselves. There are 159 fasting days in the year when only one meal is allowed which must contain no fish, eggs, cheese, milk or even oil. Meals are eaten after the morning and evening services, and the time in between is spent working, resting and praying.

The Megístis Lávras monastery, with its red *katholikón* in the centre

⓯ Kavála
Καβάλα

Macedonia. **Road map** D1.
🅼 56,000. ✈ 35 km (22 miles) SE
of Kavála. 🚢 🚌 🚇 daily.

Kavála's history goes back to its foundation in the 6th century BC by settlers from Thásos and Erétria. It became part of the Roman Empire in 168 BC, and is where St Paul first set foot on European soil in AD 50 or 51 on his way to Philippi. The biggest impact, however, was the Turkish occupation from 1371 to 1912. It was the Turks who built the 16th-century aqueduct here. Mehmet Ali (1769–1849), the Pasha of Egypt, was born in Kavála. His **birthplace**, a well-preserved house set in gardens, is marked by a bronze statue of Ali on horseback. The house is closed to the public but a bar in the grounds is open during the summer.

Kavála is a busy city, with an industrial port that also has a ferry service to the northeast Aegean islands. Life centres around the harbour below the castle, which is floodlit at night.

Sculpture by Polýgnotos Vágis

At its eastern end, there is a busy fish, fruit and vegetable market. To the west is the **Archaeological Museum**, which has finds from Avdíra *(see p260)*, including a dolphin mosaic and a painted sarcophagus. The Municipal Museum on Kapnergatis Square (closed for ongoing refurbishment) has works by local artists, in particular the sculptor Polýgnotos Vágis (1894–1965).

The **Tobacco Museum** features a unique range of artifacts and documents relating to the cultivation and production of tobacco, from the agricultural process to the commercialization of tobacco products.

🏛 **Mehmet Ali's Birthplace**
Theodórou Poulídou 63. **Open** gardens only – evenings in summer.

The town and harbour of Kavála

🏛 **Archaeological Museum**
Erythroú Stavroú 17. **Tel** 2510 222335.
Open 8am–3pm daily.
Closed main public hols. 🎫 ♿

🏛 **Tobacco Museum**
K. Paleologou 4. **Tel** 2510 223344.
Open 8am–3pm Mon–Fri,
8am–1pm Sat.
🌐 tobaccomuseum.gr

⓰ Néstos Valley
Κοιλάδα του Νέστου

Macedonia/Thrace border.
Road map D1. 🚊 🚌 Xánthi (liable to be cancelled Nov–Apr).

The Néstos river rises high in the Rodópi mountains in Bulgaria, and its meandering course down to the Aegean near the island of Thásos marks the boundary between Macedonia and Thrace. On its way, it threads through remote and inaccessible gorges, fed by other rivers and streams, until it passes under the scenic mountain road which links Xánthi in Thrace with the town of Dráma in Macedonia. This road, sometimes closed by snowdrifts in winter, makes for a spectacular scenic drive through the wooded gorge, past the valley's heavy beech forests and scattering of small villages. **Stavroúpoli**, the largest of these villages, has a good café in its village square.

⓱ Xánthi
Ξάνθη

Thrace. **Road map** E1. 🅼 25,000. 🚊
🚌 🚇 Sat.

Founded in the 11th century, it was not until the 1800s that Xánthi flourished with the development of the tobacco industry. Displays on tobacco are included in the **Folk Museum**, housed in two old mansions. The museum's collection includes embroidery, jewellery and costumes. Xánthi's main square has cafés and fountains, and east of the square is the bazaar. This is overflowing on Saturdays, when people of all nationalities and religions visit the busiest market in the area.

🏛 **Folk Museum**
Antiká 7. **Tel** 25410 25421.
Open 8:30am–2:30pm Tue–Sun. 🎫

The lush landscape of the Néstos Valley

The monastery of Agios Nikólaos on the banks of Lake Vistonída

⓲ Avdira

`Άβδηρα`

6 km (4 miles) S of modern Avdira, Thrace. **Road map** E1. 🚌 **Tel** 25410 51988. **Open** 8am–3:30pm daily. **Closed** main public hols.

The ancient city of Avdira was founded in the mid-7th century BC by refugees from Klazomenae in Asia Minor. The site is quite dispersed and overgrown. Most of what can be seen today dates from the Roman period. Some Archaic and Classical ruins are also evident, including the acropolis. The remains of its walls stand on a small headland, and ancient graves have been discovered just outside the walls. Part of the original city wall can also be seen.

Environs

Along the road from Avdira to Maróneia is **Lake Vistonída**, a haven for wildlife. At one end is Pórto Lágos (see pp240–41), an old harbour with the white monastery of Agios Nikólaos.

⓳ Komotiní

Κομοτηνή

Thrace. **Road map** E1. 🚶 38,000. 🚌 🚌 🛍 Tue.

Only 25 km (16 miles) from the Bulgarian border to the north, and less than 100 km (62 miles) from Turkey to the east, Komotiní is a fascinating mix of Greek and Turkish influence. First founded in the late 4th century AD, it was taken by the Turks in 1363, and remained part of the Ottoman Empire until 1920. Over 500 years of Turkish rule have left their mark on the town, especially since the area's Muslims were excluded from the population exchange following the Greek defeat in Asia Minor in 1922. There is a thriving market with fish, cattle and tobacco for sale, along with a good selection of fresh produce grown in fertile land. The many old wooden shops sell everything from bric-a-brac to genuine, valuable antiques.

A feel of the town's recent past is given in the well-cared-for **Museum of Folk Life and History**. Its few rooms, in an

The domed roof and tall minaret of a Turkish mosque, Komotiní

Finial from a gravestone, Archaeological Museum, Komotiní

18th-century mansion, are crammed with costumes, local copperware and domestic items. There is also a particularly good collection of embroidery, including examples of a type known as Tsevrés, used in Thracian wedding ceremonies. The town's **Archaeological Museum** displays the best of the finds from the sites at ancient Avdira and Maróneia, including gold jewellery found in 4th-century BC graves at Avdira. A 4th-century BC clay mask of Dionysos is on display, found at the god's sanctuary at Maróneia. The museum also has an extensive coin collection, painted sarcophagi, votive reliefs and maps.

🏛 **Museum of Folk Life and History**
Agíou Georgíou. **Tel** 25310 25975. **Open** 9am–2:30pm daily. **Closed** main public hols. 🚫 🚻 limited.

🏛 **Archaeological Museum**
Symeonídi 4. **Tel** 25310 22411. **Open** 8am–3pm daily. **Closed** main public hols.

⓴ Maróneia

Μαρώνεια

5 km (3 miles) SE of modern Maróneia, Thrace. **Road map** E1. 🚌 to modern Maróneia. **Open** daily. **Closed** main public hols. 🚫 🚻

The road to ancient Maróneia leads through tobacco and cotton fields, past woodland

and small rural communities. A signpost to the harbour of Agios Charálampos shows the way down a track to the remains of the site, which is in a scenic position overlooking the sea. The city flourished from the 8th century BC until AD 1400. Olive groves now cover the area, which sits between Mount Ismaros and the sea, but a small theatre has been discovered and renovated. Further down the track are the remnants of a sanctuary, thought to have been dedicated to Dionysos, whose son, Maron, is credited with founding Maróneia.

Beyond the city of ancient Maróneia is the developing harbour of **Agios Charálampos**, surrounded by red cliffs, topped by a large hotel, a taverna and a scattering of houses.

Environs

Medieval **Maróneia** is a tiny but attractive place, mainly a farming community but with some larger mansions that provide evidence of a more prosperous past.

㉑ Alexandroúpoli
Αλεξανδρούπολη

Thrace. **Road map** E1. ⛰ 36,000. ✈ 🚌 🚆 🚌 ⛴ Tue.

Alexandroúpoli lacks the cultural mix and history of other large Thracian towns. It was only built up in 1878, under the Turkish name of Dedeagaç (meaning "Tree of the Holy Man"), derived from a group of hermits who first

The landmark lighthouse in Alexandroúpoli

settled here in the 15th century. Prior to that, it was simply an unremarkable fishing village. Alexandroúpoli was renamed in 1919 after the Greek king at the time, Aléxandros.

Today, the town is a thriving holiday resort with a port, its own domestic airport, and train connections east to Istanbul, north into Bulgaria and west to Thessaloníki.

In the evening, the promenade by the long stretch of beach is thronged with people, both visitors and locals. The lighthouse, built in 1800, is situated along the seafront. It is the town's most famous feature and is lit up at night.

Inland from the promenade is a warren of narrow streets with junk shops, grocers, cobblers,

Old mansion in modern Maróneia

goldsmiths and fish restaurants. The best eating places are around tiny Plateía Polytechneíou. North from the square, beyond the main road, is the modern cathedral of Agios Nikólaos, notable for the **Ecclesiastical Art Museum** contained in its grounds. This fine collection of icons and other religious items is unfortunately seldom open, but those with a particular interest in seeing it may ask for access at the cathedral.

🏛 **Ecclesiastical Art Museum**
Palaiológou. **Tel** 25510 82282. **Open** Tue–Sat. **Closed** main public hols.

㉒ Dadiá Forest
Δάσος Δαδιάς

27km (17 miles) N of Féres, Thrace. **Road map** F1. 🚆 🚌 Féres. 🛈 1 km (0.5 miles) N of Dadiá village (25540 32209).

North of the small town of Féres in the Evros valley is the lovely Dadiá pine forest. Covering a series of hills known as the Evros Mountains, it is considered to be one of the best places in Europe for observing rare birds. Of special interest is the presence of birds of

Rare black vulture

prey, an indication of the remote location of the forest. There are 39 known species of birds of prey in Europe, 26 of which live and nest in this region.

There is an information centre in the heart of the forest, and observation huts have been placed near feeding stations, built to help preserve the rarer species that nest here. This is one of the black vulture's last refuges in eastern Europe. The forest is home to a huge number of protected and endangered species, including imperial eagles, golden eagles, griffon vultures, sparrowhawks and peregrines. Early morning is the best time to watch the different birds as they fly on the first thermals of the day.

TRAVELLERS' NEEDS

WHERE TO STAY

Accommodation in Greece is best described as functional in most cases, though a new generation of boutique and luxury hotels is sweeping across Athens, the city's outlying areas and further afield into more rural regions. However, hotel options are nearly always abundant in a country so heavily dependent on the tourist industry and, as a consequence, is good value compared with most European destinations. Despite inroads of commercialization in the busier resorts, hospitality off the beaten track can still be warm and heartfelt. Various types of accommodations are described over the next four pages. Information is included for the network of camp sites and the more limited facilities for hostelling and alpine refuge stays. The listings section (see pp268–73) includes 120 places to stay, ranging from informal *domátia* (rooms) to luxurious hotels and accommodation in restored buildings. There is a growing trend towards all-inclusive hotels and resorts, especially around the coastal areas.

Malvásia Hotel *(see p270)* at Monemvasía, restored by the EOT during the 1970s

Hotels

Most Greek hotels are of standard Mediterranean concrete architecture, although in coastal resorts, height limits restrict towering structures. Many hotels date from the 1967–74 Junta era, when massive investment in "modern" tourism was encouraged. A very few Neo-Classical or older hotels remain, now benefiting from government preservation orders. Hotels built since the 1980s are generally designed with more imagination and sensitivity to the environment. The more expensive hotels will have a correspondingly higher level of service, offered by trained personnel.

Chain Hotels

Greece, with its tradition of family business ownership, has not taken to the idea of chain hotels. However, the largest chain, **Grecotel**, comprises 27 luxury and 4-star resort hotels, many of which offer facilities such as health centres and spas, both in the capital and across the mainland. Other smaller chains, such as **Chandrís** and **Diváni**, offer accommodation in Athens, Thessaloníki, Corfu and Chios, while Diváni also has hotels in central Greece. **Club Mediterranée** and **Aldemar Hotels** are two other well-known chains.

Restored Settlements and Buildings

During the 1970s, the EOT (Greek Tourist Office) began sponsoring the restoration of derelict buildings in vernacular style. The completed units usually offer value for money and an exceptionally atmospheric environment, though preservation considerations often mean that bathrooms are shared. Such properties are found at Areópoli and Vátheia in the Máni, at Makrinítsa on the Pílio, at Megálo Pápigko in Epirus, and at Monemvasía. Some,

such as the complex at Megálo Pápigko, have been privatized, with variable effects on efficiency.

Private entrepreneurs have seized the initiative in such renovation projects, installing small and medium-sized hotels in centuries-old buildings. Particularly successful ventures can be found at Stemnítsa, Galaxídi, Náfplio, and in several villages of the Zagória region and the Pílio.

Domátia

A large proportion of Greek accommodation is in domátia, or rented rooms. In the past, these often used to be in the home of the managing family, but nowadays they are far more likely to be within a separate, modern, purpose-built structure. They tend to be good value compared with hotels of a similar standard. Increasingly, they have en suite bathrooms, are well-appointed with neutral pine furniture, and often have a kitchen for the use of guests. There is usually no communal area, however, and hot water

Front exterior of the King Othon Hotel, Náfplio *(see p271)*

◀ Little Venice, Mykonos Island

Luxurious interiors of a suite with private garden at Grand Resort Lagonissi *(see p270)*

is provided either by an electric immersion heater or by a solar heating device.

Grading

The EOT grade Greece's hotels and *domátia*. Hotel categories range from 1-star up to 5-star and are graded according to the location and the kind of facilities available. *Domátia* range from 1-star to 3-star. There is supposed to be a direct correlation between amenities and the classification, but there are many local deviations – usually the result of a dispute with local authorities.

One-star hotels, with the most basic facilities and narrow profit margins, are almost extinct. Two-star still survive, and these should have at least some en suite rooms. In a 3-star hotel, all rooms must have en suite baths, and the hotel must have some sort of common area, if only a small combination bar and breakfast area where a basic continental breakfast can be served. Four-star hotels have extra amenities such as a full-service restaurant, a more substantial breakfast, and at least one sports facility, such as a pool or tennis court. Five-star hotels are usually at seafront locations, and offer all conceivable amenities, as well as aids for the business traveller, such as conference halls and telecommunications

A sign for rooms to rent

facilities. Deluxe category hotels are effectively self-contained resort complexes.

One-star *domátia*, with baths down the hall and "jail-like" decor, are on the way out, now supplanted by modern 2-star blocks that guarantee bathrooms en suite and often have the benefit of a shared kitchen for the use of visitors. Three-star *domátia* are nearly synonymous with apartments. The furnishings are superior and there is generally landscaping outside the building. A well-equipped kitchen is fitted into each unit.

Prices

The price of hotel rooms and *domátia* should correspond to their official category, though this depends on the season and their location. In Athens, for €50 or under, it is possible to find a 1-star *domátio* for two without en suite bathroom, or a half-star hotel; €75 should cover a 2-star double *domátio*, while 3-star *domátia* and 3-star hotels charge €100. Four-star hotels ask €100 to €150 per double room; 5-star hotels typically cost €150 to €300. Deluxe resorts are exempt from the EOT price control

scheme and can run in excess of €300 per night.

All of these rate estimations are for high season, including VAT and taxes; prices can drop by almost 50 per cent in early spring or late autumn. Hotel rates include breakfast. Stays of less than three nights may carry a surcharge in high season. In mainland skiing resorts, there is often a vast difference in weekend and mid-week rates.

Opening Seasons

Mainland hotels stay open year-round, except those at seafront resorts, which operate only from May to October. Hotels in skiing areas, conversely, may open only during the winter period.

Booking

One of the most cost-effective ways of booking a room is through a package holiday agency although, increasingly, bookings are being made online. If you contact a hotel directly, do so by email, or through its website with confirmation by email, so that there is a written record of the transaction. Most hotels now have email and online facilities, even in rural areas. You may need to provide a credit card number to the value of the first night's stay.

Conservatory at Grande Bretagne hotel, Athens *(see p269)*

Monastery on Mount Athos *(see p256)*, Northern Greece

Youth Hostels

The Greek mainland has three HI (Hostelling International) recognized youth hostels *(xenón neótitos)*. They are all found in Athens. For more information, contact the **IYHA** (International Youth Hostel Association) in England, or the **YHA** (Youth Hostel Association) in Greece. In addition, there are a handful of unofficial hostels, which can provide a standard of accommodation that is just as good, if not better. Greek hostels are not nearly as regimented as their northern European equivalents. Even without an IYHF card, you can usually stay if a vacancy is available. However, if there are two of you, a less expensive *domátio* is better value.

Alpine Refuges

Mountains of the Greek mainland are dotted with over 40 alpine refuges *(katafýgia)*. Very few are continuously staffed – two on Mount Olympos *(see p245)* and one on Mount Gamíla, in the Píndos range, being notable exceptions – so you must contact the relevant branch of the **EOS** (Greek Alpine Club) to rent keys. This is expensive and not worthwhile unless you muster a large group. The **EOOA** and **SEO** *(see p267)* may also provide information on refuges. Some of the mountain huts make wonderful base camps, fully equipped with kitchens,

bed linen, and well-designed common areas; others are little more than shacks originally built for shepherds or fire-control personnel. Another complication is that, as many were built at a time when approaches to the mountain ranges were quite different, today they are often located well away from the preferred hiking routes.

Rural Tourism

Conceived during the 1980s to give women in the Greek provinces a measure of financial independence, rural tourism allows foreigners to stay on a bed-and-breakfast basis in a village house, and also provides the opportunity to participate, if desired, in the daily life of a farming community. Information on agrotourism can be obtained from **www.agro-tour.net**, from the **Hellenic Agrotourism Federation** or from the **Greek National Tourist Organisation** website *(see p303)*.

Monasteries

The less-visited monasteries and convents in Greece operate *xenónes* or hostels, intended primarily for Greek Orthodox pilgrims on weekend visits. Pilgrims will always be a priority, but it is often possible to find a vacancy at short notice. Accommodation is of the spartan-dormitory variety, with a frugal evening meal and morning coffee provided; it is customary to leave a donation in the *katholikón* (main church).

The monasteries on Mount Athos are the most accustomed to non-Orthodox visitors, though these are open to men only. Visits – especially in high season – need to be carefully planned, as the procedure for reserving space and obtaining an entry permit to this semi-autonomous monastic republic can be difficult *(see p257)*.

Camping

The Greek mainland has nearly 150 camp sites that are officially recognized. Most of them are in attractive seafront settings, and usually cater to caravanners as well. Most are privately run; the last few still owned by the EOT, or by the local municipality, are being sold off. All but the most primitive sites have hot showers heated by solar power, shady landscaping and a snack bar or café. Power hookups are generally available for an extra fee.

The most luxurious camp sites are miniature holiday villages, with swimming pool, tennis courts, laundry rooms, banking and postal facilities, and bungalows for those without tents. Established sites usually have the advantage of mature shady trees. The ground is often sun-baked and very hard, so short pegs that can be banged in with a mallet are best. For a regularly updated booklet on camp sites and their amenities, contact the **Panhellenic Camping Association**.

Mountain refuge, Kóziakas mountain, Tríkala

Travellers With Disabilities

The guide *Holidays and Travel Abroad*, published by Disability Rights UK *(see p303)*, provides details on wheelchair access to the more established hotels in Greece. Contact Tourism for All for an information sheet with hotels and useful contact numbers in Greece. The hotel listings in this guide *(see pp268–73)* indicate which establishments have suitable facilities, such as lifts and ramps, for the disabled.

Greek information sources for disabled travellers tend to be rudimentary; the EOT only publishes a questionnaire, which can be sent to specific accommodation establishments to assess their suitability.

Further Information

An invaluable booklet is published yearly by the **Hellenic Chamber of Hotels**. It is called *Guide to Hotels*, and a current copy can be obtained from their office. The booklet covers all officially registered hotels, indicating prices, facilities and their operating season. The guide does not, however, offer information on *domátia* or villas. The EOT also periodically publishes an informative leaflet entitled *Rural Tourism*. Two other hotel manuals, which are both issued by private organizations, are the **Greek Travel Pages** (GTP) and the **Tourist Guide of Greece**. They are not as complete or authoritative as the EOT guides, but are published more frequently. The GTP is monthly, offering only skeletal information unless the hotel concerned has purchased advertising space; this is also true of the quarterly publication *Tourist Guide of Greece*.

Recommended Hotels

The hotels in this section have been chosen to reflect their quality and amenities within the themes of Luxury, Historic, Resort, Rural, Boutique and Value for Money, although it is fair to say that some establishments will fall into more than one category. Greece has luxury and an especially large number of historic hotels and we have selected the best. The rural category covers hotels in villages and those standing in acres of countryside, while the boutique theme is given to the hotels that have been given a contemporary makeover in recent years. Greece has a wide selection of hotels we consider Value for Money and will stretch the budget that little bit further. The DK Choice hotels are extra special. They may have above average standards and amenities or a breathtaking location, or simply have a charm that sets them apart.

Swimming pool at Karavostasi Beach hotel *(see p271)*

DIRECTORY

Chain Hotels

Aldemar Hotels
Kifisias 262, 14562 Kifisia.
Tel 210 628 8400.
W aldemarhotels.com

Chandrís Hotels
Syngroú 377, 17564 Paleó
Fáliron, Athens.
Tel 210 948 4730.
W chandris.gr

Club Mediterranée
Tegeas 3,
16452 Argiroupoli.
Tel 210 994 7300.
W clubmed.com

Diváni Hotels
Vas. Alexándrou 2, 16121
Athens. **Tel** 210 720 7000.
W divanis.com

Grecotel
Kifissias 64b, Maroúsi,
15125 Athens.
Tel 210 728 0300.
W grecotel.gr

Hostels

IYHA (UK)
Tel 01707 324 170.
W hihostels.com

YHA (Greece)
Student & Traveller's Inn,
Kydathinaíon 16, Pláka,
10558 Athens.
Tel 210 324 4808.
W studenttravellers
inn.com

Alpine Refuges

**EOOA (Ellinikí
Omospondía
Oreivasías kai
Anarríxisis)**
(Hellenic Federation of
Mountaineering &
Climbing) Milióni 5,
10673 Athens.
Tel 210 364 5904.
W eooa.gr

**EOS (Ellinikós Orei-
vatikós Sýndesmos)**
(Greek Alpine Club)
Ipsilantou 53,
11521 Athens.
Tel 210 321 2355.
W eosathinon.gr

**SEO (Sýllogos Ellínon
Oreivatón)**
(Association of Greek
Climbers) Plateía Aristoté-
lous 5, Thessaloníki.
Tel 2310 224710.
W seoreivaton.gr

Camping

**Panhellenic Camping
Association**
Stadíou 24, 10564 Athens.
Tel 210 362 1560.
W greececamping.gr

Disabled Travellers

Disability Rights UK
Tel 020 7250 8181.
W radar.org.uk

Tourism for All
Tel 084 5124 9971.
W tourismforall.org.uk

Further Information

Greek Travel Pages
Tel 210 324 7511.
W gtp.gr

**Hellenic Chamber of
Hotels**
Tel 213 216 9900.
W grhotels.gr

**Tourist Guide of
Greece**
Tel 210 864 1688.
W tggr.com

Where to Stay

Athens

Exárcheia

Exarchion €
Value **Map** 2 F3
Themistokléous 55, 106 83
Tel 21038 00731
W exarchion.com
Well-presented rooms and an
on-site restaurant. Beautiful
rooftop views of the Acropolis.

Ilisia

Hilton €€€
Luxury **Map** 4 D5
Vasilíssis Sofías 46, 115 28
Tel 21072 81000
W hiltonathens.gr
A pre-Olympics facelift elevated
this hotel to a new level of luxury –
chic rooms with all amenities;
thermal spa; gourmet restaurants.

Kolonáki

Lion Hotel Apartments €€
Boutique **Map** 4 C5
Evzonon 7, 115 21
Tel 21072 48722
W lionhotel.gr
Complex of upmarket, nicely
decorated apartments. Located
near Plateía Syntágmatos, this is a
good base for exploring the city.

Periscope €€
Boutique **Map** 3 B5
Charitos 22, 106 75
Tel 21072 97200
W periscope.gr
Smart hotel with wooden floors
and minimalist furniture. Gym,
restaurant and a cocktail bar.

St George Lycabettus €€
Luxury **Map** 3 B4
Kleoménous 2, 106 75
Tel 21074 16000
W sglycabettus.gr
Rooms with large windows and
all modern comforts. The rooftop

pool and eatery afford views of the
Acropolis. Renowned restaurant,
La Suite Lounge, and a spa on site.

Koukáki

Art Gallery €
Value **Map** 6 D4
Erechtheíou 5, 117 42
Tel 21092 38376
W artgalleryhotel.gr
Housed in a former art gallery, this
family-run hotel has a welcoming
feel. Homely rooms and lounge.

DK Choice

Marble House €
Boutique **Map** 5 C4
Alley off Anastasíou Zínni 35, 117 41
Tel 21092 28294
W marblehouse.gr
Located near the Acropolis
Museum, this hotel offers gorgeous rooms with upmarket
fixtures and fittings. Central areas
awash with colour, tasteful
wrought-iron furniture and
plants give the Marble House a
casual but chic feel. Rooms have
furnished balconies or patios.

Makrygianni

Acropolis View €
Value **Map** 5 C3
Webster 10, 117 42
Tel 21092 17303
W acropolisview.gr
This hotel offers superb views of
the Acropolis from its dining area,
roof terrace and some rooms.

Hera €€
Boutique **Map** 6 E3
Falírou 9, 117 42
Tel 21092 36682
W herahotel.gr
Stylish hotel with deluxe suites, a
dome-lit atrium breakfast room
and a rooftop bar-restaurant with
views of the Acropolis.

Price Guide
Prices are based on one night's stay in
high season for a standard double room,
inclusive of service charges and taxes.

€	under €100
€€	€100 to 200
€€€	over €200

Monastiráki

Carolina €
Value **Map** 2 E5
Kolokotróni 55, 105 60
Tel 21032 43551
W hotelcarolina.gr
Attractive, no-frills hotel housed
in a Neo-Classical building. Located
within easy reach of Athen's main
attractions and tavernas.

Omónoia

Art Athens Hotel €
Boutique **Map** 2 D3
Márnis 27, 104 32
Tel 21052 40501
W arthotelathens.gr
Grand Neo-Classical mansion with
hi-tech lighting and cream decor
offset by wooden floors and art.
Rooms come with Jacuzzi

Delphi Art Hotel €€
Historic **Map** 2 D3
Agíou Konstantínou 27, 104 37
Tel 21052 44004
W delphiarthotel.com
A 1930s Neo-Classical building
that retains its original features.
Lavish rooms and a red foyer.

The Alassia €€
Boutique **Map** 2 D3
Sokrátous 50, 104 31
Tel 21052 74000
W thealassia.com.gr
Welcoming hotel with minimalist
decor. Lots of marble, recessed
lighting and futuristic furniture.

Pedion Áreos

Radisson Park €€
Boutique **Map** 3 A1
Leofóros Alexándras 10, 106 82
Tel 21088 94500
W athensparkhotel.gr
Lavish rooms with all modern
conveniences. Refined rooftop bar
and an outdoor swimming pool.

Pláka

Phaedra €
Value **Map** 6 E2
*Chairefontos 16, corner of
Adrianoú, 105 58*
Tel 21032 38461
W hotelphaedra.com
Comfortable rooms, larger
ones with balconies. Rooftop

Simple but comfortable interiors of a room at Marble House, Koukáki

Sweeping views from a room at New Hotel, a boutique property in Pláka

breakfast area with great city views. Located close to the Temple of Zeus.

Student And Travellers Inn
Value €
Map 6 E2
Kydathinaíon 16, 105 58
Tel *21032 44808*
W studenttravellersinn.com
Shared and private rooms, some with en suite bathrooms. Garden courtyard. Centrally located.

Acropolis House
Historic €€
Map 6 E1
Kódrou 6–8, 105 58
Tel *21032 22344*
W acropolishouse.gr
Well-preserved 19th-century mansion with many original features and antiques. Free Wi-Fi.

Central
Boutique €€
Map 6 E1
Apóllonos 21, 105 57
Tel *21032 34357*
W centralhotel.gr
Conveniently located; smart Italian designer furniture and marble bathrooms. Panoramic rooftop bar.

Electra Palace
Luxury €€
Map 6 E1
Navárchou Nikodímou 18–20, 105 57
Tel *21033 70000*
W electrahotels.gr
Housed in a splendid Neo-Classical mansion, this upscale hotel offers elegant, tasteful rooms with antique-style furniture. Full spa, pool and multiple restaurants on site.

Hermes
Boutique €€
Map 6 E1
Apóllonos 19, 105 57
Tel *21032 35514*
W hermeshotel.gr
On a quiet street. Offers stylish chic rooms, a lounge bar, kids' playroom and a roof garden.

Plaka
Value €€
Map 6 D1
7, Kapnikaréas & Mitropóleos St 105 56
Tel *21032 22706*
W plakahotel.gr
Welcoming rooms in subtle colours and quiet decor. Boasts one of the best Acropolis views in Athens.

DK Choice

New Hotel
Boutique €€€
Map 6 F1
Fillelínon 16, 105 57
Tel *21032 73000*
W yeshotels.gr
The award-winning designer duo Campana Brothers have given this hotel a dazzling decor dominated by natural wood, leather and earth colours. Rooms feature all modern comforts and bathrooms with solid brass washbasins. Superb restaurant.

Psyrrí

Arion
Value €€
Map 2 D5
Agíou Dimitríou 18, 105 54
Tel *21032 40415*
W arionhotel.gr
Tasteful rooms with marble bathrooms. Excellent rooftop bar and a bright lobby area.

Fresh
Boutique €€
Map 2 D4
Sofokléous 26 & Kleisthénous, 105 52
Tel *21052 48511*
W freshhotel.gr
Rooms with minimalist decor in white and vibrant colours. Wellness suite and a superb restaurant.

O&B Athens Boutique Hotel
Boutique €€€
Map 1 C5
Leokoríou 7, 105 54
Tel *21033 12950*
o oandbhotel.com
Very stylish, with wood and leather decor and marble bathrooms. Breakfast on the rooftop restaurant.

Sýntagma

Astor
Luxury €€
Map 6 E1
Karagiórgi Servías 16, 10562
Tel *21033 51000*
W astorhotel.gr
Well situated place; offers tasteful rooms with all modern amenities.

Athens Cypria
Value €€
Map 6 E1
Diomeías 5, 105 63
Tel *21032 38034*
W athenscypria.com
Quiet and friendly, with stylish rooms in earthy tones; some have balconies with city views.

NJV Athens Plaza
Luxury €€
Map 6 F1
Plateía Syntágmatos, 105 64
Tel *21033 52400*
W njvathensplaza.gr
Elegant rooms, superb restaurant and a full spa. The lobby boasts marble walls and chandeliers.

DK Choice

Grande Bretagne
Luxury €€€
Map 6 F1
Vassiléos Georgíou 1, Syntagma Square, 105 64
Tel *21033 30000*
W grandebretagne.gr
Built in 1842 for King Otto, this hotel exudes luxury – from its lavish lobby to its renowned gourmet restaurants, spa and stylish rooms. The Alexander's Bar is famous for its 18th-century tapestry of Alexander the Great.

Thiseío

Phidias
Value €
Map 5 B1
Apostólou Pávlou 39, 118 51
Tel *21034 59511*
W phidias.gr
Comfortable rooms with balconies and great views. Relax with a cocktail in the lovely plant-filled garden.

Chic decor in a brightly lit room at O&B Athens Boutique Hotel, Psyrrí

For more information on types of hotels *see page 267*

A luxuriously furnished suite at the upscale Grand Resort Lagonissi

Around Athens

Kifisiá: Pentelikon €€
Historic   Map D4
Diligiánni 66, 145 62
Tel *21062 30650*
W pentelikon.gr
An imposing estate hotel that has welcomed VIPs since. Opulent rooms, on-site restaurants and spa.

Kifisiá: Semiramis €€
Boutique   Map D4
Charildou Trikoúpi 48, 145 62
Tel *21062 84400*
W yeshotels.gr
Artistic decor of brilliant white with candy-inspired colour themes. Rooms boast futuristic furniture and hi-tech gadgets.

Lagoníssi: Grand Resort Lagonissi €€€
Resort   Map D4
40th km, Athens-Soúnio road, 190 10
Tel 22910 76000
W lagonissiresort.gr
Sprawling complex with villas and bungalows. Top-notch restaurants, spa and a children's club on site.

Piraeus: Hotel Mistral €€
Value   Map D4
Alexándrou Papanastasíou 105, 185 33
Tel *21041 17150*
W mistral.gr
This attractive hotel boasts picturesque views of the Mikrolímano harbour and the coast from its rooms and restaurants.

Rafína: Avra Hotel €€
Value   Map D4
Arafinídon Álon 3, 190 09
Tel *22940 22780*
W hotelavra.gr
Located right next to Rafína's harbour, this welcoming place has well-equipped rooms. The restaurant serves exquisite Greek fare.

Vouliagméni: Astir Palace €€€
Luxury   Map D4
Apóllonos 40, 166 71
Tel *21089 02000*
W astir-palace.com
Self-contained resort with acres of private beaches and

gardens. Offers suites and bungalows. Paragliding and thermal spa.

The Peloponnese

DK Choice
Corinth: Isthmia Prime Hotel €€
Luxury   Map C4
Corinth Canal, 201 00
Tel *27410 23454*
W isthmus.gr
The breathtaking location, just metres away from the Corinth Canal, is complemented by lush gardens dominated by a lagoon pool and a tennis court. Rooms are in bright summer shades with patios or balconies. The restaurant has panoramic views. Located close to ancient Corinth.

Foinikounta: Porto Finissia €€
Value   Map C5
Waterfront, 240 06
Tel *27230 71457*
W portofinissia.gr
Conveniently close to the beach. The comfortable rooms have large balconies with ironwork railings. Most have beach views.

Gýtheio: Gythion €€
Historic   Map C5
Vassiléos Pávlou 33, 232 00
Tel *27330 23452*
W gythionhotel.gr
An elegant 1864 Neo-Classical mansion with modern design features. Overlooks the harbour.

Kalámata: Akti Taygetos €€
Resort   Map C5
Mikrí Mantineía, 241 00
Tel *27210 42000*
W aktitaygetos.gr
Nestled in lovely gardens with palm trees and views of the ocean, this complex has summery rooms.

Kalávryta: Filoxenia €
Luxury   Map C4
Ethnikís Andistáseos 10, 250 01
Tel *26920 22422*
W hotelfiloxenia.gr
The use of stone and wood imparts a warm intimacy to this hotel-spa. Well-equipped rooms.

Kalógria: Kalogria Beach Hotel €€
Resort   Map B4
Kalógria Metochiou 252 00
Tel *26930 31380*
W kalogriahotel.gr
Set in lush gardens near the beach. Well-appointed rooms and villas. Watersports and a kids' playground are available.

Kardamyli: Kardamili Beach €€
Resort   Map C5
Ritsia beach, 240 22
Tel *27210 73180*
W kardamilibeach.info
Sweeping rural and sea views and private access to the waterfront. Rooms and bungalows are set in spacious gardens.

DK Choice
Messínia: The Romanos Resort €€€
Luxury   Map B5
Navarino Dunes, Costa Navarino, 240 01
Tel *27230 96000*
W romanoscostanavarino.com
This beach resort offers every amenity, from rooms with private infinity pools and a spa that uses olive oil in its therapies to a health suite and golf course. Also available are activities for children and a choice of restaurants.

Methoni: Castello €
Value   Map B5
Odós Miaoúli, 240 06
Tel *27230 31300*
W castello.gr
Close to Methoni's huge fortress. Has tasteful rooms with balconies, a roof lounge and garden.

Monemvasía: Malvásia €€
Value   Map C5
Kástro, 230 70
Tel *27320 63007*
W malvasia-hotel.gr
Rooms in warm colours with stone arches and antique-style furniture. Fabulous ocean views.

Náfplio: Byron €
Historic   Map C4
Plátonos 2, 211 00
Tel *27520 22351*
W byronhotel.gr
Elegant hotel in a restored old mansion. Boasts creamy decor and antique furniture. Breakfast terrace.

Náfplio: King Othon 1&2 €€
Historic **Map** C4
Farmakopoúlou 4, 211 00
Tel *27520 27585*
W kingothon.gr
Charming hotel in a century-old
mansion. Rooms have period
decor and wrought-iron beds.

Neos Mystras: Byzantion €
Value **Map** C5
Village Centre, 231 00
Tel *27310 83309*
W byzantionhotel.gr
Spacious, summery rooms
with castle and rural views.
Lovely gardens wrap around
a pool and a lounge-bar.

DK Choice

Olympia: Pelops €
Value **Map** B4
Varelá 2, 270 65
Tel *26240 22543*
W hotelpelops.gr
Lovely, friendly, family-run place
offering well-equipped rooms
with balconies. It has an atmospheric courtyard and a relaxed
lounge. The restaurant serves
excellent authentic Greek
cuisine. Ideal location for the
museums and arhcaeological
sites of Ancient Olympia.

Pátra: Art Primarolia €€
Boutique **Map** C4
Óthonos and Amalías 30, 262 21
Tel *2610 624900*
W arthotel.gr
Housed in a converted distillery,
this hotel has subtle decor and
art on the walls. Fabulous lobby.

Portó Heli: Aks Porto Heli €€
Luxury **Map** D4
Harbourside, 210 61
Tel *27540 98000*
W akshotels.com
Modern rooms. Amenities include
a gym, children's club, a water-
park and many dining options.

Spárti: Sparta Inn €€
Value **Map** C5
Thermopylon 109, 231 00
Tel *27310 21021*
W spartainn.gr
Located within walking distance
of Spárti's sights. Offers pleasing
rooms with traditional decor.

Stavrí Gerolimenás: Tsitsiris
Castle €€
Value **Map** C5
Tsitsiris Castle, 23 071
Tel *27330 56298*
W tsitsiriscastle.gr
A complex of stone buildings and
towers with cosy rooms in autum-
nal colours. Vaulted breakfast room.

Zachloroú: Romantzo €
Value **Map** C4
Village centre, 250 01
Tel *26920 22758*
Rustic wooden hotel by a stream.
The terrace overlooks a stopping
on the Kalávryta-Diakoftó railway.

Central and Western Greece

Aráchova: Xenonas Generali €€
Luxury **Map** C3
Village centre, 320 04
Tel *22670 31529*
This quaint stone inn is one of the
best in town and offers attractive,
themed rooms. Full spa.

DK Choice

Argalastí: Agamemnon €€
Luxury **Map** D3
Village centre, 370 06
Tel *24230 54557*
W agamemnon.gr
Housed in a beautiful, converted
mansion, this stylish hotel has
rooms in subtle colours, stone
or wood floors and antique
furniture. There are three
buildings, one of them with a
pool, bar lounge and restaurant.

Delfoí: Orfeas €
Value **Map** C3
Ifigenías & Syngroú 35, 330 54
Tel *22650 82077*
Set in lovely gardens surrounded
by countryside, the Orfeas affords
sweeping views from the rooms
and the breakfast terrace.

Delfoí: Sun View €
Value **Map** C3
Apóllonos 84, 330 54
Tel *22650 82349*
Pretty pension offering rooms and
lounges in autumnal shades with
paintings on the walls. Stunning
views of the Gulf of Corinth.

Galaxídi: Galaxa Mansion €
Value **Map** C3
Eleftherias & Kennedy 8, 330 52
Tel *22650 41620*
Welcoming place with
charming rooms, most with
sea views. Enjoy breakfast in
the lovely garden bar.

Galaxídi: Ganimede €€
Historic **Map** C3
Níkou Gourgoúri 20, 330 52
Tel *22650 41328*
W ganimede.gr
Family-run landmark 19th-
century mansion. Chic rooms.
Courtyard breakfast garden.

DK Choice

Igoumenítsa: Karavostasi
Beach €€€
Luxury **Map** B3
Pérdika, 461 00
Tel *26650 91104*
W hotel-karavostasi.gr
Attractive, family-oriented
resort located in a
secluded spot and lush
gardens. Rooms are well-
equipped, with olive grove
or sea views. Features a
swimming pool as well
as a restaurant serving
international family meals.

Ioánnina: Politeia €€
Boutique **Map** B2
Anexartisías 109, 454 44
Tel *26510 22235*
W etip.gr
Sumptuous rooms and suites with
exposed stone walls. Located in
the historic city centre area.

Kalampáka: Alsos House €
Value **Map** B2
Kanári 5, 422 00
Tel *24320 24097*
W alsoshouse.gr
Tasteful rooms and apartments
within a stone inn. Great views
of the Metéora Rocks.

Elegant exteriors and rooms with balconies at Pelops, a hotel in Olympia

For more information on types of hotels *see page 267*

Karítsa: Dohos €€
Boutique Map C2
Edge of the village, 400 07
Tel *24950 92001*
w dohos.gr
Spectacular setting, with views
of Mount Ólympos. The decor
features wood and antiques.

Konítsa: Grand Hotel Dentro €
Luxury Map B2
Kalpáki to Konítsa road, 441 00
Tel *26550 29365*
w grandhoteldentro.gr
A façade of stone and wood with
a similar decor theme in the rooms,
many with balconies. Lovely views.

Makrinítsa: Pandora €€
Luxury Map C3
Edge of village, 370 11
Tel *24280 99404*
w pandoramansion.gr
Lavish hotel with period charm
and spacious rooms. Features
fireplaces with porcelain hoods.

**Megálo Pápigko: Xenonas
Papaevangelou** €€
Value Map B2
Edge of village, 440 41
Tel *26530 41135*
w hotelpapaevangelou.gr
Rooms and studios in a stone
building in a quiet, rural setting.
Stately country-house atmosphere.

Métsovo: Kassaros €
Value Map B2
Tr Tsoumagka 3, 442 00
Tel *26560 41800*
w kassaros.gr
Cosy inn with traditional decor in
the lounges. Rooms are comfort-
able and offer views of the ravine.

**Mikró Horió: Hellas Country
Club** €€
Luxury Map C3
Village Centre, 360 75
Tel *22370 41570*
w hellascountry.gr
Opulent hotel in forested country-
side with top-notch rooms, health
suites and a superb restaurant.

Moúresi: The Old Silk Store €€
Historic Map D3
Village centre, 370 12 Tsagarada
Tel *24260 49086*
w pelionet.gr
A renovated Neo-Classical mini-
mansion, offers rooms with lovely
views. Breakfast on garden terrace.

Náfpaktos: Akti €
Value Map C3
Koridaleos 3, Gribovo, 303 00
Tel *26340 28464*
w akti.gr
Lovely hotel featuring bold, eye-
catching colours, art and antiques.
A welcoming, airy dining space.

Beautiful views of the hills in Megálo Pápigko from the hotel Xenonas Papaevangelou

Párga: Lichnos Beach €€
Luxury Map B3
Lichnos Bay, 480 60
Tel *26840 31257*
w lichnosbeach.gr
Modern resort set next to a sandy
beach. Offers watersports and an
infinity pool. Great for families.

Pórtaria: Kritsa €
Boutique Map C3
Plateía Pórtarias, 370 11 Pórtaria
Tel *24280 99121*
w hotel-kritsa.gr
Bright rooms in shades of lime
yellow and green, housed in a
former dairy. Overlooks Pórtaria's
pretty tree-lined square.

DK Choice

Tríkala: Panellinion €
Historic Map C2
Plateía Ríga Feraíou, 421 00
Tel *24310 73545*
w hotelpanellinion.com
Landmark hotel whose
renowned first-floor balcony
is from where leading Greek
politicians have delivered public
speeches for decades. Rooms
are decorated in a traditional
manner. The on-site restaurant
and lounge bar are impressive.

Tsepélovo: Gouris €
Value Map B2
Village centre, 440 10
Tel *26530 81314*
Traditional Greek-style taverna
nestled high on a mountain slope
with spectacular, panoramic views.

Voutyro: Amadryades €€
Boutique Map C3
Village centre, 361 00
Tel *22370 80921*
w amadryades.gr
Gorgeous stone boutique-style
hotel offering upscale rooms with
wooden ceilings, fireplaces,

balconies and art on the
walls. Cosy bar and lounge
and a lovely breakfast café.

**Vyzítsa: Archontiko
Karagiannopoulou** €€
Historic Map C3
Village centre, 370 10
Tel *24230 86717*
w karagiannopoulou.com
Elegantly restored 18th-century
mansion with stylish rooms and
stained-glass windows. Breakfast
is served in a lovely courtyard.

Zagóra: Archontiko Gayannis €€
Historic Map C3
Village centre, 370 01
Tel *24260 23391*
w villagayannis.gr
Old beautifully restored
mansion, with antique-filled
lounges and rooms. Breakfast
served on the garden terrace.

Northern Greece

**Ammouliani Islet:
Sunrise Hotel** €
Value Map D2
Ammouliani, 630 75
Tel *23770 51273*
w sunrise-ammouliani.gr
Outstanding setting, next to
a private beach. Traditionally
decorated rooms. Taverna-
style café.

Arnaia: Oikia Alexandrou €
Historic Map D2
*Plateía Patriárchou Vartholomaíou
tou Prótou, 630 74*
Tel *23720 23210*
w oikia-alexandrou.gr
Restored mansion dating back
to 1812 with stylish decor and
period features. Rooms are well-
equipped. Large reception hall
and lounge, gymnasium, spa
and restaurant.

DK Choice

Dadiá: Dadiaselo €
Luxury **Map** F1
Dadiá village, 684 00
Tel *25540 32333*
W dadiaselo.gr
A modern complex set around
a lagoon pool and terraces,
the Dadiaselo is popular with
visitors keen to explore this
protected region. Its six self-
contained apartments and a
restaurant in a former stable are
attractively presented. Located
close to Dadiá Forest Reserve.

Edessa: Varosi €
Value **Map** C1
Arxiereos Meletiou 45–47, 582 00
Tel *23810 21865*
W varosi.gr
Traditional, family-run place with
nice, comfortable rooms. Close to
the town's famous waterfalls.

Fanari: Fanari Hotel €
Value **Map** E1
Odós Imerou Fanariou, 691 00
Tel *25350 31300*
W fanari-hotel.gr
Family-run hotel with generous
rooms, a cheerful restaurant and
a children's playground.

**Kastoriá: Archontiko Tou
Vergoula** €
Boutique **Map** B2
Aidítras 14, 521 00
Tel *24670 23415*
W vergoulas.gr
Restored 19th-century stone man-
sion. Rooms feature antique-style
furniture and stunning sea views.

Kavála: Esperia €
Value **Map** D1
Erythroú Stavroú 44, 654 03
Tel *25102 29621*
W esperiakavala.gr
Excellent Greek hospitality at this
spacious family-run place. Elegant
rooms and a superb restaurant.

Kavála: Imaret €€€
Boutique **Map** D1
Poulídou 30–32, 651 10
Tel *25106 20151*
W imaret.gr
This restored Ottoman-era *imaret*
(a Koranic school) features 26
exquisite rooms and suites, a
dining room and a Turkish bath.

Kerkiní: Oikoperiigitis €
Value **Map** C1
Lake Kerkíni, 620 55
Tel *23270 41450*
W oikoperiigitis.gr
This traditional Greek stone-built
inn is a top bird-watching venue.
Cosy rooms and a library lounge.

Litóchoro: Villa Drosos €€
Value **Map** C2
Archeláou 20, 602 00
Tel *23520 84561*
W villa-drosos.com
Family-run inn amid woods and
lush gardens. Bright rooms with
private balconies. Swimming pool.

**Maróneia: Roxani Country
House** €€
Value **Map** E1
Edge of village, 694 00
Tel *25330 21501*
W ecoexplorer.gr
Colourful rooms, a pool and a
well-stocked bar and restaurant.
Offers birdwatching and trekking.

Néos Marmarás: Akrotiri €
Value **Map** D2
Village centre, 630 80
Tel *23750 72191*
W akrotirimarmaras.gr
Well-presented studio-style rooms
with their own kitchenettes and
balconies. Stunning views.

Néos Marmarás: Kelyfos €€
Luxury **Map** D2
Edge of village, 630 81
Tel *23750 72833*
W kelyfos.gr
Charming studios and bungalows
amid gardens full of palm trees.
Restaurant serves organic cuisine.

Nymfeo: La Moara €€
Luxury **Map** B2
Edge of village, 530 78
Tel *23860 31377*
W lamoara.gr
Country house-style hotel with
wood-floored rooms and upscale
bathrooms. Superb restaurant.

Préspa Lakes: To Petrino €
Value **Map** B1
Agios Germanós village centre, 530 77
Tel *23850 51344*
Welcoming hotel in a scenic
village of stone houses. Features
rustic furniture and wood beams.

**Préspa Lakes: Prespa
Resort & Spa** €€
Luxury **Map** B1
Préspa, Platys, 531 00
Tel *23850 51400*
W presparesort.gr
Complex of self-contained studios
with wooden floors, nice decor
and balconies. Gym, spa centre,
hot tub and a kids' playground.

Symvoli: Faraggi Hotel €
Boutique **Map** D1
Dráma–Thessaloníki road, 620 47
Tel *23240 81667*
W hotelfaraggi.gr
Lovely stone-built hotel on the
banks of a river. Tasteful rooms, a
fine-dining restaurant and a spa.

Thessaloníki: Orestias Kastorias €
Resort **Map** C2
Agnóstou Stratiótou 14, 546 31
Tel *23102 76517*
W okhotel.gr
Restored Neo-Classical building
with spacious modern rooms.
Located close to the Roman ruins.

DK Choice

Thessaloníki: Electra Palace €€
Luxury **Map** C2
Plateía Aristotélous 9, 546 24
Tel *23102 94000*
W electrahotels.gr
Landmark hotel that is superbly
opulent. The lobby features
walnut and marble decor and
deep leather sofas. Lavish rooms
and suites come with every
modern gadget. The restaurant
offers outstanding gourmet
cuisine. There is a rooftop pool.

Thessaloníki: Le Palace €€
Luxury **Map** C2
Tsimiskí 12, 546 24
Tel *23102 57400*
W lepalace.gr
Family-friendly place with artfully
decorated rooms. The restaurant
serves authentic Greek classics.

Thessaloníki: Makedonia Palace €€
Luxury **Map** C2
Megálou Alexándrou 2, 546 40
Tel *23108 97197*
W makedoniapalace.com
Popular hotel on the seafront with
comfortable rooms, a pool and
two celebrated on-site restaurants.

Thessaloníki: Nepheli €€
Luxury **Map** C2
Komninon 1, Panórama, 552 36
Tel *23103 42002*
W nepheli.gr
Modern four-star hotel with well-
equipped rooms. Rooftop bar and
restaurant afford charming views.

Welcoming façade of Fanari Hotel
in Northern Greece

For more information on types of hotels *see page 267*

WHERE TO EAT AND DRINK

To eat out in Greece is to experience the democratic tradition at work. Rich and poor, young and old, all enjoy their favourite local restaurant, taverna or café. Greeks consider the best places to be where the food is fresh, plentiful and well-cooked, not necessarily where the setting or the cuisine is the fanciest. Visitors, too, have come to appreciate the simplicity and health of the traditional Greek kitchen – olive oil, yoghurt, vegetables, a little meat and some wine, always shared with friends. The traditional three-hour lunch and siesta – still the daily rhythm of the countryside – is now only a fading memory for most city Greeks, who have adapted to a more Western European routine. But the combination of traditional cooking and outside influences has produced a vast range of eating places in Greece, and there is something on offer for everyone.

Casual dining at a restaurant in Central Athens

Types of Restaurants

Often difficult to find in more developed tourist resorts, the *estiatórion*, a traditional Greek restaurant, is one of Europe's most enjoyable places to eat. Friendly, noisy and sometimes in lovely surroundings, *estiatória* are reliable purveyors of local recipes and wines, particularly if they have been owned by the same family for decades. Foreigners unfamiliar with Greek dishes may be invited into the kitchen to choose their fare. In Greece, the entire family dines together and takes plenty of time to finish the meal, especially during weekends.

Estiatória range from the very expensive in Athens, Thessaloníki and wealthier suburbs to the incredibly inexpensive *mageirió* or *koutoúki*, popular with students and workers. There is little choice in either wines or dishes, all of which will be *mageireftá* (ready-cooked), at these eateries. The food, however, is home-made and tasty and the barrel wine is at the very least drinkable, often good, and sometimes comes from the owner's home village.

Some restaurants specialize in a particular type of cuisine. In Thessaloníki, for example, and in the suburbs of Athens, where Asia Minor refugees settled after 1923, you may find food to be spicier than the Greek norm, with lots of red peppers and dishes such as *giaurtlú* (kebabs drenched in yoghurt and served on pitta bread) or lamb-brain salad. A plethora of restaurants offering fresh fish dishes can be found in the coastal or lakeside locations.

The menu in a traditional restaurant tends to be short, comprising at most a dozen

A sign for a taverna in Párga

mezédes (starters or snacks), perhaps eight main dishes, four or five cooked vegetable dishes or salads, plus a dessert of fresh or cooked fruit, as well as a selection of local and national wines.

Many hotels have restaurants open to non-residents. Smaller country hotels occasionally have excellent kitchens and also serve good local wines. Visitors are advised to check out those close to where they are staying.

In the last few years, a new breed of young Greek chefs has emerged in *kultúra* restaurants, developing a style of cooking that encompasses Greece's magnificent raw materials, flavours and colours. This food is served with the exciting new Greek wines. In addition, Athens has seen a boom in international, French, Italian, Oriental and Indian restaurants, reflecting its multicultural identity.

Athenian restaurant interior fusing classic and contemporary styles

Waiter outside a restaurant in Pláka, Athens

Tavernas

One of the great pleasures for the traveller in Greece is the tradition of the taverna, a place to eat and drink, even if you simply snack on mezédes (Greeks rarely drink without eating). Traditional tavernas are open from mid-evening and stay open late; occasionally they are open for lunch as well. Menus are short and seasonal – perhaps six or eight mezédes and four main courses comprising casseroles and dishes cooked tis óras (to order), along with the usual accompaniments of vegetables, salads, fruit and wine.

Like traditional restaurants, some tavernas specialize in foods and wines from the owner's home region, some specialize in a particular cooking style and others in certain foods.

A psarotavérna is the place to find good fish dishes but, because fish is expensive, these tavernas often resemble restaurants and are patronized mainly by wealthy Greeks and tourists. It is quite different in small fishing villages and visitors may find the rickety tables of a psarotavérna right on the beach. Close to the lapping waves, the owner may serve fish that he himself caught that morning.

For delicious grills, try a psistariá, a taverna that specializes in spit-roasts and sta kárvouna (chargrilling). In countryside psistariés, lamb, kid, pork, chicken, game, offal, lambs' heads and even testicles are chargrilled and the whole lamb is roasted on the spit. At the harbourside, fish and shellfish are grilled and served with fresh lemon juice and olive oil. Country, family-run tavernas and cafés will invariably provide simple meals, such as omelettes and salads through-out the day, but many of these places close quite early in the evening. After your meal in the taverna, follow the Greeks and enjoy a visit to the local zacharoplasteío (see p276) for sweets and pastries.

Cafés and Bars

Cafés, known as kafeneía, are the pulse of Greek life, and even the tiniest hamlet has a place to drink coffee or wine. Equally important is the function it performs as the centre of communication – mail is collected here, telephone calls made, and newspapers read, dissected and discussed. Kafeneía serve Greek coffee, sometimes frappé (instant coffee served cold, in a tall glass), soft drinks, beer, ouzo (Greek anise-flavoured aperitif) and wine. Most also serve some kind of snack to order. All open early and remain open until late at night.

Acting as the social hub of their communities, country kafeneía, as well as many in the city, are open seven days a week.

A galaktopoleío, or "milk shop", has a seating area where you can enjoy fine yoghurt and honey; those around Plateía Omonoías in Athens remain open for most of the night.

A kapileío (wine shop with a café-bar attached) is the place to try local wines from the cask, and you may find a few bottled wines as well. The owner is invariably from a wine village or family and will often cook some simple regional special-ities to accompany the wine.

In a mezedopoleío, or mezés shop, the owner will not only serve the local wine and the mezédes that go with it, but also ouzo and the infamous spirit, raki (anise-flavoured alcoholic drink), both distilled from the remnants of the grape harvest. Their accom-panying mezédes are less salty than those served with wine.

No holiday in Greece is complete without a visit to an ouzerí. These are traditionally inexpen-sive, noisy and fun places to eat and drink. Some of the best of ouzeríes are to be found in Thessaloníki and in Athens' central arcades. You can order a dozen or more little plates of savoury meats, fish and vegetables and try the many varieties of ouzo that are served in small jugs. A jug or glass of water accompanies the ouzo to wash it down.

Bottle of ouzo

Outdoor tables on the patio at the Kritsa restaurant (see p290)

Enjoying outdoor dining in Pláka, Athens

Fast Food and Snacks

Visitors can be forgiven for thinking Greeks never stop eating, for there seem to be snack bars on every street and vendors selling sweets, nuts, rolls, and seasonal corn and chestnuts at every turn.

Although American-style fast-food outlets dominate city streets, it is easy to find traditional Greek eateries. The very cheap *souvlatzídiko* offers chunks of meat, fish or vegetables roasted on a skewer and served with bread, while an *ovelistírio* serves *yíros* – meat from a revolving spit in a pitta bread pocket. The food is sold *sto chéri* (in the hand).

Many bakeries serve savoury pies and a variety of bread rolls, and *kafeneío* serving snacks and salads can always be found in busy city areas. Street vendors sell *kouloúria* (rolls), small pies, corn on the cob, roast chestnuts, nut brittle and candies. Snacks are often local specialities – tiny pizza-like pies in Thessaloníki; pies of wild greens or cheese in Métsovo; and small flavourful sausages in Ioánnina.

Visitors with a sweet tooth will love the *zacharoplasteío* (patisserie), where bakers make traditional sweet breads, tiny sweet pastries and a whole variety of fragrant honey cakes.

Breakfast

For Greeks, breakfast is the least important meal of the day. In traditional homes and cafés, a small cup of Greek coffee accompanies *paximádia* (slices of rusk-like bread), *koulourákia* (firm, sesame-covered or slightly sweet rolls in rings or S-shapes) or pound cakes with home-made jam. In many city *kafeneía*, this has been replaced by a large cup of brewed coffee and French-style croissants or delicious brioche-style rolls, also called *kouloúria*. In the summer, some *kafeneía* will still serve fresh figs, thick yoghurt, pungent honey and slightly sweet currant bread.

Reservations

The more expensive a restaurant is, the more advisable it is to make a reservation, and it is always worth doing so during weekends. In country areas, and in the suburbs, it is the practice to visit a restaurant or taverna earlier in the day, or a day before, and check on the dishes to be served. The proprietor will take an order and reserve any dish that you request.

Wine

Restaurateurs in Greece are only now learning to look after bottled wines. If the wine list contains the better bottles, such as Ktíma Merkoúri, Seméli or Strofiliá, the proprietor probably knows how to look after the wine and it will be safe to order a more expensive bottle. For a good-value bottle, there are the nationally known Cambás or Boutári wines.

Traditional restaurants and tavernas may only stock carafe wine, which is served straight from the barrel and is always inexpensive. Carafe wines are often of the region, and among Greek wines, the rosé in particular is noted for having an unusual but pleasing flavour.

How to Pay

Greece is still largely a cash society, although more eateries now take credit cards, especially in Athens and increasingly so in smaller towns. If you need to pay by credit card, check first that the restaurant accepts them, and if so, that they take the card you intend to use – many proprietors accept some but not others. *Kafeneía* almost never take credit cards, and café-bars rarely. In rural areas, country tavernas, restaurants and *kafeneía* will generally only accept cash.

Service and Tipping

Greeks take plenty of time when they eat out and expect a high level of attention. This means a great deal of running around on the part of the waiter, but in return they receive generous tips – as much as 20 per cent if the service is good, though more often a tip is 10–15 per cent. Prices in traditional establishments do include service, but the waiters still expect a tip.

Western-style restaurants and tourist tavernas sometimes add a service charge to the bill; their prices can be much higher because of trimmings, such as telephones and air conditioning.

Patrons outside a kebab restaurant in Athens

Dress Code

The Greeks dress quite formally when dining out. Visitors should wear whatever is comfortable, but skimpy tops and shorts and active sportswear are not acceptable, except near the beach, although it is unlikely that tourist establishments would turn customers away. Some of the most expensive city restaurants, especially those attached to hotels, request formal dress; the listings indicate which places fall into this category.

In summer, if you intend dining outside, take a jacket or sweater for the evening.

Children

Greek children become restaurant and taverna habitués at a very early age – it is an essential part of their education. Consequently, children are welcome everywhere in Greece except in bars. In formal restaurants, children are expected to be well behaved, but in summer, when Greeks enjoy eating outside, it is perfectly acceptable for children to play and enjoy themselves too. Facilities such as highchairs are unknown except in the most considerate hotel dining rooms, but more casual restaurants and tavernas are fine for dining with children of any age.

Interior patio of Ouzerí Aristotélous in Thessaloníki *(see p291)*

Bread ring seller, Athens

Smoking

Smoking is commonplace in Greece and until recently, establishments maintaining a no-smoking policy have been difficult to find. However, new EU regulations make it obligatory for all restaurants to have no-smoking areas. In practice, of course, change is slow but for at least half the year, you can always dine outdoors.

Wheelchair Access

In country areas, where room is plentiful, there are few problems for wheelchair users. However, in city restaurants, access is often restricted. The streets themselves have uneven pavements and many eateries have narrow doorways and, possibly, steps. However, more restaurants in Athens and even some in rural towns, are now installing slopes and bathrooms with easier access. Restaurants that do have wheelchair access are indicated in the listings pages of this guide. Also, the organizations that are listed on page 303 provide information for disabled travellers in Greece.

Vegetarian Food

Greek cuisine provides plenty of choice for vegetarians. Greeks enjoy such a variety of dishes for each course that diners can order just vegetable dishes for first and main courses in traditional restaurants, tavernas or *kafeneía*. Vegetable dishes are satisfying, inexpensive and imaginative.

Drying octopus at a restaurant in Geroliménas, on the Máni peninsula *(see p198–203)*

Vegans may have some problems, as few places in Greece cater to special diets. However, as Greek cooking relies little on dairy products, it is possible to follow a vegan diet almost anywhere in Greece.

Picnics

The best time to picnic in Greece is in spring, when the country-side is at its most beautiful and the weather is not too hot. The traditional seasonal foods, such as Lenten olive oil bread, sweet Easter bread, pies filled with wild greens, fresh cheese and new retsina wine, all make perfect fare for picnics. Summer is the ideal time for eating on the beach. The best foods for summer snacks are peaches and figs, yoghurt and cheese, tomatoes, various breads and olives.

Recommended Restaurants

The restaurants in this section have been chosen for their quality and variety of cuisine. Greece has a large number of traditional restaurants and we have selected those that offer the most authentic dining experience. Similarly, Greece has restaurants serving international cuisine, although many of these also include classic local dishes on their menu. The best fish restaurants, and others that offer good vegetarian food have also been featured. Look out for the DK Choice restaurants, highlighted in recognition of an exceptional feature – exquisite food, an inviting atmosphere, historical charm, an unusual setting or simply great value.

The Flavours of Greece

The ancient Greeks regarded cooking as both a science and an art – even a topic for philosophy. In out-of-the-way places on the mainland and on the more far-flung islands, you will still find dishes, ingredients and culinary styles untouched by time. Elsewhere, Greek cookery has been much influenced by the Ottoman Empire, with its spiced meat dishes, and filled pastries and vegetables. In the recent past, Greek cuisine was often thought of as peasant food. Today, it is that very simplicity, and its reliance on seasonal, local produce, that makes Greek food so popular with visitors.

Oregano and thyme

Island fisherman returning to harbour with the day's catch

Athens and the Peloponnese

The capital is essentially a city of immigrants from the countryside, the islands and the shores of the eastern Mediterranean. That diversity is reflected in its markets and its cuisine. Street food is a quintessential part of Athens life. In the Peloponnese, ingredients are as varied as the

terrain: fish from the sea and, from the mountains, sheep, goat and game. From the hills come several varieties of cheese, olives and honey.

Central and Northern Greece

Mainland Greece, with its long and chequered history, is a place where regional food

boundaries are blurred and a variety of cooking traditions coexist. The meat and fruit dishes of Thessaloníki show a Jewish influence; the spices, sausages and oven cooking of Ioánnina stem from Ottoman times; while a love of sheep's cheese, pies and offal came to Métsovo and the Epirus mountains with the Vlach shepherds. The spicy food of

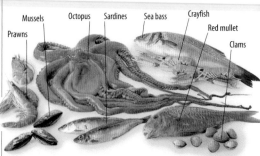

Mussels   Octopus   Sardines   Sea bass   Crayfish
Prawns   Red mullet
                                           Clams

Selection of seafood from the clear waters of Greece

Regional Dishes and Specialities

Sweets such as nougat, *pastéli* (honey-sesame candy), *loukoumádes* (yeast doughnuts in syrup) and *chalvás* (halva, or sweetmeats) have been a part of Greek street life since the days of Aristotle. They are sold in small shops or stalls. *Píttes*, or pies, are a speciality of the western Epirus region. Fillings range from game or offal to cheese and vegetables, often combined with rice or pasta. Reflecting Middle-Eastern influences, *soutzoukákia*, a speciality of northern Thrace and Macedonia, are meat patties flavoured with coriander, pepper and cumin. *Choirinó kritikó*, the classic dish of inland Crete villages, is thick pork cutlets baked until tender, while *sýka me tyrí* is a summer *mezés*, dessert or snack, of fresh figs with *mizythra* cheese, made from whey.

Olives

Fakés is a sour Peloponnese soup of green lentils, lemon juice or wine vinegar, tomatoes, herbs and olive oil.

Produce on sale in a typical Greek market

the North is the legacy of the 1922 Greek immigrants from Asia Minor, while the Balkan influence is obvious in the use of pickles, walnuts and yogurt.

The Islands

Each group of islands has a distinct culinary identity reflecting its geographical location and history. Many Ionian dishes are pasta based, a legacy of the era of Venetian occupation. Those of the Cyclades are intensely flavoured. The cooks of the Dodecanese and Northeast Aegean benefit from the rich harvest of the surrounding sea. Crete is unique in its long Turkish occupation and taste for highly spiced dishes, and Cretan cooking has a number of recipes specific to the island. The use of pork, a legacy of antiquity, is more popular here than anywhere else in Greece. Some lovely kitchen utensils and unusual

ingredients from Minoan times have been excavated by archaeologists on Crete.

Fish and Seafood

The warm and sheltered waters of the Aegean are the migratory path for tuna and swordfish, and a feeding ground for tasty anchovies and sardines. Coves and caves around the hundreds of rocky islands shelter highly prized red mullet, dentex and parrot fish, while the long

Bread being baked in an outdoor communal oven

shoreline is home to shellfish and crustaceans. Fish are usually served with their heads on: to Greeks this is the tastiest part, and it helps to identify the variety.

Other Produce

Greece is home to the largest variety of olives in the world. They are cured by methods used for thousands of years. The best quality olive oil, extra-virgin, is made by pressing just-ripe olives only. Greece produces sheep's, cow's and goat's cheeses, usually named by taste and texture, not place of origin.

WHAT TO DRINK

Wine has been part of Greek cultural life from the earliest times. Major wine-producing areas include Attica, Macedonia and the Peloponnese. Mavrodaphne is a fortified dessert wine from Pátra. Traditional Greek specialities include *tsípouro*, distilled from the residue of crushed grapes; *retsina*, a wine flavoured with pine resin (*see p151*); and the strong, aniseed-flavoured spirit *ouzo*. Coffee in Greece is traditionally made from very finely ground beans boiled up with water in a long-handled *mpríki* (coffee pot) and drunk from a tiny cup. It is served in cafés rather than tavernas.

Spetzofáï, from central Greece, is sautéed slices of spicy country sausage with herbs and vegetables.

Barboúnia, or red mullet, has been the most esteemed fish in Greece since antiquity. It is usually simply fried.

Loukoumádes are a snack of small deep-fried doughnuts soaked in honey-syrup and sprinkled with cinnamon.

The Classic Greek Menu

The traditional first course is a selection of *mezédes*, or snacks; these can also be eaten in *ouzerís*, or bars, throughout the day. Meat or fish dishes follow next, usually served with a salad. The wine list tends to be simple, and coffee and cakes are generally consumed after the meal in a nearby pastry shop. In rural areas, traditional dishes can be chosen straight from the kitchen. Bread is considered by Greeks to be the staff of life and is served at every meal. Village bakers vary the bread each day with flavourings of currants, herbs, wild greens or cheese. The many Orthodox festivals are celebrated with special breads.

Greek pitta bread

Souvlákia are small chunks of pork, flavoured with lemon, herbs and olive oil, grilled on skewers.

Choriátiki saláta, Greek salad, combines tomatoes, cucumber, onions, herbs, capers and feta cheese.

ΜΕΖΕΣ
Mezés

Olives — **Ελιές**
Eliés

Salted mullet roe dip — **Ταραμοσαλάτα**
Taramosaláta

Yogurt and cucumber dip — **Τζατζίκι**
Tzatzíki

Chickpea (garbanzo) purée — **Σουβλάκια**
Souvlákia

Ρεβυθοσαλάτα
Revythosaláta

Aubergine (eggplant) purée — **Μελιτζανοσαλάτα**
Melitzanosaláta

Vine leaves stuffed with rice — **Ντολμάδες**
Ntolmádes

Μελιτζάνες ιμάμ μπαϊλντί
Melitzánes imám baïldí

Stuffed baked aubergines (eggplant) — **Χωριάτικη σαλάτα**
Choriátiki saláta

ΨΑΡΙΑ
Psária

Fish are at their best around the coast and on the islands — **Πλακί**
Plakí

Σχάρας
Scháras

Τηγανιτά καλαμάρια
Tiganitá kalamária

Fried squid

Psária plakí is a whole fish baked in an open dish with vegetables in a tomato and olive oil sauce.

Scháras means "from the grill". It can be applied to meat or fish, or even vegetables. Here, grilled swordfish has been marinated in lemon juice, olive oil and herbs before being swiftly chargrilled.

Mezédes

Mezédes are eaten as a first course or as a snack with wine or other drinks. *Taramosaláta* is a purée of salted mullet roe and breadcrumbs or potato. Traditionally a dish for Lent, it is now on every taverna menu. *Melitzanosaláta* and *revythosaláta* are both purées. *Melitzanosaláta* is grilled aubergines (eggplant) and herbs; *revythosaláta* is chickpeas (garbanzos), coriander and garlic. *Melitzánes imám baïldí* are aubergines filled with a purée of onions, tomatoes and herbs. *Ntolmádes* are vine leaves stuffed with currants, pine nuts and rice.

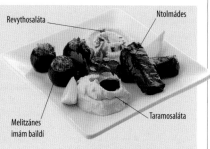

Revythosaláta
Ntolmádes
Melitzánes imám baïldí
Taramosaláta

Typical selection of mezédes

ΚΡΕΑΣ
Kréas

Μουσακάς
Mousakás

Κεφτέδες
Keftédes

Χοιρινό σουβλάκι
Choirinó souvláki

Κλέφτικο
Kléftiko

ΛΑΧΑΝΙΚΑ ΚΑΙ ΣΑΛΑΤΙΚΑ
Lachaniká kai salatiká

Μελιτζάνες και κολοκυθάκια τηγανιτά
Melitzánes kai kolokythákia tiganitá

Αγκινάρες α λα πολίτα
Agkináres a la políta

Σπαράγγια σαλάτα
Sparángia saláta

ΓΛΥΚΑ
Glyká

Φρέσκα φρούτα
Fréska froúta

Σύκα στο φούρνο με μαυροδάφνη
Sýka sto foúrno me mavrodáfni

Γιαούρτι και μέλι
Giaoúrti kai méli

Meat is more readily available on the mainland than on the islands

Moussaka (minced lamb and aubergine baked in layers)

Vegetables and salads often use wild produce

Fried aubergines (eggplant) and courgettes (zucchini)

Artichokes with potatoes, dill, lemon and oil

Asparagus salad

Desserts are simple affairs of pastry, fruit or yogurt.

Fresh fruit

Figs baked in sweet, spiced Mavrodaphne wine with orange-flower water

Keftédes are meatballs of pork with egg and breadcrumbs, flavoured with herbs and cumin and fried in olive oil.

Kléftiko is usually goat meat wrapped in parchment paper and cooked so that the juices and flavours are sealed in.

Giaoúrti kai méli (yogurt with honey) is served in speciality "milk shops", to be eaten there or taken home.

Sweet pastries filled with nuts and honey, syrup-drenched cakes, pies, doughnuts and glyká (candied fruits) are mainly eaten in cafés. The most famous of all are baklavas, with layers of filo pastry and nuts, and kataïfi, known to tourists as "shredded wheat".

Where to Eat and Drink

Athens

Exárcheia

I Lefka €
Traditional Greek **Map** 3 B2
Mavromicháli 121, 114 72
Tel 21036 14038 **Closed** *Aug*
This cosy taverna, complete
with wooden tables and barrels
of *retsina*, abounds with tradition.
Try their stuffed vine leaves,
followed by lamb *kléftiko* (lamb
with garlic, oregano and mustard,
baked in paper) in the courtyard.

Mparmpa Giannis €
Traditional Greek **Map** 2 F3
Emmanouíl Mpenáki 94, 106 81
Tel 21038 24138 **Closed** *Sun eve; Aug*
Popular eatery that serves grills
and daily specials, such as the
classic *giouvarláki* (rice and
meat balls in *avgolémono* – a
Mediterranean egg and lemon
sauce) with okra. Arrive early to
secure a table on the terrace.

Peinaleon €€
Traditional Greek **Map** 3 B2
Mavromicháli 152, 114 72
Tel 21064 40945 **Closed** *Jul & Aug*
Reserve ahead at this local
favourite famous for its *mezédes*
and home-made wine. Retro
lamps, old photos and *rempétiki*
music complete the scene.

Rifífi €€
Traditional Greek **Map** 2 F3
*Emmanouil Mpenaki 69 & Valtetsiou,
106 81*
Tel 21033 00237 **Closed** *1 week in Aug*
Rifífi serves traditional dishes made
with unusual ingredients from the
Mediterranean. Don't miss the
lamb cooked for 20 hours with
sundried tomato sauce and the
skewer of chicken breast grilled
with sweet chilli sauce and yogurt.

A tempting dish of grilled cuttlefish with
spinach at the restaurant Yiantes

DK Choice

Rozalia €€
Traditional Greek **Map** 2 F2
Valtetsíou 54, 106 81
Tel 21033 02933
Housed in a beautiful Neo-
Classical building with a garden
full of vines, olive trees and
flowers, this taverna has
been attracting diners with its
signature dish, *tiganiá* (pork in a
peppery sauce) as well as classics
like *spanakórizo* (spinach rice) and
ouzo-marinated fish and seafood
for over 35 years. Superb wine
list and choice of *ouzo* blends.

Salero €€
Spanish **Map** 2 F3
Valtetsíou 51, 106 81
Tel 21038 13358
Vibrant restaurant specialising
in cuisine from the Iberian
peninsula. Choose from over 20
tapas dishes or mains and home-
made desserts. Excellent wine
cellar and cocktails.

Yiantes €€
Mediterranean **Map** 2 F3
Valtetsíou 44, 106 81
Tel 21033 01369
Serves delectable Greek and
Mediterranean dishes such as
zucchini croquettes, couscous
with pancetta and grilled liver
with caramelised onions. Dishes
in the seasonal menus are made
with organic produce. Good
selection of wines and *ouzo*.

Ilisia

Alatsi €€
International **Map** 4 E5
Vrasida 13, 115 28
Tel 21072 10501
Award-winning eatery serving
simple, healthy dishes made with
fresh ingredients purchased from
local suppliers. Try the amberjack
tartare with onions, chilli and
capers and the calf's liver with
wild greens. Excellent service.

Fuga €€
International **Map** 2 F3
Kokkali 1 & Vas Sofias, 115 21
Tel 21072 42979
Elegant restaurant in the
gardens of the Athens Concert
Hall. Offers seasonal cuisine made
with fresh, carefully selected
ingredients. Signature dishes
include risotto a la Milanese,
lamb with aubergine and tomato
mayonnaise. Try the light *tiramisu*
for dessert. Good wine list.

Price Guide
Prices are based on one night's stay in
high season for a standard double room,
inclusive of service charges and taxes.

€	under €35
€€	€35 to 70
€€€	over €70

DK Choice

Galaxy Restaurant €€€
International **Map** 4 D5
Hilton, Vassilísis Sofías 46, 115 28
Tel 21072 81402
Everything about the Galaxy is
tasteful – from the cocktails and
finger food served at the bar to
the upscale Japanese *teppanyaki*,
Mediterranean gourmet dishes
and fine wines served at its dark
wooden tables. The highlight
of this rooftop restaurant is
the sweeping view of the
Acropolis through the floor-
to-ceiling windows.

Kerameikós

Funky Gourmet €€€
Fine Dining **Map** 1 B4
Salaminós 13, 104 35
Tel 21052 42727 **Closed** *Sun &
Mon*
Michelin-starred minimalist
restaurant serving mouthwatering
creations such as truffle *foie gras*
and smoked ice cream. The
menu also features fine wines.

Kolonáki

Il Postino €
Italian **Map** 3 A4
Grivaíon 3 & Skoufá 64, 106 73
Tel 21036 41414 **Closed** *Sun*
Osteria-style restaurant with
authentic Italian cuisine in the
heart of Athens. Choose from
delicious antipasti, meat dishes
like veal in wine, and home-
made pasta and desserts.

Kavatza €€
Traditional Greek **Map** 3 B5
Spefsipou 30, 106 75
Tel 21072 41862 **Closed** *Sun*
Landmark restaurant in Kolonáki
with wooden floors, chrome
decor and a menu of healthy
Greek food. The chicken with
oregano and lentil salad is a
house favourite.

Prytaneíon €€
International **Map** 3 A5
Milioni 7–9, 106 73
Tel 21036 43353
A stylish restaurant spread over
three floors and decorated in

Magnificent views of the Acropolis from Orizontes Lykavittou, an upscale restaurant

earthy colours and wall art. The menu tempts with Mediterranean meat and pasta dishes, Aegean fish as well as Italian desserts.

Kiku   €€€
Japanese   **Map** 3 A5
Dimokrítou 12, 106 73
Tel *21036 47033*   **Closed** *Sun; Aug*
Award-winning restaurant that serves exquisite Japanese cuisine in minimalist surroundings. There's a superb sushi bar, while sashimi and tempura dishes are presented like works of art. Good wine list.

DK Choice

Orizontes Lykavittou   €€€
Fine Dining   **Map** 3 B4
Aristippou 1, Lykavittós Hill, 106 75
Tel *21072 10701*
The views of Athens don't get much better than at this elegant venue near the hill's summit, popular with the local trendy set. Access is via funicular or a pathway through pines. Upmarket appetizers, imaginative salads as well as fish and pasta dishes are artfully plated. Meat dishes include delicious steak from central Greece. Exemplary desserts and wines.

Ouzadiko   €€€
Traditional Greek   **Map** 3 C5
Karneádou 25–29, 106 76
Tel *21072 95484*   **Closed** *Sun lunch & Mon; Aug*
Ouzadiko is a bright and breezy sort of place that attracts the literati with its vast *ouzo* selection and fine Greek cuisine. The *youvetsí* (Greek stew of meat, a rich tomato sauce and pasta) made with octopus is a must-try.

Koukáki

Mikri Venetia   €
Mediterranean   **Map** 5 C5
Olimpiou 15, 117 41
Tel *21302 59158*
The name translates as Small Venice; this cosy eatery on a beautiful pedestrian street serves flavourful dishes such as rice with *apaki* (pork marinated in spices and virgin olive oil), pasta with tomato and staka butter, and grilled sausages. Friendly atmosphere.

Makrygianni

Manimani   €€
Traditional Greek   **Map** 6 D3
Falírou 10, 117 42
Tel *21092 18180*   **Closed** *Mon*
Stylish restaurant that takes its cuisine inspiration from the Máni peninsula. *Spenzofai* (Máni sausage), oxtail-stuffed ravioli, *moussaka* and *baklava* (Turkish pastry) are among the house favourites at Manimani.

Metaxourgeio

Aleria   €€
Modern Greek   **Map** 1 B3
Megalou Alexandrou 57, 104 35
Tel *21052 22 633*   **Closed** *Sun*
Located in a beautiful renovated house, this restaurant features a lovely bar and indoor and outdoor dining areas. The exquisite food includes modern interpretations of classic Greek dishes. Seafood orzo risotto with grilled peppers, salami and basil is the house speciality.

Alexander The Great   €€
Traditional Greek   **Map** 1 C3
Megalou Alexandrou 3–7, 104 37
Tel *21052 27990*
Wooden-beamed restaurant that also offers outdoor dining in a garden. The authentic

Greek cuisine features *afélia* (pork in wine) and *spetsofáï* (sausages with tomatoes and green peppers).

Monastiráki

Café Avissinia   €
Café   **Map** 5 C1
Kinétou 7, Plateía Avissinía, 105 55
Tel *21032 17047*   **Closed** *Mon*
A superb menu of gourmet-style burgers, pasta, salads and platters has made this café one of the trendiest places in Athens. The atmosphere is warm and friendly and there is live music on weekends.

Mouses   €
Café   **Map** 5 C1
Filippou 2, 105 55
Tel *21032 19332*
Every meal from morning coffee and pasta lunches right through to candlelit dinner in the evening. The menu has delectable dishes such as *sheftalia* (beef in wine) and *kléftiko* (lamb).

Thanassis   €
Café   **Map** 6 E1
Mitropóleos 69, 105 55
Tel *21032 44705*
Located in one of the busiest streets of Monastiráki, this fast food and takeaway joint is popular for their *souvlákia* (skewered kebabs) and *yíros* (donar kebabs).

Athinaïkon   €€
Modern Greek   **Map** 6 E1
Mitropóleos 34, 105 55
Tel *21032 52688*
Twin of Athinaïkon in Omónoia, this restaurant is a trendy city venue. The menu is Greek with contemporary flourishes. Superb dishes such as swordfish *souvlákia* and smoked eel.

DK Choice

To Kouti   €€
International   **Map** 5 C1
Adrianou 23, 105 55
Tel *21032 13229*
Popular with the city's trendy set be it for morning coffee or evening dinner, To Kouti is located on a pedestrianised street beside the ancient Angora and affords views of the Acropolis. The food on offer includes gourmet-style burgers, innovative meat and fish dishes such as beef with honey, as well as salads. The vegetarian menu is also excellent. Fun and colourful decor.

Exterior of the Athinaïkon, a taverna popular for its traditional Greek cuisine

Omónoia

Obi Café Bar
International   €   **Map** 2 E5
Skouleniou 2, 105 59
Tel *21032 10089*   **Closed** *Sun*
Obi begins welcoming guests early in the day for breakfast and gradually transforms into a lively evening dining venue as well as a bar-cum-nightclub. The menu is international with Greek influences.

Athinaïkon
Traditional Greek   €€   **Map** 2 E3
Themistokléous 2, 106 78
Tel *21038 38485*   **Closed** *Sun*
Established in 1932, this traditional city taverna is popular with Greek families, especially on weekends. Fish *mezédes* and *saganáki* (Greek starter of fried cheese) are specialities.

Olive Garden
Mediterranean   €€€   **Map** 2 E3
Titania Hotel, Panepistimiou 52, 106 78
Tel *21038 38511*
Popular with locals, this award-winning rooftop restaurant combines an elegant decor with a menu of delicious Mediterranean gourmet cuisine. Enjoy dining with great Acropolis views.

Pangráti

The Sushi Bar
Japanese   €€   **Map** 7 B4
Plateía Varnáva 4, corner Stílponos, 116 36
Tel *21075 24354*
Watch chefs in the open kitchen create the most exquisite sushi and tempura dishes at this minimalist eatery. The decor is bright, with wooden floors, and the service is friendly and attentive.

Vyrinis
Traditional Greek   €€   **Map** 7 B3
Archimidous 11 & Arátou, 116 36
Tel *21070 12153*
Charming taverna decorated with ornamental wine barrels. Serves mouthwatering Greek food including salads, *mezédes*, main dishes and honey-rich *loukoumádes* (bite-sized Greek donuts).

DK Choice
Spondi
Fine Dining   €€€   **Map** 7 B4
Pyrronos 5, 116 38
Tel *21075 64021*
Housed in a glorious Neo-Classical building with a lovely interior of natural stone, the Michelin-starred Spondi serves exquisite food prepared by an expert French chef. Menu classics include terrine of *foie gras*, wild mushroom ravioli and lamb in a herb cocotte. Tasting and dessert menus are available. The wine cellar boasts a comprehensive list of 1300 labels.

Pedion Áreos

Strofi
Mediterranean   €   **Map** 6 D3
Rovertou Gkalli 25, 117 42
Tel *21092 14130*   **Closed** *Mon*
Open since 1975, this eatery serves traditional Mediterranean and Greek fare. Try the fried feta cheese with honey and sesame for starters as well as lamb wrapped in vine leaves stuffed with cheese for mains. Great views of the Acropolis from the rooftop terrace. Reserve ahead.

St' Astra Blue
Mediterranean   €€€   **Map** 2 F1
Leofóros Alexándras 10, 106 82
Tel *21088 94500*   **Closed** *Sun & Mon*
This designer-furnished rooftop restaurant of the Radisson Blu

Park Hotel is a city favourite. Enjoy superb cocktails with gourmet dishes such as salmon quinoa and pork with mango chutney.

Pláka

Bakalarákia Ouzeri Damigos
Traditional Greek   €€   **Map** 6 E2
Kydathinaion 41, 105 58
Tel *21032 25084*   **Closed** *Mon*
Rustic restaurant famous for its *bakalarákia* – battered cod in a fiery garlic sauce that has, to go by legend, been served here since 1864. Features barrels containing retsina as part of the decor.

Klimataria
Greek   €€   **Map** 2 D4
Plateia Theatrou 2, 105 52
Tel *21032 16629*   **Closed** *Mon*
Every inch a Greek taverna, Klimataria draws guests in with bouzouki music and exotic aromas. Menu classics include home-made dips such as *tzatziki*, *moussaka* and *souvlaki*.

DK Choice
Ouzeri Platanos
Greek   €€   **Map** 6 D1
Diogenous 4, 105 56
Tel *21032 20666*
A local favourite, Platanos takes its name from the plane tree outside and has been serving classic home-made Greek dishes like *pastítsio* (Greek dish of baked pasta with ground beef and white sauce) and *kléftiko* for decades. Diners wash down the delectable food here with *retsina* from a barrel. The lovely pink-washed courtyard covered with bougainvillea is a major attraction.

Sholarhio Ouzeri Kouklis
Greek   €€   **Map** 6 E2
Tripódon 14, 105 57
Tel *21032 47605*
This ouzeri has a gimmick – waiters bring *dískos* (platters) of 20 dishes to choose from, all for a set price, and diners get to keep those they want to eat. The dishes include mini *moussakas*, bread, and a traditional dessert, along with wine.

Taverna Tou Psarra
Seafood   €€   **Map** 6 D2
Erechthéos 16, corner Erotokrítou, 105 57
Tel *21032 18733*
With a name that means the Fisherman's Tavern, this eatery is

housed in two of Pláka's oldest mansions. It has earned a reputation for its superb gourmet fare, especially fresh fish, and fine wines.

Psyrrí

Oraia Penteli €
Traditional Greek **Map** 1 C5
Corner Aristofanoú & Aischyloú, 105 54
Tel *21032 18627*
A lovely old restored merchant's house beautifully restored with elegant decor, this eatery serves classic Greek cuisine, with dishes such as *souvlaki* and *kléftiko*. The *bekri meze* (Greek meat appetizer) is a must try. Features live music.

Taverna Tou Psyrri €
Traditional Greek **Map** 1 C5
Aischyloú 12, 105 52
Tel *21032 14923*
Housed in an old stone building, this traditional taverna is considered to be the oldest in Psyrrí. Enjoy hearty portions of *souvlaki, kléftiko* and *afélia* (stew of pork marinated in red wine and flavoured with coriander seeds) washed down with house wine.

To Zeidoron €€
Traditional Greek **Map** 1 C5
Agios Anargiron 17, 105 54
Tel *21032 15368*
Located on a busy street, this taverna tempts diners with mouth-watering modern Greek dishes such as *bakalarákia* (cod in garlic sauce) with zucchini fritters. Sit at the pavement tables that are perfect for people-watching.

Hytra €€€
Fine Dining **Map** 1 C5
Leof Syngrou 107-109, 117 45
Tel *21033 16767* **Closed** *Wed & Thu*
Stylish Michelin-starred eatery serving artfully prepared Cretan cuisine. The menu features dishes such as *kalitsoúnia* (herb pie) and *kolokythoanthoí* (stuffed zucchini flowers), and a *mezédes* menu.

Sýntagma

Avocado €
Café **Map** 6 F1
Nikis 30, 105 57
Tel *21032 37878*
A vegetarian eatery and juice bar, Avocado is renowned for its creative salads, pizzas and desserts. The bread is home-made. Wash down the delicious food with a smoothie or organic wine.

Mama Roux €
International **Map** 6 D1
Aiolou 48, 105 64
Tel *21300 48382* **Closed** *Sun*
Food from the world over, in unique combinations of ingredients in a friendly ambience. The wide-ranging menu features dishes such as burgers, tandoori chicken, burritos, tacos, kebab, falafel and soups. Don't miss the hummous or the delectable cheesecake.

Noodle Bar €
International **Map** 6 E1
Appollonos 11
Tel *21033 18585*
This fun, minimalist eatery has a menu that focuses on salads featuring mango, wasabi and wontons, mains of authentic Chinese and Asian dishes and creative desserts. There is a kid's menu and a good selection of beers and wines.

GB Roof Garden €€€
Fine Dining **Map** 6 F1
Grande Bretagne, Vassiléos Georgíou 1, Plateía Syntágmatos, 105 64
Tel *21033 30000*
Rooftop eatery of the Grande Bretagne hotel offering a menu of gourmet dishes inspired by Mediterranean cuisine. Enjoy the exquisite cooking with fine wines and beautiful uninterrupted views of the Acropolis.

DK Choice

The Tudor Hall €€€
Fine Dining **Map** 6 F1
King George Palace, Vassiléos Georgíou 3, Plateía Syntágmatos, 105 64
Tel *21033 30265*
Located on the 7th floor of the luxury hotel, this elegant restaurant seves enticing authentic Greek dishes such as *kakavia* (fish soup) and rabbit *stifado* (meat stew). Evening appetizers include shrimp *saganáki* and steamed octopus, and mains feature seafood risotto and chicken marinated in yoghurt and honey. Artful desserts.

Thiseío

Filoistron €€
Greek **Map** 5 B1
Apostólou Pávlou 23, 118 51
Tel *21034 22897* **Closed** *Mon*
Trendy place where platters of *mezédes* are served with glasses of quality Greek wine, *ouzo* or a cocktail. Try the *pastourmas* (cured cold cuts of meet). Sit outdoors on the rooftop terrace.

Thisseo View €€
Mediterranean **Map** 5 B1
Apostolou Pavlou 25, 118 51
Tel *21034 76754*
This restaurant is great for meals, coffee or drinks in a lively space with superb views of the Acropolis. Try the steamed mussels with ouzo and the pepper beef fillet. Great cocktails. Friendly atmosphere.

To Steki Tou Ilia €€
Traditional Greek **Map** 1 A5
Eptachálkou 5, 118 51
Tel *21034 58052* **Closed** *Mon*
Always packed with locals and tourists alike, this place is popular for its succulent *paidákia* (thinly sliced lamb chops) and *sykotária* (lamb liver).

Simply furnished dining area at Avocado, an eatery in Syntagma serving vegetarian food and juices

For more information on types of restaurants *see page 277*

Around Athens

Kessariani: Trata O Stelios €€
Seafood **Map** D4
Plateía Anagenísseos 7–9, 161 21
Tel *21072 91533* **Closed** *Sun eve*
Lively eatery that dominates the central square and is popular with the locals. Serves delicious seafood dishes and is known for its calamari, prawns and fish soup.
Superb Sunday lunches.

Kifisiá: Rakkan €€
Japanese **Map** D4
Leoforos Kifisiás 238-240, 145 62
Tel *21080 87941*
A stylish bar, that offers a varied menu of Japanese cuisine, including sushi, sashimi, tempura and teriyaki dishes.

Kifisiá: Souvlákia Kifissias €€
Traditional Greek **Map** D4
Othonos 99, 145 61
Tel *21080 11093*
Popular, informal and locally renowned for their delectable *souvlákia* and *yíros*. The menu also includes salads and grills.

Kifisiá: Berdema €€€
Fine Dining **Map** D4
Skiathou 3, 145 61
Tel *21062 01108*
The a la carte menu comprises regional Greek dishes with a modern twist. House specials include Cretan *lachmatzoun* (cheese and tomato pie) and *kousmpasi* (marinated lamb).

DK Choice

Kifisiá: Eleas Gi €€€
Fine Dining **Map** D4
Dexamenis & Olimpionikon 4 Politia, 145 63
Tel *21062 00005* **Closed** *Sun eve*
Housed in a stone mansion, this charming restaurant welcomes diners through a corridor decorated with wine bottles. The gourmet tasting menus feature *katiki domokos* (cheese with a red pepper mousse) followed by honey pork. Excellent wine list. The elegant dining area boasts crisp linens, high ceilings and a dining terrace.

Piraeus: Axinos €€
Seafood **Map** D4
Aktí Themistokléous 51, 185 34
Tel *21045 26944* **Closed** *Mon*
Local favourite specializing in top-notch fish and seafood platters, for which it is famous. Built against a cliff with great sea views and access to Freatida beach.

Sweeping views from the lovely outdoor dining area at Eleas Gi, a restaurant in Kifisiá

Piraeus: Ta Katsarolakia €€
Greek **Map** D4
Aktí Moutsopoulou 21, 185 34
Tel *21041 00609*
Located on the waterside, this eatery is always buzzing with diners. Serves classics such as home-made *moussaka*, along with fresh fish platters.

Piraeus: Jimmy And The Fish €€€
Seafood **Map** D4
Aktí Koumoundoúrou 46, Mikrolímano, 185 33
Tel *21041 24417*
A nautical theme and a deck by Mikrolímano's harbour provide the setting for a superb menu of creative dishes based on fresh sea produce. Try the prawns in *ouzo*.

DK Choice

Piraeus: Kollias €€€
Seafood **Map** D4
Syngrou 303 and Dimosthenous, 175 64
Tel *21046 29620* **Closed** *Sun*
This legendary restaurant has some unusual seafood options on the menu – appetizers such as sea urchins, *spinialo* (seafood fermented in sea water) from Kálymnos and mussels *souvlákia*, as well as mains of salt-crusted seabream, pandora, red mullet and bass. Extensive dessert and drinks menus.

Piraeus: Vassilenas €€€
Seafood **Map** D4
Aitolikoú 72, 185 45
Tel *21046 12457* **Closed** *Sun*
Tastefully decorated eatery offering contemporary fish and seafood platters and *mezédes*. There are tasting and a la carte menus comprising dishes such as pasta with shrimp and cured fish roe, and ravioli with veal tail and mushrooms. Excellent fine wines.

Porto Ráfti: Psaropoula Mpimpikos €€
Seafood **Map** D4
Leofóros Avlakíou 118, 190 09
Tel *22990 71292*
A choice of delicious *mezédes*-style seafood dishes as well as mouthwatering desserts. There is a separate menu for children, making this an ideal place for family dining, just metres away from the beach.

Rafína: Kavouria Tou Asimaki €€
Seafood **Map** D4
Limáni Rafína (harbour), 190 09
Tel *22940 24551*
Established in 1952, this is one of the oldest and best seafood eateries in Rafina. Regulars keep coming back for the freshest grilled fish. Try the fisher man's spaghetti, made with mussels, squid and octopus in a rich tomato sauce. The place is easy to find.

DK Choice

Rafína: Ioakeim €€€
Seafood **Map** D4
Limáni Rafína (harbour), 190 09
Tel *22940 23421*
Popular with Athenians, especially on weekends, Ioakeim has been a part of Rafina's picturesque harbour landscape for decades. Dine on fresh fish flavoured with *krítamo* (wild rock fennel), and oysters or barracuda with herbs. Dine al fresco on the terrace while watching hydrofoils leave for the islands.

Soúnio: Syrtaki €€
Greek **Map** D4
2km (1 mile) north of Temple of Poseidon, 195 50
Tel *22920 39125*
Frequented more by local than international tourists, Syrtaki

serves quick bites such as *mezédes*, spit-roasted meat and *souvláki* to visitors to the Temple of Poseidon. Great views from its terrace.

Varkiza: Island €€€
International   **Map** D4
27th km of Athens–Soúnio coast road, 166 72
Tel 21096 53563
A restaurant-nightclub located on a clifftop that serves creative Mediterranean and modern international cuisine. There are dedicated tapas and sushi bars. Wine cellar with over 150 labels.

The Peloponnese

Ancient Corinth: Archontiko €€
Greek   **Map** C4
Paralía Lechaíou, 200 06
Tel 27410 27968
Situated close to archaeological tourist sites with a good range of dishes. The house speciality, *kokkinistó Archontiko* (Greek beef stew), made with the taverna's own meat in red wine, is a must try.

DK Choice

Gialova: Chelonaki €€
Seafood   **Map** B5
Limáni Gialova, 240 01
Tel 27230 23080
This informal, waterside taverna is located on the harbour and looks out to the Navaríno Bay. Fish caught earlier in the day is artfully served, dressed either with lemon and herbs or a creamy home-made sauce. Sunset views from the restaurant terrace are legendary. Features live music on most weekends.

Gýtheio: I Trata €
Traditional Greek   **Map** C5
Paralia Gytheio, 232 00
Tel 27330 24429
Excellent seaside option for enjoying traditional dinner and delicious *mezédes* made with the freshest ingredients. Friendly staff. Great atmosphere.

Gýtheio: Saga €€
Greek   **Map** C5
Odós Tzanni Tzannetáki, 232 00
Tel 27330 21358
This excellent family-run eatery serves home-made fish soup and stuffed squid, along with chargrilled meats. Dishes come in generous portions. Sit at one of the outdoor tables set on the pavement by the sea.

Kalamáta: Krini €€
Seafood   **Map** C5
Evangelistrías 40, 241 00
Tel 27210 24474
Located near the marina, Krini has a menu that prominently features *saganáki* with seafood and cheese, *ouzo*-drenched prawns and chargrilled sea bass. There are grilled meats and good local wines on offer too.

Koróni: Peroulia €
Traditional Greek   **Map** C5
Peroulia Beach, Kompoi, 240 04
Tel 27250 41777
Known since 1984 for its delicious Messinian cuisine. Enjoy home-made meals of the freshest fish and ingredients, along with extra virgin Messinian olive oil. The Peroulia Beach Bar offers exotic cocktails and coffee on the beach.

DK Choice

Kosmas: Maleatis Apollion €
Greek   **Map** C5
Central plateía, 210 52
Tel 27570 31494
Located in the picturesque Párnon mountain range village of Kosmas, this is every inch a traditional Greek taverna. The food on offer includes local dishes such as *kléftiko* that has been cooked for hours in a special outdoor oven and tasty home-made bread to dip into local olive oil. Wine from the Peloponnese vineyards accompanies the superb fare.

Kyparissía: Tiris €
Greek   **Map** B4
Mitrópoli, 230 52
Tel 27320 55260
A family-run taverna whose menu focuses on whatever fish was caught earlier in the

day, along with grills and roasts. The food is fresh and tasty and the conversations are lively.

Lygourió: Leonidas €€
Traditional Greek   **Map** C4
Village centre, 210 52
Tel 27530 22115
Located near Epidaurus theatre, this taverna is decorated with old photographs and is frequented by local regulars as well as actors. The hearty *mageireftá* (meat cooked slowly in wine) is a house special.

DK Choice

Methóni: Klimataria €€
Traditional Greek   **Map** B5
Odós Miaoúli, 240 06
Tel 27230 31544
Klimataria excels in *mezédes*, *mageireftá* and vegetarian dishes. The delectable food is served artfully on tables laid out in crisp linens. Dine in the courtyard shielded from the sun by a vine-covered pergola, featuring tubs of flowers and its own bar. The wine list has something to go with every dish.

Monemvasía: Matoula €€
Traditional Greek   **Map** C5
Kástro, 230 70
Tel 27230 61660
Located inside the castle, Matoula has been serving diners for over 60 years – classic Greek with a speciality of fish *mezédes*. The walls of the eatery are lined with old photographs.

Monemvasía: Skorpios €€
Traditional Greek   **Map** C5
Géfyra coast road, 230 70
Tel 27320 62090
Situated on a waterside spot with a terrace overlooking the rock. Diners flock to this eatery to enjoy marinated fish dishes of *gávros* (anchovies) and *atherína*, and a daily *mageireftá*.

DK Choice

Monemvasía: Chrisovoulo €€€
Fine Dining   **Map** C5
Kástro, 230 70
Tel 27320 62022
This fashionable eatery inside the castle, ttempts diners with appetizers such as *saiti* pie (traditional pie filled with vegetables and herbs), mains of veal with Malvasia wine sauce as well as feta cheese ice cream. Superb wine list. The decor complements the stone walls, while a terrace looks over rooftops to the sea.

A dessert of Greek yoghurt with honey and walnuts at Chrisovoulo in Monemvasía

For more information on types of restaurants *see page 277*

Náfplio: Omorfo Tavernaki €€
Traditional Greek   Map C4
Vassilísis Ólgas 1, 211 00
Tel *27520 25944*
Charming eatery in a Neo-Classical
building on a beautiful street. Try
the home-made *tyrokafterí* (spicy
cheese dip) and the signature
dish *kolokotroneïko* (pork in wine).

Náfplio: Ta Fanaria €€
Traditional Greek   Map C4
Staïkopoulou 13, 211 00
Tel *27520 27141*
Lively taverna serving classic
dishes such as *spetzofáï* (sausage
and pepper stew), *moussaka* and
stuffed eggplants, washed down
with Mégara retsina. Dine outdoors
on the lovely vine-covered terrace.

Pátra: Mythos €
Traditional Greek   Map C4
Trión Navárhon 17, 262 22
Tel *26103 29984*
One of the oldest tavernas near
the Agios Andréas basilica. Good,
traditional food such as home-
made *moussaka* and *pastítsio*.

Plaka Leonidiou: Bekarou €
Tradtional Greek   Map C5
Limáni, 223 00 Plaka Leonidiou
Tel *27570 22379*
Housed in a lovely old seafront
building, this inn gives guests the
opportunity to dine on fresh fish
such as *gávros* and *atheerína*,
while observing the port's bustle.

Pýlos: Gregory's €€
Tradtional Greek   Map B5
Pýlos
Tel *27230 22621*
A local favourite for its hearty
mageireftá menu that also
includes *kokkinistó* (beef stew) and
spetzofáï. There is a charming
garden for alfresco dining.

DK Choice

Rio: Naut-oiko €€
Seafood   Map C4
Poseidonos 12, 265 00
Tel *26109 95992*
Imaginative fresh fish and
seafood with fine Peloponnese
wines is the deal at this elegant
restaurant. There are pergolas
and subtle lighting outside.
Add an idyllic location right
next to the beach and it's easy
to see why Naut-oiko is popular
with locals and tourists alike.

Spárti: Remo €
Pizza & Pasta   Map C5
Dinekous 8, Laconia, 231 00
Tel *27310 89089*
With its bright red decor inside
and out, Remo is something of a

landmark in Spárti. It offers pizzas
with an array of toppings, tasty
pasta dishes and charcoal grills.

Spárti: Elysse €€
Modern Greek   Map C5
Konstantínou Palaiológou 113, 231 00
Tel *27310 29896*
A pastel decor and an elegant
dining terrace create the perfect
backdrop for Elysse's innovative
mageireftá menu. Try the *keftedes*
(spiced lamb meatballs in a tomato
sauce) and the chargrilled lamb
cutlets with aromatic rice.

Vytina: Ta Kokkina Pitharia €€
Traditional Greek   Map C4
Central plateía, 220 10
Tel *27950 22540*
Charming stone eatery located in
the central square. Serves local
specialities such as *bekrí mezé* (pork
with feta sauce) and *spetzofáï*
(sausage and pepper stew).

Central and Western Greece

DK Choice

**Agios Ioánnis (Pílio):
Poseidonas** €€
Seafood   Map D3
Coast road, 370 12
Tel *24260 31222*
Charming taverna located
on the Pílio Peninsula's coast.
The ready supply of fish,
caught by the owners themselves, appears in the menu
in the form of flavoursome
creations. *Kakaviá* (fish soup)
and *baroúnia* (red mullet)
delicately cooked with
lemon are house specials.
Dine indoors or alfresco.

Neatly arranged tables in the indoor dining
area of Ta Fanaria, a restaurant in Náfplio

Aráchova: Panagióta €€
Greek   Map C3
Opposite Agios Geórgios, 320 04
Tel *22670 32735*
An elegant little place with
a menu comprising classic
Greek dishes, including
tyrokafterí (spicy cheese dip),
kléftiko and *tsakonikí* (eggplant).

Delfoí: Vakhos €€
Greek   Map C3
*Apollonos 31, Fokida,
330 54*
Tel *22650 83186*
Charming family-run taverna,
serving dishes prepared from
fine Parnassus mountain produce. Superb selection of wines.
There's a lovely veranda from
where the view can be enjoyed.

Diáva: Neromylos €€
Seafood   Map B2
*Pigí Goúra, top end of Diáva
village, 422 00*
Tel *24320 25224*   **Closed** *Sun eve*
Housed in an old watermill,
this rustic taverna has a
large local following. The
menu features meat dishes
and vegetable *mezédes*,
along with trout from the
farm on site.

DK Choice

Elati: Sta Riza €€
Traditional Greek   Map B3
Village centre, 420 32
Tel *26530 71550*   **Closed** *Wed &
Thu*
One of Elati's best kept secrets,
Sta Riza offers spectacular views,
with delicious food to match.
The speciality here is *mageireftá*
and *lachanópita* (vegetable pie
with feta cheese), served with
home-made bread and salad.
A sun terrace doubles as an
outdoor eating area with
views of the Vikos Gorge.

Galaxídi: Albatross €€
Traditional Greek   Map C3
Konstantinoú Satha 36, 330 52
Tel *22650 42233*
Known for its wholesome food,
with a daily-changing menu
typically features *mageireftá*
stews and their special *samári*
(savory pancetta).

Gavros: To Spiti Tou Psara €€
Traditional Greek   Map B3
Gavros through road, 360 75
Tel *22370 41202*
Dining on tasty Greek fare while
enjoying river and rural views is
what attracts diners to this taverna.
Tyrokafterí (spicy cheese dip) and
grilled trout are menu highlights.

Ioánnina: Fisa Roufa €€
//modern Greek **Map** B2
Avéroff 55, 452 21
Tel *26510 26262*
Family-run eatery offering classic
dishes with a modern twist. Try
the fish *mageireftá*, *spetzofáï* with
herbs and *kataïfi* (cheese pastry
soaked in a sugar-based syrup).

DK Choice

Ioánnina: To Agnanti €€€
Fine Dining **Map** B2
Pamvotides 2, Molos, 452 21
Tel *26510 22010*
Elegant restaurant with a large
terrace looking out over the Isle
of Ali Pasha. The elaborate menu
includes *arnáki lemonato* (lamb
in lemon sauce), *kolokythoanthoí*
(stuffed zucchini flowers) and
sweet *glyká* (traditional Greek
sweet made with fruit).
Excellent wine cellar.

Kalampáka: Archontariki €€
Traditional Greek **Map** B2
Plateía Riga Fereou, 422 00
Tel *24320 22449*
Diners flock to Archontariki for its
traditional taverna-style food such
as *mezédes* and dips, as well as
dishes such as *zygoúri* (lamb stew).

Kastráki: Paradeisos €€
Traditional Greek **Map** B2
Village centre, 422 00
Tel *24320 22723*
Grillhouse popular with locals for
its pumpkin with garlic speciality,
as well as the delicious *souvlákia*
or *yíros* with a *choriátiki saláta*
(Greek salad). The terrace affords
charming views.

Katigiorgis: Flisvos €
Seafood **Map** D3
On the beach, 370 06
Tel *24230 71071*
Family-run eatery on the beach
always bustling with visitors.
The food on offer features the
must-try dish, *scháras* – fresh
grilled fish drizzled in lemon.

DK Choice

Kipoí: Stou Mihali €€
Modern Greek **Map** B2
Main road through village, 440 10
Tel *26530 71630*
Breathtaking views from its
terrace and a superb menu of
contemporary cuisine have put
Stou Mihali on the map. The
emphasis is on using Zagórian
produce. Try the dishes of wild
boar roasted in a claypot or the
venison *stifádo*, accompanied
by a local red wine.

Stylish, contemporary interiors of Bourazani, a rural taverna in Konítsa

Konítsa: To Dendro €
Greek **Map** B2
Approach road, 441 00
Tel *26550 22055*
To Dendro has a daily-changing
menu that features dishes
such as *gástra* (baked goat)
and wild boar cooked in
wine until tender. The wine
is local and plentiful.

Konítsa: Bourazani €€
Greek **Map** B2
Ioánnina to Konítsa road, 441 00
Tel *26550 61283*
Rural taverna at a resort
near an environmental
park. The menu features
dishes prepared with fresh
and naturally produced
ingredients, such as the
deer and rabbit *mezédes*.

DK Choice

**Koronisiá: Myrtaria
Patentas** €€
Seafood **Map** B3
Coast road, 471 00
Tel *26810 24021*
Looking out over the
picturesque Amvrakikós Gulf,
this laidback taverna has
garnered a reputation for its
exquisitely cooked and presented fresh fish and seafood
dishes. The speciality here are
prawns – caught straight from
the gulf and served drenched
in *ouzo*. Superb wine list.
There's an outdoor dining
area on a terrace.

Lamía: Alaloum €
Traditional Greek **Map** C3
Androutsou 24, 351 00
Tel *22310 44470*
A lively taverna off Lamía's
Plateía Laoú. The quick bites
served here include tasty
souvlákia and *píttes* (pies
of stuffed filo pastry).

Lamía: En Aristotelous €
Macedonian **Map** C3
Aristotélous 3, 351 00
Tel *22310 31502*
Housed in a 19th-century
building with a courtyard for
summer dining, this popular
eatery serves excellent
Macedonian cuisine like
tavče gravče (a traditional
dish of baked beans).

Lamía: Fitilis €
Modern Greek **Map** C3
Plateía Laoú 6, 351 00
Tel *22420 26761*
Since it opened a few years
ago, Fitilis has earned itself a
great reputation for creative
mageireftá dishes. The slow-
cooked goat with herbs is a
must-try speciality.

DK Choice

Miliés: To Salkimi €€
Traditional Greek **Map** D3
Central plateía, 37 010
Tel *24230 86010*
A buzzing eatery in a smart
wooden building. The food
served here features classic
dishes made with fresh local
produce. Its signature dish
is *salkimi*, made with veal,
aubergines and courgettes in
a brandy and *béchamel* sauce.
Good wine selection and lovely
outdoor dining that makes
the most of sweeping views
across the Pagasitikos gulf.

Milina (Pílio): Sakis €
Seafood **Map** D3
Waterfront, 370 06
Tel *24230 66078*
An established, inviting
taverna offering outdoor
seating at tables set on the
waterfront. Excellent *mezédes*
as well as specials such as
soupiés (cuttlefish).

Néo Mikro Horió: To Horiatiko €
Traditional Greek **Map** C3
Central plateía, 360 75, near Karpenisi
Tel 22370 41257
Welcoming taverna in a stone
building offering home-made
food in generous portions. Try the
kokoretsi (a dish of lamb or goat
intestine) and lamb *souvláki*a.

Párga: Golfo Beach €€
Mediterranean **Map** B3
Agiou Athanasiou, 480 60
Tel 26840 32336
This restaurant serves wholesome
meals such as home-made
mageireftá, *moussaka* and *tzatzíki*
as well as fresh fish dishes all day.
Features regular music nights.

DK Choice

Párga: Kastro 1380 €€
Mediterranean **Map** B3
Kástro entrance, 480 60
Tel 26840 32164
Situated atop a hill by the
castle with fabulous views.
The innovative menu includes
Mediterranean meat and
fish dishes and specials such
as *psária plaki* (baked fish),
*souvláki*a and veal *stifádo*.
Always bustling with diners.

DK Choice

Portaria: Kritsa €€
Fine Dining **Map** C3
Hotel Kritsa, Central plateía, 370 11
Tel 24280 90006
Atmospheric place housed in a
Neo-Classical former dairy. The
elegant ambience, crisp linens
and good wine make it the local
favourite for special occassions.
The menu has a good selection
of appetizers and salads, as
well as dishes such as *spetzofái*
and a *mageireftá* of rabbit
with mustard and brandy.

Préveza: Skaloma €€
Seafood **Map** B3
Limáni Lygia, 481 00
Tel 26820 56240
Prawn *saganáki*, calamari and
seafood *mezédes* top the crowd
favourites at this harbourside fish
taverna. Offers great views of Paxós
from its terrace. Good wine list.

Sarakíniko Bay: Taverna
Tou Christou €€
Traditional Greek **Map** B3
Beside the beach, 480 60, near Párga
Tel 26840 35207
Beachside taverna with a dining
terrace and a pool, serves top
notch meat, fish and vegetarian
dishes. Very popular with locals.

Tríkala: Diachroniko €
Traditional Greek **Map** C2
Hatzipetroú, 421 00
Tel 24310 77522
Traditional *tsipourádika* that
must be visited if only for
the ambience! The food is
good too – hearty fare, along
with *mezédes* and *ouzo*.

Tríkala: Mezedokomomata €
Traditional Greek **Map** C2
Ypsilántou 16–18, 421 00
Tel 24310 76741
Set amidst the timber-framed
homes of Tríkala, this welcoming
family-run *ouzerí* offers a good
selection of Greek dishes such
as *ntolmádes* (stuffed vine
leaves) and beef *stifádo*.

Tríkala: Palaia Istoria €€
Modern Greek **Map** C2
Ypsilántou 3, 421 00
Tel 24310 77627
Authentic flavours, but with a
touch of the modern at this
popular alleyway *ouzerí*. Pork
and lamb with creamy sauces
and garnishes like *ftéri* (fried
fern) are a must-try.

Tsagkarada: Agnati €
Traditional Greek **Map** D3
Village centre, Píliou
Tel 24260 49210
Tasty *spetzofái* and meat in
home-made sauces are menu
classics served at this taverna.
Tables are laid out under the
village's famous plane tree.

Tsagkarada: Dipnosofistis €
Traditional Greek **Map** D3
Village centre, Píliou
Tel 24260 49825
One of several *psistariés*
(grillhouses) in scenic
Tsagkarada. *Ntolmádes* and
mageireftá combos as well as
tasty grilled dishes are on offer.

Tsoumerka: Panorama €€
Traditional Greek **Map** B3
Central plateía, Agnata, 471 00
Tel 26850 31000
As its name suggests, Panorama
affords fabulous mountain views
from the terrace where diners
feast on home-made *spetzofái*
and the *mageireftá* of the day.

Zagóra (Pílio): Petros
Landis €
Traditional Greek **Map** C3
Plateía Agíou Georgíou, 370 01
Tel 24260 23666
Set high in the mountains,
with great views of the
Sporádes. The kitchen
excels in *píttes*, *souvláki*a
and charcoal grills. Has a
large local following.

Charming outdoor dining area at Kritsa,
a restaurant in Portaria

Northern Greece

Alexandroúpoli: Nea Klimataria €
Greek **Map** E1
Plateía Kyprou 8, 681 00
Tel 25510 26288
Rest your feet and people
watch while enjoying superb
Greek food in one of the
town's busiest squares. Try
their *ntolamádes* or one of
the charcoal grills.

Alexandroúpoli: Psarotaverna
Tis Kyra Dimitras €€
Seafood **Map** E1
Karaoli Dimitriou 104, 681 00
Tel 25510 34434
Freshly-caught fish and seafood,
such as *atherína* and *tsipoúra*
(sea bream), are displayed on
ice at the entrance for diners
to choose the one they want to
eat. It is then exquisitely cooked
and served. Try the mussels.

Alexandroúpoli:
To Nisiotiko €€€
Seafood **Map** E1
Zarífi 3, 681 00
Tel 25510 20990
An upmarket fish taverna
with a nautical decor located
right on the waterfront. Has a
variety of grills and specials
such as *psária plaki*.

DK Choice

Kastoriá: Krontíri €€
Modern Greek **Map** B2
Orestiádos 13, 521 00
Tel 24670 28358
A setting right by a lake, with
tables laid out on the shoreline,
paired with creative modern
Greek cuisine attracts diners to
Krontíri. Menu highlights
include home-made cabbage
ntolamádes and *mageireftá*
combos such as veal with plums
and *píttes*. Good wine selection.
Cosy interior for winter dining.

Kavála: Elia €
Traditional Greek Map D1
Batis beach, 653 02
Tel *25102 43181*
The aroma of fresh fish such as *tsipoúra* and chicken or beef on the grill is a huge draw at this delightful taverna on Batis beach. Superb salad bar and wine list.

Kavála: Panos & Zafira €€
Traditional Greek Map D1
Plateía Karaóli & Dimitríou 20, 653 02
Tel *25102 27978*
Harbourside taverna that is usually full of locals keen to dine on delicious authentic Greek *mageireftás, pastítsio* and *stifádo*.

Komotiní: To Petrino €
Seafood Map E1
Serron 25, 691 00
Tel *25310 73650* **Closed** *Dinner*
Sample exquisite and authentic Thracian cuisine, the speciality at this restaurant. Don't miss the *trahanas* (soup) and tender *pligouri* (goat) with *gioufkas* (pasta).

Komotiní: Kouti €€
Balkan Map E1
Orfeos 45, 691 00
Tel *25310 25774*
Upscale, modern restaurant is located in a city that is close to the Bulgarian border. Balkan cuisine features strongly on the menu.

DK Choice

Litóchoro: Gastrodromio' En Olympo' €€€
Fine Dining Map C2
Agiou Nikolaou 36, 602 00
Tel *23520 21300*
The place to enjoy al fresco dining and renowned gourmet fare. The meat and fish menu lists a few surprises such as octopus with saffron and *tsoukaliasto* (braised) rabbit. Good wine list, salad selection and over 30 Greek cheeses.

Psarádes: I Syntrofia €
Greek Map B1
Village centre, 530 77
Tel *23850 46107*
Dine indoors at this welcoming hotel taverna or on the summer terrace that looks out over the lakes. The menu focuses on fish, especially *tsironia* from the lake.

Thessaloníki: I Myrovolos Smyrni €
Café Map C2
Komninón 32, 546 24
Tel *23102 74170*
This busy *ouzerí* is a local favourite and serves wholesome dishes such as meatballs and *souvlákia* all through the day.

Thessaloníki: Ta Koumparakia €
Macedonian Map C2
Egnatía 140, 546 22
Tel *23102 71905*
Meat dishes with a spicy kick are the main draw at this *ouzerí*. Its *tavče gravče* is popular, enjoyed with the Balkan drink *mastika*.

Thessaloníki: Tiffany's Grill €
International Map C2
Iktínou 22, 546 22
Tel *23102 74022*
Trendy eatery with wooden floors and art displayed on the walls. Serves steaks and grills as well as Greek classics such as home-made *moussaka*.

DK Choice

Thessaloníki: Aristotélous €€
Seafood Map C2
Aristotélous 8, 546 23
Tel *23102 33195*
Popular restaurant that serves mouthwatering fish dishes in its arcaded dining halls and courtyard. Menu highlights include *Galéos skordaliá* (shark with garlic sauce) and *mydopílafo* (mussels served with rice). Excellent wine list. Located off Aristotelous Square.

Thessaloníki: Kamares €€
Modern Greek Map C2
Plateía Agíou Georgíou 11
Tel *23102 19686*
Outdoor tables located near the Rotónda. On the menu are staples such as grilled meat and fish served with tasty, creative salads.

Thessaloníki: Kitchen Bar €€
International Map C2
Limani Thessaloníki, 546 27
Tel *23105 02241*
A fun, trendy place housed in a restored warehouse on the jetty. The open kitchen

allows diners to watch European and Mediterranean food being prepared by the chefs.

Thessaloníki: Louloudadika €€
Greek Map C2
Komninón 20, 546 24
Tel *23102 25624* **Closed** *Sun dinner*
Named after the flower market in which it is situated, this charming *ouzerí* offers a good mix of fish dishes and Greek classics such as *moussaka*.

Thessaloníki: To Yenti €€
Traditional Greek Map C2
Paparéska 13, 54634
Tel *23102 46495*
Rustic, traditional old town *ouzerí* that serves hearty classic Greek dishes such as *ntolmádes, spetzofái* and *mageireftás* of the day.

Thessaloníki: Vrotos €€
Traditional Greek Map C2
Metropolítou Gennadíou 6, 546 30
Tel *23102 23958* **Closed** *Sun*
Popular *ouzerí* with tasteful decor of old movie posters and a menu of Greek classics with a Middle Eastern twist. The signature dish is *hunkiar beyendi* (lamb served on an eggplant puree).

Thessaloníki: Ergon €€€
Fine Dining Map C2
Kouskoura 3-5, 546 23
Tel *23210 84224*
Run by a celebrity chef, Ergon often plays host to famous guests. Try the pumpkin risotto, lamb with *ouzo* and *millefeuille* (French pastry). There's a separate food shop selling local and organic produce.

Xánthi: Ta Fanarakia €
International Map E1
Georgíou Stávrou 18, 671 00
Tel *25410 73606*
Lovely little *ouzerí* with a courtyard that is usually packed with locals enjoying the food. Serves classic Greek but with a Turkish influence. Features music on weekends.

Food shop selling local and organic products at Ergon, a high end restaurant in Thessaloníki

For more information on types of restaurants *see page 277*

SHOPPING IN GREECE

Shopping in Greece can be entertaining, particularly when you buy directly from the producer. There is a wide range of shops and boutiques, as well as corner stores and department stores. Markets provide a colourful shopping experience, whether you are looking for olives, sugary sweets or traditional handi-

crafts. In smaller villages, embroiderers, lace makers and potters can often be seen at work. Leather goods, carpets, rugs and jewellery are also widely available, as are religious icons. Most other goods in Greece have been imported and carry a heavy mark-up. For information on shopping in Athens, see pages 118–19.

Vat and Tax-Free Shopping

Almost always included in the price, FPA *(Fóros Prostitheménis Axías)* – the equivalent of VAT – is about 23 per cent in Greece.

Visitors from outside the EU who stay less than three months may claim this money back on purchases over €120. A "Tax-Free Cheque" form must be completed in the shop, a copy of which is then given to the customs authorities on departure. You may be asked to show your receipt or goods as proof of purchase.

Tax-free shop symbol

Opening Hours

Allowing for plenty of exceptions, shops and boutiques are generally open on Monday, Wednesday and Saturday from 9am to 2:30pm, and on Tuesday, Thursday and Friday from 9am to 1:30pm and 5 to 9pm. Department stores remain open Monday to Friday from 9am to 9pm and Saturday from 9am to 6pm. Supermarkets, found in all but the smallest communities, are often family-run and open long

hours, typically Monday to Saturday from 8 or 9am to 8 or 9pm. Sunday shopping is possible in most tourist resorts and also in some of the suburban shopping malls in Athens. The corner *perÍptero* (street kiosk), found in nearly every town, is open from around 7am to 11pm or midnight, selling everything from aspirins to ice cream, as well as bus tickets and phonecards.

Markets

Most towns in Greece have their weekly street market *(laïkí agorá)*, a colourful selection of fresh fruit and vegetables, herbs, fish, meat and poultry – often juxtaposed with shoes and underwear, fabrics, household items and sundry electronic equipment. In the larger cities, the street markets are in a different area each day, usually opening early and packing up by about 2pm, in time for the siesta. Prices are generally cheaper than in the supermarkets, and a certain amount of bargaining is also acceptable, at least for non-

perishables. This guide gives market days in the information under each town entry.

In Athens, there is a famous Sunday-morning flea market that is held around Plateía Monastirakíou and its radiating streets, which should not be missed if you are in the city *(see p91).*

"Brettos" distillery and liquor store, in Athens

Food and Drink

Culinary delights to look out for in Greece include honey – the best varieties coming from the mountain villages – a wide selection of cured olives, high quality olive oil, and fresh and dried herbs and spices. A great selection of nuts is also available, including pistachios, hazelnuts and sunflower seeds.

The famous Greek feta cheese is widely available, and delicious in a salad or with rustic bread. The sweet breads and biscuits of the *zacharoplasteío* (cake and pastry shop) are another must. Sweetened with honey and syrup, Greek pastries are mouthwateringly good.

Greece is also renowned for several alcoholic drinks, including *oúzo* (an aniseed-flavoured spirit), *retsína* (a resinated wine), brandy, the firewater *tsípouro* and *rakí* (a type of distilled wine).

Souvenir shop window in Párga, central Greece

What to Buy in Greece

Traditional handicrafts, though not particularly cheap, do offer the most genuinely Greek souvenirs. Handicrafts cover a range of items from finely wrought gold reproductions of ancient pendants to rustic pots, wooden spoons and handmade sandals. Some of the country's best ceramics can be found in the markets and shops of Athens' northern suburb, Maroúsi. Brightly coloured embroidery and wall-hangings are produced in many villages throughout Greece, where they are often seen hanging out for sale, along with thick *flokáti* rugs, which are handwoven from sheep or goat's wool. These are made mainly in the Píndos Mountains and can also be found at Aráchova, near Delphi *(see p225)*. In the small, rural communities, crafts are often cottage industries, earning the family a large chunk of its annual income. Here, there is room to engage in some bartering over the price. The *Shopping in Athens* section, on pages 118–19, indicates places within the capital where traditional crafts may be bought.

Gold jewellery is sold in larger towns or cities. Modern designs are found in jewellers such as Lalaounis, and reproductions of ancient designs in museum gift shops.

Icons are generally sold in shops and monasteries. They range from very small portraits to substantial pictures. Some of the most beautiful, and expensive, use only age-old traditional techniques and materials.

Ornate utensils, such as these wooden spoons, are found in traditional craft shops. As here, they are often hand-carved into the shapes of figures and produced from the rich-textured wood of the native olive tree.

Kombolói, or worry beads, are a traditional sight in Greece; the beads are counted as a way to relax. They are sold in souvenir shops and jewellers.

Kitchenware is found in most markets and in specialist shops. This copper coffee pot *(mpríki)* is used for making Greek coffee.

Leather goods are sold throughout Greece. The bags, backpacks and sandals make useful and good-value souvenirs.

Ornamental ceramics come in many shapes and finishes. Traditional earthenware, often simple, functional and unglazed, is frequently for sale by the roads on the outskirts of Athens and the larger towns.

SPECIALIST HOLIDAYS AND OUTDOOR ACTIVITIES

Many organized tours and courses cater for the special interests of visitors to Greece. You can follow in the footsteps of the apostle Paul or take a train ride through history; you can visit ancient archaeological sites with a learned academic as your guide, sample Greek wine, improve your writing skills, draw wild flowers or paint the Greek landscape. Sailing and windsurfing holidays are available, as are walking tours and botanical and birdwatching expeditions. There are also plenty of opportunities to watch sporting events. Many organized holidays include food and accommodation in the price.

A scenic railway journey through the Greek countryside

Archaeological Tours

For those interested in Greece's ancient past, a tour to some of the famous archaeological sites can make a fascinating and memorable holiday. You can choose from an array of destinations and itineraries, all guided by qualified archaeologists. As well as visiting ancient ruins, many tours also take in Venetian fortresses, Byzantine churches and frescoes, museums and monasteries en route to the archaeological sites. **Andante Travels** runs specialist tours guided by archaeologists, while **Ramblers Holidays**, **ACE Study Tours**, **Travelsphere** and **Martin Randall** all organize tours of Classical sites.

Writing and Painting

With its vivid landscape and renowned quality of light, Greece is an inspirational destination for artistic endeavour. Courses in creative writing or drawing and painting are available at all levels and are conducted by professional tutors, well established in their craft. **Greeka.com** offers a range of painting and drawing courses, as well as creative writing workshops.

Wine Tasting

The quality of Greek wine has increased enormously in recent years, with some vineyards winning international medals, a prospect that was unlikely a decade ago. A variety of tours of vineyards around Athens are arranged by the wine tour specialists **Arblaster and Clarke**.

Railway Holidays

The rail network in Greece is not extensive, nor is it used much by visitors, who tend to prefer the country's excellent bus system. It does, however, have one of the greatest railway journeys in Europe, on the narrow-gauge track to the mountain town of Kalávryta (*see p172*) from Diakoftó. A trip on this railway can be arranged as part of a larger Greek tour through **Great Rail Journeys** in the UK. **Ffestiniog Travel** also arranges tailor-made rail trips around Greece, going east as far as Alexandroúpoli (*see p261*).

Beautiful spring wildflowers

Nature Tours

Much of the Greek countryside is rich in birdlife and noted for its spring flowers. The shorelines are also good for wildlife. Specialist tour operators, such as **Limosa Holidays**, **The Travelling Naturalist**, **Naturetrek** or **Sunbird**, offer package holidays that guide visitors through the ornithology and botany of Northern Greece and the Peloponnese. The **Hellenic Ornithological Society** can also be contacted for advice on birdwatching in Greece.

An archaeological guided tour

A horse-riding holiday along the azure coast

Walking and Cycling

Greece is a paradise for walkers, particularly in the spring when the countryside is at its greenest and the wild flowers are in bloom. The best locations are in the mountain ranges of the Taÿgetos in the Peloponnese *(see p199)* and the Píndos range in central Greece *(see p210)*, where **Sherpa Expeditions** has both guided and self-guided tours. **Trekking Hellas** arranges walking holidays in these regions as well as tours to the remote mountain areas of Agrafa and Stereá, offering a harsh landscape to explore at the southern end of the Píndos range. **Exodus** offers a similar service in these and other regions, using its own hiking leaders and tour guides.

Greek Options includes walking holidays in the Máni, based in the resort of Stoúpa *(see p199)* and organized by a local travel agent. The Máni also features in the **Inntravel** programme of walking holidays, as does the Pílio peninsula *(see pp222–4)*.

Travelsphere offers a week's trekking in Chalkidikí *(see p253)*, while walking and cycling trips in and around Athens, using a local company, can be booked through **Hidden Greece**. **Bikegreece** offers coast to coast cycling tours that are suitable for all abilities and can also arrange tailor-made holidays for families.

Riding

The Pílio peninsula *(see pp222-4)*, home to the legendary Centaurs – half-man and half-horse – is an ideal place for a riding holiday. **Ride World Wide** offers two different riding itineraries. One follows a coastal route, while the other takes you into the lushly wooded hills of this unspoiled corner of Greece.

Downhill skiing on Mount Parnassus

Skiing

There are several ski centres throughout the mainland, including some within easy reach of Athens – the closest being Mount Parnassus, near Delphi *(see p225)*. Depending on snow conditions, the season runs from the start of January to the end of April.

Costs are low compared with other European resorts, though facilities are quite basic. However, the Greek mountain resorts certainly provide an interesting alternative to the all-too-familiar names elsewhere in southern Europe.

For more information on skiing in Greece, contact the **Hellenic Skiing Federation**, or pick up a copy of the EOT's booklet entitled *Mountain Refuges and Ski Centres;* it is free from tourist offices and describes all the major ski centres.

Watersports

All along Greece's coastline, facilities for watersports are numerous. Visitors will find everything from windsurfing and water-skiing to jet-skiing and parasailing in the larger resorts, and many of the shops and beach huts that rent equipment also offer instruction. Kayaking, white-water rafting and canoeing holidays are organized by **Trekking Hellas**. Canoeing and rafting trips on the Gulf of Corinth near Pátra can also be booked through **Hidden Greece**.

Windsurfing in the Peloponnese

Snorkelling and Scuba Diving

The amazingly clear waters of the Mediterranean reveal a world of submarine life and archaeological remains. Snorkelling can be enjoyed almost anywhere along the coast, though scuba diving is restricted due to many submerged ancient artifacts. Greece is highly protective of its antiquities, and it is forbidden to remove them, or even to photograph them. The law is quite strict, so make sure you go with a reputable company.

A list of places where oxygen equipment may be used is available from the Greek National Tourism Organization (GNTO) *(see p303)*. The Athens-based organizes diving trips along the Attica coast, and tuition is available for those with no previous diving experience.

Scuba diver exploring the submarine life

Sailing Holidays

Sailing holidays can be booked through charter companies either in Greece or abroad. The season runs from April to late October, and itineraries range from a few days to several weeks.

Charters fall into four main categories. Bareboat charter,

A sailboat under power along the Corinth Canal in the Peloponnese *(see p171)*

without a skipper or crew, is available to anyone with sailing experience (most companies require at least two crew members to have a basic skipper's licence). Crewed charters range from the services of a paid skipper, assistant or cook to fully crewed yachts with every imaginable luxury. Chartering a yacht as part of a flotilla – typically in a group of six to 12 yachts – provides the opportunity of independent sailing with the support of a lead boat contactable by radio. **Sunsail** and **Thomas Cook** offer this kind of holiday, as well as holidays that mix cruiser sailing with shore-based dinghy sailing and windsurfing. Contact the **Hellenic Sailing Federation** for more information.

Cruises and Boat Trips

Running from April to October, cruise options range from the luxury of a large liner or handsome tall sailing ship to inexpensive mini-cruises and boat trips. The former can be booked through the big operators such as **Swan Hellenic**, **Sunvil** or **Voyages of Discovery**, while the tall ships belong to **Star Clippers**. Mini-cruises and boat trips can be organized locally and are best booked through **Ghiolman Yachts** or at a

travel agent on the spot. For a listing of cruise companies sailing to Greece, visit the Passenger Shipping Association website (www.discovercruises.co.uk).

A luxury cruise ship

Spas

The Greek mainland is not as well served with spas as some of the islands, such as Crete and Santorini, but several of the resort hotels on Chalkidikí *(see p253)* do have excellent facilities. Many tour operators feature them, including **Seasons** in the UK.

Unusual Activities

Not everyone wants to do a bungee-jump into the Corinth Canal, but for those who do, it can be arranged. The tour operator **Hidden Greece** specializes in finding places off the beaten track and also offers unusual activities. In addition to the bungee-jump they can book you two actor-guides in character as citizens from 460 BC to take you on a tour around Athens.

DIRECTORY

Archaeological Tours

ACE Study Tours
Babraham, Cambridge, CB22 5BP, UK.
Tel 01223 841 055.
W acestudytours.co.uk

Andante Travels
The Clock Tower, Unit 4, Southampton Road, Whaddon, Salisbury SP5 3HT, UK.
Tel 01722 713800.
W andantetravels.co.uk

Martin Randall
Voysey House, Barley Mow Passage, London W4 4GF, UK.
Tel 020 8742 3355.
W martinrandall.com

Ramblers Holidays
Lemsford Mill, Lemsford Village, Welwyn Garden City, Herts, AL8 7TR, UK.
Tel 01707 331133.
W ramblersholidays. co.uk

Travelsphere
Compass House, Rockingham Road, Market Harborough, Leicestershire, LE16 7QD, UK.
Tel 0844 567 9966.
W travelsphere.co.uk

Writing and Painting

Greeka.com
Makrigianni 26A, 18537 Piraeus. Tel 210 4526 900.
W greeka.com

Wine Tasting

Arblaster and Clarke Wine Tours
Cedar Court, 5 College Street, Petersfield, Hampshire, GU31 4AE, UK.
Tel 01730 263111.
W winetours.co.uk

Railway Holidays

Ffestiniog Travel
First Floor, Unit 6, Snowdonia Business Park, Penrhyndeudraeth, Gwynedd, LL48 6LD, UK.
Tel 01766 772 030.
W festtravel.co.uk

Great Rail Journeys
Saviour House, 9 St Saviourgate, York, YO1 8NL, UK.
Tel 01904 521936.
W greatrail.com

Nature Tours

Hellenic Ornithological Society
Themistokleous 80, 10681 Athens.
Tel 210 822 7937.
W ornithologiki.gr

Limosa Holidays
West End Farmhouse, Chapel Field, Stalham, Norfolk, NR12 9EJ, UK.
Tel 01692 580623.
W limosaholidays.co.uk

Naturetrek
Cheriton Mill, Cheriton, Alresford, Hants, SO24 0NG, UK.
Tel 01962 733051.
W naturetrek.co.uk

Sunbird
26B Market Sq, Potton, Bedfordshire, SG19 2NP, UK. Tel 01767 262522.
W sunbirdtours.co.uk

The Travelling Naturalist
PO Box 3141, Dorchester, Dorset, DT1 2XD, UK.
Tel 01305 267994.
W naturalist.co.uk

Walking and Cycling

Bikegreece
Karaiskáki 13, 10554 Athens.
Tel 210 453 5567.
W bikegreece.com

Exodus
Grange Mills, Weir Road, London, SW12 ONE, UK.
Tel 020 8772 3760.
W exodus.co.uk

Greek Options
26 High Street, Tring, Herts, HP23 5AH, UK.
Tel 0844 800 4787.
W greekoptions.co.uk

Hidden Greece
10 Upper Square, Old Isleworth, TW7 7BJ, UK.
Tel 020 8758 4707.
W hiddengreece.co.uk

Inntravel
Whitwell Grange, York, YO60 7JU, UK.
Tel 01653 617 001.
W inntravel.co.uk

Sherpa Expeditions
131a Heston Road, Hounslow, Middlesex, TW5 0RF, UK. Tel 020 8577 2717. W sherpa-walking-holidays.co.uk

Travelsphere
See Archaeological Tours.

Trekking Hellas
Saripolou 10, 10682 Athens. Tel 210 331 0323.
W trekking.gr

Riding

Ride World Wide
Staddon Farm, North Tawton, Devon, EX20 2BX, UK. Tel 01837 82544.
W rideworldwide.co.uk

Skiing

Hellenic Skiing Federation
28 Oktovriou 71, 10434 Athens. Tel 210 323 0182.
W eox.gr

Watersports

Hidden Greece
See Walking and Cycling.

Trekking Hellas
See Walking and Cycling.

Scuba and Snorkelling

Athina Diving
38Km Coastal Road, Sounio, Lagonissi, Athens.
Tel 229 102 5434.
W athinadiving.gr

Sailing Holidays

Hellenic Sailing Federation
Naftathlitiki Marina, 78550 Kallithea. Tel 210 940 4825. W eio.gr

Sunsail
TUI Travel House, Crawley Business Quarter, Fleming Way, Crawley, West Sussex RH10 9QL, UK.
Tel 0140 414 201.
W sunsail.eu

Thomas Cook
The Thomas Cook Headquarters, London WC2E 7EN, UK.
Tel 0844 895 0045.
W thomascook.com

Cruises and Boat Trips

Ghiolman Yachts
8 Propileon St, Acropolis, Athens.
Tel 210 325 5000.

Star Clippers
Olympus House, 2 Olympus Close, Ipswich, Suffolk, IP1 5LN, UK.
Tel 0845 200 6145.
W starclippers.co.uk

Sunvil
Upper Square, Old Isleworth, Middlesex, TW7 7BJ, UK.
Tel 020 8568 4499.
W sunvil.co.uk

Swan Hellenic Cruises
Lynnem House, 1 Victoria Way, Burgess Hill, West Sussex, RH15 9NF, UK.
Tel 0844 871 4603.
W swanhellenic.com

Voyages of Discovery
Lynnem House, 1 Victoria Way, Burgess Hill, West Sussex, RH15 9NF.
Tel 0844 822 0802.
W voyagesofdiscovery. co.uk

Spas

Seasons
Lakeside, St David's Park, Nr Chester, CH5 3YE, UK.
Tel 01244 202020.
W seasons.co.uk

Unusual Activities

Hidden Greece
See Walking and Cycling.

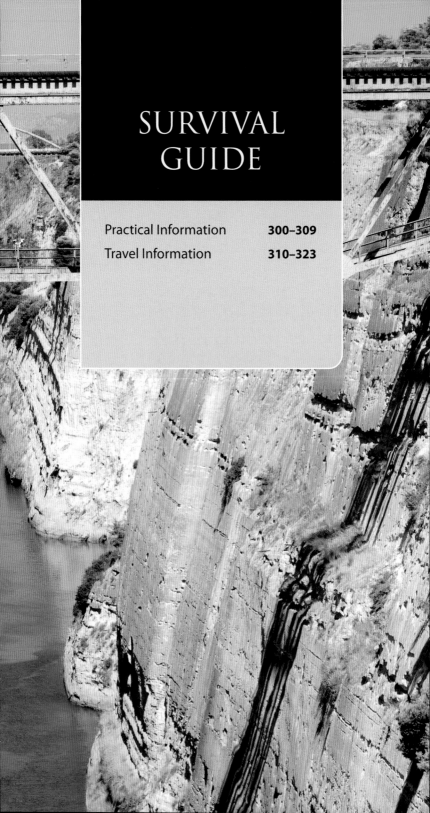

SURVIVAL
GUIDE

PRACTICAL INFORMATION

Greece's appeal is both cultural and hedonistic. The country's physical beauty, hot climate and warm seas, together with the easy-going outlook of its people, are all conducive to a relaxing holiday. It does pay, however, to know something about the nuts and bolts of Greek life – when to visit, what to bring, how to get around and what to do if things go wrong – to avoid unnecessary frustrations. Greece is no longer the cheap holiday destination it once was, though public transport, vehicle hire, eating out and hotel accommodation are still fairly inexpensive compared to most west European countries. The many tourist offices (see p303) offer information on all the practical aspects of your stay.

Boats near the Greek coast in high summer

When to Go

High season – July and August – is the hottest (see p53) and most expensive time to visit Greece; it is also very crowded on the coast. December to March are the coldest and wettest months, with many hotels and restaurants closed for the winter.

Skiing in Greece is possible from January to April, with around 20 mainland resorts to choose from (see p295).

Spring (late Apr–May) is one of the loveliest times to visit – the weather is sunny but not debilitatingly hot, there are relatively few tourists about, and the countryside is ablaze with brightly coloured wild flowers (see pp26–7).

Visas and Passports

Visitors from EU countries need a valid passport or ID card to enter Greece and do not need a visa. Some non-EU citizens such as those from the US, Canada, Australia and New Zealand, do not need a visa, but do need a valid passport for a stay of up to 90 days (there is no maximum stay for EU visitors). For longer stays, a resident's permit must be obtained from the **Aliens' Bureau** in Athens or the local police. Visitors should check visa requirements with a Greek embassy before travelling.

Any non-EU citizen planning to work or study in Greece should contact their local Greek consulate about visas and work permits.

Customs Information

EU residents can import alcohol, perfumes and tobacco without limits so long as they are for personal use. Visitors entering Greece from non-EU countries should check the following website for details of quantities that they can import free of charge: http://greece.visahq.com/customs.

Note that the unauthorized export of antiquities and archaeological artifacts from Greece is a serious offence, with strong penalties ranging from hefty fines to prison sentences.

Any prescription drugs that are brought into the country should be accompanied by a copy of the prescription (see pp304–5).

Tourist Information

Tourist information is available in many towns and villages in the form of government-run EOT offices (*Ellinikós Organismós Tourismoú*, also often referred to as **Greek National Tourism Organization, GNTO**), municipal tourist offices, the local tourist police (see p304) or travel agencies. Many of these offices operate only in summer. The GNTO publishes an array of tourist literature and brochures, but be aware that not all of this information is always up to date or reliable.

The addresses and phone numbers of the GNTO and municipal tourist offices are listed throughout this guide. A list of major Greek festivals and cultural events is given on pages 48–52, but it is also worth asking your nearest tourist office about what's happening locally.

Getting information at a City of Athens infopoint

◀ Canal of Corinth near the city of Athens

Ticket for the National Archaeological Museum

Admission Prices

Most state-run museums and archaeological sites charge an entrance fee of €3–€12. However, visitors aged 18 or under from EU countries are entitled to free admission, as are EU travellers carrying an International Student Identity Card (ISIC) *(see p302)*. Reductions of around 25 per cent are granted to EU citizens aged 65 and over (use your passport as proof of age), and reductions of 50 per cent to non-EU students armed with an ISIC card.

Though most museums and sites are closed on public holidays *(see p52)*, the ones that do stay open are free of charge. Admission to all state-run museums and archaeological sites is free on Sundays between November and April.

Opening Hours

Opening hours tend to be vague in Greece, varying from day to day, season to season and place to place. In addition to this, the financial crisis that the country has been experiencing since 2010 is having significant impact on many attractions, causing staff budget cuts and reduced opening hours. Although the opening times in this book have been checked at the time of going to print, they are likely to keep changing. It is advisable to use the times in this book as a rough guideline only and to check with local information centres before visiting a sight.

Most attractions usually close on Mondays and main public holidays. Small and private museums may be closed on local festival days in addition to main public holidays.

Monasteries and convents are open during daylight hours but will close for a few hours in the afternoon.

Most shops and offices are also closed on public holidays and local festival days, with the exception of some shops in tourist resorts. The dates of major local festivals are included in the Visitors' Checklists in each main town entry in this guide.

Social Customs and Etiquette

For a carefree holiday in Greece, it is best to adopt the local philosophy: *sigá, sigá* ("slowly, slowly"). Within this principle is the ritual of the afternoon siesta, a practice that should be taken seriously, particularly during the hottest months, when it is almost a physiological necessity.

Like anywhere else, common courtesy and respect are appreciated in Greece, so try speaking a few words of the language, even if your vocabulary covers only the basics *(see pp344–8)*.

Though formal attire is rarely needed, modest clothing (trousers for men and skirts for women) is de rigueur for churches and monasteries. Topless sunbathing is generally tolerated, but nude bathing is officially restricted only to a few designated beaches.

In restaurants, the service charge is always included in the bill, but tips are still appreciated – the custom is to leave around 10 per cent if you were satisfied with the service. Public toilet attendants should also be tipped. Taxi drivers do not expect tips, but they are not averse to them either; likewise, hotel porters and chambermaids.

In 2010, Greece introduced a law officially banning smoking in enclosed public spaces, including in restaurants, bars and cafés. An estimated forty per cent of Greeks smoke, and many ignore this law. Restaurant and café owners prefer to turn a blind eye to this, for fear of losing custom. Many bar staff smoke too. All the same, visitors should avoid smoking in enclosed public spaces; smoking in outdoor areas such as café terraces is permitted.

Note that Greek police will not tolerate rowdy or indecent behaviour, especially when fuelled by excessive alcohol consumption; Greek courts impose heavy fines or even prison sentences on people who behave indecently.

Religion

About 97 per cent of the population is Greek Orthodox. The symbols and rituals of the religion are deeply rooted in Greek culture, and they are visible everywhere. Saints' days are celebrated throughout Greece *(see p52)*, sometimes on a local scale and sometimes across the entire country. Greek Orthodox monasteries and churches, many dating back centuries, are among the country's top cultural attractions. Visitors to these sacred places should dress respectably (shoulders and legs covered for both men and women) and refrain from taking photographs (this is officially forbidden, though rules do vary).

A Greek priest

Regarding religious minorities, the largest group are the Muslims of Thrace, which constitute only about 1.2 per cent of the country's total population. Many immigrants from Muslim countries such as Bangladesh, Pakistan, Afghanistan and Somalia, as well as Albania, now live in Athens. In addition, there is a sizeable community of Roman Catholics, including ethnic Greeks and immigrants from Poland and the Philippines, who are catered for by the Roman Catholic Archdiocese of Athens.

Sign for disabled parking

Travellers with Special Needs

There are few facilities for the disabled in Greece, so careful advance planning is essential; sights that have wheelchair access will have a wheelchair symbol at the start of their entry in this guide. Organizations such as **Disability Rights UK** and **Tourism for All** are invaluable sources of information. Agencies such as **Accessible Travel and Leisure** and **Responsible Travel** arrange holidays specifically for disabled travellers.

Note that disabled visitors (with a person assisting them) are entitled to free entry to state-run museums and archaeological sites.

Travelling with Children

Children are much loved by the Greeks and welcomed just about everywhere, including restaurants, where waiters will be happy to suggest special dishes for them. Babysitting facilities are provided by some hotels on request, but always check before booking. Some coastal resorts also have special amenities such as playgrounds, children's pools and even Kids' Clubs with organized activities.

Those aged 18 or under from EU countries enjoy free admission to state-run museums and archaeological sites, as do children aged five and under from non-EU countries. Concessions of up to 50 per cent are offered on most forms of public transport for children aged ten and under (in some cases, eight and under).

Swimming in the sea is generally safe for kids, but keep a close eye on them, as lifeguards are rare in Greece. Choose sandy beaches in sheltered bays with shallow water. Be aware of the hazards of overexposure to the sun and dehydration *(see p305)*.

Student and Youth Travellers

Concessions are offered on train, metro and bus travel in Greece to students below the age of 25 with a valid **International Student Identity Card (ISIC)**. They may also need to show their passport. There are plenty of deals to be had getting to Greece, especially during low season. Agencies for student and youth travel include **STA Travel**. Before setting off, it is worth joining **Hostelling International** to enjoy discounts in Greek hostels. Most state-run museums and archaeological sites are free to EU students with a valid ISIC card; non-EU students with an ISIC card are usually entitled to a 50 per cent reduction.

There are no youth concessions available, but occasional discounts are possible with an International Youth Travel Card (IYTC), which can be obtained from any STA office by travellers under the age of 26.

An International Student Identity Card

Women Travellers

Greece is by and large a very safe country, and local communities are generally welcoming. Foreign women travelling alone are usually treated with respect, especially if they are dressed modestly. Although local men openly display their interest in women, making it clear that you are not interested in them is usually enough to curtail any flirtation. Like elsewhere, hitchhiking alone in Greece carries potential risks and is not advisable.

Time

Greece is 2 hours ahead of Britain, 1 hour ahead of countries on Central European Time (such as France and Italy), 7 hours ahead of New York, 10 hours ahead of Los Angeles and 8 hours behind Sydney.

Greece puts the clock forward to summertime, and back again to wintertime, on the same days as other EU countries, in order to avoid any confusion when travelling around Europe.

Electricity

Greece, like other European countries, runs on 220 volts/ 50 Hz AC. Plugs have two round pins (those for appliances that need to be earthed have three). The adaptors needed for British electrical appliances and the transformers for North American equipment are difficult to find in Greece, so bring one with you.

Conversion Chart

Greece uses the metric system, with two small exceptions: sea distances are expressed in nautical miles and land is measured in *strémmata*, the equivalent of about 0.1 ha (0.25 acre).

Kids enjoying the shallow waters at a sandy beach

Imperial to Metric
1 inch = 2.54 centimetres
1 foot = 30 centimetres
1 mile = 1.6 kilometres
1 ounce = 28 grams
1 pound = 454 grams
1 pint = 0.6 litres
1 gallon = 4.6 litres

Metric to Imperial
1 millimetre = 0.04 inches
1 centimetre = 0.4 inches
1 metre = 3 feet 3 inches
1 kilometre = 0.64 miles
1 gram = 0.04 ounces
1 kilogram = 2.2 pounds
1 litre = 1.8 pints

Responsible Tourism

Greece is lagging behind most EU countries in environmental awareness – recycling is scarcely practised, illegal dumping in rural areas is the norm, and waste management is a major problem.

However, there is much interest in renewable energy sources. Greece has great potential for developing solar energy – many families already have solar panels for heating water (they can sell the surplus to the National Grid), and there have been talks about producing solar power on a far larger scale. Wind energy is already used to some extent on the islands, but here too there is potential for further exploitation.

Agrotourism (working farms that offer accommodation and meals to visitors) is well established on the island of Crete and is being developed on the mainland too. Contact the **Hellenic Agrotourism Federation** or **Guest Inn** for a list of agrotourism establishments.

Visitors can support local communities by shopping for local produce at the Central Market in Athens (see p121) and Modiáno Market in Thessaloníki (see p248), as well as the open-air street markets held weekly in various neighbourhoods of Athens. In some areas, you can buy local specialities directly from the producers – for example, formaella cheese in Araxova (near Delphi) and metsovone cheese in Metsovo – and visit vineyards for wine tastings and direct purchases.

Ethical tour operators include the UK-based **Responsible Travel** and the Athens-based **Trekking Hellas**; both run adventure sports packages including activities such as hiking, mountain biking, sea kayaking and rafting. The Athens-based **Ecotourism Greece** is a useful source of ideas for rural destinations, activities and small family-run hotels.

DIRECTORY

Visas and Passports

Aliens' Bureau
Petrou Ralli 24, Tavros, Athens.
Tel 210 340 5828.

Embassies

Australia
Level 6, Thon Building, Kifissias & Alexandrias Avenue, Ambelokipi, 11523 Athens.
Tel 210 870 4000.

Canada
Gennadíou 4, 11521 Athens.
Tel 210 727 3400.

Ireland
Vassiléos Konstantínou 7, 10674 Athens.
Tel 210 723 2771.

New Zealand (Consulate)
Kifissias 76, Ambelokipi, 11526 Athens.
Tel 210 692 4136.

United Kingdom
Ploutárchou 1, 10675 Athens.
Tel 210 727 2600.

United States
Vasilíssas Sofías 91, 10160 Athens.
Tel 210 721 2951.

Tourist Information Offices

Greek National Tourism Organization (GNTO)
Head office: Tsoha 7, 11521 Athens.
Tel 210 870 7000.
W visitgreece.gr
Information centre: Dionysiou Areopagitou 18–20, 11742 Athens.
Tel 210 331 0392.

GNTO Australia and New Zealand
Underwood House, Suite 307, 37–49 Pitt St, Sydney, NSW 2000.
Tel (2) 9241 1663.

GNTO United Kingdom and Ireland
4 Great Portland St, London, W1W 8QJ.
Tel 020 7495 9300.

GNTO USA
305 E 47th Street, New York, New York 10017.
Tel (1212) 421-5777.

Travellers With Special Needs

Accessible Travel and Leisure
Tel 01452 729 739.
W accessibletravel.co.uk

Disability Rights UK
Tel 020 7250 8181.
W radar.org.uk

Responsible Travel
Tel 01273 823 700.
W responsibletravel.com

Tourism for All
Tel 0845 124 9971.
W tourismforall.org.uk

Student Travellers

Hostelling International
2nd Floor, Gate House, Fretherne Road, Welwyn Garden City, Herts, AL8 6RD.
Tel 01707 324 170.
W hihostels.com

International Student Identity Card (ISIC)
W isic.org

STA Travel
52 Grosvenor Gardens, London, SW1W 0AG.
Tel 0800 988 6884.
W statravel.co.uk

Responsible Tourism

Ecotourism Greece
Tel 211 770 3877.
W ecotourism-greece.com

Guest Inn
Tel 210 960 7100.
W guestinn.com

Hellenic Agrotourism Federation (SEAGE)
Tel 693 650 0670.
W agroxenia.net

Responsible Travel
Tel 01273 823 700.
W responsibletravel.com

Trekking Hellas
Tel 210 331 0323.
W trekking.gr

Personal Health and Security

Strikes and protest marches have always been regular features of Greek life. However, the rise in unemployment and in the cost of living caused by the ongoing economic crisis have led to higher levels of public unrest. Despite this, Greece remains a safe country to visit, although it is best to avoid protest marches and demonstrations, which can turn violent – especially in Athens, and most notably on Sýntagma Square, in front of the Greek Parliament. Crime is rare outside Athens, where the biggest danger is the road – Greece has one of the highest accident rates in Europe. Considerable caution is recommended, for both drivers and pedestrians.

Police

Regular Greek police officers wear blue uniforms and keep a relatively low profile. However, there are several special units, the most conspicuous being the riot police (MAT), who wear a khaki military-type uniform and a helmet with a visor. The MAT are usually only seen at unruly demonstrations.

In addition, there are the tourist police, who combine normal police duties with dispensing advice to tourists. Tourist police wear a cap with a white band, a white belt and white gloves, as well as a badge saying "Tourist Police" on their shirt. Should you suffer a theft, lose your passport or have cause to complain about restaurants, shops, taxi drivers or tour guides, your case should first be made to them. Every tourist police officer speaks several languages and each office claims to have at least one English speaker, so they can also act as interpreters if the case needs to involve the local police.

What to be Aware of

Most crime-related problems centre on Athens. Crime levels outside large cities are low. Visitors are advised to avoid public demonstrations, in particular those in Athens' Sýntagma Square, which have become increasingly violent due to widespread public discontent. There has also been a rise in street muggings, especially around Omónoia Square, which is a gathering point for drug addicts, the homeless and other communities on the margins of society. Burglaries have also become more common than they once were. Visitors should take sensible precautions such as keeping an eye on their bags in public, especially in crowded places, and keeping important documents and valuables in the hotel safe. If you do have anything stolen, contact the police or tourist police.

In an Emergency

In case of emergencies, the appropriate services to call are listed in the directory on the opposite page. For accidents and other medical emergencies, a 24-hour ambulance service operates within Athens. Outside the capital, in rural towns and on the islands, it is unlikely that ambulances will be on 24-hour call. If necessary, patients can be transferred from local ESY (Greek National Health Service) hospitals or surgeries to a main ESY hospital in Athens by ambulance or helicopter.

A complete list of ESY hospitals, private hospitals and clinics is available from the tourist police.

Hospitals and Pharmacies

Emergency medical care in Greece is free for all EU citizens in possession of a European Health Insurance Card (EHIC), available from main post offices. For minor health problems, go to an IKA (Social Security Institute) polyclinic. All the main hospitals are in Athens, so if you have more serious issues, you will probably need to be taken to the capital. Also in Athens, **SOS Doctors** is a service that carries out emergency home visits for a fee. Public hospitals are often understaffed, and it is not unusual for relatives to help feed and provide basic nursing care for patients. Note that corruption is rife within the Greek healthcare system, and it is considered perfectly normal to offer doctors under-the-table payments for priority treatment.

Greek pharmacists are highly qualified and can not only advise on minor ailments, but also dispense medication not usually available over the

Greek police officers wearing typical blue uniforms

Ambulance

Police car

counter back home. Their premises, *farmakeía*, are identified by a green cross on a white background. Pharmacies are open from 8:30am to 2pm Monday to Friday, and they are usually closed in the afternoon and at weekends. However, in larger towns, a rota system is usually in place to maintain a daily service from morning to night. Details of on-duty pharmacies are posted in pharmacy windows.

Be sure to bring an adequate supply of any medication you may need while away, as well as a copy of the prescription with the generic name of the drug – this is useful not only in case you run out, but also for the purposes of customs when you enter the country.

Several international pharmaceutical companies have stopped selling to Greece due to delayed payments, so some drugs are now in short supply. Also be aware that codeine, a painkiller commonly found in headache tablets, is illegal in Greece.

Minor Hazards

The most obvious thing to avoid is overexposure to the sun, particularly for the fair-skinned; always wear a hat and good-quality sunglasses, as well as a high-factor suntan lotion. Heat stroke is a real hazard for which medical attention should be sought immediately; heat exhaustion and dehydration are also serious. Be sure to drink plenty of water, even if you don't feel thirsty; if in any doubt, invest in a packet of electrolyte tablets (a mixture of potassium salts and glucose) to replace lost minerals. These are available at any pharmacy.

Tap water in Greece is generally safe to drink, but in remote communities, it is a good precaution to check with the locals. Bottled spring water, for sale in shops and kiosks, is reasonably priced and often has the advantage of being chilled.

When swimming in the sea, hazards to be aware of are weaver fish, jellyfish and sea urchins. The latter are not uncommon and are extremely unpleasant if trodden on. If you do tread on one, the spine will need to be extracted using olive oil and a sterilized needle. Jellyfish stings can be relieved by applying vinegar, baking soda or various remedies sold at Greek

Pharmacy sign

pharmacies to the affected area. The sand-dwelling weaver fish has a powerful sting, its poison causing extreme pain. The immediate treatment is to immerse the affected area in very hot water to dilute the venom's strength.

No inoculations are required for visitors to Greece, though tetanus and typhoid boosters may be recommended by your doctor.

Travel and Health Insurance

EU citizens should carry a European Health Insurance Card (EHIC) to receive free emergency medical care. Private medical insurance is needed for all other types of treatment. Visitors are strongly advised to take out comprehensive travel insurance – available from travel agents, banks and insurance brokers – covering both private medical treatment and loss or theft of personal possessions. Be sure to read the small print – not all policies, for instance, will cover you for activities of a "dangerous" nature, such as motorcycling and trekking; not all policies will pay for doctors' or hospital fees direct, and only some will cover you for ambulances and emergency flights home. Paying for your flight with a credit card such as VISA or American Express will provide limited travel insurance, including reimbursement of your air fare if the agent happens to go bankrupt.

DIRECTORY

Countrywide Emergency Numbers

Ambulance
Tel 166.

Coastguard patrol
Tel 108.

Emergencies
Tel 112.
W sos112.info

Fire
Tel 199.

Police
Tel 100.

Road assistance
Tel 10400.

Tourist Police
Tel 171.

Athens Emergency Numbers

Pharmacies
Tel 14944 (information on 24-hour pharmacies).

Poison treatment centre
Tel 210 779 3777.

SOS Doctors
Tel 1016.
W sosiatroi.gr

Banking and Currency

Greece adopted the euro in 2002. Hit by the economic crisis of 2010, the country procured massive loans, but it soon emerged that it might be unable to repay them and therefore be forced to declare bankruptcy. In 2011, Greece's future within the Eurozone began to look uncertain. The impact of this situation on visitors remains to be seen. At the time of going to press, the economy had been stabilized thanks to yet more loans. Prices have risen, but the government may introduce tax exemptions in the tourism sector to encourage holiday-makers. If Greece did leave the Eurozone and readopt the drachma, foreign exchange rates would make the country a more competitive destination.

Visitors changing money at a foreign exchange bureau

Banks and Bureaux de Change

Towns throughout Greece, as well as tourist resorts, have the usual banking facilities, including 24-hour cash machines (ATMs). Alternatively, you can change foreign currency and travellers' cheques into euros at a bureau de change. Some travel agents, hotels, tourist offices and car-hire agencies are also willing to do this. Always take your passport with you when cashing travellers' cheques, and check exchange rates and commission charges beforehand, since these vary greatly.

The main banks in the country are Ethniki Trapeza tis Ellados (National Bank of Greece), Alpha Bank, ATE Bank, Pireaus Bank, Emporiki Bank and Eurobank. Banks are open 8am–2pm Monday to Thursday and 8am–1:30pm on Friday. They are closed on public holidays (see p52) and may also be closed on any local festival days.

ATMs

Easily found in all Greek towns and resorts, ATMs can be used to withdraw cash using internationally recognized credit and debit cards. There has been a rise in ATM crime the world over, so exercise caution when using one, and always shield your PIN from passers-by.

Credit and Debit Cards

VISA, **MasterCard**, **American Express** and **Diners Club** are the most widely accepted credit cards in Greece. A credit card is the most convenient way to pay for air tickets, international ferry journeys, car hire, some hotels and large purchases. However, some small tavernas, shops and hotels do not take credit cards, so be sure to have cash with you when visiting these establishments.

A credit card can be used for drawing local currency at a cash machine. A 1.5 per cent processing charge is usually levied for VISA at banks and

ATMs, but this does not apply to other cards. Cirrus and Plus debit card systems operate in Greece. Cash can be obtained using Cirrus at National Bank of Greece ATMs, and Plus at Commercial Bank ATMs. Be sure to tell your bank that you are travelling to Greece, so that your card is not blocked while you are away.

Travellers' cheques are the safest way to carry large sums of money. They are refundable if lost or stolen, though the process can be time-consuming. American Express and VISA are the best-known brands of travellers' cheques in Greece.

Queueing at an ATM

The Euro

The euro (€) is the common currency of the European Union. It went into general circulation on 1 January 2002, initially for 12 participating countries, including Greece. The Greek drachma was phased out in March 2002.

EU members using the euro as sole official currency are known as the Eurozone. Several EU members have opted out of joining this common currency. Euro notes are identical throughout the Eurozone countries, each one including

designs of fictional architectural structures and monuments. The coins have one side identical (the value side), and one side with an image unique to each country. Both notes and coins are exchangeable in each of the Eurozone countries.

Bank Notes

Euro bank notes have seven denominations. The €5 note (grey in colour) is the smallest, followed by the €10 note (pink), €20 note (blue), €50 note (orange), €100 note (green), €200 note (yellow) and €500 note (purple). All notes show the stars of the European Union.

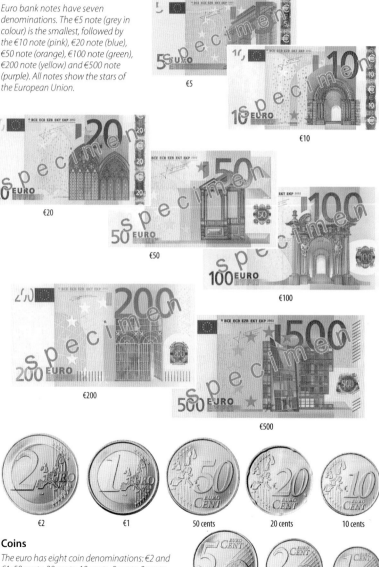

€5

€10

€20

€50

€100

€200

€500

€2

€1

50 cents

20 cents

10 cents

Coins

The euro has eight coin denominations: €2 and €1; 50 cents, 20 cents, 10 cents, 5 cents, 2 cents and 1 cent. The €2 and €1 coins are both silver and gold in colour. The 50-, 20- and 10-cent coins are gold. The 5-, 2- and 1-cent coins are bronze.

5 cents

2 cents

1 cent

Communications and Media

The Greek national telephone company is OTE (Organismós Tilepikoinonión Elládos). Telecommunications in Greece are good, and there are direct lines to all major countries; these are often better than local lines. Mobile phones are widespread and telecom companies compete for customers. There are Internet cafés in all main towns and resorts. Greek post is reasonably reliable and efficient, especially from the larger towns and resorts. The Greeks are avid newspaper readers, and in addition to a vast array of Greek publications, there are a few good English-language papers and magazines. Foreign newspapers are also available.

Useful Dialling Codes

- Directory enquiries for calls within Greece: 11888
- International operator and directory assistance: 139
- For reverse-charge call instructions, call the international operator
- For international calls from Greece, dial 00, followed by the country code (see the list below), the local area code (minus the initial 0) and then the number.
  Australia 61
  Ireland 353
  New Zealand 64
  UK 44
  USA & Canada 1
- To call Greece from abroad, dial the international access code (see list below), followed by 30 (country code for Greece), the area code and then the number.
  Australia: 0011
  Ireland, New Zealand & UK: 00
  USA & Canada: 011

International Telephone Calls

Public telephones have become increasingly rare on the streets of Greece as more and more people now have mobile (cell) phones.

Making long-distance calls from a hotel can be very expensive. The best deals on long-distance calls are to be found at privately run call centres, which have sprung up in all the larger cities (often close to the train or bus station) to serve Greece's immigrant communities. Each call centre displays specific rates, as well as information about peak and cheap times, which vary depending on the country you are phoning.

Mobile Phones

The main mobile phone network providers are **Cosmote**, **Vodafone Greece** and **WIND Hellas**. To reduce the cost of calls while in Greece, it might be a good idea to purchase a Greek SIM card from one of these companies; however, this will work only if your phone is unlocked. Alternatively, you could use your network's roaming facility, but this can be expensive. All Greek mobile phone numbers begin with the digit "6".

Internet

There are many Internet cafés in all the main towns and resorts in Greece and their prices are very reasonable. Two of the best ones in Athens are **Deligrece Café** and **Bits and Bytes**.

Some public spaces in Athens offer free Wi-Fi, notably around Sýntagma Square, Kotzia Square and Thiseío metro station. An increasing number of hotels also offer free Wi-Fi to their residents.

A sign advertising the services of an Internet café

Postal Services

The Greek postal service is run by **ELTA**. Greek post offices (tachydromeía) are generally open 7:30am–2pm Monday to Friday, with some main branches, especially in larger towns or cities, staying open as late as 8pm and occasionally for a few hours at weekends. All post offices are closed on public holidays (see p52).

Post boxes are usually bright yellow; some have two slots, marked esoterikó (domestic) and exoterikó (overseas).

Bright-red post boxes are reserved for express mail, both domestic and overseas. Express is a little more expensive, but it cuts delivery time by a few days. Airmail letters take three to six days to most European countries, and anywhere from five days to a week or more to North America, Australia and New Zealand.

Stamps (grammatósima) can be bought at post offices and occasionally from vending machines inside post offices.

The poste restante system – whereby mail can be sent to, and picked up from, a post office – is widely used in Greece, especially in more remote regions. Mail should be clearly marked "Poste Restante", with the recipient's surname underlined so that it gets filed in the right place. Proof of identity is needed when collecting the post, which is kept for a maximum of 30 days before being returned to the sender. If you are sending a parcel to a

A standard Greek bright-yellow post box

non-EU country, do not seal it before heading to the post office – its contents will need to be inspected by security before it is sent.

The main post offices in central Athens – on Sýntagma Square and at Aiólou 100 (just off Omónoia Square) – are indicated on the Street Finder maps *(see pp126–39)*.

International courier services such as **ACS** and **DHL**, both of which have offices in Athens and other major cities, offer the best solution for express deliveries.

Newspapers and Magazines

The trusty corner *períptera* (kiosks), bookshops in larger towns and tourist shops in the resorts often sell day-old foreign newspapers and magazines, though the mark-up is substantial. **Athens Views** is an English-language weekly paper published in Athens on Fridays. It's a good source of information on local entertainment, festivals and other cultural goings-on, and it also provides decent

A typical street kiosk, selling a wide variety of newspapers and magazines

coverage of domestic and international news. Also in English, **Athens In Your Pocket** is a useful bi-monthly guide available at newspaper kiosks in the capital; it has listings and details of restaurants, bars and museums. **Odyssey**, a glossy English-language bi-monthly magazine about all things Greek, appeals mainly to the Greek diaspora.

The most popular Greek-language newspapers are **Kathimeriní**, *Eleftherotypía* and *Ta Néa*. The weekly Greek-language **Athinorama** *(see p122)* details cultural events in Athens.

Television and Radio

There are three state-run and several private TV channels, plus a host of cable and satellite stations from across Europe. The state-owned TV and radio broadcasting corporation is **NERIT**. Most Greek stations cater to popular taste, with a mix of dubbed foreign soap operas, game shows, sport and films. Foreign-language films tend to be subtitled rather than dubbed. Satellite stations CNN and Euronews have international news in English around the clock. Guides detailing the coming week's television programmes are published in all the English-language papers.

With three state-owned radio channels and a plethora of local stations, the airwaves are positively jammed in Greece, and reception is not always dependable. Many stations are devoted exclusively to Greek music, either traditional or contemporary. There are also classical music web stations, such as NERIT-Trito Programma (95.6 FM), one of the three state channels, and modern music stations such as

Rock FM (96.9 FM). For the daily news in English, you can pick up the BBC World Service (90.2 FM in the Greater Athens area; frequency varies in other parts of Greece). The BBC can also be received over the Internet. Athens International Radio (AIR; 104.4 FM) broadcasts news bulletins, current affairs discussions and local information in English, German, French and a dozen more languages.

DIRECTORY

Mobile Phones

Cosmote
Tel 13838. W cosmote.gr

Vodafone Greece
Tel 13830. W vodafone.gr

WIND Hellas
Tel 13800. W wind.gr

Internet

Bits and Bytes
Akadimías 78, Athens.
Tel 210 381 3830.

Deligrece Café
Akadimías 87, 10678 Athens.
Tel 210 330 1895.

Postal Services

ACS
Tel 210 819 0000.
W acscourier.gr

DHL
Tel 210 989 0000.
W dhl.gr

ELTA
W elta.gr

Newspapers and Magazines

Athens In Your Pocket
W inyourpocket.com

Athens Views
W athensviews.gr

Athinorama
W athinorama.gr (Greek only)

Kathimeriní
W ekathimerini.com

Odyssey
W odyssey.gr

Television and Radio

NERIT
W nerit.gr

TRAVEL INFORMATION

Reliably hot, sunny weather makes Greece a popular destination for holiday-makers, particularly from northern Europe. From mid-May to early October, there are countless flights to Greece. For those with more time, it is also possible to reach the country by car, rail and coach. Travelling on the mainland is easy enough. An extensive bus network reaches even the tiniest communities, with frequent services on all major routes. Greece's rail network is skeletal by comparison, and aside from the intercity expresses, service is much slower. Travelling by car offers the most flexibility, allowing visitors to reach places that are not accessible by public transport. However, road conditions are variable, and in remoter parts can be rough and dangerous (see p316). Some of the larger cities and popular tourist destinations can also be reached by plane from Athens and Thessaloníki. Note that strikes (a regular occurrence in Greece) can cause disruption to public transport both to and within the country, and that demonstrations in the capital often see the roads of central Athens closed to all traffic.

Green Travel

To limit smog and traffic congestion in central Athens, driving restrictions apply – cars with registration numbers ending in an even number may drive in the city centre only on even dates of the month; cars with registrations ending in an odd number may drive in the city centre only on odd-numbered dates of the month (see p322).

The city buses run on natural gas, while trolley-buses are powered by electricity, making them both environmentally friendly.

Cycling in Athens is only for the brave. Local drivers have little respect for bicycles, and cycle lanes are non-existent. However, more people have started to use bicycles in the capital, and cyclists are now allowed to ride in the bus lanes.

For long-distance travel, Greeks have always preferred buses to trains. This has been even more true since 2011, when the already limited rail network suffered further cuts as a result of the economic crisis (see p314). The only fast and reliable railway line is the one linking Athens to Thessaloníki.

In rural areas (notably the Peloponnese), cycling and hiking holidays are ever more popular; visitors relish the glorious unspoilt landscapes.

Arriving by Air

The main airlines operating direct scheduled flights from London to Athens are **Aegean Airlines** and **British Airways**. In addition, several budget airlines – including **easyJet** (from London Gatwick, Manchester and Edinburgh to Athens; and from London Gatwick to Thessaloníki) and **Ryanair** (from London Stansted to Thessaloníki and Pátra) – also connect the UK to the Greek mainland. The Irish airline **Aer Lingus** runs scheduled flights from Dublin to Athens, while all the major European carriers such as **Air France** and **Alitalia** also operate scheduled flights.

There are about 15 inter-national airports around Greece that can be reached directly from Europe; how-ever, most of these are located on the islands. On the mainland, Athens and Thessaloníki handle most scheduled flights. The other mainland international airports – such as Préveza, Kalamáta, Kavála and Vólos – can be reached directly mainly by charter flights.

All scheduled long-haul flights to Greece land in Athens although many are not direct and will require changing at a connecting European city. There are direct flights to Athens from New York with **Delta** and from Philadelphia with **US Airways**, while **Air Canada** and **Air Transat** fly from Montreal and Toronto. **Air China** flies directly from Beijing to Athens. Although there are no direct flights to Athens from Australia or New Zealand, there are more than five flight routes daily from that part of the world that involve changing to a connecting flight at hubs in the Middle East.

Athens Elefthérios Venizélos International Airport

Light and spacious interior of Athens airport

Charter Flights and Package Deals

Charter flights to Greece are nearly all from within Europe, and mostly operate between the months of May and October. They are usually the cheapest option during peak season (Jul–Aug), when air fares rise steeply, though discounted scheduled flights are worth considering in low season, when there are few charters available.

Tickets are sold through airline websites and, to a lesser extent, by travel agencies either as part of an all-inclusive package holiday or as a flight-only deal. Companies operating charter flights to Thessaloníki from the UK throughout the summer are **Thomson Airways** (from East Midlands, London Gatwick, Luton and Manchester) and **Fly Thomas Cook** (from London Gatwick and Manchester).

Some real bargains can be found by buying tickets through price comparison websites such as **Kayak**, **Momondo**, **Skyscanner** and **www. airtickets.gr**.

Athens Airport

Greece's largest and most prestigious infrastructure development project for the millennium, **Elefthérios Venizélos – Athens International Airport** opened to air traffic in 2001. Located at Spata, 27 km (17 miles) southeast of the city centre, the airport handles the majority of Greece's international and domestic flights, as well as all of Athens' passenger and cargo flights.

It has two runways, designed for simultaneous, round-the-clock operation, and a Main Terminal Building for all arrivals and departures. Arrivals are located on the ground floor (Level 0) and departures on the first floor (Level 1). Passengers are advised to check in as early as possible and to contact their airline in advance to find out the recommended time to arrive at the airport for their flight.

Service facilities include a shopping mall, restaurants and cafés in the Main Terminal Building and a five-star Sofitel hotel in the airport complex. Car-rental firms, banks, bureaux de change and travel agencies are all located in the arrivals area. There is also a small museum displaying archaeological findings from digs carried out in the airport area.

Transport from Athens Airport

Metro line 3 (blue line) links the airport to Sýntagma and Monastiráki in the city centre from 6:33am until 11:33pm every 30 minutes, while the Proastiakos suburban rail service runs from 5:26am until 9.44pm from the airport to Ano Liosia just north of Athens (every 20 minutes) and to Kiato (every hour). From these, it is possible to connect to the rest of the suburban or intercity rail network. Tickets for both metro and suburban rail journeys from the airport to the city centre cost €8 (single) and €14 (return).

Visitors who prefer to use road transport (for those arriving or departing between 11:30pm and 5:30am this is the only option), can take a bus, a taxi or a hired car. The X95 bus runs from the airport to Sýntagma Square, in the city centre, every 10–15 minutes (journey time: about 70 minutes). Bus X96 runs to Piraeus port every 20–25 minutes (journey time: about 90 minutes). Bus X93 runs to Kifisos and Liosion intercity bus stations in Athens every 25–30 minutes (journey time: about 65 minutes). Bus X97 runs to Dáfni metro station every 45–60 minutes (journey time: about 70 minutes). All four buses run 24 hours a day, and a single ticket costs €5. A taxi ride to the centre of Athens costs €35 by day and €50 by night (fixed prices). A six-lane toll motorway links the airport to the Athens ring road. Several car hire companies are also based at the airport (*see p316*).

Bus outside Athens Elefthérios Venizélos International Airport

Thessaloníki and Other International Airports

Makedonia-Thessaloníki Airport is located 15 km (9 miles) southeast of Thessaloníki, in the north of the country. It handles a number of international scheduled flights, but only from the rest of Europe.

The number 78 bus, which runs 24 hours a day, links Thessaloníki airport to the city's central train station, a journey of about 45 minutes, costing €0.90. A taxi covering the same route takes about 20 minutes depending on traffic, but is considerably more expensive (€15–€20).

Greece's other mainland international airports (such as Kalamáta, Kavála and Préveza) are served by charter flights only, mostly from the United Kingdom, Germany, the Netherlands and Scandinavia, during the summer season (May through September).

Domestic and Connecting Flights

Greece's domestic airline network is fairly extensive. The majority of internal flights are operated by two Greek airlines: **Olympic Air** and **Aegean Airlines**; however, there are also a number of small private companies, including **Astra Airlines**, that provide flight connections between Thessaloníki and the rest of the country.

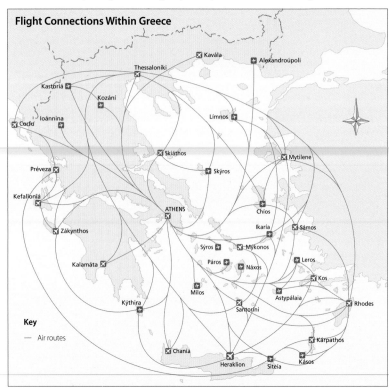

Flight Connections Within Greece

Key
— Air routes

Island	Distance	Flying Time	Island	Distance	Flying Time
Corfu	381 km (237 miles)	40 minutes	Crete (Chaniá)	318 km (198 miles)	45 minutes
Rhodes	426 km (265 miles)	45 minutes	Santoríni	228 km (142 miles)	40 minutes
Skýros	128 km (80 miles)	40 minutes	Kos	324 km (201 miles)	45 minutes
Skiáthos	135 km (84 miles)	30 minutes	Mykonos	153 km (95 miles)	30 minutes
Límnos	252 km (157 miles)	45 minutes	Páros	157 km (98 miles)	35 minutes

For keys to symbols *see back flap*

Olympic Air planes on an airport runway

As well as having the largest number of international flights in Greece, Athens has the most connecting air services to other parts of the country. Both international and domestic flights use the city's Elefthérios Venizélos airport *(see p311)*.

Olympic Air operates direct flights from Athens to four mainland destinations (Thessaloníki, Ioánnina, Alexandroúpoli and Kavála); in addition, it runs services to more than two dozen island airports. A number of inter-island services operate during the summer months, and about a dozen of these fly all year round.

Aegean Airlines operates direct flights from Athens' Elefthérios Venizélos to two mainland towns (Thessaloníki in the north and Kalamáta in the south) and to around a dozen islands.

Fares

Fares for domestic flights are often at least double the equivalent of a bus journey or deck-class ferry trip. Tickets and timetables for Olympic Air and Aegean Airlines flights are available from the respective websites, as well as from most major travel agencies. Bear in mind that flights tend to sell out quickly during the busy summer months – reservations are essential.

Airport Taxes

A small airport departure tax (€8.51) is charged on domestic flights of between 62 and 466 air miles. For "international" flights (that is, those exceeding 466 air miles), the tax rises to €12.15. This tax applies only to flights departing from Athens International Airport. In a bid to strengthen the country's tourism industry, this tax was waived from all other Greek airports in 2011.

DIRECTORY

Arriving by Air

Aegean Airlines
Viltanioti 31, 14564 Athens.
Tel 801 112 0000.
W aegeanair.com

Aer Lingus
W aerlingus.com

Air Canada
W aircanada.ca

Air China
214 Síngrou Avenue, 17672 Athens.
Tel 210 722 0630.
W airchina.com

Air France
7 Megalou Alexandrou & Karaiskaki, 16452 Athens.
Tel 210 998 0222.
W airfrance.com

Air Transat
W airtransat.com

Alitalia
80 Poseidonos Avenue, 17455 Alimos.
Tel 210 998 8888.
W alitalia.com

British Airways
Building Strovolos, PO CY2001, Nicosia, Cyprus.
Tel 801 115 6000.
W british-airways.com

Delta
Tel 210 998 0444.
W delta.com

easyJet
Tel 210 353 0300.
W easyjet.com

Ryanair
W ryanair.com

US Airways
Tel 210 353 0365.
W usairways.com

Charter Flights and Package Deals

Fly Thomas Cook
W flythomascook.com

Thomson Airways
W flights.thomson.co.uk

Flight Comparison Websites

Airtickets.gr
W airtickets.gr

Kayak
W kayak.co.uk

Momondo
W momondo.com

Skyscanner
W skyscanner.net

Athens Airport

Elefthérios Venizélos – Athens International Airport
5th km Spata-Loutsa Ave, 19019 Spata.
Tel 210 353 0000.
W aia.gr

Thessaloníki Airport

Makedonia – Thessaloníki Airport
PO Box 22605, GR-55103 Kalamaria, Thessaloníki.
Tel 2310 985 000.
W thessalonikiairport.com

Domestic flights

Aegean Airlines
See Arriving by Air.

Astra Airlines
12 km Thessaloníki Moudania Road/ Airport Area, GR 57001 PO Box 608 04, Thermi Thessaloníki.
Tel 2310 489 390.
W astra-airlines.gr

Olympic Air
1st km Varis Koropiou & Ifaistou, 19400 Koropi.
Tel 210 355 0500.
W olympicair.com

Travelling by Train

Greece's rail network is limited to the mainland and was always fairly skeletal by European standards. However, in 2011, as part of the restructuring of the debt-ridden Greek railways, train services were cut even further and some routes completely suspended.

Except for the intercity express train linking Athens to Thessaloníki (a trip of about 5 hours), services tend to be extremely slow. On the plus side, non-express tickets are not expensive (cheaper than coach fares), and some lines allow you to experience Greece's rugged and beautiful countryside. An overnight sleeper service is available on the Athens–Thessaloníki route.

First- and second-class carriages of a non-express train

Arriving by Train

Travelling to Greece by train is expensive and difficult due to the reduction in rail services into and within the country since 2011, though there is an extensive bus network *(see p318)*. However, travelling to Greece by train may be a good option if you wish to make stopovers en route. From London to Athens, the main route takes around three days. The journey is through France, Switzerland and Italy, then by overnight ferry from an Italian port such as Ancona or Bari to the Greek port of Pátra, followed by a bus to Athens.

While some international train services may run into Greece, as of 2011, due to Greece's ailing economy, all Greek train services to and from the country have been suspended until further notice. These include routes into neighbouring Bulgaria and Turkey, though there is a TrainOSE bus service from Thessaloníki to Sofia in Bulgaria.

Travelling Around Greece by Train

Greece's railway infrastructure is owned by **OSE** (Organismós Sidirodrómon Elládos), and train services are run by **TrainOSE**. Athens forms the principal hub of the system. A northbound line from Laríssis station connects Athens to Thessaloníki, with branch lines to Vólos, and to Kardítsa, Tríkala and Kalampáka.

From Thessaloníki, there is a line travelling west to Edessa (going through Véroia) and another travelling east to Alexandroúpoli (passing through Xánthi and Komotiní).

Destinations on the Peloponnese are no longer served by train, with the exception of Corinth. Trains depart from Laríssis station on the **Proastiakos** network, stopping at Corinth shortly before terminating at Kiato. Passengers heading for Pátra then have to change to a TrainOSE bus service to reach their final destination. There are plans to build a new standard-gauge line from Kiato to Pátra, but no dates have been set for this project. Proastiakos also runs a service from Athens' airport to Kiato via Nerantziotissa *(see p311)*.

There is a picturesque heritage route, the rack-and-pinion line between Diakoftó and Kalávryta on the Peloponnese *(see p172)*; this is not connected to the rest of the national rail network.

Train Tickets

Train tickets can be bought at any OSE office or railway station, as well as through the TrainOSE website.

There are two basic types of ticket: first and second class. Tickets for intercity express trains on the Athens–Thessaloníki line are more expensive, but worth it for the time they save.

When booking through the TrainOSE website there is a 10 per cent reduction on ticket prices, a 15 per cent reduction if you buy tickets at least two days before the beginning of your journey

Laríssis station, the main railway station in Athens

Train station ticket window

and a 20 per cent reduction on all return journeys. With the Intercity 6+1 ticket, you get six intercity train tickets plus an extra ticket for free.

Travellers aged over 65 are entitled to a 25–50 per cent reduction on tickets. Children up to age four travel free; those aged 4–12 get a 50 per cent reduction, while teenagers and students below the age of 25 receive a 25% discount with an International Student Identity Card.

Rail passes issued by **InterRail** (a global pass

for European residents that covers 30 countries) and **Eurail** (a global pass for non-European residents that covers 23 countries) are both honoured in Greece, though supplements are charged on some lines. The passes also allow reductions on some ferries between Italy and Greece. InterRail pass holders travel free of charge with Superfast (see p319) from Ancona to Pátra, while Eurail pass holders can travel free with both Superfast and Minoan (see p319) on the same route. There may be a small surcharge in high season (Jun–Sep) and a port tax.

A modern commuter train run by Proastiakos, linking Athens with Corinth

Railway Stations in Athens and Thessaloníki

Athens has one main terminal, **Laríssis Station**, which is located a 15-minute walk northwest of Omónoia Square and is served by metro Line 2 (red line). There are baggage storage facilities inside the station.

Thessaloníki Station is located a 15-minute walk west of the city centre. There are plans to build a one-line metro system in Thessaloníki (running from the east to the west of the city), with a stop at the train station. This project is already underway and will be completed by the year 2018.

DIRECTORY

Travelling Around Greece by Train

OSE
Sína 6, Athens.
Tel 1110.
Aristotélous 18, Thessaloníki.
Tel 2310 598 120.
Tel 14511 (customer service).

Proastiakos
Ⓦ trainose.gr/proorismoi/proastiakos-athinon

TrainOSE
Ⓦ trainose.gr
(Greek only)

Train Tickets

Eurail
Ⓦ raileurope.co.uk

InterRail
Rail Europe Travel Centre, 193 Piccadilly, London, W1J 9EU.
Tel 08448 485 848.
Ⓦ interrailnet.com

Railway Stations in Athens and Thessaloníki

Laríssis Station
Deligiánni, 10439 Athens.
Tel 210 527 0700.

Thessaloníki Station
Monastiriou 28, 54629 Thessaloníki.
Tel 2310 599 421.

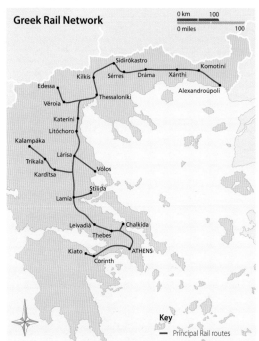

Greek Rail Network

Key — Principal Rail routes

Travelling by Road

Travelling by car allows you to explore at your own pace. Greece's express highways (motorways) are the A1 (north–south from Thessaloníki to Athens, passing Lárisa en route); the A2 (east–west from Evros to Igoumenítsa, passing Thessaloníki en route); the A8 (east–west from Athens to Pátra, passing Corinth en route); and the A7 (under construction; north–south from Corinth to Kalamáta, passing Tripoli en route). Some stretches of these motorways are being upgraded, and roadworks may cause delays. However, the roads are designed to be fast, and tolls are charged for their use. The maps in this guide categorize the roads into four groups, from motorways in blue to non-asphalt roads in yellow *(see back flap)*.

You have priority

You have right of way

Do not use car horn

Wild animals crossing

Hairpin bend ahead

Roundabout ahead

Arriving by Car

The most direct overland routes to Greece are through the countries that made up the former Yugoslavia. Anybody considering this should be aware that road quality is poor through some parts of this route. Instead, many visitors choosing to drive from the UK to Greece head for Italy, then catch an overnight ferry from Ancona port to Pátra.

For a small fee, the **AA** and **RAC** will compile individual itineraries for motorists. They can also supply up-to-date information on route closures and potential hotspots. It is also worth asking their advice on insurance needs and on any special driving regulations for those countries en route.

In order to drive in Greece, you will need to have a full, valid national driving licence and insurance cover (at least third party is compulsory). **ELPA** (the Automobile and Touring Club of Greece) offers useful information on driving in Greece.

Rules of the Road

Driving is on the right in Greece. Road signs conform to European norms and are usually in both Greek and Roman scripts. However, on rural back roads, the names of villages are sometimes signposted in Greek only.

The speed limit for cars on national highways is 120 km/h (75 mph), on country roads it is 110 km/h (68 mph) and in towns 50 km/h (30 mph). For motorbikes, the speed limit on national highways is 90 km/h (55 mph), while on country roads it is 70 km/h (45 mph).

The use of seatbelts in cars is required by law, and children under the age of ten are not allowed to sit in the front seat. Using a mobile phone (without hands-free) while driving is prohibited, although many Greeks ignore this law. Parking and speeding tickets must be paid at the local police station or at your car-hire agency.

Tolls

Tolls are payable on all Greek motorways and on the Attiki Odos (the Athens ring road). There are also tolls to be paid when passing over the spectacular Rion-Antirio bridge (close to Pátra), and through the Artemission tunnel (on the Corinth–Tripoli motorway) and the Aktion undersea tunnel (close to Préveza). On major public holidays, be prepared for long tailbacks (and a lot of irate drivers) at busy toll booths on the motorways.

Car Hire

There are scores of car-hire agencies in every major city and resort, all offering a full range of cars and four-wheel-drive vehicles. International companies such as **Budget**, **Avis**, **Hertz**, **Enterprise** and **Europcar** (which have offices at Athens airport, as well as in the city centre) tend to be slightly more expensive than their local counterparts, though the latter are generally just as reliable.

The car-hire agency should have an agreement with an emergency recovery company, such as **Express Service** or **InterAmerican**, in the event of a vehicle breakdown. Also, be sure to check the insurance policy cover: third party is required by law, but personal accident insurance is also strongly recommended. A valid driving licence that has been held for at least one year is necessary, and there is a minimum age requirement, ranging from 21 to 25 years.

An emergency recovery vehicle

Rack of bicycles for hire at a coastal resort

Motorbike, Moped and Bicycle Hire

Motorbikes and mopeds are readily available for hire in all the tourist resorts. Mopeds are ideal for short distances on fairly flat terrain, but for travel in more remote or mountainous areas, a motorbike is essential.

Always make sure that the vehicle you hire is in good condition before you set out, and that you have adequate insurance cover; also check whether your own travel insurance covers you for motorbike accidents (many do not). Speeding in Greece is penalized by fines, drink-driving laws are strict, and helmets are compulsory.

Though less widely available, bicycles can be hired in some tourist resorts. The hot weather and tough terrain make cycling extremely hard work, though. On the positive side, bikes can be transported for free on most Greek ferries, and for a small fee on trains.

Petrol

Petrol stations are plentiful in urban centres, but few and far between in rural areas – always set out with a full tank to be on the safe side. Fuel is sold by the litre, and the price is comparable to most other European countries. There are usually either three or four grades available: super (95 octane), unleaded, super unleaded and diesel, which is confusingly called *petrélaio*. Filling stations set their own working hours in Greece. They are generally open from around 7am or 8am to between 7pm and 9pm daily, and are closed on Sundays in many areas. Some stations in the larger towns are open 24 hours a day.

Taxis

Taxis provide a reasonably priced way of making short trips around Greece. All taxis are metered, but for longer journeys, a price can usually be negotiated per day or per trip. Also, drivers are generally amenable to dropping you off somewhere and returning to pick you up a few hours later.

In Athens, taxis are plentiful and can simply be hailed on the street. In smaller towns, it is best to find a taxi rank, which is likely to be either in the centre or by the bus or train station. Most rural villages have at least one taxi, and the best place to arrange for one is at the local *kafeneío* (café).

Although taxis are metered, it is worth getting a rough idea of the price before setting out. Round up to the nearest euro as a tip; luggage will incur an additional charge. In Greece, taxis are often shared with other passengers, each paying for their part of the journey.

Hitchhiking

Greece is a relatively safe place for hitchhiking but, like anywhere else, there are potential risks. Women especially are advised against hitching alone. If you do hitchhike, finding a lift is usually easier in the less populated rural areas than on busy roads heading out from major towns and cities. Note that it is illegal to hitchhike on motorways.

Δράμα
Drama 36
Θεσσαλονίκη
Thesaloniki 161

Dual-language road sign, found on most routes

Maps

Visitors who intend to do much motoring around the country are advised not to give too much reliance to the maps issued by local travel agents and car-hire agencies, since these are rarely detailed enough. Instead, they should invest in the regional Orama Editions maps (available in Greece), or bring with them the Geo-Center regional road maps (1:300,000 range) or the single-sheet Freytag & Berndt maps (1:650,000).

DIRECTORY

Arriving by Car

AA
Tel 0800 887 766 (UK).
W theaa.com

ELPA
Mesogeíon 395,
15343 Agía Paraskeví.
Tel 210 606 8800.
Tel 10400 (road assistance).
W elpa.gr

RAC
Tel 0800 015 6000 (UK).
W rac.co.uk

Car Hire (Athens Offices)

Avis
Tel 210 687 9600.
W avis.gr

Budget
Tel 210 898 1444.
W budget-athens.gr

Enterprise
Tel 0800 781 358.
W enterpriserentacar.gr

Europcar
Tel 210 921 1444.
W europcar-greece.gr

Express Service
Tel 1154.
W expressservice.gr

Hertz
Tel 210 626 4000.
W hertz.gr

InterAmerican
Tel 1158.
W interamerican.gr

Travelling by Coach and Bus

Time permitting, bus travel is a good way of experiencing the country. Greece's bus system is operated by KTEL (Koinó Tameío Eispráxeon Leoforeíon), a syndicate of dozens of regional private companies. The network is comprehensive in that it provides every community with services of some sort: in rural villages this may be once a day; in remoter places, once or twice a week. Services between the larger centres are frequent and efficient.

International coaches also connect Greece with some of its neighbouring countries; these services are used mainly by immigrants who work in Greece.

Domestic coach, run by KTEL

Arriving by Coach

Coach journeys from London to Athens take many days, involve several changes, and are not as cheap as a bargain air fare. Coaches are, however, cheaper than taking the train.

Top Deck is an adventure tour operator used mainly by young travellers. Some of their longer coach tours include Greece but do not necessarily depart from the UK – their 18-day European Horizons tour, for example, starts from Rome, Italy, and finishes in London, covering ten countries in total and including three days' flotilla sailing in Greece.

Travelling by Coach

The Greek coach system is operated by a network of regional private companies under the umbrella of **KTEL**. It is extensive, with services to even the remotest destinations and frequent express coaches on all the major routes. Large cities usually have more than one terminal, each serving a different set of destinations.

Ticket sales are computerized for all major routes, with reserved seating on modern, air-conditioned coaches. Buy your ticket in advance, as seats often sell out on popular routes and Greek coaches tend to leave a few minutes early.

In country villages, the local *kafeneío* (café) often serves as the coach station. You can usually buy your ticket from the owner; if not, it is possible to buy a ticket upon boarding.

Coach Tours

In the resort areas, travel agents offer a wide range of excursions on air-conditioned coaches accompanied by qualified guides. These trips include visits to major archaeological and historical sites, other towns and seaside resorts and special events. Note that coach tours are best booked a day in advance.

In Athens, **Key Tours** and **Fantasy Travel** offer a range of mainland excursions, including one- and two-day coach tours to places like Mycenae, Delphi, Epidaurus or Metéora.

Coach Services from Athens & Thessaloníki

From Athens, there are frequent coach services to all the larger mainland towns, apart from those in Thrace, which are served by coaches departing from **KTEL Thessaloníki**. Athens' **Terminal A** is situated 4 km (2 miles) northeast of the city centre. The terminal serves Epirus, Macedonia, the Peloponnese and the Ionian islands of Corfu, Kefaloniá, Lefkáda and Zákynthos (ferry crossings are included in the price of the ticket). It takes 6 hours to reach Thessaloníki, and 2 hours 30 minutes to the port of Pátra.

Terminal B is situated north of Agios Nikólaos metro station, but is most easily reached by taxi. It serves most destinations in central Greece, such as Delphi (3 hours) and Vólos (6 hours).

Coaches to destinations around Attica (Soúnio, Lávrio, Rafína and Marathónas) leave from the Mavrommataíon coach terminal, on the corner of Leofóros Alexándras and 28 Oktovríou (Patisíon).

DIRECTORY

Arriving by Coach

Top Deck
Level 1, 107 Power Road,
Chiswick, London, W4 5PY.
Tel 0845 257 5212.
Ⓦ topdecktours.co.uk

Travelling by Coach

KTEL
Tel 14505.
Ⓦ ktel.org

Coach Tours

Fantasy Travel
Filellinon 19, 10557
Athens.
Tel 210 331 0530.
Ⓦ fantasy.gr

Key Tours
Athanasiou Diakou 26, 11743
Athens. **Tel** 210 923 3166.
Ⓦ keytours.gr

Coach Services from Athens & Thessaloníki

KTEL Thessaloníki
Giannitson 244, Thessaloníki.
Tel 2310 500 111.
Ⓦ ktel-thes.gr

Terminal A
Kifisoú 100, Athens.
Tel 210 512 4910.

Terminal B
Liosíon 260, Athens.
Tel 210 831 7096.

Travelling by Sea

The sea has always played an important role in the life and history of Greece. Today, the sea is a major source of revenue for the country, with millions of tourists descending each year for beach holidays on the Mediterranean and the Aegean, and thousands coming here for yacht-charter sailing holidays too. The Greek mainland and islands are linked by a vast network of ferries, catamarans and hydrofoils that serves the local population all year round, as well as tourists through the summer.

Arriving by Sea

There are ferry crossings from the Italian ports of Ancona, Bari, Brindisi and Venice to Igoumenítsa in Epirus and Pátra in the Peloponnese. **Minoan** and **Superfast** are the main Greek companies covering these routes. In summer, reservations are advisable, especially if you have a car or want a cabin.

Greek Ferry Service

Athens' port, **Piraeus**, is the largest passenger port in Europe and one of the busiest in the world. From here, there are frequent ferry services (run by several private companies) to the islands of the Argo-Saronic, the Cyclades, the Dodecanese, the Northeast Aegean and Crete. Northeast of Athens, the smaller port of

Rafína sees ferry departures for Evvia, plus some islands in the Cyclades.

Hellenic Seaways runs high-speed catamarans and hydrofoils, plus several ferries, from Piraeus to many islands in the Aegean Sea. The high-speed services cost about twice as much as the ferries, but the journey times are often twice as fast. However, catamarans and hydrofoils are more likely to be cancelled in the event of adverse weather.

Tickets can be purchased online or from travel agents in Athens. Advanced bookings are recommended for ferries in high season (especially if you have a car), and they are essential for high-speed catamarans and hydrofoils. Out of season, services (and prices) are reduced.

DIRECTORY

Arriving by Sea

Minoan
25th August Street 17,
712 02 Heraklion, Crete.
Tel 2810 330 308.
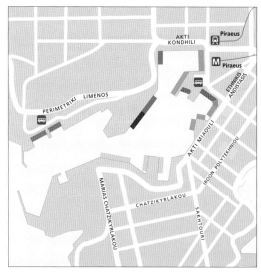 minoan.gr

Superfast
Syngrou Avenue 123–125
& Torva 3, 11745
Athens.
Tel 210 891 9500.
superfast.com

Greek Ferry Service

Hellenic Seaways
Astiggos 6, Karaiskaki
Square, 185 31 Piraeus.
Tel 210 419 9000.
hellenicseaways.gr

Piraeus Port Authority
Tel 210 406 0900 (for emergencies outside working hours).
Tel 14541 (for ferry timetables).
olp.gr

Cruises

Most cruise ships sailing the Mediterranean stop at Piraeus to give passengers a day in Athens. The port has 11 modern berths for cruise ships and can accommodate even the largest vessels.

Piraeus Port Map

This shows where you are likely to find ferries to various destinations.

Piraeus Port Authority:
Tel 210 455 0000.

Coastal Services Timetables
Tel 14541.

Key To Departure Points

- Argo-Saronic Islands
- Northeast Aegean Islands
- Dodecanese
- Cyclades
- Crete
- International ferries
- Hydrofoils and catamarans

For keys to symbols *see back flap*

Getting Around Athens

The sights of Athens' city centre are closely packed, and almost everything of interest can be reached on foot. Walking is the best way of sightseeing in the city, especially in view of the traffic congestion, which can make both public and private transport slow and inefficient. The bus and trolleybus network provides the majority of public transport in the capital for Athenians and visitors alike; the three-line metro system offers a good alternative to the roads for some journeys. Taxis are another option and, with the lowest tariffs of any EU capital, they are worth considering even for longer journeys.

One of the fleet of yellow, blue and white buses

Bus Services

Athens is served by an extensive bus network. Buses are white, yellow and blue. The network covers over 300 routes, connecting various districts to each other and to the city centre. All buses are ecologically friendly and run on natural gas.

Bus journeys are inexpensive but can be slow and uncomfortably crowded, particularly in the city centre and during rush hours; the worst times are from 7am to 8:30am, from 2pm to 3:30pm and from 7:30pm to 9pm.

Note that to reach Piraeus port, metro Line 1 (green line) is infinitely faster and more convenient than the bus. Timetables and route maps (only in Greek) are available from **OASA**, the Athens Urban Transport Organization.

Tickets must be purchased in advance from a metro station or a *perínptero* (street kiosk). Tickets can be bought individually or in a book of ten. The same ticket can be used on any bus, trolleybus, metro or tram, but must be validated in a ticket machine upon boarding. There is a penalty fine for not stamping your ticket, and tourists who are unfamiliar with this may be caught out by inspectors who board buses to carry out random checks. Tickets are valid for one ride only, regardless of the distance.

Trolleybuses

Athens has a good network of trolleybuses, which are yellow and purple in colour and run on electricity. There are more than 20 routes that criss-cross the city centre and connect many of the main sights. Routes 7 and 8 are useful to reach the National Archaeological Museum from Sýntagma Square, while route 1 links Laríssis railway station with Omónoia Square and Sýntagma Square.

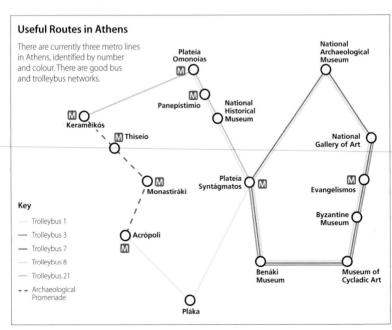

Useful Routes in Athens

There are currently three metro lines in Athens, identified by number and colour. There are good bus and trolleybus networks.

Plateía Omonoías Ⓜ
Panepistimio Ⓜ
Keramèikós Ⓜ
Thiseío Ⓜ
/ Monastiráki Ⓜ
Acrópoli Ⓜ
National Historical Museum
National Archaeological Museum
National Gallery of Art
Plateía Syntágmatos Ⓜ
Evangelismos Ⓜ
Byzantine Museum
Benáki Museum
Museum of Cycladic Art
Pláka

Key
— Trolleybus 1
— Trolleybus 3
— Trolleybus 7
— Trolleybus 8
— Trolleybus 21
–– Archaeological Promenade

An Athens trolleybus

Tickets can be bought at ticket machines at metro stations and at most street kiosks and must be validated upon boarding the trolleybus.

Trams

Athens' tram system, a project inaugurated for the 2004 Olympics, connects the city centre and the coast. There are just three lines, confusingly numbered 3, 4 and 5. Line 3 runs along the coast between Néo Fáliro and Voúla; Line 4 runs from Sýntagma Square to Néo Fáliro; and Line 5 runs from Sýntagma Square to Voúla. The trams operate 5am–1am Sun–Thu (24 hours on Fridays and Saturdays).

Tickets can be bought at ticket machines at tram stops and must be validated at a machine at the tram stop before entering the tram.

Metro

The metro is fast and reliable. It was a key element in the restructuring of urban public transport for the 2004 Olympics, leading to the reduction in the number of private cars, as well as buses, in the city centre.

The metro has three lines: Line 1 (green line) runs from Kifissiá in the north to the port of Piraeus in the south, with central stops at Thiseío, Monastiráki, Omónoia and Victória. Most of the line is overland and only runs underground between Attikí and Monastiráki stations. The green line is used mainly by commuters who live in the northern suburbs, but it also offers visitors the fastest way of reaching Piraeus.

Line 2 (red line) and Line 3 (blue line) form part of a huge expansion of the system, most of which was completed in time for the 2004 Olympic Games. These two lines, which intersect at Sýntagma, were built 20 m (66 ft) underground in order to avoid interfering with material of archaeological interest. Both Sýntagma and Acrópoli stations feature impressive displays of archaeological finds uncovered during construction work.

Line 2 (red line) runs from Anthoupoli in northwest Athens to Elliniko in the southeast. Line 3 (blue line) runs from Agia Marina to Doukissis Plakentias in the northeast, with some trains continuing on to Eleftherios Venizélos airport.

One ticket allows travel on any of the three lines and is valid for 90 minutes in one direction. You cannot exit a station and then go back to continue your journey with the same ticket. Tickets must be validated before boarding the train – use the machines at the entrances to all platforms. Trains run every five minutes,

Evangelismos
metro sign

5am–midnight on Line 1, and 5:30am–midnight on Lines 2 and 3. At weekends, trains run from 5am to 2am.

Walking

The centre of Athens is very compact, and most major sights and museums are within a 25-minute walk of Sýntagma Square, which is regarded as the city's centre.

Since the 2004 opening of the Archaeological Promenade, Athens has become infinitely more pleasant to navigate on foot. A broad car-free walkway running 4 km (2.5 miles), the promenade skirts the foot of the Acropolis to link the city's main ancient sites, as well as four metro stations. The streets of Dionissiou Areopagitou and Apostolou Pavlou run between Acrópoli metro station and Thiseío metro station (passing the Acropolis and the New Acropolis Museum); Adrianou street runs from Thiseío metro station to Monastiráki station (passing the Ancient Agora); and Ermou runs from Thiseío metro station to Kerameikós metro station (passing the Kerameikós archaeological site).

By day, Athens is still one of the safest European cities in which to walk around. However, it pays to be vigilant at night.

Archaeological remains on display at Sýntagma metro station

A yellow taxi on a street in Athens

Taxis

Swarms of yellow taxis can be seen cruising the streets of Athens at most times of the day or night. However, trying to persuade one to stop can be a difficult task, especially between 2pm and 3pm, when taxi drivers usually change shifts. Then, they will only pick you up if you happen to be going in a direction that is convenient for them.

To hail a taxi, stand on the edge of the pavement and shout out your destination to any cab that slows down. If a cab's "taxi" sign is lit up, then it is definitely for hire (though often a taxi is also for hire when the sign is not lit). It is common practice in Athens for drivers to pick up extra passengers along the way, so it is worth flagging the occupied cabs too. If you are not the first passenger on board, make a note of the meter reading immediately; there is no fare sharing, so you should be

No parking on odd-numbered months (Jan, Mar, etc)

No parking on even-numbered months (Feb, Apr, etc)

charged for your portion of the journey only.

Despite a rise in prices, Athenian taxis are still very cheap by European standards – depending on traffic, you should not have to pay more than about €5 to travel to any destination within the downtown area, and between €6 and €9 from the centre to Piraeus. Higher tariffs come into effect between midnight and 5am and for journeys that exceed certain distances from the city centre. Fares to the airport, which is out of town at Spata, are now fixed at €35 in the daytime and €50 at night (midnight–5am).

There are also small surcharges for extra pieces of luggage weighing more than 10 kg (22 lbs), and for journeys from the ferry or railway terminals. Taxi fares are increased during holiday periods, such as Christmas and Easter.

For an extra charge (€3.50–€6), you can make a phone call to a radio taxi company and arrange for a car to pick you up at an appointed place and time. Radio taxis are plentiful in the Athens area. Telephone numbers of a few companies are listed in the Directory box.

Driving

Driving in Athens can be a nerve-racking experience and best avoided, especially if you are not accustomed to Greek road habits. Many streets in the centre are pedestrianized, and there

are also plenty of one-way streets, so you need to plan your route carefully.

Finding a parking space can be very difficult too. Despite appearances to the contrary, parking in front of a no-parking sign or on a single yellow line is illegal. There are pay-and-display machines for legal on-street parking, as well as underground car parks, though these usually fill up quickly.

In an attempt to reduce dangerously high air pollution levels, there is an "odd-even" driving system in force. Cars that have an odd number at the end of their licence plates can enter the central grid, also called the *daktýlios*, only on dates with an odd number, and cars with an even number at the end of their plates are allowed into it only on dates with an even number. To avoid being unable to access the *daktýlios*, some people have two cars – with odd and even plates. The "odd–even" rule does not apply to foreign cars; however, if possible, avoid taking your car into the city centre.

Sign for a pedestrianized area

DIRECTORY

Public transport

Metro
Tel 210 519 4012.
🅦 amel.gr

OASA (buses/trolleybuses)
Metsovou 15.
Tel 111 85.
🅦 oasa.gr

Trams
Tel 210 997 8000.
🅦 tramsa.gr

Taxis

Athina 1
Tel 210 921 2800
(central Athens).

Ermis
Tel 210 411 5200
(Piraeus).

Hellas
Tel 210 645 7000 (central Athens).
Tel 210 801 4000 (north Athens).

Athens Transport Links

The hub of Athens' public transport is the area around Sýntagma Square and Omónoia Square. From this central area, the metro and various buses can be taken to Elefthérios Venizélos International Airport, the port at Piraeus and Athens' Laríssis train station. In addition, three tram lines connect the city centre with the Attic coast.

Bus X95 runs between the airport *(see p311)* and Sýntagma Square, and bus X96 links the airport to Piraeus *(see p319)*. The airport is also served by Line 3 (blue line) of the metro, from Sýntagma and Monastiráki.

Metro Line 1 (green line, from Omónoia and Monastiráki) extends to Piraeus; the journey from the city centre to the port takes about half an hour. Trolleybus route 1 goes past Sýntagma metro station and Laríssis train and metro stations. Laríssis train station is also served by metro Line 2 (red line), from both Sýntagma and Omónoia.

Tram line 3 runs along the coast from Néo Fáliro to the seaside suburb of Voúla; tram line 4 runs from Sýntagma Square in the city centre to Néo Fáliro; and tram line 5 runs from Voúla to Sýntagma Square.

These lines are especially useful if you are staying in a hotel along the coast, or if you wish to have a day on the beach.

Though more expensive than public transport, the most convenient way of getting to and from any of these destinations is by taxi. The journey times vary greatly, but if traffic is free-flowing, the journey from the city centre to the airport takes about 40 minutes; the journey from the city centre to Piraeus takes around 30 minutes; and the journey from Piraeus to the airport takes about 60 minutes.

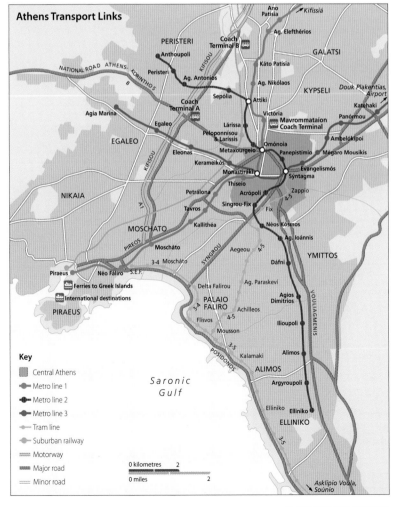

Athens Transport Links

Key

- Central Athens
- Metro line 1
- Metro line 2
- Metro line 3
- Tram line
- Suburban railway
- Motorway
- Major road
- Minor road

For keys to symbols *see back flap*

General Index

Page numbers in **bold** refer to main entries

Acknowledgments

Dorling Kindersley would like to thank the following people whose contributions and assistance have made the preparation of this book possible.

Main Contributors

Marc Dubin is an American expatriate who divides his time between London and Sámos. Since 1978 he has travelled in every province of Greece. He has written or contributed to many guides to Greece.

Mike Gerrard is a travel writer and broadcaster who has written several guides to various parts of Greece, which he has been visiting annually since 1964.

Andy Harris is a travel and food journalist based in Athens. He is the author of *A Taste of the Aegean*.

Tanya Tsikas is a Canadian writer and travel guide editor. Married to a Greek, she has spent time in Crete and currently lives in Oxford.

Deputy Editorial Director Douglas Amrine

Deputy Art Director Gillian Allan

Managing Editor Georgina Matthews

Managing Art Editor Annette Jacobs

Additional Illustrations

Richard Bonson, Louise Boulton, Gary Cross, Kevin Goold, Roger Hutchins, Claire Littlejohn.

Design and Editorial Assistance

Emma Anacootee, Hilary Bird, Julie Bond, Elspeth Collier, Michelle Crane, Catherine Day, Mariana Evmolpidou, Jim Evoy, Emer FitzGerald, Jane Foster, Michael Fullalove, Emily Green, Lydia Halliday, Emily Hatchwell, Leanne Hogbin, Kim Inglis, Despoina Kanakoglou, Lorien Kite, Esther Labi, Maite Lantaron, Felicity Laughton, Delphine Lawrance, Nicola Malone, Alison McGill, Andreas Michael, Rebecca Milner, Ella Milroy, Lisa Minsky, Robert Mitchell, Adam Moore, Jennifer Mussett, Tamsin Pender, Marianne Petrou, Rada Radojicic, Jake Reimann, Ellen Root, Simon Ryder, Collette Sadler, Sands Publishing Solutions, Rita Selvaggio, Ellie Smith, Susana Smith, Claire Stewart, Claire Tennant-Scull, Amanda Tomeh, Helen Townsend, Dora Whitaker, Maria Zygourakis.

Revisions and Relaunch Team

Ashwin Adimari, Dipika Dasgupta, Carole French, Mohammad Hassan, Bharti Karakoti, Rupanki Kaushik, Zafar Khan, Darren Longley, Anwesha Madhukalya, Deepak Mittal, Tanveer Abbas Zaidi.

Dorling Kindersley would also like to thank the following for their assistance: The Greek Wine Bureau, Odysea.

Additional Research

Anna Antoniou, Garifalia Boussiopoulou, Anastasia Caramanis, Michele Crawford, Magda Dimouti, Shirley Durant, Jane Foster, Panos Gotsi, Zoi Groummouti, Peter Millett, Eva Petrou, Ellen Root, Tasos Schizas, Linda Theodora, Garifalia Tsiola, Veronica Wood.

Additional Photography

Stephen Bere, Mariana Evmolpidou, John Heseltine, Ian O'Leary, Steven Ling, Tony Souter, Clive Streeter, Jerry Young.

Artwork Reference

Ideal Photo S.A., The Image Bank, Tony Stone Worldwide.

Photography Permissions

Dorling Kindersley would like to thank the following for their assistance and kind permission to photograph at their establishments:

Ali Pasha Museum, Ioannina; City of Athens Museum; Museum of Greek Folk Art, Athens; V Kyriazopoulos Ceramic Collection; Kavala Modern Art Gallery; National Gallery of Art, Athens; National War Museum, Athens; Nicholas P Goulandris Foundation Museum of Cycladic and Ancient Art, Athens; Theatrical Museum, Athens; University of Athens Museum; Polygnotos Vagis Museum, Thassos. Also all other cathedrals, churches, museums, hotels, restaurants, shops, galleries, and sights too numerous to thank individually.

Picture Credits

a = above; b = below; c = centre; f = far; l = left; r = right; t = top.

Works of art have been reproduced with the permission of the following copyright holders: Vorres Museum *Water Nymph* (1995) Apostolos Petridis 154tl.

The publisher would like to thank the following individuals, companies and picture libraries for permission to reproduce their photographs:

AISA Archivo Icongrafico, Barcelona: Museo Archeologique Bari 61cra; **AKG, London:** Antiquario Palatino 57bl; *Bilder aus dem Altherthume*, Heinrich Leutemann 232cla; British Museum 99bc; Edward Dodwell 91cr; Erich Lessing Akademie der Bildenden Künste, Vienna 58cr; Musée du Louvre 57tc; Museum Narodowe, Warsaw 149br; Mykonos Museum 59tr; National Archaeological Museum, Athens 30–1(d), 31tc; Staatliche Kunstsammlungen, Albertinum, Dresden 35crb; Liebighaus, Frankfurt/Main 37crb; Staatliche Antikensammlungen und Glyptotek, München 4tr, 56bl; **Alamy Images:** The Art Archive 8-9; Art Directors & TRIP/ Bob Turner 311br; CW Images/Chris Warren 294bl; David Crousby 302tl; Danita Delimont 308cb; FAN Travelstock/ Katja Kreder 276tl; funkfood London - Paul Williams 194-5; Greece 162; GreekSportStock 295c; Andrew Holt 154b,

279tl, 294cla; Just Greece Photo Library/Terry Harris 51bl; Hercules Milas 172t; Werner Otto 294crb; Picpics 295br; Kostas Pikoulas 305tl; Robert Harding World Imagery 279c, Peter Titmuss 305cla; Aristidis Vafeiadakis 123br; Jan Wlodarczyk 86; **Allsport**: Mike Hewitt 124tr; **Ancient Art and Architecture**: 33crb, 38ca, 39cb, 41tl, 60cb, 60bc(d), 250cl, 258c; **Antikenmuseum Basel und Sammlung Ludwig**: 64–5c(d), 189br(d); **Aperion**: John Hios 188c; **Apollo Editions**: 189tl; **Argyropoulos Photo Press**: 49t, 49c, 51c, 51tr, 52crb; **Centre for Asia Minor Studies**: Museum of Greek Popular Musical Instruments Fivos Anoyianakis Collection 108tr; **Athens International Airport**: 310bl, 311tl; **Athens Urban Transport**: 320cl; 321tl; **Athinaïkon**: 284tl; **Avocado**: 285b.

Beau Brummel Restaurant: 274br; **Benaki Museum**: 29b, 40cl, 43tl, 43crb, 45cra, 69br, 82–3 all; **Paul Bernard**: 37tc; **Bibliotheque National**, Paris: Caoursin folio 179 42–3(d); **Bodleian Library**, Oxford: MS Canon Misc 378, 174v, 38clb; **Bourazani**: 289tr; **Bridgeman Art Library**, London: Birmingham City Museums and Art Galleries *Pheidias Completing the Parthenon Frieze*, Sir Lawrence Alma-Tadema 62tr; Bradford Art Galleries and Museums *The Golden Fleece* (c.1904), Herbert James Draper 224br; British Museum, London *Cup, Tondo, with Scene of Huntsmen Returning Home* 33cb, *Black-necked Amphora, Depicting Boxers and Wrestlers* (c.550–525 BC) Nidosthenes 177cra; Fitzwilliam Museum, University of Cambridge *Figurine of Demosthenes*, Enoch Wood of Burslem (c.1790) (lead glazed earthenware) 61tl, House of Masks, Delos *Mosaic of Dionysus Riding a Leopard* (c.AD 180) 39t; Guildhall Art Library *Clytemnestra*, John Collier 183cr; National Archaeological Museum, Athens *Bronze Statue of Poseidon* (c.460–450 BC) photo Bernard Cox 56cl; Private Collection *Two-tiered Icon of the Virgin and Child and Two Saints, Cretan School* (15th century) 42cl; © **The British Museum**: 30clb, 31cb, 34cb, 35clb, 57tr(d), 57br, 59cl(d), 65tc, 65ca, 104cl, 177cla(d), 189bl.

Camera Press, London: Anag 47bl(d); Wim Swaan 247t; **Jean Loup- Charmet**: L Dupré Bibliotheque des Artes Decoratifs 28(d); **Chrisovoulo**: 287bc; **Bruce Coleman Ltd**: Udo Hirsch 240bl; Dr Eckart Pott 261cr; Hans Reinhard 27ca, 210bc; **Courtesy of the City of Athens Development and Destination Agency**: 300br; **C M Dixon Photo Resources**: 31cr; Staatliche Antiken-sammlung und Glyptotek, München 36tr; **Corbis**: John Heseltine 278cl; JAI/Walter Bibikow 245t.

Dreamstime.com: Costas Aggelakis 254-5; Airphoto 15br; Georgios Alexandris 14tl, Anastasios71 218-9; Michael Avory 168-9; Pietro Basilico 140-1; Dudau 306bl; Emicristea 10bl; Enmanja 11tl; Freesurf69 66-7; Imagin.gr Photography 96-7; Javarman 262-3; Kalousp 300cla; Panagiotis Karapanagiotis 200-1; Andreas Karelias 204b; Milosk50 100cl; Ollirg 11crb; Pajche 298-9; Yiannis Papadimitriou 54-5 Lefteris Papaulakis 13bc; Picturefan1414 13tl; Preisler 14b; Sborisov 110-1, 152b; Nikolai Sorokin 230-1; Valery109 12br; Dejan Veljkovic 236; Ivonne Wierink 190cl; **Marc Dubin**: 23tl, 172bc, 210t, 212cr, 257cl, 256br.

Ecole Nationale Superieure Des Beaux Arts, Paris: *Delphes Restauration du Sanctuaire Envoi Tourn-aire* (1894) 34–5; **ECB**: 307 all; **Ekdotiki Athinon**: 25br, 30crb; **Eleas Gi**: 286tr; **Ergon**: 291br; **ET Archive**: British Museum 189cr; National Archaeology Museum, Naples 36cl; **Mary Evans Picture Library**: 245br.

Fanari Hotel: 273br; **Ferens Art Gallery**: Hull City Museums and Art Galleries and Archives *Electra at the Tomb of Agamemnon* (1869), Lord Frederick Leighton 59br; **Folk Art Museum**, Athens: 114t, 114bl.

g7ahn/Flicker: 315c; **Getty Images**: © Dimitris Sotiropoulos Photography 242-3; Lonely Planet 122cra; George Papapostolou 2-3; Lizzie Shepherd 206; George Tsafos 50bl; **Giraudon**, Paris: Laruros Versailles Chateau *Le Batille de Navarin*, Louis Ambroise Garneray 204tr; Louvre, Paris 64cl, *Scene de Massacres de Scio*, Delacroix 44ca(d); Musee Nationale Gustave Moreau *Hesiode et Les Muses* Gustave Moreau 60cla; Musee d'Art Catalan, Barcelona 99br; National Portrait Gallery, London *Portrait of George Gordon Byron*, Thomas Phillips (1813) 153tr(d); **Grande Bretagne Hotel**: 265br; **Grand Resort Lagonissi**: 265tl, 270tl; **Greek National Tourist Organization**: 300tc; **Nicholas P Goulandris Foundation Museum of Cycladic and Ancient Greek Art**: 69cr, 78–9 all.

Robert Harding Picture Library: David Beatty 48br; Tony Gervis 48cl, 48bl; Adam Woolfitt 50c; **Helio Photo**: 258b; **Hellenic Post Service**: 47tl, 309tl; **Michael Holford**: British Museum 36cl, 56tr; **Hotel Kritsa**: 275br, 290tr; **Hotel Pelops**: 271br; **Hulton Getty Collection**: 45crb(d); Central Press Photo 46clb(d); **Hutchison Library**: Hilly Janes 102tr.

Ideal Photo SA: N. Adams 120clb; T Dassios 49br, 179tl, 256cl, 256bl, 257bl, 266bc; C. Vergas 52bl,182bl; **Images Colour Library**: 103bl; **Impact Photos**: Caroline Penn 49bl.

Karavostasi Beach Hotel: 267cl; **Kostos Kontos**: 30ca, 46cra, 46cla, 49crb, 124br, 144, 156tr, 156cla,157tl, 157cra, 174tr, 179cr, 183bc, 188tr, 193tr, 321br; **KTEL Bus**: 318cla.

Ilias Lalaounis: 293cla; **Lampropoulos**:118c.

Mansell Collection: 56–7; **Marble House**: 268bl; **Municipal Art Gallery of Athens**: *Despinis TK* Mitarakis Yannis 92tl.

National Gallery of Victoria, Melbourne: Felton Bequest (1956) *Greek by the Inscriptions Painter Challidian* 58bl; **National Historical Museum**, Athens: 44–5(d), 45tl, 46bl, 177clb, 192cr(d), 198crb; **Natural Image**: Bob Gibbons 27br; Peter Wilson 241cr; **Nature Photographers**: S C Bisserot 240cr; Brinsley Burbridge 27cb, 27br; N A Callow 26bl; Andrew Cleave 27bc, 241bl; Peter Craig Cooper 241cl; Paul Sterry 27cra, 27cr, 229cr; **New Acropolis Museum**: 104cl.

O&B Athens Boutique Hotel: 269br; **Octopus Sea Trips**: Peter Nicolaides 296tr; **Olympic Airways**: 313tl; **Orizontes Lykavittou**: 283tl; **Oronoz Archivo Fotografico**: 215bc; Biblioteca National Madrid *Invasions Bulgares Historia*

Matriksiscronica FIIIV 40clb(d); Charlotten- berg, Berlin 58tr; El Escorial, Madrid *Battle Lepanto Cambiaso Luca* 42cr(d); Museo Julia 57cr(d); Musee Louvre 64br; Museo Vaticano 61b, 65bl, 225tr.

Romylos Parisis: 18t, 108bl, 222cr; City of Athens Museum 44clb; **Pictures Colour Library**: 20bl, 48crb; **Popperfoto**: 46bc, 47ca, 47cb, 47br, 102br, 184tl, 266tl; **Michalis Pornalis**: 222br, 223crb, 223br; **Private Collections**: 221tc, 221br.

Ride World Wide: 295tl; **Rex Features**: 21cr; Sipa/ Argyropoulos 52t; Sipa/C.Brown 47tr.

Scala, Florence: Gallerie degli Uffizi 32clb; Museo Archeologico, Firenze 33tl; Museo Mandralisca Cefalu 34cl; Museo Nationale Tarquinia 65bc; Museo de Villa Giulia 32-3, 64tr; **Spatherio Shadow Theatre Museum**: 155c; **Spectrum Colour Library**: 248bl; **STASY/Attiko Metro Operation Company S.A. (AMEL)**: 321cr; **Maria Stefossi**: 122b; **Theodoros-Patroklos Stellakis**: 158br; **Carmel Stewart**: 277c; **Sunvil**: 296bl; **Swan Hellenic**: 296cr.

Ta Fanaria: 288bc; **Tap Service Archaeological Receipts Fund Hellenic Republic Ministry of Culture**: A Epharat of Antiquities 9b, 47cb, 62br, 98clb, 98br, 99tl, 99cb, 100br, 101c, 101tl, 102cl, 103crb; Ancient Corinth Archaeological Museum 170c; B Epharat of Antiquities 145b, 148 all, 150 all, 151cla, 152cr; Byzantine Museum, Athens 80 all; D Epharat of Antiquities 143c, 143br, 166–7 all, 171bl, 181br, 182tr, 183tl, 183ca, 184cla; Delphi Archaeological Museum 234tl, 235c, 235br; E Epharat of Antiquities 178cb; Elefis Archaeological Museum 160cb; 11th Epharat of Byzantine Antiquities 241tr; 5th Epharat of Byzantine Antiquities 25cla, 25c, 41ca, 196bc; 1st Epharat of Byzantine Antiquities 143cra, 157bl, 226–7 all; I Epharat of Antiquities 142ca, 209tl, 232br, 233tl, 234tr, 234bl; IB Epharat of

Antiquities 215tr, 216c; IO Epharat of Antiquities 260c; IST Epharat of Antiquities 245c; Keramikos Archaeological Museum 93t, 93cr, 93br, 95t, 95car; Marathon Archaeological Museum 149c; National Archeological Museum, Athens 1, 7c, 32tr, 69tr, 72-3 all, 74–5 all, 103tl, 161cr; 9th Epharat of Byzantine Antiquities 252c, 252b; Pireaus Archaeological Museum 159tl; 2nd Epharat of Byzantine Antiquities 25cra; 6th Epharat of Byzantine Antiquities 17t, 25cr; 7th Epharat of Byzantine Antiquities 25bl, 223ca; Thebes Archaeological Museum 225tl; Thessaloniki Archaeological Museum 35tl, 143tc, 246bl(d), 250tr, 250br, 251 all; I Epharat of Antiquities 92ca, 92cb, 93tc, 93c, 93bl, 94-5 all, 160tr, 160cla, 161 all; Z Epharat of Antiquities 142clb, 174cl, 174bl, 175tc, 175bc, 176 all, 205b; **Yannis Tsarouhis Foundation**: Private Collection *Barber Shop in Marousi* (1947) 46tr.

Wadsworth Atheneum, Hartford Connecticut: T Pierpont Morgan Collection 193bc; **Peter Wilson**: 63bl, 98cla, 101br, 220clb; **Woodfin Camp & Associates**: John Marmaras 258tr; **Adam Woolfitt** 49clb.

Xenonas Papaevangelou: George Papaevangelou 272tr.

YES! Hotels: 269tl; **Yiantes**: Kamilo Nollas 282bl.

Front Endpaper: **Alamy Images**: Greece Lbl; **Dreamstime. com**: Freesurf69 R bc; Dejan Veljkovic Rcr; **Getty Images**: Lizzie Shepherd cla.

Map Cover: **AWL Images**: Marco Simoni.

Jacket
Front and Spine top- **AWL Images**: Marco Simoni.

All other images © Dorling Kindersley. For further information see: www.dkimages.com

Phrase Book

There is no universally accepted system for representing the modern Greek language in the Roman alphabet. The system of transliteration adopted in this guide is the one used by the Greek Government. Though not yet fully applied throughout Greece, most of the street and place names have been transliterated according to this system. For Classical names, this guide uses the k, os, on and f spelling, in keeping with the modern system of transliteration. In a few cases, such as Socrates, the more familiar Latin form has been used. Classical names do not have accents. Where a well-known English form of a name exists, suchas Athens or Corfu, this has been used. Variations in transliteration are given in the index.

Guidelines for Pronunciation

The accent over Greek and transliterated words indicates the stressed syllable. In this guide, the accent is not written over capital letters nor over monosyllables, except for question words and the conjunction ή (meaning "or"). In the right-hand "Pronunciation" column below, the syllable to stress is given in bold type.

On the following pages, the English is given in the left-hand column with the Greek and its transliteration in the middle column. The right-hand column provides a literal system of pronunciation and indicates the stressed syllable in bold.

The Greek Alphabet

Α α	A a	**a**rm
Β β	V v	**v**ote
Γ γ	G g	**y**ear (when followed by e and i sounds) **no** (when followed by ξ or γ)
Δ δ	D d	**th**at
Ε ε	E e	**e**gg
Ζ ζ	Z z	**z**oo
Η η	I i	bel**ie**ve
Θ θ	Th th	**th**ink
Ι ι	I i	bel**ie**ve
Κ κ	K k	**k**id
Λ λ	L l	**l**and
Μ μ	M m	**m**an
Ν ν	N n	**n**o
Ξ ξ	X x	ta**xi**
Ο ο	O o	**fo**x
Π π	P p	**p**ort
Ρ ρ	R r	**r**oom
Σ σ	S s	**s**orry (zero when followed by μ)
ς	s	(used at end of word)
Τ τ	T t	**t**ea
Υ υ	Y y	bel**ie**ve
Φ φ	F f	**f**ish
Χ χ	Ch ch	lo**ch** in most cases, but **h**e when followed by a, e or i sounds
Ψ ψ	Ps ps	ma**ps**
Ω ω	O o	**fo**x

Combinations of Letters

In Greek, there are two-letter vowels that are pronounced as one sound:

Αι αι	Ai ai	**e**gg
Ει ει	Ei ei	bel**ie**ve
Οι οι	Oi oi	bel**ie**ve
Ου ου	**Ou ou**	l**u**te

There are also some two-letter consonants that are pronounced as one sound:

Μπ μπ	Mp mp	**b**ut, sometimes nu**mb**er in the middle of a word
Ντ ντ	Nt nt	**d**esk, sometimes u**nd**er in the middle of a word
Γκ γκ	Gk gk	**g**o, sometimes bi**ng**o in the middle of a word
Γξ γξ	Nx	a**nx**iety
Τζ τζ	Tz tz	ha**nds**
Τσ τσ	Ts ts	i**t's**
Γγ γγ	Gg gg	bi**ng**o

In an Emergency

Help!	Βοήθεια! *Voítheia*	vo-**ee**-theea
Stop!	Σταματήστε! *Stamatíste*	sta-ma-**tee**-steh
Call a doctor!	Φωνάξτε ένα γιατρό! *Fonáxte éna giatró*	fo-**nak**-steh **e**-na ya-**tro**!
Call an ambulance/ the police/the fire brigade!	Καλέστε το ασθενοφόρο/την αστυνομία/την πυροσβεστική! *Kaléste to asthenofóro/tin astynomía/tin pyrosvestikí*	ka-**le**-steh to as-the-no-**fo**-ro/teen a-sti-no-**mia**/teen pee-ro-zve-stee-**kee**
Where is the nearest telephone/hospital/ pharmacy?	Πού είναι το πλησιέστερο τηλέφωνο/νοσοκο-μείο/φαρμακείο; *Poú eínai to plisiés-tero tiléfono/nosoko-meío/farmakeío?*	poo **ee**-ne to plee-see-**e**-ste-ro tee-**le**-pho-no/no-so-ko-mee-o/far-ma-**kee**-o?

Communication Essentials

Yes	Ναι *Nai*	neh
No	Όχι *Ochi*	**o**-chee
Please	Παρακαλώ *Parakaló*	pa-ra-ka-**lo**
Thank you	Ευχαριστώ *Efcharistó*	ef-cha-ree-**sto**
You are welcome	Παρακαλώ *Parakaló*	pa-ra-ka-**lo**
OK/alright	Εντάξει *Entáxei*	en-d**ak**-zee
Excuse me	Με συγχωρείτε *Me synchoreíte*	me seen-cho-**ree**-teh
Hello	Γειά σας *Geiá sas*	yeea sas
Goodbye	Αντίο *Antío*	an-**dee**-o
Good morning	Καλημέρα *Kaliméra*	ka-lee-**me**-ra
Good night	Καληνύχτα *Kalinýchta*	ka-lee-**nee**ch-ta
Morning	Πρωί *Proí*	pro-**ee**
Afternoon	Απόγευμα *Apógevma*	a-**po**-yev-ma
Evening	Βράδυ *Vrádi*	**vrath**-i
This morning	Σήμερα το πρωί *Símera to proí*	**see**-me-ra to pro-**ee**
Yesterday	Χθές *Chthés*	chthes
Today	Σήμερα *Símera*	**see**-me-ra
Tomorrow	Αύριο *Avrio*	**av**-ree-o
Here	Εδώ *Edó*	ed-**o**
There	Εκεί *Ekeí*	e-**kee**
What?	Τί; *Tí?*	**tee**?
Why?	Γιατί; *Giatí?*	ya-**tee**?
Where?	Πού; *Poú?*	**poo**?
How?	Πώς; *Pós?*	**pos**?
Wait!	Περίμενε! *Perímene!*	pe-**ree**-me-neh

Useful Phrases

How are you?	Τι κάνεις;	tee ka-nees
	Ti káneis?	
Very well, thank you	Πολύ καλά,	po-lee ka-la, ef-cha-
	ευχαριστώ	ree-sto
	Polý kalá, efcharistó	
How do you do?	Πώς είστε;	pos ees-te?
	Pós eíste?	
Pleased to meet you	Χαίρω πολύ	che-ro po-lee
	Chaíro polý	
What is your name?	Πώς λέγεστε;	pos le-ye-ste?
	Pós légeste?	
Where is/are…?	Πού είναι;	poo ee-ne?
	Poú eínai?	
How far is it to…?	Πόσο απέχει…;	po-so a-pe-chee?
	Póso apéchei…?	
How do I get to?	Πώς μπορώ να	pos bo-ro-na pa-o?
	πάω…;	
	Pós mporó na páo…?	
Do you speak	Μιλάτε Αγγλικά;	mee-la-te an-glee-ka?
English?	Miláte Angliká?	
I understand	Καταλαβαίνω	ka-ta-la-ve-no
	Katalavaíno	
I don't understand	Δεν καταλαβαίνω	then ka-ta-la-ve-no
	Den katalavaíno	
Could you speak	Μιλάτε λίγο πιο	mee-la-te lee-go pyo
slowly?	αργά παρακαλώ;	ar-ga pa-ra-ka-lo?
	Miláte lígo pio argá	
	parakaló?	
I'm sorry	Με συγχωρείτε	me seen-cho-ree teh
	Me synchoreíte	
Does anyone have a	Έχει κανένας	e-chee ka-ne-nas
key?	κλειδί;	klee-dee?
	Echei kanénas	
	kleidí?	

Useful Words

big	Μεγάλο	me-ga-lo
	Megálo	
small	Μικρό	mi-kro
	Mikró	
hot	Ζεστό	zes-to
	Zestó	
cold	Κρύο	kree-o
	Krýo	
good	Καλό	ka-lo
	Kaló	
bad	Κακό	ka-ko
	Kakó	
enough	Αρκετά	ar-ke-ta
	Arketá	
well	Καλά	ka-la
	Kalá	
open	Ανοιχτά	a-neech-ta
	Anoichtá	
closed	Κλειστά	klee-sta
	Kleistá	
left	Αριστερά	a-ree-ste-ra
	Aristerá	
right	Δεξιά	dek-see-a
	Dexiá	
straight on	Ευθεία	ef-thee-a
	Eftheía	
between	Ανάμεσα / Μεταξύ	a-na-me-sa/me-tak-
	Anámesa / Metaxý	see
on the corner of….	Στη γωνία του…	stee go-nee-a too
	Sti gonía tou…	
near	Κοντά	kon-da
	Kontá	
far	Μακριά	ma-kree-a
	Makriá	
up	Επάνω	e-pa-no
	Epáno	
down	Κάτω	ka-to
	Káto	
early	Νωρίς	no-rees
	Norís	
late	Αργά	ar-ga
	Argá	
entrance	Η είσοδος	ee ee-so-thos
	I eísodos	
exit	Η έξοδος	eee-kso-dos
	I éxodos	
toilet	Οι τουαλέτες /WC	ee-too-a-le-tes
	Oi toualétes / WC	
occupied/engaged	Κατειλημμένη	ka-tee-lee-me-nee
	Kateiliméni	

unoccupied/vacant	Ελεύθερη	e-lef-the-ree
	Eléftheri	
free/no charge	Δωρεάν	tho-re-an
	Doreán	
in/out	Μέσα /Έξω	me-sa/ek-so
	Mésa/ Exo	

Making a Telephone Call

Where is the nearest	Πού βρίσκεται ο	poo vrees-ke-teh o
public telephone ?	πλησιέστερος	plee-see-e-ste-ros
	τηλεφωνικός	tee-le-fo-ni-kos tha-
	θάλαμος;	la-mos?
	Poú vrísketai o	
	plisiésteros	
	tilefonikós thálamos?	
I would like to place	Θα ήθελα να κάνω	tha ee-the-la na ka-
a long-distance call	ένα υπεραστικό	no e-na ee-pe-ra-sti-
	τηλεφώνημα	ko tee-le-fo-nee-ma
	Tha íthela na káno éna	
	yperastikó tilefónima	
I would like to	Θα ήθελα να	tha ee-the-la na chre-
reverse the charges	χρεώσω το	o-so to tee-le-fo-nee-
	τηλεφώνημα στον	ma ston pa-ra-lep-tee
	παραλήπτη	
	Tha íthela na	
	chreóso to tilefónima	
	ston paralípti	
I will try again later	Θα ξανατηλεφωνήσω	tha ksa-na-tee-le-fo-
	αργότερα	ni-so ar-go-te-ra
	Tha xanatilefoníso	
	argótera	
Can I leave a	Μπορείτε να του	bo-ree-te na too a-
message?	αφήσετε ένα	fee-se-teh e-na mee-
	μήνυμα;	nee-ma?
	Mporeíte na tou	
	afísete éna mínyma?	
Could you speak up	Μιλάτε δυνατότερα,	mee-la-teh dee-na-to-
a little please?	παρακαλώ;	te-ra, pa-ra-ka-lo
	Miláte dynatótera,	
	parakaló	
Local call	Τοπικό τηλεφώνημα	to-pi-ko tee-le-fo-
	Topikó tilefónima	nee-ma
Hold on	Περιμένετε	pe-ri-me-ne-teh
	Periménete	
OTE telephone office	Ο ΟΤΕ / Το	o O-TE/To tee-le-fo-
	τηλεφωνείο	nee-o
	O OTE / To	
	tilefoneío	
Phone box/kiosk	Ο τηλεφωνικός	o tee-le-fo-ni-kos tha-
	θάλαμος	la-mos
	O tilefonikós	
	thálamos	
Phone card	Η τηλεκάρτα	ee tee-le-kar-ta
	I tilekárta	

Shopping

How much does this	Πόσο κάνει;	po-so ka-nee?
cost?	Póso kánei?	
I would like….	Θα ήθελα…	tha ee-the-la…
	Tha íthela…	
Do you have….?	Έχετε…;	e-che-teh
	Echete…?	
I am just looking	Απλώς κοιτάω	a-plos kee-ta-o
	Aplós koitáo	
Do you take credit	Δέχεστε πιστωτικές	the-ches-teh pee-sto-
cards/travellers'	κάρτες / travellers'	tee-kes kar-tes/
cheques?	cheques;	travellers' cheques?
	Décheste pistotikés	
	kártes / travellers'	
	cheques?	
What time do you	Ποτέ ανοίγετε/	po-teh a-nee-ye-teh/
open/close?	κλείνετε;	klee-ne-teh?
	Póte anoígete/	
	kleínete?	
Can you ship this	Μπορείτε να το	bo-ree-teh na to
overseas?	στείλετε στο	stee-le-teh sto e-xo-
	εξωτερικό;	te-ree-ko?
	Mporeíte na to	
	steílete sto	
	exoterikó?	
This one	Αυτό εδώ	af-to e-do
	Aftó edó	
That one	Εκείνο	e-kee-no
	Ekeíno	

expensive	Ακριβό *Akrivó*	*a-kree-vo*		art gallery	Η γκαλερί *I gkalerí*	*ee ga-le-ree*
cheap	Φθηνό *Fthinó*	*fthee-no*		beach	Η παραλία *I paralía*	*ee pa-ra-lee-a*
size	Το μέγεθος *To mégethos*	*to me-ge-thos*		Byzantine	βυζαντινός *vyzantinós*	*vee-zan-dee-nos*
white	Λευκό *Lefkó*	*lef-ko*		castle	Το κάστρο *To kástro*	*to ka-stro*
black	Μαύρο *Mávro*	*mav-ro*		cathedral	Η μητρόπολη *I mitrópoli*	*ee mee-tro-po-lee*
red	Κόκκινο *Kókkino*	*ko-kee-no*		cave	Το σπήλαιο *To spílaio*	*to spee-le-o*
yellow	Κίτρινο *Kítrino*	*kee-tree-no*		church	Η εκκλησία *I ekklisía*	*ee e-klee-see-a*
green	Πράσινο *Prásino*	*pra-see-no*		folk art	λαϊκή τέχνη *laïkí téchni*	*la-ee-kee tech-nee*
blue	Μπλε *Mple*	*bleh*		fountain	Το συντριβάνι *To syntriváni*	*to seen-dree-va-nee*

Types of Shop

				garden	Ο κήπος *O kípos*	*o kee-pos*
antique shop	Μαγαζί με αντίκες *Magazí me antíkes*	*ma-ga-zee me an-dee-kes*		gorge	Το φαράγγι *To farángi*	*to fa-ran-gee*
bakery	Ο φούρνος *O foúrnos*	*o foor-nos*		grave of….	Ο τάφος του…	*o ta-fos too*
bank	Η τράπεζα *I trápeza*	*ee tra-pe-za*		hill	Ο λόφος *O lófos*	*o lo-fos*
bazaar	Το παζάρι *To pazári*	*to pa-za-ree*		historical	ιστορικός *istorikós*	*ee-sto-ree-kos*
bookshop	Το βιβλιοπωλείο *To vivliopoleío*	*to vee-vlee-o-po-lee-o*		island	Το νησί *To nisí*	*to nee-see*
butcher	Το κρεοπωλείο *To kreopoleío*	*to kre-o-po-lee-o*		lake	Η λίμνη *I límni*	*ee leem-nee*
cake shop	Το ζαχαροπλαστείο *To zacharoplasteío*	*to za-cha-ro-pla-stee-o*		library	Η βιβλιοθήκη *I vivliothíki*	*ee veev-lee-o-thee-kee*
cheese shop	Μαγαζί με αλλαντικά *Magazí me allantiká*	*ma-ga-zee me a-lan-dee-ka*		mansion	Η έπαυλις *I épavlis*	*eee-pav-lees*
department store	Πολυκατάστημα *Polykatástima*	*Po-le-ka-ta-stee-ma*		monastery	Μονή *moní*	*mo-ni*
				mountain	Το βουνό *To vounó*	*to voo-no*
fishmarket	Το ιχθυοπωλείο/ ψαράδικο *To ichthyopoleío/ psarádiko*	*to eech-thee-o-po-lee-o/psa-ra-dee-ko*		municipal	δημοτικός *dimotikós*	*thee-mo-tee-kos*
greengrocer	Το μανάβικο *To manáviko*	*to ma-na-vee-ko*		museum	Το μουσείο *To mouseío*	*to moo-see-o*
hairdresser	Το κομμωτήριο *To kommotírio*	*to ko-mo-tee-ree-o*		national	εθνικός *ethnikós*	*eth-nee-kos*
kiosk	Το περίπτερο *To períptero*	*to pe-reep-te-ro*		park	Το πάρκο *To párko*	*to par-ko*
leather shop	Μαγαζί με δερμάτινα είδη *Magazí me dermátina eidi*	*ma-ga-zee me ther-ma-tee-na e-ethee*		river	Ο τάφος του… Το ποτάμι *To potámi*	*to po-ta-mee*
street market	Η λαϊκή αγορά *I laïkí agorá*	*ee la-ee-kee a-go-ra*		road	Ο δρόμος *O drómos*	*o thro-mos*
newsagent	Ο εφημεριδοπώλης *O efimeridopólis*	*O e-fee-me-ree-tho-…-loes*		saint	άγιος/άγιοι/αγία /αγίες *ágios/ágioi/agía/agíes*	*a-yee-os/a-yee-ee/a-yee-a/a-yee-es*
pharmacy	Το φαρμακείο *To farmakeío*	*to far-ma-kee-o*		spring	Η πηγή *I pigí*	*ee pee-yee*
post office	Το ταχυδρομείο *To tachydromeío*	*to ta-chee-thro-mee-o*		square	Η πλατεία *I plateía*	*ee pla-tee-a*
shoe shop	Κατάστημα υποδημάτων *Katástima ypodimáton*	*ka-ta-stee-ma ee-po-dee-ma-ton*		stadium	Το στάδιο *To stádio*	*to sta-thee-o*
				statue	Το άγαλμα *To ágalma*	*to a-gal-ma*
souvenir shop	Μαγαζί με "souvenir" *Magazí me "souvenir"*	*ma-ga-zee meh "souvenir"*		theatre	Το θέατρο *To théatro*	*to the-a-tro*
supermarket	Σουπερμάρκετ/ Υπεραγορά *"Supermarket"/ Yperagorá*	*"Supermarket"/ee-per-a-go-ra*		town hall	Το δημαρχείο *To dimarcheío*	*To thee-mar-chee-o*
tobacconist	Είδη καπνιστού *Eidi kapnistoú*	*Ee-thee kap-nees*		closed on public holidays	κλειστό τις αργίες *kleistó tis argíes*	*klee-sto tees aryee-es*
travel agent	Το ταξειδιωτικό γραφείο *To taxeidiotikó grafeío*	*to tak-see-thy-o-tee-ko gra-fee-o*				

Transport

				When does the …. leave?	Πότε φεύγει το …; *Póte févgei to…?*	*po-teh fev-yee to…?*
				Where is the bus stop?	Πού είναι η στάση του λεωφορείου; *Poú eínai i stási tou leoforeíou?*	*poo ee-neh ee sta-see to le-o-fo-ree-oo?*

Sightseeing

tourist information	Ο ΕΟΤ *O EOT*	*o E-OT*		Is there a bus to…?	Υπάρχει λεωφορείο για….; *Ypárchei leoforeío gia…?*	*ee-par-chee le-o-fo-ree-o yia…?*
tourist police	Η τουριστική αστυνομία *I touristikí astynomía*	*ee too-rees-tee-kee a-stee-no-mee-a*		ticket office	Εκδοτήρια εισιτηρίων *Ekdotíria eisitiríon*	*Ek-tho-tee-reea ee-see-tee-ree-on*
archaeological	αρχαιολογικός *archaiologikós*	*ar-che-o-lo-yee-kos*		return ticket	Εισιτήριο με επιστροφή *Eisitírio me epistrofí*	*ee-see-tee-ree-o meh e-pee-stro-fee*
				single journey	Απλό εισιτήριο *Apló eisitírio*	*a-plo ee-see-tee-reeo*

bus station	Ο σταθμός λεωφορείων *O stathmós leoforeíon*	*o stath-mos leo-fo-ree-on*
bus ticket	Εισιτήριο λεωφορείου *Eisitírio leoforeíou*	*ee-see-tee-ree-o leo-fo-ree-oo*
trolley bus	Το τρόλλεϋ *To trólley*	*to tro-le-ee*
port	Το λιμάνι *To limáni*	*to lee-ma-nee*
train/metro	Το τρένο *To tréno*	*to tre-no*
railway station	σιδηροδρομικός σταθμός *sidirodromikós stathmós*	*see-thee-ro-thro-mee-kos stath-mos*
moped	Το μοτοποδήλατο / το μηχανάκι *To motopodílato / To michanáki*	*to mo-to-po-thee-la-to/to mee-cha-na-kee*
bicycle	Το ποδήλατο *To podílato*	*to po-thee-la-to*
taxi	Το ταξί *To taxí*	*to tak-see*
airport	Το αεροδρόμιο *To aerodrómio*	*to a-e-ro-thro-mee-o*
ferry	Το φερυμπότ *To "ferry-boat"*	*to fe-ree-bot*
hydrofoil	Το δελφίνι / Το υδροπτέρυγο *To delfíni / To ydroptérygo*	*to del-fee-nee/To ee-throp-te-ree-go*
catamaran	Το καταμαράν *To katamarán*	*to catamaran*
for hire	Ενοικιάζονται *Enoikidzontai*	*e-nee-kya-zon-deh*

Staying in a Hotel

Do you have a vacant room?	Έχετε δωμάτια; *Echete domátia?*	*e-che-teh tho-ma-tee-a?*
double room with double bed	Δίκλινο με διπλό κρεβάτι *Díklino me dipló kreváti*	*thee-klee-no meh thee-plo kre-va-tee*
twin room	Δίκλινο με μονά κρεβάτια *Díklino me moná krevátia*	*thee-klee-no meh mo-na kre-vat-ya*
single room	Μονόκλινο *Monóklino*	*mo-no-klee-no*
room with a bath	Δωμάτιο με μπάνιο *Domátio me mpánio*	*tho-ma-tee-o meh ban-yo*
shower	Το ντουζ *To douz*	*to dooz*
porter	Ο πορτιέρης *O portiéris*	*o por-tye-rees*
key	Το κλειδί *To kleidí*	*to klee-dee*
I have a reservation	Έχω κάνει κράτηση *Echo kánei krátisi*	*e-cho ka-nee kra-tee-see*
room with a sea view/balcony	Δωμάτιο με θέα στη θάλασσα/μπαλκόνι *Domátio me théa sti thálassa / mpalkóni*	*tho-ma-tee-o meh the-a stee tha-la-sa/bal-ko-nee*
Does the price include breakfast?	Το πρωινό συμπεριλαμβάνεται στην τιμή; *To proinó symperilamvánetai stin timí?*	*to pro-ee-no seem-be-ree-lam-va-ne-teh steen tee-mee?*

Eating Out

Have you got a table?	Έχετε τραπέζι; *Echete trapézi?*	*e-che-te tra-pe-zee?*
I want to reserve a table	Θέλω να κρατήσω ένα τραπέζι *Thélo na kratíso éna trapézi*	*the-lo na kra-tee-so e-na tra-pe-zee*
The bill, please	Τον λογαριασμό, παρακαλώ *Ton logariazmó parakaló*	*ton lo-gar-yas-mo pa-ra-ka-lo*
I am a vegetarian	Είμαι χορτοφάγος *Eímai chortofágos*	*ee-meh chor-to-fa-gos*
What is fresh today?	Τι φρέσκο έχετε σήμερα; *Ti frésko échete símera?*	*tee fres-ko e-che-teh see-me-ra?*

waiter/waitress	Κύριε / Γκαρσόν / Κυρία (female) *Kýrie/Garson/Kyría*	*Kee-ree-eh/Gar-son/Kee-ree-a*
menu	Ο κατάλογος *O katálogos*	*o ka-ta-lo-gos*
cover charge	Το κουβέρ *To "couvert"*	*to koo-ver*
wine list	Ο κατάλογος με τα οινοπνευματώδη *O katálogos me ta oinopnevmatódi*	*o ka-ta-lo-gos meh ta ee-no-pnev-ma-to-thee*
glass	Το ποτήρι *To potíri*	*to po-tee-ree*
bottle	Το μπουκάλι *To mpoukáli*	*to bou-ka-lee*
knife	Το μαχαίρι *To machaíri*	*to ma-che-ree*
fork	Το πηρούνι *To piroúni*	*to pee-roo-nee*
spoon	Το κουτάλι *To koutáli*	*to koo-ta-lee*
breakfast	Το πρωινό *To proinó*	*to pro-ee-no*
lunch	Το μεσημεριανό *To mesimerianó*	*to me-see-mer-ya-no*
dinner	Το δείπνο *To deípno*	*to theep-no*
main course	Το κυρίως γεύμα *To kyríos gévma*	*to kee-ree-os yev-ma*
starter/first course	Τα ορεκτικά *Ta orektiká*	*ta o-rek-tee-ka*
dessert	Το γλυκό *To glykó*	*to ylee-ko*
dish of the day	Το πιάτο της ημέρας *To piáto tis iméras*	*to pya-to tees ee-me-ras*
bar	Το μπαρ *To "bar"*	*To bar*
taverna	Η ταβέρνα *I tavérna*	*ee ta-ver-na*
café	Το καφενείο *To kafeneío*	*to ka-fe-nee-o*
fish taverna	Η ψαροταβέρνα *I psarotavérna*	*ee psa-ro-ta-ver-na*
grill house	Η ψησταριά *I psistariá*	*ee psee-sta-rya*
wine shop	Το οινοπωλείο *To oinopoleío*	*to ee-no-po-lee-o*
dairy shop	Το γαλακτοπωλείο *To galaktopoleío*	*to ga-lak-to-po-lee-o*
restaurant	Το εστιατόριο *To estiatório*	*to e-stee-a-to-ree-o*
ouzeri	Το ουζερί *To ouzerí*	*to oo-ze-ree*
meze shop	Το μεζεδοπωλείο *To mezedopoleío*	*To me-ze-do-po-lee-o*
take away kebabs	Το σουβλατζίδικο *To souvlatzídiko*	*To soo-vlat-zee-dee-ko*
rare	Ελάχιστα ψημένο *Eláchista psiméno*	*e-lach-ees-ta psee-me-no*
medium	Μέτρια ψημένο *Métria psiméno*	*met-ree-a psee-me-no*
well done	Καλοψημένο *Kalopsiméno*	*ka-lo-psee-me-no*

Basic Food and Drink

coffee	Ο καφές *O Kafés*	*o ka-fes*
with milk	με γάλα *me gála*	*me ga-la*
black coffee	σκέτος *skétos*	*ske-tos*
without sugar	χωρίς ζάχαρη *chorís záchari*	*cho-rees za-cha-ree*
medium sweet	μέτριος *métrios*	*me-tree-os*
very sweet	γλυκύς *glykýs*	*glee-kees*
tea	τσάι *tsái*	*tsa-ee*
hot chocolate	ζεστή σοκολάτα *zestí sokoláta*	*ze-stee so-ko-la-ta*
wine	κρασί *krasí*	*kra-see*
red	κόκκινο *kókkino*	*ko-kee-no*
white	λευκό *lefkó*	*lef-ko*
rosé	ροζέ *rozé*	*ro-ze*

raki	Το ρακί	to ra-kee
	To rakí	
ouzo	Το ούζο	to oo-zo
	To oúzo	
retsina	Η ρετσίνα	ee ret-see-na
	I retsína	
water	Το νερό	to ne-ro
	To neró	
octopus	Το χταπόδι	to chta-po-dee
	To chtapódi	
fish	Το ψάρι	to psa-ree
	To psári	
cheese	Το τυρί	to tee-ree
	To tyrí	
halloumi	Το χαλούμι	to cha-loo-mee
	To chaloúmi	
feta	Η φέτα	ee fe-ta
	I féta	
bread	Το ψωμί	to pso-mee
	To psomí	
bean soup	Η φασολάδα	ee fa-so-la-da
	I fasoláda	
houmous	Το χούμους	to choo-moos
	To houmous	
halva	Ο χαλβάς	o chal-vas
	O chalvás	
meat kebabs	Ο γύρος	o yee-ros
	O gyros	
Turkish delight	Το λουκούμι	to loo-koo-mee
	To loukoúmi	
baklava	Ο μπακλαβάς	o bak-la-vas
	O mpaklavás	
klephtiko	Το κλέφτικο	to klef-tee-ko
	To kléftiko	

Numbers

1	ένα	e-na
	éna	
2	δύο	thee-o
	dýo	
3	τρία	tree-a
	tría	
4	τέσσερα	te-se-ra
	téssera	
5	πέντε	pen-deh
	pénte	
6	έξι	ek-si
	éxi	
7	επτά	ep-ta
	eptá	
8	οχτώ	och-to
	ochtó	
9	εννέα	e-ne-a
	ennéa	
10	δέκα	the-ka
	déka	
11	έντεκα	en-de-ka
	énteka	
12	δώδεκα	tho-the-ka
	dódeka	
13	δεκατρία	de-ka-tree-a
	dekatría	
14	δεκατέσσερα	the-ka-te-se-ra
	dekatéssera	
15	δεκαπέντε	the-ka-pen-de
	dekapénte	
16	δεκαέξι	the-ka-ek-si
	dekaéxi	
17	δεκαεπτά	the-ka-ep-ta
	dekaeptá	
18	δεκαοχτώ	the-ka-och-to
	dekaochtó	
19	δεκαεννέα	the-ka-e-ne-a
	dekaennéa	
20	είκοσι	ee-ko-see
	eíkosi	
21	εικοσιένα	ee-ko-see-e-na
	eikosiéna	
30	τριάντα	tree-an-da
	triánta	
40	σαράντα	sa-ran-da
	saránta	
50	πενήντα	pe-neen-da
	penínta	
60	εξήντα	ek-seen-da
	exínta	
70	εβδομήντα	ev-tho-meen-da
	evdomínta	

80	ογδόντα	og-thon-da
	ogdónta	
90	ενενήντα	e-ne-neen-da
	enenínta	
100	εκατό	e-ka-to
	ekató	
200	διακόσια	thya-kos-ya
	diakósia	
1,000	χίλια	cheel-ya
	chília	
2,000	δύο χιλιάδες	thee-o cheel-ya-thes
	dýo chiliádes	
1,000,000	ένα εκατομμύριο	e-na e-ka-to-mee-ree-o
	éna ekatommýrio	

Time, Days and Dates

one minute	ένα λεπτό	e-na lep-to
	éna leptó	
one hour	μία ώρα	mee-a o-ra
	mía óra	
half an hour	μισή ώρα	mee-see o-ra
	misí óra	
quarter of an hour	ένα τέταρτο	e-na te-tar-to
	éna tétarto	
half past one	μία και μισή	mee-a keh mee-see
	mía kai misí	
quarter past one	μία και τέταρτο	mee-a keh te-tar-to
	mía kai tétarto	
ten past one	μία και δέκα	mee-a keh the-ka
	mía kai déka	
quarter to two	δύο παρά τέταρτο	thee-o pa-ra te-tar-to
	dýo pará tétarto	
ten to two	δύο παρά δέκα	thee-o pa-ra the-ka
	dýo pará déka	
a day	μία μέρα	mee-a me-ra
	mía méra	
a week	μία εβδομάδα	mee-a ev-tho-ma-tha
	mía evdomáda	
a month	ένας μήνας	e-nas mee-nas
	énas mínas	
a year	ένας χρόνος	e-nas chro-nos
	énas chrónos	
Monday	Δευτέρα	thef-te-ra
	Deftéra	
Tuesday	Τρίτη	tree-tee
	Tríti	
Wednesday	Τετάρτη	te-tar-tee
	Tetárti	
Thursday	Πέμπτη	pemp-tee
	Pémpti	
Friday	Παρασκευή	pa-ras-ke-vee
	Paraskeví	
Saturday	Σάββατο	sa-va-to
	Sávvato	
Sunday	Κυριακή	keer-ee-a-kee
	Kyriakí	
January	Ιανουάριος	ee-a-noo-a-ree-os
	Ianouários	
February	Φεβρουάριος	fev-roo-a-ree-os
	Fevrouários	
March	Μάρτιος	mar-tee-os
	Mártios	
April	Απρίλιος	a-pree-lee-os
	Aprílios	
May	Μάιος	ma-ee-os
	Máios	
June	Ιούνιος	ee-oo-nee-os
	Ioúnios	
July	Ιούλιος	ee-oo-lee-os
	Ioúlios	
August	Αύγουστος	av-goo-stos
	Avgoustos	
September	Σεπτέμβριος	sep-tem-vree-os
	Septémvrios	
October	Οκτώβριος	ok-to-vree-os
	Októvrios	
November	Νοέμβριος	no-em-vree-os
	Noémvrios	
December	Δεκέμβριος	the-kem-vree-os
	Dekémvrios	

Road Map of Mainland Greece

Key

- Area covered by this guide
- International airport
- Domestic airport
- Mainland ferry port
- Railway line
- Motorway
- Major road
- Minor road
- National boundary
- Motorway under construction

0 kilometres 50

0 miles 50